GLOBALIZATION AND INTERNATIONALIZATION
IN HIGHER EDUCATION

Also available from Continuum

The Future of Higher Education, Les Bell, Howard Stevenson and Michael Neary

Internationalizing the University, Yvonne Turner and Sue Robson

Comparative and International Education, David Phillips,
Erwin Epstein and Michele Schweisfurth

'This book brings much needed conceptual rigour to understanding the dynamics of globalization and internationalization of higher education, two terms that are often used loosely and interchangeably. In addition to making clear theoretical distinctions between different forms of globalization and internationalization, it provides important insights into the development of institutional strategies and their management. It also provides a wide range of empirical studies – from China to Spain, from student mobility to intercultural experiences. Above all the book offers an intelligent and comprehensive account of higher education's efforts to respond to the challenges of globalization.'

Peter Scott, Vice Chancellor of Kingston University, London, UK

'Universities have always regarded themselves as playing both an international and a global role, sometimes to the irritation of stakeholders with more limited horizons. This timely and comprehensive set of essays sets out the range of contemporary dilemmas that result. It also usefully explores some perspectives that are (in the 800 year history of the modern university) new and troubling, including the ethical challenges of a global market in students and staff, the cultural tensions between North and South, and the institutional responsibilities of higher education beyond state boundaries. It should prove valuable to all who are trying to think about as well as manage the consequences.'

*Sir David Watson, Professor of Higher Education Management,
Institute of Education, University of London, UK*

Globalization and Internationalization in Higher Education

Theoretical, Strategic and Management Perspectives

Edited by Felix Maringe and Nick Foskett

continuum

Continuum International Publishing Group
A Bloomsbury company
50 Bedford Square   80 Maiden Lane
London   New York
WC1B 3DP   NY 10038

www.continuumbooks.com

First edition published 2010
This paperback edition published 2012

British Library Cataloguing-in-Publication Data
A catalogue record for this book is available from the British Library.

ISBN: 978-1-4411-3277-2 (hardcover)
      978-1-4411-7709-4 (paperback)

Library of Congress Cataloging-in-Publication Data
Globalization and internationalization in higher education : theoretical, strategic and
management perspectives / Felix Maringe and Nick Foskett, [editors].
     p. cm.
  ISBN 978-1-4411-3277-2 (hardback)
  1. Education, Higher—International cooperation. 2. Transnational education. 3.
Education and globalization. I. Foskett, Nicholas, 1955– II. Maringe, Felix. III. Title.
  LB2324.G56 2010
  378'.016–dc22   2010002891

Typeset by Pindar NZ, Auckland, New Zealand
Printed and bound in Great Britain

Contents

List of Tables and Figures

Tables

Figures

Notes on Contributors

Joanna Al-Youssef is a part-time Teaching Fellow at the Foreign Languages Centre at the University of Bath. She has an EdD from the University of Bath and an MA in English Language Teaching from the University of Nottingham. Her research interests are in the areas of Internationalization of Higher Education, International Policy, International students' issues, and language and culture. She is currently looking at implications of the internationalization of HE for students' experiences on university campus.

Rodney Arambewela is a Senior Lecturer in Marketing at Deakin University, Australia. His research interests include International Education, Issues in Higher Education, Teaching and Learning, Customer Satisfaction, International Marketing and Services Marketing.

Bruce Barnett is a Professor in the Educational Leadership and Policy Studies Department at the University of Texas at San Antonio. His research interests include cohort-based learning, mentoring and coaching, leadership for school improvement, school-university partnerships, and international research and program development.

Roberta Malee Bassett is a Tertiary Education Specialist in the Human Development Network at The World Bank. She has had several years of experience as an academic in Universities in the UK and the US. Her research is around issues of the liberalization of HE through the GATS and policy at both government and institutional levels associated with this.

Vivienne Caruana is Reader in Internationalization of the Curriculum at Leeds Metropolitan University, UK. This recently acquired role consolidates research in the field conducted in an academic development capacity and experience as Lecturer in Modern Economic and Social History, teaching international and local students.

Nick Foskett has been Dean of the Faculty of Law, Arts and Social Science (LASS) at the University of Southampton, UK, and has worked extensively in the field of Higher Education. He is currently involved in research on globalization and internationalization in Higher Education. In August 2010, Nick will be the next Vice-Chancellor of University of Keele.

Rosalind Foskett is Professor of Higher Education and Deputy Vice-Chancellor at The University of Worcester UK, and has specific research interests in education and business partnerships, widening participation and career development.

Paul Gibbs is Professor at the Work Based Institute at Middlesex University, UK. He has research interest in marketing, markets and work based learning; he researches in aspects of educational management and has contributed extensively to what may be called a philosophy of educational marketing.

Dr Jane Hemsley-Brown is a Reader in Marketing in the School of Management, University of Surrey, Guildford, UK. Jane previously worked in the School of Education at the University of Southampton, UK as Senior Researcher and Lecturer; and as a Principal Researcher with the National Foundation for Educational Research (NFER) Slough, UK. Jane is the author of over 70 papers and articles on education decision-making and choice in education markets and is the co-editor of the *Journal of Marketing for Higher Education* with Dr Anthony Lowrie of Minnesota State University, Moorhead, USA.

Stephen Jacobson is Professor and Associate Dean for the Graduate School of Education at University at Buffalo, USA. His research interests include teacher compensation and labour market behaviour, the reform of school leadership preparation and practice, and effective principal leadership in challenging schools.

John Lowe is a Lecturer in Education at the University of Bath, UK. His research interests are in the relationship between education and socio-economic change, particularly in the context of globalization and with an emphasis on higher education. He is currently engaged in a range of Higher Education research projects with partners in China, examining issues of internationalization in Chinese universities.

Felix Maringe is Senior Lecturer in Education at the University of Southampton, UK. He researches into leadership and management perceptions of transforming Higher Education environments. His current research focus is on the impact of globalization in Higher Education.

Izhar Oplatka is Associate Professor in Educational Administration, and the Head of Division of Educational Administration and Leadership in the School of Education, at Tel Aviv University, Israel. His main research fields are educational marketing, and the careers of school principals and teachers.

Laura E. Rumbley is Research Associate at the Boston College Center for International Higher Education, USA. She leads the Center's Podcast Initiative, coordinates the International Network for Higher Education in Africa (INHEA), and serves as an adjunct assistant professor in the graduate programme in higher education administration.

John Taylor is Professor of Higher Education and Director of the Centre for Higher Education Management and Policy at Southampton (CHEMPaS) at the

University of Southampton, UK. He researches into HE Policy and contributes significantly to leadership and management literature in HE.

Mei Tian is a lecturer at the School of International Studies, Xi'an Jiao Tong University, China. She researched into experiences of Chinese students in a British university during her PhD study. Her current research interest involves internationalization of higher education in China.

Dianmin Wang is associate professor of English at Nanjing University, China. As the director of the graduate English division of the Department of Applied Language Studies, he is responsible for the curriculum design. His current research is cross-cultural pragmatics and internationalization of curriculum.

Steve Woodfield is Senior Researcher in the Higher Education Policy and Management Research Group at Kingston University, UK. His research focuses on internationalization in higher education (international student mobility, international partnerships and networks, quality assurance in cross-border education, and international strategy development); and leadership and management in UK higher education.

Jiang Yumei is a doctoral student of higher education at Nanjing University, China. Her interests include Teaching English as a Foreign Language (TEFL) theories and methodology and materials development as well as higher education administration.

Hongshia Zhang is Professor in Education at Nanjing University, China, and is the Head of the Department of Education, with specific interests in teaching and learning in higher education, science education, comparative education and educational internationalization.

Chapter 1

Introduction: Globalization and Universities

Felix Maringe and Nick Foskett

Introduction

Globalization as a social phenomenon has a long history, but its impact on world affairs and other facets of human development and endeavour has strengthened in the last two or three decades. Primarily, globalization has replaced postmodernism as a theory and framework for understanding world development. The concept is an emotive and complex one, with many shades of meaning arising from its multiplicity of dimensions and differentiated impacts in different parts of world. It has both positive and negative consequences and as such has protagonists, cynics and critics in abundance. Although there is no single universal definition of the concept, it is broadly understood to mean the creation of world relations based on the operation of free markets (see, for example, Giddens, 2000; Albrow, 1997; Held *et al.*, 1999; Robertson, 1992; Mittelman, 2000; Steger, 2003). Universities are knowledge-producing entities and have social, cultural, ideological, political and economic responsibilities to society. A key strategy for responding to the influence of globalization adopted by universities across the world is internationalization, generally understood to mean the integration of an international or intercultural dimension into the tripartite mission of teaching, research and service functions of Higher Education (HE) (see, for example, Knight, 2004; de Wit, 1997; Scott, 2000; and Teichler, 1996). This chapter provides a broad overview of the concepts of globalization and internationalization and maps out a proposition for the global context of HE in which some of the key challenges for universities operating in the global environment are outlined. It then provides a rationale for the book, explains its organization and how each chapter contributes to its overall purpose.

Globalization and internationalization: an overview

These two concepts are two sides of the same coin yet are not synonymous with each other, although they perhaps share many common characteristics. Globalization entails the opening up and coming together of business, trade and economic activities between nations, necessitating the need for greater homogenization of fundamental political, ideological, cultural and social aspects of life across different countries of the world. Such processes have been taking place for a long time, but have been accelerated and intensified in the past few decades because of developments in technology, computers and the Internet. The impact these changes are having on universities is profound and, within universities, the key strategic responses to globalization have come to be known as internationalization. However, while internationalization in HE constitutes a group of strategic responses to globalization, it is important to acknowledge the reciprocity that exists between these two concepts. For example, the intensification of student mobility that may result from an institutional strategy to increase overseas student recruitment contributes to the further intensification of globalization. Similarly, intensifying curriculum internationalization processes will result in making the university educational product more attractive and therefore help to increase student mobility in recruitment markets.

Discussions of globalization have tended to utilize the analytic discourse of its dimensions. The most recent and useful contribution to this discussion is by Steger (2003), who identified political, economic, ideological and cultural dimensions. The problem with this approach is that it tends to reify rather than integrate globalization conceptualizations. However, it provides a useful analytical framework for understanding what obviously is a complex concept. These globalization dimensions will be explored in some detail in Chapter 2. Fundamentally, because universities have a political, economic, social and cultural mission, a good understanding of changes taking place globally within these areas will help shape both institutional response and strategy for current and future development.

Propositions about a global HE system

Most universities operate primarily in their own national space and context, and are part of the educational system within their own country. Shaped in many ways by history and legislative/governmental acts and policies in relation to education in general and HE in particular, their key accountabilities lie within their own national boundaries. So in what way can we conceive of a global HE system and what are its chief characteristics?

First and foremost, the global HE system is not uniform and homogeneous. It is characterized by diversity in relation to every dimension of what it means to be a university. With diversity comes differentiation caricatured by performance rankings and league tables both within countries and internationally. Different tables emphasize different priorities in their ranking criteria, of course. For example, in the UK, the *Guardian* newspaper tables (*Guardian*, 2009) rank universities in terms of excellence in teaching while the *Times Higher Education* magazine tables (2009) tend to emphasize research performance more highly than other criteria. International tables such as the Shanghai Jiao Tong University tables (2009) place greater emphasis on graduate destinations and their impact in society (see Chapter 3 for a discussion of this aspect). The outcome of such comparative performance, of course, is the ascribing of relative value and the identification of a hierarchy of institutions at a national and global scale. Such a hierarchy in turn influences investment decisions by outside organizations, application decisions by students, staff recruitment patterns and overall student and staff mobility patterns, reinforcing the differentiation and diversity within the global system.

Second, because of the World Trade Organization (WTO) and the General Agreement in Trade and Services (GATS) initiative to diminish and ultimately eliminate barriers to trade and services in service industries including HE (Bassett, 2006), it is clear that HE across the world is increasingly being subjected to international law, rather than ordinary local and national legislation. Fundamentally, HE is now legitimately viewed as a tradable commodity despite heavy criticism of this apparent commodification of HE (see Chapter 16 for a discussion of this contentious concept). The route to an open global HE market is a challenging one. Foster (2000) identifies a range of economic obstacles needing reform in order to open up and allow HE institutions to work together in the global environment. These include:

• the need to remove specific taxes to education imposed in some countries;
• the need to review the issue of outright bans of educational materials and services from other countries;
• the need to review the issue of restrictions on online instructional materials from abroad;
• reviewing delays in government approval of foreign programmes;
• the need to facilitate staff and student mobility across nations.

The third element of the global HE system is one in which the overall direction of student and staff mobility, and hence the financial flow, is from poor, underdeveloped countries to the rich, industrialized nations of the West. Also known as human capital flight, the idea of the 'brain drain' describes the emigration of educated and highly skilled workers due to a whole range of push and pull factors (Emeagwali, 2003). While some writers have argued that globalization will exacerbate brain drain, others look more positively at the emergence of what has been termed 'brain gain', in the global context. Freidman *et al.* (2004), for example, argue that the world is flattening and that drains and gains are becoming reciprocal across different parts of the world.

Fourth, HE is increasingly coming under the influence of international organizations where the roles of national governments in state HE systems are becoming subordinated to regional and international influence. For example, in Europe, the Lisbon and Bologna Processes have given a new role to a more regionally controlled HE sector across the countries of the EU by opening up free trade agreements and mechanisms for cross-border movement of students without restrictions. International organizations such as the United Nations Educational, Scientific and Cultural Organization (UNESCO) have a mission to:

> promote the global vision of HE in which people are enabled to function in their personal, professional and community lives and are able to be perpetrators and repositories of knowledge, ideas and local and national cultural traditions. (Sadlak, 1998, p. 107)

UNESCO also has a responsibility for promoting culturally sensitive approaches to cross-border education. The WTO and the Organization for Economic and Cultural Development (OECD) share responsibilities for encouraging nations to open up their state regulations for HE in order to encourage more interaction with outside partners (Altbach, 2002). The World Bank position on financing HE has been based on the assumption that HE provides greater private than public benefits and, as such, nations are encouraged to cut back their public funding for HE to spread the burden of financing HE provision to private individuals (see, for example, Psacharopoulos, 1994). Thus, despite the great expectation of universities to be entirely autonomous institutions, the influence of external, local, regional and international organizations appears to have intensified over the last decade.

 A fifth proposition is that the demand for HE will increase in years to come. This is due to the new demands placed by a knowledge- and information-based economy which will require more highly skilled global workers. Van Damme (2009) contends that HE will become a booming market and associated changes will include the emergence of a borderless HE market, controlled externally by international bodies. The implications of this for credentialism, quality and equity across HE providers are likely to be profound, though difficult to quantify and measure.

A sixth proposition for a global HE system is that it is characterized by increasing competition for students, resources, staff and funding. The number of international students on university campuses is currently being used as one of the best proxies for institutional competitiveness (Douglass *et al.*, 2009). Nations are investing more in educational attainment and human capital, as these are the desired outcomes of a competitive HE system. Consequently, the world's developed nations are scrambling for the best talent across different parts of the globe. A range of strategies is being utilized in various regions of the world to increase the competitiveness of HE systems, including: creating a more 'open door' policy for educational migrants; branding and re-branding nations as places of opportunity for educational advancement; increasing financial support for foreign students; and commercializing student recruitment (for example, in Australia, IPD International recruits approximately 20 per cent of all international students to Australia, according to the *World Education News and Reviews*, 2009). There is also some evidence which suggests that staff mobility is increasing as universities tend to get into the business of tracking the 'big hitters' in order xto enhance their research outputs for research assessment (RAE, 2008).

The final proposition about a global HE system is the focus contemporary universities have on the notions of global citizenship and the necessary graduate attributes required in students who engage with these global universities. The arguments for global citizenship are wide-ranging, encompassing political, social, cultural and economic dimensions (see, for example, Beck, 1998; Parekh, 2003; Dower, 2003; Hicks, 2002). Many universities are reviewing their graduate attributes in line with globalization imperatives and as another way to foster internationalization. As Barrie (2004, p. 263) states: 'Graduate attributes sit at a vital intersection of many of the forces shaping higher education today.' Most of the research on graduate attributes has been carried out in Australia and, although universities provide different sets of attributes, the theme of operating in global scenarios is repeatedly referred to in the literature, as are competences in intercultural communication, international literacy, international consciousness, global awareness and global perspectives (see, for example, Whalley *et al.*, 1997; Sadiki, 2001; Knight, 1999; Briguglio, 2007). Chapter 4 provides an in-depth analysis of issues of global citizenship and debates the idea of graduate attributes in an incisive way.

The above provide an overarching, though not entirely exhaustive, perspective of the global nature of HE today. Below we provide a few illustrative examples of the extent of this global nature of HE.

Estimates of numbers of students emigrating for purposes of study vary enormously, according to the source. Globally, it is estimated that there are about 150 million students in HE across the world, up from 68 million in 1991 (Bhandari *et al.*, 2008). At the same time many countries, especially the less developed ones, are failing to keep up with the demand for HE places. For example, demand for university places in China, India and Malaysia is said to have doubled in the last five years, outstripping the number of available places in the system (UNESCO, 2008). This partly explains why those countries have become the major exporting countries in the HE marketplace today. An Australian study has estimated that more than 7.2 million students will be studying outside their home countries in 2015 (Bohm *et al.*, 2002). Eight countries host 72 per cent of the world's international students. These include the US (20 per cent); the UK (13 per cent); Germany and France each (8 per cent); Australia (7 per cent); China (7 per cent); Canada (5 per cent); and Japan (4 per cent). Newer host countries in this global market include China, New Zealand, Malaysia and Singapore. Some argue that, while this will have the net effect of shrinking the international recruitment markets for the traditional hosts, it evens out the previously unidirectional mobility of students, if only somewhat (Teferra, 2005). Sub-Saharan Africa has the highest proportion of outward-bound students, while North America and Canada have the lowest.

Other forms of international education have been developed over the years, aimed at providing cost-effective forms of international learning with limited or no overseas travel. These have generally been described as internationalization at home (see Chapter 3 for an elaboration). Such programmes include distance education, joint degrees, branch campuses and sandwich programmes involving limited study-abroad provision.

Universities have now become key players in the global economy, contributing significantly to the knowledge stock of the world and to the financial economy of their countries. It is estimated that foreign students and their dependants contributed approximately US$15.54 billion to the US economy during the 2007–08 academic year (Association of International Educators, 2008). In the UK, in the same period, the British Council Global Value Report (2008) noted that the export value of UK HE was approximately £8.5 billion.

Different universities will be expected to respond in different ways to globalization forces as much as they are also expected to have different conceptualizations of what it means to internationalize the tripartite roles of teaching, research and enterprise. However, a review of the research on internationalization in HE suggests that many universities have adopted a two-pronged approach to the internationalization process, encompassing home-based (internationalization at home) and overseas-based (internationalization abroad) activities (see, for example, Crowther *et al.*, 2000). A range of models has also been developed which shows the variety of internationalization processes in universities in different parts of the world (see, for example, Neave, 1992; Davies, 1992; Van Dijk *et al.*, 1994; Rudzki, 1995; de Wit, 1995). Knight (1994) criticizes many of these models for being linear and static and proposes a cyclical model of internationalization processes in universities which has the key elements of developing an awareness of need; developing institutional commitment to the need; and planning; implementation, review and reinforcement. However, these models all seem to ignore the important aspect of recognizing the globalization context in which the internationalization processes are being developed. This is why we have developed a book which addresses the two concepts in the context of HE.

Overall, Maringe (2008) has categorized the variety of approaches into five distinct sets of activities encompassing a focus on international student recruitment; student and staff mobility programmes; collaborative teaching programmes such a joint degrees, overseas campuses and distance learning programmes; collaborative research and enterprise programmes; and curriculum reform programmes.

A range of studies has been undertaken on the impact of globalization in HE in different countries (see, for example, Burnett, 2008; Van Damme, 2001) and these seem to identify some common issues and challenges which have helped shape the rationale for this book. These include:

- the prevalence of a limited view of internationalization;
- the dominance of Western models of globalization;
- lack of coherence in the nature of university products suited to a globalized world;
- lack of strategies for measuring internationalization performance;
- incoherent strategies for curriculum internationalization;
- difficulties in making transitions from isolated to participative staff working models;
- a lack of suitable leadership for university internationalization.

Given the plethora of internationalization activities in universities across the world and the wide-ranging nature of the challenges faced by universities, the absence of a coherent theory of globalization and internationalization in HE fails to provide a basis for effective analysis, implementation and evaluation of institutional responses and strategic choices concerning the impact of globalization. The editors of this book, Felix Maringe and Nick Foskett, both then based at the University of Southampton, developed a proposal for a book which was commissioned by Continuum Educational Publishers.

Rationale and aims of the book

Universities all over the world increasingly recognize the challenges of globalization and the pressures for internationalization. The world's leading universities aspire to become global institutions involved in and leading world-class research at the cutting edge, drawing the highest calibre students and staff from different parts of the world, focused on scientific and social issues of global significance. Most universities, whether large or small and irrespective of their national market position, have begun to recognize the importance of developing teaching and instructional programmes that have both local and international relevance, both to recruit students in a global market and also to prepare all their students for lives in a globalized world.

International political organizations are driving a global HE agenda, too, for example through the decisions of the WTO to recognize education as a global service business, and of the European Union to promote convergence through the Bologna Process. In response to the economic importance of HE, many national governments are investing in promoting the internationalization of their own domestic university systems. All universities, therefore, are facing key issues about their own responses to the forces of globalization and the pressures to internationalize.

However, in trying to address these issues, universities face multiple challenges. A common strategic response has been the development of an 'internationalization agenda' – a programme of development and operational activities which may or may not be integrated into a wider institutional strategic plan. This has happened most frequently, though with little reference to supporting theoretical and strategic frameworks, and without a sound or substantial evidence base for either policy-making or operational activities. While the volume of literature supporting the theoretical, practical and strategic responses to the influence of globalization has grown significantly in business, economics and politics, there is as yet not much available with direct relevance to the HE sector. Furthermore, there is relatively little empirical evidence from research to underpin appropriate strategic responses.

The primary aim of this book, therefore, is to provide evidence from an analysis of emerging patterns of strategy and practice and, from research studies, how universities in different parts of the world are responding to the influences of globalization, the assumptions behind their chosen internationalization activities and strategies and the impact that internationalization is having at both local and international levels. In order to address this broad aim, the book was developed on the basis of a specific set of questions:

- How is the concept of globalization in the context of HE understood by those who lead universities across the world?
- What local, national and international pressures drive institutions to plan for globalization?
- How does this understanding help to shape institutional strategic responses to globalization?
- What conceptual models do universities adopt when considering the internationalization of HE?
- What strategies do HE institutions across the world adopt and develop as part of their internationalization agenda?
- What new challenges are being created as universities seek to become more international?
- What new leadership forms are needed in these transforming institutions and how are they being prepared?

To address these and other questions, the book is divided into four broad sections. The first section has five chapters and is devoted to a review of theoretical and strategic perspectives on the two concepts of globalization and internationalization.

In the opening chapter of the book the editors, Felix Maringe and Nick Foskett, provide a broad exploration of the concepts of globalization and internationalization highlighting the centrality of the force of the 'free markets' idea as an underpinning philosophy behind world globalization (see Kaskarelis, 2009). Internationalization is identified as an umbrella term for the range of institutional strategic responses to globalization in universities. The chapter makes significant propositions for what a global HE environment could mean and identifies key challenges universities face in their internationalization processes.

In the second chapter, Felix Maringe provides an in-depth discussion of globalization and internationalization, exploring a range of theoretical orientations and dimensions. The chapter recognizes the central importance, at both the global and the local level, of economic imperatives to the decisions of organizations and institutions concerning their cultural, ideological and political responsibilities to society. The need for a theoretical perspective on globalization in HE is underlined and the discussion identifies possibilities for developing this theory around four key elements. These include the overarching influence of the economic, political, cultural and knowledge elements of the global and local environments on the tripartite mission of universities in teaching/learning, research and enterprise. In discharging these key responsibilities, universities incorporate a range of internationalization strategies which fall into five broad categories of student recruitment and student and staff mobility, and collaborative partnership in research, in teaching, and in curriculum internationalization practices. A key element that is still missing in universities, but which needs to be incorporated, is assessment and evaluation of the success or otherwise of these strategies in terms of equity, quality and overall impact on students and on the institution. This model will be further developed in the final chapter of the book.

In Chapter 3, Nick Foskett draws on research into the internationalization strategies of a range of universities in different global settings in Asia and the UK. It identifies a range of strategies being deployed in these universities, but also discusses challenges for university leaders and synthesizes key themes emerging from the analysis. The chapter argues that being strong both domestically and internationally provides the best mix of internationalization strategies for universities. On this basis, the chapter provides a classification of universities based on their patterns of internationalization. These include: Domestic focused universities; imperialist universities; internationally-aware universities; internationally engaged universities; and internationally focused universities.

Vivienne Caruana provides Chapter 4 of the book, in which she explores the notion of global citizenship. In the chapter, Vivienne discusses the concept of global graduates and asks whether universities are engaging sufficiently with the reality of global graduates' skills, knowledge and competences.

Chapter 5 was jointly written by Izhar Oplatka and Jane Hemsley-Brown.

It provides an alternative view of globalization using the lens of institutional theory. The key argument is that universities are more institutions than organizations. As such, institutional theory is best suited to illuminate issues of response to globalization in the university sector. It uses a three-pronged analytical framework based on conformity to institutional rules; isomorphism, myth-making and the theory of rational choice to explore the extent to which university marketization is progressing. The chapter ends with an illuminating commentary on possible future directions of university marketization in the HE sectors. It concludes the first section of the book on theoretical perspectives of globalization in HE.

John Taylor opens the next section, on management and empirical perspectives, contributing two consecutive chapters. In Chapters 6 and 7, John explores the strategic and management implications for universities working under globalization. In Chapter 6 he explores the patterns of responses of national governments to the influence of globalization in HE. In Chapter 7, he focuses on specific management models emerging in HE designed to address the impact of globalization in HE.

In Chapter 8, Steve Woodfield deals with trends and emerging issues in international students' mobility. He identifies and discusses two factors of growth and diversity as driving the changing nature of student mobility. A range of models and types of student mobility are explored, including physical mobility, and virtual mobility in the context of national- and transnational student mobility. Challenges brought about through increasing student mobility are also discussed and include: economic and job disputes in host nations; increased terrorist threats; and the need to promote greater intercultural learning and understanding

In Chapter 9, Hongshia Zhang explores the impact of globalization on the Chinese education system. She deploys a descriptive and historical approach, describing how globalization has been embedded in the Chinese education system generally, and in Chinese HE specifically.

In Chapter 10, Rosalind Foskett discusses the impact of globalization on partnership development in the context of a project in which her university worked with a range of university partners in Africa. The chapter provides a well-argued discussion about how partnership working is likely to be the future *modus operandi* for university business in research, teaching and enterprise, and also points out potential pitfalls that need to be avoided when working in partnership. This chapter concludes the section on management and empirical perspectives.

The third section of the book focuses on several case studies of internationalization in different parts of the world. Rodney Arambewela discusses in Chapter 11 the notion of the student experience in the globalized HE environment. He examines the issues of a growing customer orientation, the increasingly litigious nature of the HE experience and the impact of the commodification of HE. He also explores the relevance of customer services in universities.

In Chapter 12, Dianmin Wang describes a case study on the introduction of classic literature into English studies in a Chinese university as a strategy for enhancing the international awareness of students of the increasingly international context in HE. Finally, he explores the impact of this institutional intervention.

Chapter 13, by Joanna Al-Youssef, discusses the notion of the institutionalization of internationalization in UK universities and explores the extent to which strategies developed to support the growth of internationalization are becoming an integral part of universities' focus and culture.

In Chapter 14, Laura Rumbley provides an excellent case study of how Spanish universities are internationalizing. Based on models developed by Knight, she evaluates the nature and extent of internationalization in a number of Spanish universities.

Chapter 15, by Yumei Jiang, focuses on the role of English language teaching in university internationalization in China. She discusses a variety of curriculum internationalization models and explores the extent to which they fulfil the requirements for fundamental curriculum internationalization.

The final section draws on several themes and issues in HE emerging from the context of globalization and internationalization. Paul Gibbs, in Chapter 16, examines the issue of standards and the commodification of HE. Paul raises several important questions regarding who should take responsibility for standards in a globalized HE system. Should HE be treated as a commodity, or a force for good? The chapter critiques the notion of the growing consumer orientation in HE.

In Chapter 17, Bruce Barnett and Steve Jacobson discuss the leadership needs for the globalized HE system, focusing on how leadership preparation should be improved and how partnership working will require new skills and leadership competences in twenty-first century universities.

In Chapter 18, Roberta Bassett provides an in-depth discussion of the role and increasing influence of global organizations such as the World Bank, the International Monetary Fund (IMF), UNESCO and the WTO and how the international agendas of these institutions are to impact on strategic and policy aspects of contemporary universities.

Mei Tian and John Lowe, in Chapter 19, focus on intercultural experience in English universities, with a case study of Chinese students. The chapter raises questions about the meaning attached to internationalization in UK universities and the efficacy of the strategies used to support its development.

In the final chapter of the book, Foskett and Maringe draw key lessons from the individual chapters and use the propositions of an HE system discussed earlier to evaluate where HE is today and where it might be in the next decade. The book concludes with a model that institutions can use to analyse their global orientation and on the basis of which they can evaluate progress in making university experience truly global and international.

References

Albrow, M. (1997), *The Global Age: State and Society Beyond Modernity*. Stanford: Stanford University Press.

Altbach, P. G. (2002), 'Knowledge and education as international commodities: The collapse of the common good', *International Higher Education*, 28, 2–5.

Association of International Educators (Nafsa) (2008), 'The economic benefits of
    international education to the United States for the 2007–2008 academic year: A
    statistical analysis', at http://www.nafsa.org (accessed 8 October 2009).
Barrie, S. (2004), 'A research-based approach to generic attributes policy', *Higher
    Education Research & Development*, 23, (3), 261–76.
Bassett, R. M. (2006), *The WTO and the University; Globalization, GATS and American
    Higher Education*. London: Routledge.
Beck, U. (1998), 'The cosmopolitan manifesto', in *New Statesman*, 20 March, 28–30.
Bhandari, R. and Blumenthal, P. (2008), *The Europa World of Learning*. London:
    Routledge.
Bohm, A., Davis, D., Meares, D. and Pearce, D. (2002), *Global Student Mobility 2005*.
    Sydney, Australia: IDP Education.
Briguglio, C. (2007), 'Educating the business graduate of the 21st century:
    Communication for a globalized world', *International Journal of Teaching and
    Learning in Higher Education*, 19, (1), 8–20.
British Council (2008), report by Davidson, M., CEO, *Annual Report for the British
    Council 2007–08*, at http://www.britishcouncil.org/annual-report/introduction_
    chief.htm (accessed 8 October 2009).
Burnett, S-A., 2008, 'The impact of globalisation on higher education institutions in
    Ontario'. Thesis (Doctor of Business Administration (DBA)). University of Bath.
Crowther, P., Joris, M., Otten, M., Nilsson, B., Teekens, H. and Wächter, B. (2000),
    'Internationalisation at home: A position paper', European Association for
    International Education in cooperation with the Academic Cooperation
    Association, IAK, IÉSEG, Nuffic, Katholieke Hogeschool Limburg and Malmö
    University.
Davies, J. (1992), 'Developing a strategy for internationalisation in universities:
    Towards a conceptual framework', in C. Klasek (ed.), *Bridges to the Future: Strategies
    for Internationalising Higher Education*. Carbondale: Association of International
    Education Administration, 177–90.
Douglass, J. A. and Edelstein, R. (2009), 'The global competition for talent: The
    rapidly changing market for international students and the need for a strategic
    approach in the US', Research and Occasional Paper Series, CSHE, August.
    Centre for Studies in HE: University of California, Berkeley.
Dower, N. (2003), *An Introduction to Global Citizenship*. Edinburgh University Press.
Emeagwali, P. (2003). 'How do we reverse the brain drain?', a paper presented at
    the Pan African conference on brain drain, Elsah, Illinois, USA, 24 October, at
    http://www.addistribunecom/Archives/2004/09–01–04/How.htm (accessed
    15 October 2009).
Foster, A. (2000), 'College, fighting US trade proposals, says it favors for-profit
    distance education', *The Chronicle of Higher Education*, 33.
Freidman, J. and Randeria, S. (2004), *Worlds on the Move: Globalization, Migration, and
    Cultural Security*. London: I. B. Tauris Publishers.
Giddens, A. (2000), *Runaway World: How Globalization is Reshaping Our Lives*. New
    York: Routledge.
Guardian University Guide League Tables (2009), at http://www.guardian.co.uk/
    education/table/2009/may/12/university-league-table (accessed 8 October
    2009).
Held, D. and McGrew, A. (eds) (1999), *The Global Transformations Reader: An
    Introduction to the Globalisation Debate*. New York: Wiley Blackwell.
Hicks, D. (2002), *Lessons for the Future: The Missing Dimension in Education*. London
    and New York: Routledge Falmer.
Kaskarelis, I. (2009), 'Free market economy, representative democracy, cultural

globalisation and the protection of the environment', *International Journal of Environment and Sustainable Development (IJESD)*, 8, (2), 132–50.

Knight, J. (1994), 'Internationalisation: Elements and checkpoints', CBIE Research, No. 7, CBIE, Ottawa.

—— (1999), 'A time of turbulence and transformation for internationalization', Proceedings of Internationalization of the Curriculum seminar, 5 October, Fremantle, Western Australia: IDP.

—— (2004). 'Internationalization remodelled: Definition, approaches, and rationales', *Journal of Studies in International Education*, 8, (1), 5–31.

Maringe, F. (2008), 'Globalisation and internationalisation in HE', a paper presented at the ICHEM conference at University of Minho, Portugal, 1–3 April.

Mittelman, J. H. (2000), *The Globalisation Syndrome*. Princeton: Princeton University Press.

Neave, G. 1992, *Managing Higher Education International Cooperation: Strategies and Solutions*. Reference Document, UNESCO, pp. 166–69.

Parekh, B. (2003), 'Cosmopolitanism and global citizenship', *Review of International Studies*, 29, 3–17.

Psacharopoulos, G. (1994), 'Returns to investment in education: A global update', *World Development*, 22, (9), 1325–43.

Research Assessment Exercise (RAE) (2008), Managers' Report at http://www.rae.ac.uk/pubs/2009/manager/manager.pdf (accessed 20 October 2009).

Robertson, R. (1992), *Globalisation*. London: Sage.

Rudzki, R. J. (1995), 'The application of a strategic management model to the internationalisation of higher education institutions', *Higher Education* 2, (June), 421–41.

Sadiki, L. (2001), *Internationalising the curriculum in the 21st century*. Canberra: CEDAM, Australian National University.

Sadlak, J. (1998), 'Globalisation and concurrent challenges for HE', in P. Scott (ed.), *The Globalisation of HE*. Buckingham, UK: Open University Press.

Scott, P. (2000), 'Globalisation and higher education: Challenges for the 21st century', *Journal of Studies in International Education*, 4, (1), 3–10.

Shanghai Academic Rankings of World Universities (2009), at http://www.arwu.org/ (accessed 8 October 2009).

Steger, M. B. (2003), *Globalisation: A Very Short Introduction*. Oxford: Oxford University Press.

Teferra, D. (2005), 'Brain circulation: Unparalleled opportunities, underlying challenges and outmoded presumptions', *Journal of Studies in International Education*, 9, (3), 229–50.

Teichler, U. (1996), 'Research on academic mobility and international cooperation in higher education: An agenda for the future', in P. Blumenthal, C. Goodwin, A. Smith and U. Teichler (eds), *Academic Mobility in a Changing World*. London: Jessica Kingsley, pp. 338–58.

Times Higher Education Sector (2009), World university rankings, at http://www.timeshighereducation.co.uk/WorldUniversityRankings2009.html (accessed 8 October 2009).

UNESCO (2008), *Global Education Digest, Comparing Education Statistics across the World*. Montreal, Canada: UNESCO Institute of Statistics.

Van Damme, D. (2001), 'Higher education in the age of globalisation: The need for a new regulatory framework for recognition, quality assurance and accreditation', introductory paper for the UNESCO Expert Meeting Paris, 10–11 September.

—— (2009), *European Universities in a Changing World*. Centre for Educational Research and Innovation, OECD/EDU-CERI.

Van Dijk, H. and Meijer, C. (1994), *Internationalization of Higher Education for the 21st Century*. Washington, DC: US Advisory Commission on Public Diplomacy.

Whalley, T., Langley, L., Villareal, L.and College, D.(1997), *Best Practice Guidelines for Internationalising the Curriculum*. Centre for Curriculum, Transfer and Technology. British Columbia: British Columbia Ministry of Education and Training.

de Wit, H. (1997), 'Studies in international education: A research perspective', *Journal of Studies in International Education*, 1, (1), 1–8.

de Wit, H. (ed.) (1995), *Strategies of Internationalisation for Higher Education: A Comparative Study of Australia, Canada, Europe, and the USA*. Amsterdam: European Association for International Education.

World Education News and Reviews (2009), July/August 2009, at http//:www.wes.org.

PART I

Theoretical and Strategic Perspectives

Chapter 2

The Meanings of Globalization and Internationalization in HE: Findings from a World Survey

Felix Maringe

Introduction

The concepts of globalization and internationalization have attained household status in many fields of human endeavour, including higher education (HE). To a large extent, globalization has replaced postmodernism (Giddens, 1990), a period in which development was broadly perceived within the confines of national rather international spaces as a framework for analysing social issues and societies. There seems to be an increasing political socio-economic, cultural and ideological homogeneity across many countries of the world. This is being driven by the increasing digitalization of the world; the accelerating cross-border financial flows and integration of economic activity; the accelerating human traffic across national borders; the blurring of national boundaries in favour of free cross-border movement and increasing use of common currencies and languages across different nations. The two concepts are complex and multifaceted and tend to exhibit a North-South, East-West divide in the way they are understood and responded to in different parts of the world. It can be argued that universities have always had an underlying international mission and focus, and as such are essentially international organizations. However, globalization has accelerated internationalization activity within universities. This chapter views globalization and internationalization as mutually reinforcing ideas, especially in the field of HE. Globalization largely provides the external impetus for accelerated institutional internationalization. On the other hand, the intensification of university internationalization activity reinforces accelerated globalization. Therefore, it seems logical to assume that how globalization is understood will influence the nature of internationalization activity in different universities. This chapter aims broadly to explore how these two concepts are understood in different universities across the world and to review the variety of internationalization activity that grows out of these understandings. To achieve this broad aim, the chapter will: (a) utilize a definitional and theoretical approach to explore the meanings of the concepts of globalization and internationalization; (b) use empirical evidence from the World Survey of the Impact of Globalization in Universities Project (Maringe *et al.*, 2009) to examine how the two concepts are understood in different universities, including the nature and types of internationalization activities that these understandings are driving at institutional levels; (c) identify and discuss key internationalization strategies that may privilege the development of a theory of globalization and internationalization in HE. We begin with a theoretical review of the two concepts.

Popular meanings of globalization

The terms hyper-globalizers, globalizers, and anti-globalizers have been used to describe the spectrum of opinions, reactions and responses of different people to the phenomenon of globalization (see Steger, 2003). Hyper-globalizers and globalizers sit at the positive end of the spectrum of opinion about globalization and tend to see it as a force for good, as the engine for greater world prosperity and as an unstoppable and uncontrollable force influencing world development in a positive way. They look positively at the impact of the Internet and its great contribution to knowledge generation and development. On the other hand, anti-globalizers emphasize the negative impact of globalization, especially the widening of poverty differentials between the rich nations of the North and the poor countries of the South.

The concept has also been closely associated with other ideas with which it is often used interchangeably in popular discourse. Such ideas include cosmopolitanism, which captures a sense of the universality of the human condition in which the boundaries between nations, cultures and societies are morally irrelevant (Appiah, 2006); deterritorialization, a kind of 'borderlessness' between nations where goods, services, money and people are free to move across countries without any restriction (Held *et al.*, 1999); glocalization, the idea that there are certain fundamental cultural characteristics shared locally by groups of nations or people which warrant regional and local cooperation, but which remain informed by more global events and structures. The African Union, for example, is a miniature version of the United Nations, while Bollywood is the Indian version of Hollywood (Robertson, 1992); and Westernization, a concept associated with consumerism, materialism, competitiveness, democracy, individual freedom and liberal values spearheaded by what has come to be known as the McDonaldization or Coca-colonization of the world. McDonald's and Coca-Cola are major world brands which have a worldwide presence and appeal. On the other hand, the East tends to be associated with notions of social and cooperative existence, hierarchical and highly structured lifestyles, unquestioning obedience, and centralized leadership verging on dictatorship. The term 'Westernization' is often used pejoratively to imply some kind of cultural imperialism in relations between West and East (Steger, 2003). Thus, globalization is perceived through the lenses of a complex web of subsidiary concepts, making it very difficult to pin down. Each of these ideas contributes to some degree towards our understanding of globalization. Often the various conceptualizations compete for a position of prominence in shaping peoples' understanding of globalization. Even when this happens, the same idea can have totally different connotations about globalization for different people. Problems often arise when the view one has about globalization is privileged entirely by one or a limited number of such conceptualizations. The point being made here is that a key characteristic of the idea of globalization is that it is a multi-dimensional and complex concept which is best understood from a holistic rather than a restricted perspective.

The complexity of globalization was captured by an anonymous writer responding to a call on the Internet to define the concept. The writer noted:

> Globalization is the death of Diana, Princess of Wales, beamed to 10 billion viewers simultaneously, a young Christian lady who was having an affair with an Afro-Arabian Muslim man, who died in the French capital of Paris, crushed in a German made car with a Dutch engine, driven by a Belgian driver who had drunk a few glasses of scotch whisky made in Scotland, hotly pursued by Italian paparazzi riding on Japanese scooters made in Malaysia using underpaid labour from Afghanistan.

Although the above does not count as a definition in the strictest sense, it captures a scenario befitting of Giddens' notion of a runaway world (Giddens, 2003) characterized by speed and spontaneity of human action and events; intercultural fusion; great fascination with celebrity news; economic interconnectedness; labour export and exploitation of labour from poor countries. It can be argued that all these constitute legitimate and powerful descriptions of the concept of globalization.

Dimensions of globalization

Steger (2003) devotes an entire book to discussing the nature of globalization in which he identifies and elaborates four broad dimensions: the economic, the political, the ideological and the cultural. The dimensions are intricately related to one another, since what happens to the economy is often dictated by political decisions and imperatives, and political decisions themselves are embedded within deep ideological and philosophical contexts. It can also be argued that the economy, ideology and politics are part of the cultural fabric of any nation. To talk about these dimensions of globalization separately, as Steger does, seems to suggest an independent existence of the ideas of politics, ideology, culture and economy. However, each of these has a plethora of issues that deserve separate treatment for the purposes of analysis. Essentially the economic dimension of globalization refers to the intensification and interconnectedness of economic activities, increased monetary and trade flows and the increasing importance of the Breton Woods institutions, the World Trade Organization, the GATS and the liberalization of trade, including in education. The political dimension focuses on the intensification of political interrelations across the world, the gradual demise of the nation state, and the development of global cities and global governance based on strengthening of international rather than national governance structures. The ideological dimension deals with the systems of shared values about globalization across different parts of the world. For example, where do people in different parts of the world stand in relation to claims and assumptions about globalization, such as its inevitability and irreversibility, its capacity to integrate markets, its spontaneity, its ability to benefit all, and equally, and its ability to usher a new world peace among other beliefs? Finally, the cultural dimension of globalization focuses on the intensification of cultural flows across the globe, with several potential consequences or outcomes, such as the rise of a homogenized world culture underwritten by the West in terms of the expanding use of English as the language of choice for international business, trade and commerce and as the preferred medium of learning and instruction in universities and other education environments. American sociologist George Ritzer talks of McDonaldization to describe the worldwide spread of the fast food concept in different parts of the globe. Conversely, the spread of Jihad, which to a large extent is the antithesis of McDonaldization, has brought international political and cultural resistance to a global scale.

The essences of these dimensions of globalization are further explored through the lens of theoretical perspectives, to which we now turn.

Globalization and higher education: a theoretical perspective

As yet, we do not have a coherent theory of globalization and internationalization in HE. In this section, we shall explore four theoretical perspectives of globalization borrowed from business, politics and international relations and assess the extent to which they can be used to explain developments in universities.

The first is 'world systems theory', which assumes that the world is divided into three broad areas or layers, with a core of about twenty super-rich nations, all with nuclear capability and all of which are technologically advanced. These countries basically dictate to the rest of the world and are host to key international financial institutions which control world economic ideas and financial systems. They control and dictate world prices for international labour, goods and services. In HE, we have elite universities which belong to cartels such as the Ivy League in the USA and the Russell Group in the UK. Rarely do these universities enter into partnership agreements with universities that do not belong to the same league, a strategy for the preservation of purity and maintenance of the group status quo. Entry to such elite groups is not easy and is jealously guarded. The second layer of the system, known as the periphery, is a group of poor countries that operate on the fringes and margins of poverty and underdevelopment. These countries supply raw materials and labour to rich countries in the core at prices that are dictated by the rich nations. Human migration patterns are generally from poor to rich countries and so too are recruitment patterns in universities. The best staff members from the periphery are often taken up by the good universities. It is very rare for staff to move from elite universities to those in the fringes. This serves to preserve the status quo in that institutions on the periphery are always struggling to recruit, while those in the core enjoy unlimited access to the best staff. In between the core and the periphery is a group of countries which are neither very rich nor very poor. These are termed the semi-periphery and are often used as a buffer in times of conflict to deflect responsibility. For example, in the Zimbabwe–UK conflict, South Africa (RSA) has been used as overseer of negotiations for power sharing and the formation of the government of national unity (GNU). In the event of failure, blame is effectively deflected from the UK to RSA. The system is self-selecting, self-fulfilling and self-preserving and is engineered to serve the best advantage of those in the core. The world systems theory thus explains the flows of capital, good and services across nations and the need to preserve economic and poverty differentials in service of the core. The theory legitimates inequality, which defines the fundamental organization of society.

The second is world polity theory. Boli *et al.* (1997) talk of a growing political isomorphism across nations of the world. They argue that political systems across the world are increasingly legitimated on the basis of a small set of values such as democracy and democratic governance; and diminished sovereignty and increasing subordination to regional or transnational governmental organizations. However, resistance exists in certain parts of the world to this underplaying of the importance of national sovereignty, especially where there might be suspicion of cultural imperialism or neo-colonialism, as is the case between Zimbabwe and the UK. However, despite a convergence on the values of democracy and democratic governance, its practice in different parts of the world varies quite significantly. For some countries in Africa, including Zimbabwe, coercion is an essential element of the democratic process. The outcome of elections, not the process which delivers these outcomes, is the important thing. As long as the supposedly right people are placed in power to rule, then the means by which they got there is inconsequential. In universities, the aspiration to become or be seen as international or global institutions is all-pervasive. Universities across the world also hold dearly to three fundamental freedoms related to teaching what they want, to who they choose, in the way they consider best. Another area where there is striking isomorphism in universities is in their tripartite mission of teaching, research and service/enterprise. To that extent, it can be argued that there is ideological isomorphism in universities, especially in regard to their overall mission, social relevance and purpose, which can be explained through the world polity theory. Areas where there is significant ideological isomorphism in universities in recent times include a growing managerialism in response to increasing market forces (Foskett, 1995); a growing strategic focus on institutional internationalization (Massoud *et al.*, 2007); and a convergence of thought regarding the overall mission and purpose of universities in society. However, the ways in which institutions choose to develop strategies about being management/marketing focused or about becoming international or global universities will vary. Such variations though are as important a part of universities as their ideological capital.

A third theoretical perspective of globalization is world culture theory (Robertson, 1992). It can be argued that this theory is closely aligned to world polity theory, as ideology is a key element of the cultural capital of any group of people. Culture is a very difficult word to pin down and, as indicated earlier, tends to encompass everything that defines a specific group of people in terms of fundamental beliefs, norms, values, language, symbols, technological implements, dress and food, among others. The central argument behind the theory is that the world is gradually becoming culturally homogeneous and that Western culture seems to be the blueprint upon which this cultural influence and transformation is based. For example, in more than 70 per cent of universities in the world, as in other fields of human endeavour, English is the preferred language of communication and teaching. Science and mathematics and their derived disciplines tend to occupy positions of strength and influence in universities. Of the vice-chancellors (VCs) in eight thousand universities across the world, nearly 30 per cent have science-related qualifications while the rest have qualifications shared between all other subject areas (*International Handbook of Universities*, 2009). Similarly, universities share an undergirding belief about being independent centres of unfettered thought and knowledge development. An opposing culture being underwritten by Islam is increasingly taking root in many parts of the world under the name of Jihad, a force designed to oppose Western cultural forms and influences. It can be assumed that universities, because of their culture of permissiveness, tolerance and openness, can potentially become the epicentres for the development, strengthening and spreading of Jihad as both a political and cultural ideology which will have an influence equal to or greater than the dominant Western culture.

The final theory is the neo-liberal theory of globalization. Essentially, neo-liberalism is about freeing trade between countries so that trade relations operate on the basis of free market principles. The problem is that the free market itself is a humanly contrived ideology and not a naturally or freely occurring framework for international and business or economic relations. There is always someone in control of the major decisions. As it turns out, such decisions are vested with large international corporate organizations such as the World Trade Organization (WTO), the Organization for Economic and Cultural Development (OECD), the World Bank (WB), and the United Nations Educational, Scientific and Cultural Organization (UNESCO), all of which are Western organizations. In HE, similar international organizations have been created to oversee key decisions and monitor the quality of university education. These include the Council for Higher Education Accreditation (CHEA), the Consortium on Financing Higher Education (COFHE),the Centre for Quality Assurance in International Education (CQAIE), the Association of Commonwealth Universities (ACU), and the Association of European Union Universities (AEUU). The free market is based on the notion of profit, which has resulted in the merchandization of knowledge under conditions that subject its content, structures and modes of accessibility to the pressures of a global market (Prasad, 2007). It is a philosophy which seeks to open up the world as a marketplace and not as a constellation of nation states dictating to one another about the conditions of trade and business. However, nation states have always sought to preserve their right to have the universities they want; which serve, first and foremost, local needs in political, social and economic development terms. As such, a tension arises in that neo-liberalism seeks to limit the role of the state in decisions about business and trade while elevating the role of international organizations in overseeing and legislating for international trade. Friedman (2006) argues that neo-liberalism is about free market capitalism, based on a range of free market policies such as competition, markets, deregulation, privatization and reduction of the welfare state.

Arguing that neo-liberalism and globalization are two sides of the same coin, Friedman notes:

> The driving force behind globalization is free market capitalism – the more you let market forces rule and the more you open your economy to free trade and competition, the more efficient your economy will be. Globalization means the spread of free market capitalism to virtually every country in the world. (Friedman, 1999, p. 9)

The impact of this on HE has been substantial over the years. Universities are no longer just places that generate knowledge for its own sake or for society; they are increasingly partnered with commercial and business corporations to create knowledge that has economic value. They have also become corporate organizations in their own right, maintaining a watchful eye on the bottom line and, in some cases, seeking to generate profit using minimum resources. In some institutions today, the VC does not have to be an academic, but should be an astute corporate leader and manager overseeing an organization that seeks to make money to a much greater extent than it seeks to generate knowledge (Goddard, 2006). In the UK, for example, a key reason for the increasing closure of some departments is lack of profitability. Knowledge which does not create money is thus increasingly being shunned. Conversely, education which does not lead to profitable employment and jobs is also being sidelined by students (Goddard, 2006).

Table 2.1 provides a summary of key definitions of globalization teased out of the literature which exemplify the key elements we think characterize the concept.

Table 2.1 Conceptualization of globalization

View of globalization	*Illustrative definition*	*Source*
As a capitalist world system	. . . the process, completed in the twentieth century, by which capitalist world systems spread across the globe	Wallerstein, 1988
As world economic integration	. . . a process associated with increasing economic openness, growing economic interdependence and deepening economic integration in the world economy	Deepak Nayyar, 2006
As increasing social, political and ideological interdependence between nations	. . . the intensification of worldwide social relations which link distant localities in such a way that local happenings are shaped by events occurring many miles away and vice versa	Giddens, 2000

(continued)

Table 2.1 (*cont.*)

View of globalization	Illustrative definition	Source
As a multi-dimensional concept defining the deepening of interdependencies	. . . a multi-dimensional set of social processes that create, multiply, stretch, and intensify worldwide social interdependencies and exchanges, while at the same time fostering in people a growing awareness of deepening connections between the local and the distant	Steger, 2003
As a neo-liberal philosophy	. . . the development of international relations based on the values of the free market	Harvey, 2003

Before turning to the idea of internationalization, we offer a definition of globalization of our own, which draws upon these key ideas:

Excellent

Globalization is a multidimensional concept that relates to creating a world in which the social, cultural, technological, political and ideological aspects of life become increasingly homogeneous and in which economic interdependence and growth are driven by the principles of the free market.

Internationalization

Universities have always had an international mission and character. The word university itself subsumes the notion of the universe, a kind of international space for the development of universal knowledge by individuals and groups of staff working locally and internationally with students and resources from different parts of the world. However, as globalization has intensified over the last few decades, organizations including HE have turned to internationalization as both a response and a proactive way of meeting the demands of greater globalization, both in the immediate and as preparation for envisaged futures. It has been argued earlier in this paper that the two concepts are mutually reinforcing. The term became part of the lexicon of HE in the late eighties and especially became formalized following the General Agreement on Trade in Services (GATS) conference in 2003. Following neo-liberal prescriptions of the WTO, the GATS sought to liberalize trade in goods and services in industries and in education. In particular, HE was defined in this agreement as 'an international service industry to be regulated through the marketplace and through international trade agreements' (Bassett, 2006, p. 4). As a consequence of this, internationalization became a buzz-word in university sectors across the world as institutions and nations prepared themselves to become strong and effective actors on a new global HE platform.

How internationalization is defined in the literature

There is a growing base of literature on internationalization in HE which explores a wide variety of internationalization conceptualizations. Such conceptualizations include sectoral, national and institutional strategies or activities designed to incorporate international education into existing curricula. Other conceptualizations focus on enhancement of educational quality; growth of enterprise or entrepreneurial education and the associated managerialism in HE; a focus on recruiting international students; and the development of partnership education and research in HE. Table 2.2 provides a summary of definitions and perspectives of internationalization by some of the most influential writers in this field.

Motives/rationales and strategies for internationalization

Knight (2006) has identified four broad rationales for internationalization in HE, driven primarily by globalization forces in the political, economic and the socio-cultural dimensions. However, while these forces provide an external impetus for internationalization, there is also a powerful internal driver of internationalization based purely on academic arguments, providing the fourth rationale for internationalizing the university. The economic argument operates at the institutional and national level and more recently at regional levels, such as the EU level. Maringe and Gibbs (2009) found that university institutions that exhibit high levels of internationalization tend to have the following characteristics:

- They have highly diversified income generating sources.
- They have high annual income turnovers.
- They contribute more strongly to local and regional economic development.
- They have diversified employment profiles.
- They attract more foreign staff and students.

The above institutional characteristics have been shown to be positively associated with organizational economic performance. At the national level, universities that have a strong international focus make a significant contribution to the national economy. For example, Adams (2004) found that international students contribute approximately 10 per cent of all UK receipts from UK visitors and that expenditure by international students generates about £2.4 billion across the economy and creates about 22,000 jobs. The local, regional and international impact of international universities has thus been well documented. Adams (2004), for example, observed that UK universities with the strongest international focus, located mainly in London, the East and South East tend to have the highest numbers of research-active staff, the highest research grants and contract income, the highest PhD awards and the most published papers. In addition, these regions account for 60 per cent of the money jointly spent on research and development by university/business collaborations. The economic case for internationalization is thus quite clear.

Table 2.2 Conceptualizations of internationalization in HE

View of internationalization	Definition/perspective	Source
Integration of the international dimension	. . . internationalization at the national, sector, and institutional levels is defined as the process of integrating an international, intercultural, or global dimension into the purpose, functions or delivery of postsecondary education.	Knight, 2004
Enhancing the quality of HE	. . . increasing focus on international education raises the quality of HE in the global labour market, but equally raises issues about how to measure that quality	Van Damme, 2001
Focus on international education	. . . ranges from traditional study abroad programs, which allow students to learn about other cultures, to providing access to higher education in countries where local institutions cannot meet the demand. Other activities stress upgrading the international perspectives and skills of students, enhancing foreign language programs, and providing cross-cultural understanding	Altbach and Knight, 2006
Growth of enterprise, entrepreneurialism and managerialism in HE	. . . internationalization as crucial for universities to retain competitiveness through university business models which underpin an entrepreneurial culture. . . universities as entirely business entities	Goddard, 2006
Overseas student recruitment and staff mobility focus	. . . flows of staff and students in both directions, strategic alliances, joint programmes with external institutions	Fielden, 2008
Partnership development in HE	. . . a focus on the development of partnerships to reduce risk, increase competitiveness, enhance image and broaden the knowledge base for research, enterprise and education	Teichler, 2004

The political argument for internationalization also operates at institutional and regional levels. However, the political argument has been changing over the years. In colonial times, education was seen as a tool for both political and economic domination, in terms of developing a desired workforce and much-needed leadership in the colonized countries. Higher education especially was specifically aimed at the development of educated elites as an integral part of this political process of domination and economic expansion (Maringe *et al.*, 2009). In the post-colonial era, international education has become an important tool for economic migration. Maringe and Carter (2007) identified the international nature of university provision as one of the key drivers of overseas study migration decisions by students from less developed to more developed countries. Thus, attracting and recruiting international students has become a key strategic goal of universities in the West, for economic, political and cultural motives.

The socio-cultural rationale for university internationalization can be explained in a variety of ways. However, the dominant interpretations derive from the reality of globalization. HE is seen as having the potential to contribute to the increasing cultural homogenization of the world (de Wit, 2003). It is assumed that the attainment of a stable and peaceful world rests broadly on greater cultural integration and understanding. The spread of English as a language of communication and learning and as a tool for world business and commerce is part of this cultural homogenization project. However, in times when major world powers are seeking greater influence across the globe, knowledge and understanding of other people's cultures, language and socio-political systems has become increasingly important. Universities are seen as well suited to nurture this greater socio-cultural understanding and the more they can do in this regard, the more international their profile becomes.

The academic rationale for internationalization is based on a wide range of arguments, including the cultural relevance of international learning; the need to contribute to evolving global labour market needs; the growing importance of international and comparative learning in a globalizing world; the need for curricula redesign to face new challenges in a globalizing world and the importance of deconstructing Western models of knowledge and understanding in order to accommodate other models from different parts of the world (Rudolph, 2005; Resnik, 2008). A key aspect of the academic rationale for internationalization is the notion of the type of graduate required in the new global world. The new global worker is expected to have a cognitive, emotional, social and ethical multiculturalism, or what others refer to as 'international mindedness' (Resnik, 2008, p. 153).

Research suggests that there is a wide variety of strategies for internationalization adopted in different universities (Massoud *et al.*, 2007). Maringe (2008), however, developed five broad categories of internationalization strategies based on research carried out in 37 UK universities. These strategies were accorded varying importance and significance by staff in different universities, as summarized in Table 2.3.

The findings suggest that newer universities tend to emphasize student recruitment, development of offshore teaching programmes and curriculum internationalization while older universities place more emphasis on student and staff mobility and partnerships in research and enterprise. These differences in approach may be due to the focus that the new and old universities tend to place on research and teaching. Older universities tend to be more research-intensive while newer institutions are more teaching-focused. Clearly, activities which generate money are prioritized more highly in the internationalization processes of universities. Thus, despite the centrality of the curriculum in the business of universities, curriculum internationalization does not appear to be a top priority strategy in the majority of universities. This might be linked to the fact that changing the purpose, content and methodology of teaching

Table 2.3 Range and importance of university internationalization strategies

5 Strategies

Internationalization strategy	Rank	Type of university
① Recruitment of international students	1	All but especially in newer universities, former polytechnic and privately funded institutions
② Student and staff exchange programmes	2	All but especially in the older universities
③ Development of international partnerships for teaching, including joint programmes, offshore teaching and learning	3	All but especially in the newer universities
④ Development of international collaborative partnerships for research, entrepreneurship and development	4	All but especially in the older universities
⑤ Curriculum internationalization, ranging from minor changes in content to fundamental redesign of objectives, teaching methods and assessment	5	All, but especially in newer universities

is perhaps the most deskilling and risky decision university staff might make and one that they would not embrace wholesale without some resistance. That decision requires significant re-learning and frankly, university staff, especially those in research-intensive universities, would rather invest more learning time in their research than in their teaching.

Although there is a multiplicity of strategies in different universities, there seems to be greater convergence on the understanding of the idea of internationalization than there is on the idea of globalization. While some emphasize the notion of cultural compatibility in education (Ebuchi, 1989), or the importance of providing an educational experience in an integrated global environment (Association of Universities and Colleges of Canada, 1993), it is Knight and de Wit's integration of an international or intercultural dimension into the tripartite mission of universities in teaching, research and enterprise that seems to have struck a resonance with scholars and practitioners in this area.

The bulk of literature on globalization and internationalization in HE has been produced by Western writers who base their arguments on research and evidence in Western countries. This piecemeal approach is an affront to the ideals of globalization and appears to endorse the dominance of Western models in shaping understanding and practice in this area. Recognizing this weakness, we decided to undertake a global survey of the impact of globalization and internationalization in HE, which we now turn to in the next section of this chapter.

The global survey (Maringe *et al.*, 2009)

The survey had three main aims: to explore how key senior university staff in different parts of the world interpret and define the ideas of globalization and internationalization; to explore the key internationalization strategic choices of universities in different parts of the world; and to develop a mapping of the status of internationalization as a strategic option and as an area of practice in universities in different parts of the world. A questionnaire survey was developed and sent out to two hundred universities across major regions of the world. Response rate was low (49 returns; about 25 per cent) despite repeated (three waves) postal questionnaire administrations. Responses came from: the USA (8); Canada (5) Australia (4); UK (5); Africa South of the Sahara (4); South America (3); China (6); North Africa and the Middle East (7); Japan and the Koreas (4); and Continental Europe (3). The findings are statistically representative, but show some interesting patterns. Despite a global recognition of the importance and impact of globalization on universities and recognition of the need to intensify the internationalization processes as a key strategic response, there is a North–South or East–West divide in the way the concepts are understood and in the specific strategic internationalization choices made in different universities. Findings were collated and compared in three broad categories for each of the aims of the research, that is, Western universities (USA, Canada, Australia, UK and continental Europe); Non-Western Universities (South America, Africa South of the Sahara, China, Japan and the Koreas); and North Africa and the Middle East universities.

Meanings attached to globalization

Table 2.4 Views about globalization across universities

Views about globalization	Western universities n=25	Non-Western universities n=17	North Africa and the Middle East n=7
Spontaneous inevitable world social, political and economic integration	About 80%	About 60%	About 30%
Contrived Western ideology for political and economic domination	About 10%	About 30%	About 75%
Postmodern form of imperialism designed to establish Western models of democracy	About 10%	About 30%	About 75%
Results in skewed development favouring rich nations	About 60%	About 80%	About 75%
Results in general improvement of people's lives across the world	About 60%	About 40%	About 15%

Using Steger's normative classification of globalization views, it is clear that views in Western universities tend to be pro-globalization, with a few exhibiting hyper-globalist views, while those in non-Western universities are somewhat sceptical. Clearly those in North Africa and the Middle East are generally anti-globalization and sometimes quite cynical.

In terms of the perceived impact of globalization, the differences in views are less clear. [There is general agreement that globalization is accelerating uneven development across the world; that it has resulted in the net migration of students from poor to rich nations and that it has improved access to resources for teaching and learning. However, staff in North African and Middle East universities believe more strongly than staff in other categories that globalization has had the net effect of accelerating the brain drain from less developed to developed nations.]

Be aware

Views about internationalization

Generally, staff across the universities saw internationalization as an HE response to the influences of globalization. A small number in Western universities captured the reciprocal nature of the two concepts. The importance attached to the five internationalization strategic responses was different across the universities. While Western universities prioritized student recruitment, collaborative teaching and research, the strategies of choice in North Africa and the Middle East tended to show concern for enhancing the quality of the curriculum through a variety of curriculum internationalization approaches. Table 2.5 shows this variation in perception and strategic choice in the different countries.

The variations in internationalization strategic options in different countries in this research mirror those found within different types of universities in the UK (Maringe, 2008), where new (and hence still developing) universities placed greater emphasis on mobility-related strategies while the more stable older universities tended to focus on research-related activities.

The status of internationalization in universities

Data obtained from the global survey show that across all universities, internationalization is currently viewed as a key strategic issue. Activities around this strategic option are generally headed by very senior academics, the majority of whom are female, except in North Africa and the Middle East where all strategy heads were male. Their job titles also reflect this seniority as presidents, provost or deputy provosts, pro vice-chancellors and deputy vice-chancellors, directors and deans of faculties. The majority of these staff are educated to doctoral levels, although a few have master's degrees in some universities. However, the PhDs are generally not in areas of management or strategy. The majority of the universities which took part describe their institutions as international and almost half of them have a separate strategy document for internationalization. More than two thirds of those that do not have a separate strategy document

Table 2.5 Views and internationalization strategic choices across universities

Views about internationalization	*Western universities n=25*	*Non-Western universities n=17*	*North Africa and the Middle East n=7*
HE response to impact of globalization	80%	80%	75%
Intensifies globalization	60%	40%	15%
Largely about international student recruitment	80%	80%	15%
Largely about student and staff exchange programmes	80%	80%	60%
Development of international partnerships for teaching, including joint programmes, offshore teaching and learning	80%	80%	30%
Development of international collaborative partnerships for research, entrepreneurship and development	80%	80%	75%
Curriculum internationalization, ranging from minor changes in content to fundamental redesign of objectives, teaching methods and assessment	20%	20%	75%

are in non-Western universities and in North Africa and the Middle East. The above findings partly confirm those by Massoud and Ayoubi (2007), but could point to a new understanding about the relatively lower status of internationalization as a strategic option in non-Western universities generally and those in the Middle East and North Africa specifically.

Summary and conclusion: towards a theoretical model of globalization and internationalization in HE

The chapter provided a theoretical reflection on the meanings and understandings of the concepts of globalization and internationalization. It began by identifying the fact that we do not yet have a coherent theory of globalization in HE. What is currently available draws heavily from Western models and understandings of the concepts. Clearly, globalization is a multifaceted concept with several dimensions which we know to have a potential impact on education. One of the most obvious impacts of globalization in HE has been the intensification of internationalization activities on many university campuses.

Four theoretical models of globalization have been explored, all of which emphasize some fundamental ideas which have relevance to our understanding of how globalization is influencing HE in different parts of the world. The models highlight the development of political, cultural, ideological and economic homogeneity around the world as the basis of globalization. Equity, in terms of fairness and justice; quality and the creation of value for who engage with HE are assumed to be the outcomes of this spread of goodwill across the world. The success or failure of responses to globalization in any field of endeavour will necessarily have to be measured against these criteria. Beyond these criteria, questions need to be asked about the worth of seeking greater homogeneity across nations in the first place. Might celebrating difference be a more noble and achievable goal and might a focus on difference rather than sameness lead to greater fairness, justice, equity and quality?

The privileging of Western models as a basis for our understanding of globalization and internationalization need to be challenged. There is a need to develop new understandings based on global-scale projects which draw evidence from a broader platform of countries across the world. Our research on the global survey at Southampton has hopefully started that process and its findings, though limited by the size of the sample, provide a good basis for exploring the impact of globalization on HE and an opportunity for integrating non-Western models into our current understanding of the concepts.

The above discussion and empirical findings lead us to construct a tentative theoretical model which helps bring together understandings about globalization and internationalization in the context of HE. The model, to be developed more extensively in the final chapter, highlights the importance of economic imperatives at both the global and local levels and places HE responses at the centre as the unit of analysis. The economic imperatives are filtered through and operate within the contexts of political, ideological cultural and socio-economic university responsibilities which relate to the tripartite mission of universities in teaching, research and enterprise. As a response to these global and local imperatives, universities across the world seem to be developing their mission through a range of strategies which include international student recruitment, staff and student exchange programmes, collaborative partnerships in research enterprise and teaching, and in curriculum reform. The emphasis and focus placed on any one or a combination of these strategies depends on the local context of the institution and the imperatives of globalization in that part of the world. In order to execute these responsibilities in a way which reflects sensitivities to the global impacts, universities need to constantly evaluate their programmes in equity, quality and career effectiveness terms.

The model can be both an analytical or evaluative tool which personnel in universities can utilize to develop a good understanding of both the processes and impact of globalization and internationalization in their institution.

References

Adams, K. (2004), 'Modelling success: Enhancing international postgraduate research students' self-efficacy for research seminar presentations', *Higher Education Research & Development*, 23, (2), 10–26.

Altbach, P. G. and Knight, J. (2006), 'The internationalization of higher education: Motivations and realities', *Journal of Studies in International Education*, 11, (3–4), 290–305.

Appiah, K. A. (2006), *Cosmopolitanism: Ethics in a World of Strangers*. New York: Norton & Company.

Association of Universities and Colleges of Canada (1993), *Guide to Establishing International Academic Links*. Ottawa: The AUCC.

Bassett, R. M. (2006), *The WTO and the University: Globalisation, GATS, and American Higher Education*. London: Routledge.

Boli, J. and Thomas, G. M. (1997), 'World culture in the world polity', *American Sociological Review*, 62, (2), 171–90.

Van Damme, D. (2001), 'Quality issues in the internationalisation of higher education', *Higher Education*, 41, 415–41.

Deepak, N. (2006), 'Globalisation, history and development: A tale of two centuries', *Cambridge Journal of Economics*, 30, 137–59.

Ebuchi, K. (ed.) (1989), *Foreign Students and Internationalisation of HE*. Hiroshima: Research Institute for HE.

Fielden, J. (2008). *The Practice of Internationalisation: Managing International Activities in UK Universities*. UK Higher Education International Unit.

Foskett, N. (1995), 'Marketing, management and the school: A study of a developing marketing culture in secondary schools', unpublished doctoral thesis, University of Southampton.

Friedman, T. (1999), *The Lexus and the Olive Tree*. London: HarperCollins.

—— (2006), *The World is Flat: The Globalised World in the Twenty-First Century*. London: Penguin.

Giddens, A. (1990), *The Consequences of Modernity*. London: Polity Press.

—— (2000), *Runaway World: How Globalization is Reshaping Our Lives*. New York: Routledge.

Giddens, A. (ed.) (2003), *The Progressive Manifesto. New Ideas for the Centre-Left*. Cambridge: Polity.

Goddard, S. E. (2006), 'Uncommon ground: Indivisible territory and the politics of legitimacy', *International Organization*, 60, (1), 35–68.

Harvey, D. (2003), *The New Imperialism*. Oxford: Oxford University Press.

Held, D. and McGrew, A. (eds) (1999), *The Global Transformations Reader: An Introduction to the Globalisation Debate*. New York: Wiley Blackwell.

International Association of Universities (2009), *The International Handbook of Universities*, 20th edn. Palgrave Macmillan in association with: International Association of Universities.

Knight, J. (2004), 'Internationalization remodelled: Definition, approaches, and rationales', *Journal of Studies in International Education*, 8, (1), 5–31.

—— (2006), *Internationalisation of HE: New Directions, New Challenges: The 2005 IUA Global Survey Report*. Paris: International Association of Universities.

Maringe, F. (2008), 'Globalisation and internationalisation in HE: A survey of UK universities', paper presented at the ICHEM Conference at the University of Minho, Portugal, April 1–3.

—— (2009), 'Internationalisation strategies in UK universities: An exploratory study', paper presented at the ICHEM Conference at Minho University April 1–3.

Maringe, F. and Carter, S. (2007), 'International students' motivations for studying in UK HE: Insights into the choice and decision making of African students', *International Journal of Educational Management*, 21, (6), 459–75.

Maringe, F. and Foskett, N. (2009), 'Globalisation and internationalisation of HE: An international survey', School of Education, University of Southampton.

Maringe, F. and Gibbs, P. (2009), *Marketing Higher Education: Theory and Practice*. London: McGraw Hill/Open University Press.

Massoud, H. K. and Ayoubi, R. M. (2007), 'The strategy of internationalization in universities: A quantitative evaluation of the intent and implementation in UK universities', *International Journal of Educational Management*, 21, (4), 329–49.

Prasad, M. (2007), *The Politics of Free Markets: The Rise of Neo-Liberal Economic Policies in Britain, France, Germany, and the United States*. Chicago: University of Chicago Press.

Resnik, J. (ed.) (2008), *The Production of Educational Knowledge in the Global Era*. Rotterdam: Sense Publishers.

Ritzer, G. (2005), *The McDonaldisation of Society*. London: Sage.

Robertson, R. (1992), *Globalisation*. London: Sage.

Rudolph, C. (2005), Sovereignty and Territorial Borders in a Global Age. *International Studies Review*, 7, 1–20.

Steger, M. B. (2003) *Globalisation: A Very Short Introduction*. Oxford: Oxford University Press.

Teichler, U. (2004), 'The changing debate on internationalisation of higher education', *Higher Education*, 48, 5–26.

Wallerstein, I. (1988), *The Modern World System*, vol. 3. New York: New York University Press.

de Wit, K. (2003), The consequences of European integration for higher education', *Higher Education Policy*, 16, (2), 161–78.

Chapter 3

Global Markets, National Challenges, Local Strategies: The Strategic Challenge of Internationalization

Nick Foskett

Introduction

Higher education (HE) is an international business operating in a global market, with some 100,000 institutions describing themselves as universities. Universities are not only a significant service sector in their own right (Breton, 2003), however, but are an important contributor to the whole global economy as a primary engine of economic growth. Governments in almost every country are committed to increasing the proportion of their workforce with tertiary-level qualifications and to using the research and enterprise 'products' of universities as key contributions to their nation's economic and social well-being. Increasing the proportion of the workforce educated to tertiary level by one per cent is estimated to produce a 6 per cent growth in Gross Domestic Product (GDP) (OECD, 2007). The recognition that higher education is a key driver in economic and social development is, therefore, now central to national government perspectives on the role of universities (Stephens, 2009).

The three principal activities of universities (education, research and enterprise/knowledge transfer) all offer global prospects. An underpinning principle of research is that 'knowledge' is a consistent and global 'good', and that the advancement of knowledge is optimized by drawing together the expertise of academics from around the world. Journals, conferences, academic visits and research collaborations provide the mechanism for such an international perspective on research questions, and make the research community inherently international.

Such a pressure towards global collaboration, however, sits alongside strong pressures for global competition among universities. The demand for education at tertiary level in a different country has grown significantly in the last decade, and universities have sought to acquire an increasing share of this global market. Universities in all countries have responded to the increased transnational mobility of students through strategies ranging from direct marketing to the provision of overseas campuses and the establishment of student mobility partnerships. While this is partly (even predominantly) driven by economic motives, there is an important element of this mobility driven by the desire to share cultures and emphasize the global nature of the academic enterprise.

The third activity of universities, enterprise and knowledge transfer, is perhaps the least well-developed characteristic of HE, but business and innovation opportunities are available to universities from the local to the global scale, and the success of HE innovations such as Google show the global potential for university enterprise.

The local, regional and national perspectives still feature large in the focus of all universities, of course, and for most institutions it is those scales of operation that will continue to dominate their activity. Increasingly, though, the international perspective has become an important focus of universities, and especially for those regarded as the leading institutions in their own country. This pressure to respond to global markets is also becoming an increasingly heightened challenge. As Neubauer and Ordonez (2008, p. 51) have indicated:

> The challenge that rapid globalization presents to universities is whether they can continue to adapt, no longer slowly or organically but in the quantum leaps required by new realities. Knowledge . . . is now created, transmitted and stored through modalities, institutions and configurations that were previously unknown and at speeds once unimaginable.

Universities are obliged to develop their strategies for the future, therefore, to include an international dimension to their profile, balanced with their commitments and engagement to the local and national context. Global markets raise challenges for universities and governments at national level and require local strategies by institutions to stake a place in those global arenas.

This chapter draws on research into the internationalization strategies of a range of universities in different global settings. The universities studied are all based in Asia or in the United Kingdom (UK), but represent a diverse set of operational contexts. The analysis identifies the key strategies being deployed to promote internationalization, and considers the challenges for university leaders in developing and operationalizing such strategies. It focuses particularly on the development of strategy by the senior leadership of universities in response to the rapidly changing context within which they operate, and it offers, therefore, both a specific view of internationalization in higher education and also a perspective on how university leaders 'manage' and 'strategize' in response to dynamic and often ambiguous and unclear external environments (Shiel *et al.*, 2008). Internationalization challenges the skills of leaders to scan, sense and respond to changing social, economic and political circumstances at an international scale, and then to plan and implement change on an institutional scale in the context of universities whose academic staff are still principally engaged in the conservative and monastic dialogue and discourse of research, scholarship and 'the academy'. The chapter concludes that the most challenging management issues relate to a number of perceived 'deficits' in the skill sets of senior leaders in universities in relation specifically to the availability of effective marketing insights, the development of senior colleagues with appropriate externally focused management skills, and the skills of university presidents in adjusting their operational approaches to adapt to globalized HE markets.

Although most leading universities have had a degree of international engagement since their foundation, internationalization has emerged on their strategic agenda to a significant extent principally over the last decade, and has risen rapidly up that agenda in the last three to five years (Weber *et al.*, 2008). 'Internationalization' is a complex and multifaceted concept, which makes precise definition elusive. All definitions, however, share a common perspective that it is about universities increasing the international dimension in all aspects of their work. Knight (2003, p. 5) defines internationalization as '. . . the process of integrating international dimensions into teaching, research and service'. This is helpful as it emphasizes that internationalization is not simply about recruiting students from other countries, but is about changing the nature, perspective and culture of all of the functions of a university. Internationalization reaches to the heart of the very meaning of 'university' and into every facet of its operation, from teaching and education to research and scholarship, to enterprise and innovation and to the culture and ethos of the institution.

We have already touched on some of the high-level reasons for the growth of an international perspective, but the motivation for universities to engage with internationalization is complex in detail. Its emergence can be seen as an inevitable consequence and component of globalization (Deem, 2001). Waters' (1995) analysis distinguishes distinct but strongly intertwined processes which he differentiates as political, economic and cultural globalization. All three have a direct connection to the world of universities, for in most countries universities are at the heart of economic and cultural development, and are key players in the political arena, not only by influencing political thought and process but in their role as a mechanism used by governments to shape social and economic change.

From the perspective of governments, the encouragement of universities to engage internationally may be seen as largely having an economic motive – in the UK, for example, knowledge services contribute 25 per cent of all exports and 6.3 per cent of GDP. Governments have been strongly motivated to invest in the development of research in their universities. Zhang (2006) has described the investment in the '973 Project' universities by the Chinese government (Ministry of Science and Technology, 1997), and Shin (2009) has considered the effect of the South Korean government's Brain Korea21 (BK21) Project. But most countries are also investing heavily in HE, however, so that although the BK21 Project has been successful in its aim of developing world class research universities, Shin concludes that the project did not lessen the gap between Korean universities and world-class research universities in the US, China or Japan as they too were strongly investing in similar developments.

At the same time governments have been investing in schemes to attract overseas students to their universities. For example, international students bring £5.5 billion per annum to the UK economy, and the work of the British Council through its Education UK programme, and of the British Government through the Prime Minister's Initiatives (PMI1 and PMI2), has been focused on at least retaining market share.

For the universities themselves, though, the motives are more diverse and are underpinned by both economic and more altruistic perspectives. While globalization has stimulated a growing 'economization of society and the erosion of all that is considered public' (Wolin, 1981, p. 23), universities strive to retain their wider social mission. Fielden (2006), for example, identifies three underpinning motivations for universities in internationalizing:

1 Developing human resources for competitive global markets. This perspective recognizes that most graduates will be employed in fields that have an international dimension to the work, whether they are working overseas, working for a TNC (transnational corporation) or simply in an organization which engages with other countries or other cultures. Preparing students to be able to work in such a context is seen as an important educational priority by universities.

2 Researching and contributing to the resolution of global problems. Most of the major research challenges relate to global issues (health, climate change, food supply and global security, for example) which, by definition, require international collaboration with academics, universities, businesses and governments.

3 An educative role in promoting international values. This perspective recognizes that a key priority for universities is in ensuring students are 'global citizens', understanding and valuing cultural diversity, promoting economic and social development and engaged with global issues such as poverty, health and environmental change.

Scott (2005) offers a different perspective on university motivations towards internationalization by considering the strategic position that institutions might adopt, and identifies three specific stances:

1 An economic position in which universities regard themselves as 'knowledge businesses battling for market share'.

2 A cultural position in which universities act as 'key cultural mediators in the encounter between world culture and national cultures'.

3 A stewardship position in which they fulfil 'guardian roles alerting societies to major emerging issues'.

Whatever the motivation and perspective, though, it is clear that internationalization is a central concern of universities. Foskett (2008a) has shown that in 2007 in the UK, for example, there were five national conferences on aspects of HE internationalization (ranging from student recruitment to developing international research partnerships) (for example, see CIHE, 2007), four reports for national organizations considering the development of internationalization in universities (for example, see Fielden, 2007), and every government HE policy document referred to the importance of internationalization. Of the 22 advertisements for university vice-chancellors (presidents) during 2007, every one stipulated that candidates should have an international perspective, and 43 per cent of universities were identified as having a deputy vice-chancellor (or equivalent) with a brief for internationalization.

The focus on internationalization can also be seen in a range of characteristics of higher education, globally. The number of students worldwide pursuing HE has risen from 40 million in 1975 to 150 million in 2007 and, of this number, figures for those opting to study abroad has been growing significantly, from 600,000 in 1975 to 1.3 million in 1995 and 2.8 million by 2005 (UNESCO, 2007), with an expectation that this will grow to 4.5 million by 2020. The United States (23 per cent), the UK (12 per cent), Germany (11 per cent), France (10 per cent) and Australia (7 per cent) are the main global destinations, but, increasingly, traditional 'source' countries such as Singapore and China are seeking to become 'destination' countries for international students too (UNESCO, 2007). In addition, many universities have been pursuing international education strategies through other means – these include, for example:

a   the establishment of transnational programmes and/or campuses abroad (in 2006 there were 82 HE branch campuses globally, principally operated by US and Australian universities);

b   the establishment of distance learning programmes (for example the Indira Ghandi National Open University in India);

c   the increasing establishment of student exchange and 'study abroad' programmes;

d   the development of articulation agreements between universities, in which students spend an initial period at a university in their home country and then spend the final one, two or three years of the programme at a partner institution overseas.

The strategies are varied, therefore, but the competition is strong – and the growth of such significant international business for HE has inevitably attracted the attention of private sector providers, ranging from private universities (for instance, the University of Phoenix) to private HE businesses (for instance, Kaplan).

In the arena of research and enterprise, too, the evidence of internationalization is strong. Research is increasingly interdisciplinary and international, focused on global issues, with large-scale corporate and charitable funding (for example, through The Gates Foundation or The Wellcome Trust). International collaborations and partnerships are essential to compete for such funding, and a number of high-profile global partnerships of research-intensive universities have emerged (for example, Universitas 21, and WUN – the Worldwide Universities Network). While the direct benefit accruing from such international partnerships is difficult to determine, in that few educational or research activities have emerged from within these organizations, membership of such elite research groups identifies a university as being regarded by their peers as a leading global institution. Such an indicator of esteem enables strong leverage in relation to research funding, a presence at the table in the development of international and national policy, and a premium market value in the recruitment of both domestic and international students. Profile and reputation is everything in such arenas, and as a result the emergence of global league tables has been important to all universities with international aspirations. A high position in the Times Higher Education International League Tables or in the Shanghai Jiaotong tables is increasingly an institutional priority, being seen both as an indicator of international credibility and as an entrance ticket to the major global research, education and enterprise fora.

Developing an international strategy

So what might be the main elements of an internationalization strategy for a university? Notwithstanding the inevitable reality gap between the published strategy documents of universities and the actual strategic emphasis as demonstrated by operational activities, it is nevertheless possible to gain a picture of such strategies from published documentation. Foskett (2008b) has summarized the aims of a sample of university internationalization strategies, and shows that the common themes are:

1 Recognition that 'being international' has both geographical and quality dimensions, in that it involves both working with organizations and people from other countries and ensuring that the quality of research and education in the institution is of a standard that would be seen as 'international' in peer evaluation.

2 For universities with a strong research profile, a clear aim that the university should be engaged in leading research/academic debate at international levels in some or all of its disciplines.

3 A view that the university, through its leading academics, should be contributing to political, economic, social, and technological developments internationally.

4 An explicit aim that the institution should provide an education (curriculum) for all of its students (whether from the home country or overseas) that is international in quality and equips graduates to be both global citizens and employable in a globalized economy.

5 An aim to develop organization, systems and culture within the university that promote an international community, attractive to and meeting the needs of students and staff (both faculty and professional service staff) from both the home country and from overseas.

An important distinction of context is that identified by Knight (2003) as the difference between 'internationalization at home' and 'internationalization abroad'. This distinguishes the location of the key focus activities. 'Internationalization at home' describes those changes undertaken in the university's home context. This might include a wide range of specific implementing activities, but frequently is expressed through:

• redevelopment of the curriculum to ensure international coverage and focus, and relevance for international students as well as 'home' students;

• internationalizing teaching and learning, by recognizing different cultural perspectives on learning styles and employing a diverse international staff;

• providing student services that meet the practical and cultural needs of international students as well as 'home' students;

• benchmarking educational provision not just against national comparator institutions, but against comparators in other countries.

'Internationalization abroad' refers to 'offshore' activities, and often has a higher profile in internationalization strategies in their early phases of development. Its most obvious expression is in substantial marketing activities seeking to recruit students to join academic programmes in the home university, a function characterized by recruitment fairs, promotional materials and engagement with student recruitment agents and agencies. However, it also includes, *inter alia*:

- increasing student and staff mobility between universities in different countries, encouraging students to spend time in overseas universities as part of their programmes and encouraging faculty to spend research time working with partner institutions abroad;
- the formal inclusion of an 'overseas' element to projects, programmes and research, for example by including international field study opportunities;
- the establishment of joint teaching programmes with overseas institutions. This may include, for example, articulation agreements, joint degree programmes or split-site PhD programmes;
- setting up overseas branch campuses, often in partnership with other private or public sector organizations;
- building research partnerships with overseas universities.

This initial picture of international strategy in universities therefore raises a number of key research questions related to HE leadership:

- What internationalization strategies are being adopted by universities?
- How are strategies being developed?
- What are the organizational arrangements being made to develop and deliver internationalization?
- What different leadership skills are needed for such developments and how are these being developed?

It is these questions which are the focus of the research reported here.

Methodology

The research evidence in this chapter was gathered over a two-year period from July 2006 to June 2008. It was drawn from an initial analysis of the changing strategies of a number of universities as they consider and respond to the challenges they perceive coming from 'internationalization'.

The sample comprises two groups of universities. The first, the UK universities, consists of seven institutions, differentiated in terms of their location within the UK, their standing within UK university rankings, and by their mission. Three describe themselves as strongly research-led, two present a strategic profile which emphasizes a mixed mission with a clear balance and interplay between research and teaching, and two highlight the teaching-led dimension of their mission, while still indicating an engagement with scholarship, research and knowledge transfer. The second group comprises 16 universities from Asia, distributed geographically as indicated in Figure 3.1. The pattern of missions of the universities is diverse, as with the UK universities, and the spread across the main 'mission' types is also shown in Table 3.1.

The sample was an opportunity sample, where the author was able to undertake an enquiry into the university's internationalization strategy and strategy

Table 3.1 Location and mission of the Asian universities within the study

Country	Number of universities	Overall mission		
		Research-led	Balanced	Teaching-led
China	3	2	1	
India	3	3		
Pakistan	3		2	
Singapore	3	1	1	1
Malaysia	2		2	1

processes through visits or existing professional contacts. In that sense the sample cannot be regarded as representative of any specific set of universities. However, the universities within the UK represent a cross-section of British institutions, and the Asian universities are all engaging to some extent in a strategy of internationalization. The picture they present might therefore be regarded as within the boundaries of common strategic behaviours of universities either in the UK or globally. The individual universities, of course, remain anonymous within this analysis.

The data collection process consisted of:

a a semi-structured interview with a senior leader within the university holding a post at vice-chancellor (president), or deputy vice-chancellor level;

b a semi-structured interview with a senior officer with responsibility for the institution's international relationships (for example, the director of the international office);

c a review of a range of documentation relating to internationalization. This varied in detail, but included, typically, public domain policy documents and prospectuses. In some cases the researcher was given access to confidential policy documents.

Analysis and key themes

The interpretation of the interviews and the documentary analysis is presented here in relation to the four key research questions.

1 What internationalization strategies are being adopted by universities?

The pattern of strategies in relation to internationalization, and hence the pattern of strategic behaviours, varied between the universities within the study. Two examples illustrate the contrasting strategic positions observed. One of the UK universities has an institutional mission which prioritizes its relationship with its local region in terms of providing programmes and knowledge transfer that support economic and social growth and development in that region. While not eschewing international engagement, it is clear that it is not a high priority for resource allocation, and its international engagement is therefore seen in terms of:

a accepting (enthusiastically) international students onto its programmes, despite not investing substantially in an international student recruitment activity;

b ensuring its teaching programmes contain curriculum elements that will support business and other sectors in their international engagement, illustrated by its undergraduate programme in 'International Business and Marketing', for example;

c providing consultancy and research to regional organizations which engage in international markets or arenas.

By way of contrast, one of the universities in China has internationalization as a key strategic priority, emphasized strongly within all of its strategic documentation and seen as an important arena for resource allocation. The university is one of the leading universities in China and within the world's top one hundred institutions, according to the Times Higher Education World Rankings. Its strategy is characterized by:

a the recruitment of overseas students to its programmes (principally from other East Asian countries);

b the development of articulation agreements with British, US and Australian institutions to enable its students to spend time overseas within their programmes or to undertake '2+2' programmes, with the final two years of their undergraduate studies completed overseas;

c ensuring every student experiences an international engagement as part of their programme (whether a placement abroad, or an 'internationally focused' taught unit, or a language programme);

d building a small number of multifaceted research partnerships with global leading research-led universities;

e investing in overseas research time for its academic staff and in bringing researchers from world-leading universities to spend time in the institution.

These two examples represent extreme positions within the analysis, of course, and other universities demonstrated a pattern of strategy between these extremes. From the analysis of the stance of each of the universities in the study it has been possible to construct an initial model of internationalization strategies. The model is shown in Figure 3.1. It is constructed on a two-by-two matrix which relates the orientation of the institution towards 'internationalization at home' and 'internationalization abroad'. Each dimension of the model indicates a range from 'low engagement' to 'high engagement', and in this way four broad categories of institutional strategic position can be defined. In addition, detailed analysis suggests that one of the broad categories should itself be divided into two sub-categories. The categories identified in this model are:

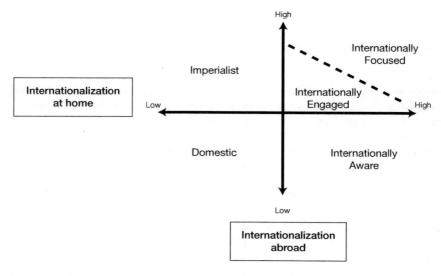

Figure 3.1 A model of university internationalization strategies

1 Domestic universities

Institutions in this category are focused on their own national and regional context. While content to recruit international students who apply, they invest little in active recruitment. Their mission, too, is to support regional and national business and communities, and while this may contain international dimensions these are not the priority for the university. One of the UK universities fitted this category, together with two of the Asian universities.

2 Imperialist universities

These are universities which have strong international recruitment activities to draw students from overseas, but have done relatively little to change their organization, facilities or services 'at home'. International students are expected largely to experience college life in just the same way as home students, the curriculum is a 'domestic national' curriculum, and facilities for overseas students (for example, cultural facilities) are poorly developed. Few of the staff are from overseas. Such a perspective largely sees internationalization as a financial strategy, by enhancing 'home' income with overseas student income. Two of the UK universities and two of the Asian universities were categorized in this group.

3 Internationally aware universities

These are universities which are changing their organization and culture to have a profile that is international, but who have not yet really engaged with overseas recruitment or overseas partner universities. Typically they recognize the global nature of economy and society and even of higher education, but have not yet engaged with 'overseas'. None of the UK universities was seen as within this category, whereas four of the Asian universities were interpreted as being 'internationally aware'.

4 Internationally engaged universities

Internationally engaged universities are those which are operating in international arenas, for example through institutional partnerships and student recruitment, but are also driving an internationalization agenda 'at home'. This typically includes curriculum review to make the teaching programmes global in perspective and to provide an international experience (such as a placement abroad); ensuring that services and cultural facilities on the home campus support international and ethnic diversity; recruiting international staff; and encouraging staff to seek research and education partnerships overseas. Three UK universities and four Asian universities were identified as being within this category.

5 Internationally focused universities

Among the internationally engaged universities are a small number where the level of progress and achievement in internationalization is strong in many dimensions, and where the cultural change within the institution has been transformational. These have been identified, therefore as internationally focused universities, as they are strong in terms of both internationalization at home and internationalization abroad. One university in the UK and two in Asia (both in China) were identified as falling into this category.

This analysis shows the broad picture of internationalization strategies among the universities within the study. It reflects, of course, an external perspective on the reality of strategy rather than an account of internationalization strategy as the institutions themselves see it. It is helpful, therefore, to distinguish between strategic aspiration and strategic reality and to recognize that, for some of the institutions, there is a 'gap' between the two. It has not been possible to present to all of the participating universities the analysis of their strategic position, but from the evidence of those institutions where this has happened it is possible to offer some observations on this 'gap'. For those universities identified as strategically positioned, as 'internationally engaged', there is no reality gap, as this reflects the position to which they aspire – and while there may be differences in view of how far they have progressed towards the 'internationally focused' position, there is a close match between aspiration and reality. Among some of the institutions in the 'domestic' category there was a similar match between aspiration and reality, for here there was a good understanding of the institution's strategic position. This position may have been achieved by default or strategic action, but there is recognition that this is the position at which these institutions operate.

More problematic are those universities in the 'imperialist' category. This is not a position to which any of the universities in the study explicitly aspired, for, although they confirmed the economic value of recruiting international students, they perceived that their strategy was placing them as an internationally engaged university. There is an ethical dimension in this observation of course, in that there may be a view that such an 'imperialist' position is simply a 'quick win' exploitation of a market position – yet, even if this is a key motivation, it is unlikely that institutions will openly state that this is their position. This reality gap, however, is of significance within this study as it suggests that it may be in this group of universities where there is the least well-developed managerial understanding of the processes and strategies of internationalization. We shall consider this below.

2 How are strategies being developed?

Having identified the strategic positions of the institutions, the study considered the ways in which internationalization strategies were being developed. While some universities are adopting their strategies in a deliberate way, others are in their strategic position by default. Those universities within the 'domestic' group may be positioned there from either of these two directions. One of the UK universities, a medium-sized regional institution, had a clearly articulated internationalization strategy which recognized the university's regional and national focus. This reflected a careful market analysis of its own position and a recognition that it did not have the resource base to become a significant player in any of the existing international markets. Its choice to remain as a 'domestic' institution was a well-articulated strategic decision, and its internationalization strategy was clearly defined. In contrast, one of the universities in Pakistan which had a similar regional focus was in that position because it had not yet given much consideration to an international role. There had been little or no debate about how the university might engage with international perspectives, and so its lack of an internationalization strategy was in effect a default position.

The 'imperialist' universities seem to have adopted their position because of an absence of well-developed strategy. In most cases they have simply set up an international recruitment programme to raise income, rather than looking at the way forward in a strategic way. In each of these universities the initial impetus to engaging internationally appears to be finance driven, as a way of growing income to support the university's wider mission. Questions of wider engagement, of cultural change and curriculum change seem to emerge as a product of the growth of international student numbers rather than being part of the initial conceptualization of such a growth strategy. In such institutions, while the president/vice-chancellor had a strong commitment to the concept of internationalization, the strategic and operational dimensions were delegated to a functional area such as the international office or the marketing office, and most international visits by senior staff were to attend recruitment events or marketing conferences. Hence the internationalization strategy seems to be the result of operational practices rather than the determinant of them.

In those universities identified as 'internationally engaged', strategy in this domain has emerged through a developmental process but with strong leadership from one of the senior team in conjunction with the president/vice-chancellor. In each case, a number of key organizational and operational features could be identified:

a   The president had a well-articulated vision of what it means to be an international university.
b   A further member of the senior leadership within the university shared this vision and had responsibility for its operationalization. Typically this was a vice-president (pro vice-chancellor) with a brief for international activities.
c   The president and the senior colleague actively discussed the strategy, and engaged colleagues in institutional governance, academic leadership and administrative functions in discussion about strategy and operations.
d   Each of the key functional areas (research, teaching, administration and enterprise) incorporated an international dimension into its key strategic documents.
e   Identifiable resources (including finance) are channelled to international activities other than student recruitment, for example into supporting staff international exchanges or academic conference attendance.

What emerges from this analysis is that carefully articulated and developed strategy for internationalization appears to characterize the two extreme positions within the model. For all the universities within the internationally engaged sector and for some of those in the 'domestic' sector, their position is the product of strategy. For those in the 'imperialist' sector and for some of those in the 'domestic' sector, the position is either a default position or has emerged as a product of recruitment activity, driven by financial goals rather than as the outcome of a strategic analytical process.

3 What are the organizational arrangements being made to develop and deliver internationalization?

Organizational structures, systems and processes vary in form and detail between universities in relation to most aspects of the institutions' functions, and reflect the complex interaction of cultures, histories, resources, strategies and power relations within each university. In detail this is as true of internationalization processes as any other professional function, yet the key elements of organizational arrangements show some clear similarities across the universities within this study. Those commonalities lie in a number of features:

a   The president/vice-chancellor has the overall strategic leadership role for internationalization vested in her/him.
b   A senior member of the institution's leadership has a delegated responsibility for international activities.

c   The university has an international office or office of international affairs.

Within and beyond these elements, diversity characterizes the sector. The scope of the role of the senior leadership for internationalization varies from strong, formal line management leadership for all dimensions of international activity, to a nominal reporting role, to a role in which the international function is but a small part of a much wider portfolio. International offices, similarly, may take a broad-ranging strategic lead or simply be responsible for student recruitment or arranging incoming and outgoing international visits. The role of individual academic departments or schools in internationalization also varies from a position of total devolution of all international activities to departments, to one where there is a strongly centralized function.

From the evidence of this study there is no simple relationship between strategic position and organizational arrangements for internationalization. The key distinguishing feature, rather, relates to the location of strategic development, for in those institutions within the 'internationally engaged' sector this function is retained at the most senior levels of the university, with strong leadership from a vice-president/pro vice-chancellor and active engagement by the president/vice-chancellor.

4 What different leadership skills are needed for such developments and how are these being developed?

The growing importance of internationalization within institutional strategies has brought with it the requirement for strategic and operational skills hitherto not well developed in the sector. At the strategic level this may be seen simply as extending the operational environment to a global rather than national scale, but this brings with it the need to read and assess much more complex scopes of knowledge and activities set in a diverse cultural setting. The growth of internal markets (that is, within their own country) for the universities within the study, as a consequence of growing participation rates, has brought with it the need for a broad swathe of partnership, external relations and marketing skills. Internationalization requires that those skills now operate in global arenas rather than national ones.

Although universities have sought to professionalize their internationalization activities, there is still a large degree of learning by experience. Within this study, while those with leadership roles in this field expressed an interest and enthusiasm for international activities, few had any form of professionally recognized expertise or training. Some of the directors of the international offices had a background in marketing in the commercial sector or educational sector, but at institutional leadership level none of the presidents or vice-presidents had any formal background in the field. Some had leadership experience in other sectors, some had undertaken senior leadership development or training, but in most cases their knowledge of internationalization in HE was rooted simply in their own experience as academics, teachers, researchers and managers.

Despite the lack of formal training and development for managing and leading internationalization, those universities which had a strategic position within the 'internationally engaged' sector of the model had senior leadership teams that had significant international experience from their own academic or other professional background. The presidents and vice-presidents of all of the universities in this category had a personal track record of working internationally with their research or teaching. Most had been actively part of global academic networks with a long experience of attending events overseas, spending time on academic placements in other countries, and hosting international students and faculty. This experience may have provided them with an international perspective on universities which enables them to understand better the arena of international HE, and hence a good conceptualization of the needs and challenges of developing an internationalization strategy for their institution. So, although there is only limited formal training experience, those who are most actively leading and promoting internationalization have considerable experience of working in the international higher education arena.

There is, therefore, a clear picture of a priority for appropriate international leadership development, and also for training at all levels for those engaged in the operational dimensions of internationalization. At the most senior level it is clear, though, that of key importance is a personal history of international engagement that enables the strategic process for the institution to have a well-informed perspective on the reality of working in international arenas.

In conclusion

This chapter has provided the background and some early and initial findings about the strategic management of internationalization in a range of universities in the UK and Asia. The research shows some diversity of approach to internationalization, together with some common challenges that university leaders are facing. The model that emerges may provide an interesting first benchmark for institutions to consider their strategic approach and to identify a range of aims that go beyond economic objectives and help to re-assert the role of universities as a social as well as an economic good.

References

Breton, G. and Lambert, M. (eds) (2003), *Universities and Globalization: Private Linkages, Public Trust.* Paris: UNESCO.

Council for Industry and Higher Education (CIHE) (2007), *Internationalising Higher Education: A Financial or Moral Imperative?* Summary of a conference at St. George's House, Windsor Castle, January 2007.

Deem, R. (2001), 'Globalisation, new managerialism, academic capitalism and entrepreneurialism in universities: Is the local dimesion still important?', *Comparative Education,* 37, (1): 7–20.

Fielden, J. (2006), 'Internationalisation and leadership: What are the issues?', paper presented to The Leadership and Development Challenges of Globalisation and Internationalisation Summit 2006, London, at http://www.lfhe.ac.uk/

international/internationalconferences/summit2006/index.html (accessed 10 November 2009).

—— (2007), *Global Horizons for UK Universities*. London: Council for Industry and Higher Education.

Foskett, N. H. (2008a), 'Internationalisation and the marketing challenge for universities', *International Academy of Marketing Conference*, Krakow, Poland, April.

—— (2008b), 'Global markets, national challenges, local responses – the management challenge for universities of the internationalisation of higher education', *Commonwealth Council for Educational Administration Conference*, Durban, South Africa, September.

Knight, J. (2003), 'Updating the definition of internationalization', *International Higher Education*, Fall.

Ministry of Science and Technology (1997), *Profile of 973 Program*, from http://www.973.gov.cn/English/Index.aspx (accessed 10 November 2009).

Neubauer, D. and Ordonez, V. (2008), 'The new role of globalized education in a globalized world', in P. Taylor on behalf of GUNI (The Global University Network for Innovation) (ed.), *Higher Education in the World 3: Higher Education: New Challenges and Emerging Roles for Human and Social Development*. London: Palgrave Macmillan.

OECD (2007), *Higher Education and Regions: Globally Competitive, Locally Engaged*. Paris: OECD.

Scott, P. (2005), 'Universities and the knowledge economy', *Minerva*, 43, (3), 297–309.

Shiel, C. and McKenzie, A. (eds) (2008), *The Global University: The Role of Senior Managers*. London: Development Education Association.

Shin, Jung Cheol (2009), 'Building world-class research university: The Brain Korea21 Project', *Higher Education*, 58, (5), 669–88.

Stephens, D. (ed.) (2009), *Higher Education and International Capacity Building: Twenty Five Years of Higher Education Links*. London: Symposium Books.

UNESCO (2007), *Global Education Digest*. Montreal: UNESCO.

Waters, M. (1995), *Globalization*. London: Routledge.

Weber, L. E. and Duderstadt, J. J. (2008), *The Globalization of Higher Education*. London: Economica.

Wolin, S. S. (1981), 'The new public philosophy', *Democracy*, 1, (4), 23–36.

Zhang, H. (2006), 'Principles of higher education reform in research universities: The international perspective', *Higher Education Research*, 12: 60–5 (in Chinese).

Chapter 4

Global Citizenship for All: Putting the 'Higher' Back into UK Higher Education?

Vivienne Caruana

Introduction

It has been argued that there is a lack of consensus surrounding the concept of global citizenship and global citizenship education in UK higher education. A lack of definition contributes towards incoherent and often contradictory goals which make it difficult to understand the impact of teaching and learning in the field. This chapter explores concepts inherent in characterizations of global citizenship, particularly as they relate to the internationalized curriculum, by engaging with a sociological literature which demonstrates how this lack of consensus is the outcome of tensions created by globalization and knowledge economy and learning society discourses within UK higher education.

The central argument is that, in order to understand their practice, higher education teachers need to reflect on the moral and political attitudes, values and beliefs that are influential and presuppose particular renditions of what global citizenship in the context of an internationalized curriculum means. Furthermore, if learning in universities is to constitute 'higher learning', engagement with particular concepts in terms of curriculum and pedagogy are necessary in order to counter the influence of popular academic discourses in the global age.

The influence of globalization on UK higher education: process and discourse

The term globalization has been used to describe almost any and every aspect of contemporary life. Undoubtedly, it does capture some of the changes that have transformed the world over the last three decades. The most fundamental processes popularly ascribed to globalization include increased velocity and density of information flows, speeding up of time, a collapse of space and the breaking down of national barriers. With rapid flows of people, ideas, goods and images in addition to information, worldwide social relations are intensified, linking 'distant localities in such a way that local happenings are shaped by events occurring many miles away' (Blackmore, 2002; Giddens, 1990 as cited in Rizvi, 2007). Castells (1996), as cited in Rizvi (2007), also speaks of the way in which cultural and political meanings are under siege from global eco-nomic and technological restructuring. He argues that, in the 'informational mode of development', networks make up the new social morphology of our societies. As the boundaries between home and away, local and global, here and there are increasingly blurred, new global interdependencies give rise to new kinds of sociability, captured in terms such as ethnoscapes, technoscapes, finanscapes, mediascapes and ideoscapes, all indicative of the power of inter-national flows (Norris, 2003; Shultz *et al.*, 2008; Rizvi, 2007; Schattle, 2007; Skirbis *et al.*, 2004; Blackmore, 2002).

It has been argued that, while international flows in themselves are not new, what is new is that, as the entire world becomes compressed, so human aware-ness of the world as an entity is heightened. As globalization strengthens the sources of global interconnectedness, eroding national boundaries and integ-rating national economies, cultures, technologies and governance, for some writers the attendant relations of mutual interdependence will strengthen a resurgent cosmopolitan orientation which will spread well beyond elite circles to the mass public, under the influence of globalized communications. Furthermore, the younger generation in particular, who are relatively more comfortable with cosmopolitan identities, may be well disposed to pervasive structural trends that offer the potential to transform values (Norris, 2003).

While globalization has been associated with cosmopolitanism, cultural uniformity and homogenization within the embrace of MacDonalds, Disney Corporation and CNN (Norris, 2003), some authors differentiate between globalization and cosmopolitanism, arguing that the former is an empiri-cal phenomenon while the latter denotes an ideal. There are therefore two strands of debate associated with globalization, the first associating it with uniformity and the second with diversity (increasing interconnectedness of varied local cultures) (Gunesch, 2004). It is important to note that in reality the process of globalization is generated in unequal, divergent, and sometimes contradictory ways; in effect there are the 'globalized' and the 'globalizers'. In other words, globalization affects countries in different ways depending on individual nations' history, traditions, culture and priorities (Gacel-Ávila, 2005). Globalization is associated with global competitiveness, but also with intensified collaboration as a global division of labour has developed. As new regional economic blocs have emerged, the status quo has been re-ordered with old enemies becoming new allies and vice versa (Scott, 2000).

In light of these realities it is argued that the explanatory power of the concept of globalization is questionable, since it is based on a false universal-ism where the concept is reified and assumed to be an objective, self-evident entity (Rizvi, 2007). Fairclough (2001) entertains the idea that globalization is simply an empty word, 'just discourse, just ideology', and concludes that, while globalization undoubtedly involves real processes, those who benefit from it seek to extend it by perpetuating a discourse which represents processes not only more complete than they are, but as a simple fact of life which cannot be questioned or challenged (Fairclough, 2001). In this sense, globalization should be viewed as a problematic rather than a descriptor. Globalization is associated with discourses about privatization, marketization, managerializa-tion and commodification prevalent in the 1990s. Feminists argue, then, that 'globalizing discourses' reproduce old, and at the same time reconstitute new forms of identity, race, ethnicity and class. Globalization is therefore 'both dangerous and seductive'; seductive in the promise of new governance frameworks through which issues of equity can be mobilized, yet dangerous in exacerbating old, and indeed introducing new, inequalities (Blackmore, 2002). Globalization may then be regarded as a neo-liberal ideological construct which gives primacy to economic relations, limits the widening of access and contribution from across the globe and serves a particular set of interests and powerful social forces, namely the transnational corporation and financial elite (Rizvi, 2007; Blackmore, 2002).

As far as higher education is concerned, globalization is regarded as a driving force for unsettling the 'idea' of the modern university. The challenges posed involve universities' close identity with the promulgation of national cultures, the demise of the high public expenditure welfare states on which universities depended for the bulk of their income, and the impact of information and communication technology, which potentially standardizes teaching and promotes global research networks and cultures. Perhaps it is information and communication technologies (ICT), time compression and the emerging forms of global education made possible, that are most unpredictable in their impact on higher learning. Birketts (1994, p. 27), as cited in Edwards *et al.* (2008) refers to possible cognitive losses: the loss of duration experience, impatience with sustained inquiry, and divorce from a vital sense of history as a cumulative, organic process. Given the possibilities of distance learning, conventions of discipline may be challenged since learners can engage with a wide range of bodies of knowledge and be subject to different norms (Edwards *et al.*, 2008). Indeed, as early as 1994 Gibbons described a shift in modes of knowledge production, with 'older, homogenous modes of knowledge being replaced by complexity, hybridity, non-linearity, reflexivity, heterogeneity and transdisciplinarity representative of a more systemic and holistic was of seeing the world (Shultz *et al.*, 2008).

Notwithstanding the unpredictability of the impact of ICT on universities it seems clear that, since the level of economic competitiveness has become the prime indicator of a country's well-being, so business models have come to prevail in higher education and universities are primarily used for business purposes via marketing and commercialization. Within this business model, the core work of universities is management of knowledge. Generic non-academic managers manage the academic work of production, dissemination and legitimation of knowledge while the professoriate is valued largely for its capacity to attract funds, grants and students (Shultz *et al.*, 2008; Blackmore, 2002; Scott, 2000). As for students, they themselves have been influenced by the forces of globalization. Values have been transformed and fundamental identities altered, since the fee-paying student has higher expectations and is increasingly an instrumentalist, creating tensions within higher education over the balance between theory and practice, with a pull towards practice and vocationalism (Blackmore, 2002).

Deconstructing 'knowledge economy and learning society' in the context of 'higher learning'

Globalization often provides the rationale for restructuring education to better meet the needs of the national economy. In the 'knowledge economy and learning society' economic success is seen to rely on the production of higher value-added products and services which depend on scientific and technological knowledge and on continual innovation. Since information is the source of national wealth in the knowledge-based economies of many Western nation states seeking to re-position themselves in the face of rapid capital and information flows, universities are prey to many pressures which challenge identity. Arguably, in producing, transferring and disseminating economically productive knowledge, the university plays a vital role in maintaining global competitive edge. Mass higher education also provides the skilled workers required in a contemporary labour market dominated by the rhetoric of the knowledge economy. Curriculum and pedagogical practices are increasingly becoming those required by the economic base for participation in the post-industrial age. Pedagogy embracing active learning strategies, inquiry and discovery might, on the face of it, appear progressive, liberating and geared towards the 'practice of freedom' in the Frieirean sense but, in reality, cooperative learning, group work, role play and simulation are also the strategies deployed in developing the 'soft skills' – being a good listener, speaker or writer – characteristic of the dialogical element of a new labour process based on team work (Mocombe, 2004; Gacel-Ávila, 2005; Naidoo *et al.*, 2005; Blackmore, 2002).

It is argued that the economic forces influencing higher education may lead to the erosion of academic capital, the valorization of economic capital and the attendant commodification of knowledge, where education assumes an 'exchange' rather than intrinsic 'use value'. Pedagogical relationships transformed by dependency on market transactions, where the lecturer produces the commodity to be consumed by the student, may become commonplace. Furthermore, if students do indeed see themselves as consumers of the learning product, divorced from the intellectual community, they will be more likely to regard educational success as a right, and be less willing to engage with education as a process (Naidoo *et al.*, 2005). The emphasis on the centrality of the knowledge-based economy, technology and skill development is reinforced by the rhetoric of the 'learning society' in which cyclical, lifelong learning is not only a norm, but a culture and attitude. Participation is couched in terms of economistic forms of lifelong learning that can apparently help learner workers to avoid the implicit risk of social and economic exclusion that non-participation implies. Lifelong learning suggests that, in order to engage with changing circumstances, we need to continue learning throughout our lives, to make the most of opportunities to learn at home, in the workplace and the community as well as in the formal provision of learning opportunities. However, it has also been characterized as 'learning by conscription' arising from an internalized 'ought', rather than any voluntary inclination (Edwards, 2001; Grace, 2006).

Given the pragmatic-technicist view of work characteristic of the knowledge economy and learning society, where the transference of technical, instrumental knowing is what ensures good productivity for business and industry, it is perhaps unsurprising that higher education has been viewed as a means of enculturation, where the younger generation are encouraged to conform to the present system (Mocombe, 2004). Yet, the concept of the knowledge economy and learning society is paradoxical when viewed from the perspective of the information flows characteristic of globalization. Barnett (2000) maintains that – consistent with the forces of globalization – knowledge is expanding faster than we can comprehend it. This surfeit of data in itself creates a situation of complexity which, when couched within multiple frameworks of understanding, of action and of self-identity, constitutes 'supercomplexity'. For Barnett (2000) this scenario gives rise to 'the ignorance explosion' (Lukasiewicz, 1994 as cited in Barnett, 2000) whereby academic texts become simply data, and data-handling skills assume primacy rather than understanding, interpretation and adjudication. The world of supercomplexity, however, requires that students should be aware of the uncertainty, contestability, challengeability and unpredictability that surround them and this awareness can only be developed if the pedagogical situation itself manifests such characteristics. For Barnett (2000), education must 'create epistemological and ontological disturbance in the minds and in the beings of students' to enable them to 'live at ease with this perplexing and unsettling environment' and 'make a positive contribution to the supercomplex world'. The pedagogy implied by Barnett's notion of supercomplexity is complementary to critical pedagogy and the process of 'conscientization' attributed to Freire (1996). This 'problem-solving pedagogy', with teachers and learners as 'co-investigators in dialogue', encourages learners to reflect critically on and question ideas, and look beyond the limits within which they think about and live their lives; drawing out the implicit contradictions that provide the critical framework to enable them not only to interpret, but to transform the world. Advanced forms of learning to think through ill-defined problems require risk-taking, acts of faith, dissent and teachers who are reliable guides. All this does not sit well with the commodification of the learning relationship. Audacity, daring, and creativity accompanied by critique are the capacities that our world of uncertainty and contestability require. Critical dialogue with the past, questioning authority and its effects and struggling with ongoing relationships of power are the trappings of critical, active citizens in the interrelated local, national and global public spheres. Rather than compounding 'the ignorance explosion' by succumbing to economistic learning designs and a pragmatic preoccupation with skill development implicit in knowledge economy rhetoric, the university has a responsibility to critique the rival ideologies with which we are bombarded and to provide the space to enable students to develop their own voices and engage purposively with their own sense of self (Ainley *et al.*, 2006; Giroux *et al.*, 2006; Naidoo *et al.*, 2005; Barnett, 2000; Grace, 2006).

Global citizenship: contested terrain

Citizenship is usually tied into the emergence of a polity with specific privileges and duties. The nation was originally forged on exclusiveness, or a clear defining of 'other', and in many ways that is equally true of supranational organizations like the European Community (EC), where individuals of member states have a distinct and exclusive relationship with the Community which confers social status and power. For Benjamin Barker, 'Citizenship is a dynamic relationship among strangers who are transformed into neighbours, whose commonality derives from expanding consciousness rather than geographical proximity', and this more inclusive characterization of citizenship may serve to legitimize the notion of global citizenship (Schattle, 2007; Davies *et al.*, 2005; Lagos, 2002). However, in terms of citizenship encompassing status and power in the context of privileges and duties, global citizenship is problematical. Global citizenship cannot be expressed in any legal sense; it is not tied down to one's land of birth and it is not the result of rights and obligations granted by any central authority. Rather, global citizenship is said to be a 'down-up' scenario where grassroots activism is exercised within new arenas and allegiances. Falk (1993) identifies five categories of global citizen – global reformers, global environmental managers, politically conscious regionalists, transnational activists and elite global business people, all of whom, with the exception of the last, have grassroots activism at their core (Lagos, 2002).

For individuals, global citizenship represents self-awareness and being 'at ease in one's own skin'. Responsibility is framed in connection with learning and voluntary participation, rather than as a coercive derived from formal membership of a country (Lagos, 2002). Those who embrace the idea of global citizenship tend to think about citizenship in expansive terms, encompassing ways of thinking and living that evolve over time. Yet the notion of political participation and belonging may extend not only outward but inward, influencing domestic politics and local civil life. 'These days you don't have to leave home to be a global citizen, or . . . to see yourself as a global citizen in continual formation' (Schattle, 2007, p. 3).

Responsibility, participation and activism may be regarded as key elements of global citizenship, but how these are specifically played out in reality is dependent on three contrasting approaches to globalization, according to Shultz *et al.* (2008). First, the neo-liberal approach, which centres on the ability of individuals in privileged positions to travel across national borders, perpetuates global citizenship as global economic participation. The radical approach focuses on global structures that create and perpetuate global inequality. In this context global citizens tend to be active in opposing global institutions, resisting the forces of globalization and seeking to strengthen local and national institutions. Third, the transformationalist perspective views globalization as a complex set of local, national and international relationships that has generated new kinds of inclusion and exclusion. From this perspective, the global citizen seeks to include and engage others based on a common humanity, a shared planet and a shared future (Shultz *et al.*, 2008).

The concept of global citizenship in its outward orientation is informed by cosmopolitanism, which is itself a contested notion quite difficult to define. Gunesch (2004) refers to the popular catchword phrase, 'feeling at home in the world', straddling global and local spheres with a particular interest in or determination to engage with cultural diversity. In this context cosmopolitanism may constitute a state of readiness in which one is able to make excursions into other cultures through listening, looking, intuiting and reflecting. Given the vast array of alien cultures to be encountered, Gunesch (2004) argues that cosmopolitans will be connoisseurs of some, but dilettantes regarding the majority of cultures.

The phrase 'mundane cosmopolitans' has been used to describe those who simply consume media images in an unreflexive manner, which influences the type of food they eat, and encourages indulgence in heavily packaged or mediated cultural and tourist experiences and ethnic 'styles' in dress or music (Marshall, 2009; Skirbis *et al.*, 2004). Global citizenship educators may ask which agenda is more dominant when global citizenship issues are portrayed in the media, and Marshall (2009) maintains that the knowledge economy discourse and economic instrumentalist agendas are dominant, rather than any social justice agenda.

Skirbis *et al.* (2004, p. 116) regard cosmopolitanism as 'a progressive human-istic ideal' reminiscent of Kantian assumptions about cosmopolitanism as a normative ideal. However Turner (2002), as cited in Calcutt *et al.* (2009), deploys the Kantian position to argue for an active cosmopolitan virtue involv-ing commitments to protect diversity and consensus against the tolerance of human suffering. Nussbaum (1994), similarly, advocates 'world citizenship' based on Kantian principles whereby the global citizen is not devoid of local affiliations, but is rather surrounded by a series of concentric circles, the first constituting self, moving out to immediate family, extended family, neigh-bours and progressing outward to the largest circle of humanity as a whole. For Nussbaum, the global citizen seeks to draw all circles to the centre. Such moral positions are based on a core of universalism based on locally specific cultural forms which collectively share universal concerns, universal values, a fundamental belief in human rights and a shared, philosophical commitment to the primacy of world citizenship over all other affiliations (Calcutt *et al.*, 2009; Beck *et al.*, 2006; Gunesch, 2004).

A second proposition is the cross-cultural consumption approach to cos-mopolitanism whereby individuals actively pursue engagement, particularly through travel, in a quest for cultural competence. In a globalized world, social status is maintained by accumulating new forms of capital and the members of the world-class business elite are rich in cultural, social and intellectual capital as well as concepts, connections and competence. The metaphor of the palimpsest suggests how this new cosmopolitan identity masks the citizen of the advanced, liberal-democratic 'national' state and the privileged individual from elsewhere who just happens to be mobile (Calcutt *et al.*, 2009; Skirbis *et al.*, 2004). Beck *et al.* (2006) argue that, besides these forms of intended cosmo-politanism, there is an unintended, lived and 'realistic' cosmopolitanism which is primarily the function of coerced choices or a side-effect of unconscious decisions. Refugees, peoples of the diaspora, migrants and exiles effectively lack the free will to move and may, indeed, prefer to be locals and parochials 'rather than suffering the tragedy of their cosmopolitanism' (Gunesch, 2004). A 'banal' cosmopolitanism exists below the surface of these involuntary deci-sions based on acute need, repression or the threat of starvation. In the context of this reality, intended cosmopolitanism may be rendered trivial and unworthy of comment, simply an ideal of the elite (Beck *et al.*, 2006).

The concept of 'realistic cosmopolitanism' therefore poses a particular challenge to other forms which have been contested on a number of counts in the context of contemporary society. For example, the principle of global openness within cosmopolitanism is vague and diffuse; not defined in terms of observable practices. Is it consciously assumed or circumstantially induced? How is it manifested? What are the sentiments embedded within the general attitudinal category of openness? A cosmopolitan 'intoxicated' by unspecified openness and universalism may be a 'risky fantasy' for, in their perceived detachment from the nation state, for example, they may feel no ethical compulsion to pay taxes to national authorities, despite possessing healthy accumulations of various forms of capital.

Contemporary discourses of cosmopolitanism have also been criticized for their idealistic sentiment, which indulges in excessive self-reflexivity, fostering an 'armchair philosophy' of cosmopolitan attitudes. This, the criticism continues, generates a politically naïve kind of cross-cultural goodwill and inclusive global outlook reflecting a utopian drive to construct a new world of tolerant world-sensitive sensibilities (Calcutt *et al.*, 2009; Skirbis *et al.*, 2004). Political naivety may indeed degenerate into political apathy when bombarded with global media images via television and the Internet which embrace knowledge economy discourse and economic instrumentalist agendas rather than social justice agendas. Furthermore, models of cosmopolitanism grounded in Kantian principles have been criticized as a form of 'imperial cosmopolitanism' where discourse centres around a Western view of the world, a profoundly colonial engagement of the West with the rest – which is tantamount to colonialism under another banner – and a cosmopolitan appreciation of global diversity which is based on the privileges of wealth and citizenship in certain states (Mendieta, 2008; Skirbis *et al.*, 2004). Andreotti (2006) criticizes the literature and discourse of the global dimension in the UK for articulating the notion that different cultures have traditional values and beliefs, while the West possesses universal knowledge, with no discussion of the historical processes that led to this position.

Critical cosmopolitanism overcomes Kant's imperialistic and naïve form of cosmopolitanism, opening the way for forms of dialogical cosmopolitanism where the primary task is to rescue, retrieve and make audible and visible the voices of local histories rendered silent by the imperial ethos. Critical cosmopolitanism, in contrast to other forms, is oriented towards a form of universality that Mignolo (2000) calls 'diversality' (a form of diversity and universality). Critical cosmopolitanism therefore makes cosmopolitanism cosmopolitan by the concept of diversality that gives voice to the excluded other, the stranger and the marginalized. In this way, purely normative conceptions of cosmopolitanism and approaches that reduce cosmopolitanism to empirical, but empty, expressions of diversity are challenged in a framework that transcends the Western context to acknowledge non-Western expressions and interpretations of cosmopolitanism (Mendieta, 2008; Delanty, 2006).

Global citizenship education and the internationalized curriculum in UK higher education: complementary concepts and tensions

Schattle (2007) poses the question, 'what sort of life experiences lead individuals to think of themselves as global citizens or to take the idea seriously?' He suggests that international travel, experience close to home in diverse communities, career decisions or study abroad programmes (where global citizenship finds expression in civic engagement with local communities overseas), state of mind or an aspiration and political activism or expanding cultural horizons are all appropriate experiences. Such experiences are generally synonymous with the internationalized curriculum in higher education. International travel (often in the form of volunteering), study abroad, and engagement with local diverse communities (internationalization at home) all enable the fostering of engagement across cultures, which entails sharing as well as taking perspectives in order to heighten awareness. This conscious thinking from the perspective of another person is termed cross-cultural empathy in the context of global citizenship and cross-cultural capability in the internationalized curriculum. It fosters a particular state of mind or aspirations based on expanding cultural horizons.

While this chapter thus far has suggested that the concept of global citizenship embraces notions of cosmopolitanism, the internationalized curriculum is also influenced by traditions of multicultural education. Multicultural education is commonly described as the study of 'other' which, particularly in the US, focuses on commonality (Ladson-Billings, 2004). Arguably, multicultural education originates in a liberal pluralistic paradigm which is limited in its capacity for long-standing social change. Multicultural education attempts to address the concerns of all groups equally without disturbing existing power structures. While the emphasis on 'sameness' functions as a 'form of appeasement' in this human relations approach to curriculum internationalization, sometimes the internationalized curriculum can emphasize cultural differences to the point of exoticism in uncritically celebrating difference yet failing to engage with the socio-historical and cultural perspectives of the politics of difference (Ladson-Billings, 2004; Pavel, 1995). While minority voices are invited in the multicultural classroom, the invitation is often proffered in the spirit of paternalism and 'empty idealism' which, in the absence of any critical language of social analysis, fails to address how minority voices engage with those occupying privileged positions. Thus 'marginalizing inclusion' is justified on the grounds of 'common culture'. In this way the language of tolerance and recognition becomes a patronizing language which pays lip-service to the celebration of cultural distinction while containing and restraining expressions of difference (Ladson-Billings, 2004; Pavel, 1995; Rizvi *et al.*, 1998).

In the context of international experience gained from opportunities for study abroad and international volunteering as part of the internationalized curriculum, outcomes are, at best, unpredictable. Experience may not foster social engagement, awareness, participation and responsibility; rather, such experience may have more to do with professional opportunities and lifestyle options (Schattle, 2007). Willingness to engage with the 'other' via travelling may not be sufficient for transformative experiences. 'Global nomads' and 'third culture kids' possess characteristics which transcend a single culture and adopt aspects of many cultures. They may indeed feel at home anywhere, but the issue remains one of maturity and reflexivity (Gunesch, 2004). The experience of teachers and students, whether gained internationally or locally, has legitimacy in the context of the internationalized curriculum but it should not be 'uncritically patronized', since experience 'never speaks for itself and needs always to be problematized for the ideological interests that it inevitably carries' (Pavel, 1995).

The internationalized curriculum gives universities the opportunity to develop global citizens, but becoming one involves student choice. They need to be able to derive meaning from international experience within the context of a myriad of social, historical, economic and cultural relations which influence the quality of life if they are to be able to apply it to their future lives. The incentive to include an international dimension in higher education curricula derives partly from labour market effects and partly from the emergence of a multicultural and globally minded society. However, the current rhetoric of intercultural and international education is all too often located within a discourse of economic necessity which emphasizes the acquisition of intercultural communications skills like flexibility, open-mindedness and empathy as the means of survival within a highly competitive global market (Pavel, 1995; Shultz *et al.*, 2008).

Clearly, the concepts of the internationalized curriculum and global citizenship within higher education are, at least partially, reflective of the impact of globalization on curriculum and pedagogy (Edwards *et al.*, 2008). However, as previously suggested, localities may be connected to outside forces, but they do not exist in a reified fashion and most education does, after all, occur at the local level (Rizvi, 2007). It is argued, therefore, that the shape of global citizenship education and the internationalized curriculum in universities will be influenced by how they perceive their role within society. For Barnett (2009), a university is only a university insofar as it is in a perpetual state of becoming a university. In looking to future options he identifies a number of possibilities. These include the research university, where the knowledge society and knowledge transfer are prioritized; the entrepreneurial university, which views itself as being in a constant state of change governed by the criterion of knowledge products and services; the bureaucratic university, governed by human resource and quality management rules and procedures; the therapeutic university, which cares particularly about students and seeks to help the world live with its differences; the ecological university, which acknowledges its responsibilities in and to the world; and the authentic university, which helps society to learn about itself and contemplate new 'imaginaries'.

Davies (2006) envisages four possible permutations in respect of global citizenship education: global citizenship plus education, with definitions of the 'global citizen' and the implied educational framework to provide or promote this; global plus citizenship education, making citizenship education more globally or internationally relevant – think global, act local; global education plus citizenship (international awareness plus rights and responsibilities); and education plus citizenship plus global, introducing dimensions of citizenship and of international understanding, but with no essential connection between the two. Clearly, in universities any one of these permutations is possible, dependent partially on institutional mission and on the disciplinary context within which global citizenship education is encountered. Furthermore, it is interesting to note that, referring to global citizenship education in the compulsory sector, Davies *et al.* (2005) maintain that in reality it does not exist in England; rather, there is citizenship education and global education. Either international content is added into citizenship activities, or global education activities introduced to citizenship programmes. However, it is suggested that global citizenship curriculum and pedagogy facilitated within the framework of an internationalized curriculum in UK higher education tends overwhelmingly to be influenced by cosmopolitanism of either the moral or cross-cultural consumption persuasion, or multicultural education. The cross-cultural consumption approach (otherwise known as the human capital approach) is geared towards the accumulation of a new form of cultural capital in a highly competitive, globalized world of knowledge economies. This may simply perpetuate a model of global citizen education which produces tomorrow's elite, who, like the global corporation, wield power and status in the global labour market. In considering the implications of the moral brand of global citizenship education in the context of Vanessa Andreotti's (2006) characterization of soft versus critical global citizenship education, it is argued that higher education institutions may tend to address the economic and cultural roots of the inequalities in power and wealth which exist across the globe by indulging in a form of 'soft' global citizenship education. This 'soft' approach makes global citizenship a politically neutral if not banal concept, promoting a new 'civilizing mission' to a generation who willingly assume the 'burden' of saving, civilizing or educating the world, under the influence of media images and slogans that emphasize the need to be charitable, compassionate and active in recognition of a moral obligation to humanity. Moral obligation thus substitutes for any sense of political responsibility for the causes of poverty. Andreotti (2006) cites the work of Dobson (2005), who makes a useful distinction between being a human being, which raises issues of morality, and being a citizen, which raises political issues.

Internationalized curricula aimed at fostering global citizenship need to strike a balance between empowerment and cultivating a sense of humility in the face of a complex world (Marshall, 2009). It may well be the case that Western students can only understand social injustice by being disempowered in a pedagogical approach which challenges their sense of interpretive privilege and cultural superiority. The concept of 'border pedagogy' is useful in formulating pedagogic practice in response to contemporary challenges. Border pedagogy is a strategy for learning about the cultural 'other' by looking critically at how experience, images, representations and texts are constructed and at their hidden messages (Edwards *et al.*, 2008). In this way, students learn to share, listen, step aside and take a back seat while learning to unlearn (for example, the colonial mentality) and relearn with a global perspective that genuinely reaches out and engages with those considered 'other' (Pavel, 1995; Shultz *et al.*, 2008). In the context of morality in a world of uncertainty, the words of Maria Morris cited in Mohanty (2003) resonate: 'we can never be too sure, or too arrogant, to think that good intentions will lead to good things'.

In this sense, activism may be the defining element of global citizenship, an element which requires affective ties and social solidarity elusive in cosmopolitan approaches to global citizenship which offer only a 'thin' civic identity (Philippou *et al.*, 2009).

Summary and conclusions

This chapter has drawn on what might be broadly termed a sociological literature in order to understand the influence of globalization on UK higher education, to deconstruct the concept of the 'knowledge economy and learning society' within the context of 'higher' learning and to acknowledge the complexity of the concept of global citizenship within the context of the internationalized curriculum. A central proposition is the need to engage with sociological perspectives in order to give meaning to academic practice in the field and to acknowledge how values, beliefs and attitudes play a pivotal role in determining the outcomes of educational processes.

It is argued that the notion of 'higher 'learning in UK universities is being challenged by globalization processes, in the form of increased competition and globalization discourse, which serve particular interests. The challenge to universities is reinforced by knowledge economy and learning society discourse, which promotes a pragmatic-technicist view of work and learning. In order to counter instrumentalist influences, universities need to acknowledge the supercomplexitiy of the world in which we live if they are to develop capable and active global citizens. At the practice level this implies an internationalized curriculum for global citizenship which embraces the concept of critical cosmopolitanism and a 'border pedagogy' which deconstructs Western paradigms and influence, challenges popular assumptions and attitudes and enables learners to authentically engage with the 'other' in order to understand their own position within the globalized world and challenge inequalities and injustices. The words of Giroux *et al.* (2006) succinctly capture the essence of the challenge faced by UK universities in the globalized world. They acknowledge how, in 'tough economic times', providing students with anything other than work skills 'threatens their viability in the future labour market', but argue that higher education is about more than job preparation or even critical consciousness. Rather, it is about 'imagining different futures'.

References

Ainley, P. and Canaan, J. E. (2006), 'Critical hope at the chalkface: An English perspective', *Cultural Studies Critical Methodologies*, 6, (1), 94–106.

Andreotti, V. (2006), *Soft Versus Critical Global Citizenship Education. Open Space for Dialogue and Enquiry*, available at http://www.osdemethodology.org.uk/texts/softcriticalvan.pdf.

Barnett, R. (2000), *Realising the University in an Age of Supercomplexity*. Buckingham, UK: Society for Research into Higher Education/Open University Press.

—— (2009), *Realising the University in the Twenty-First Century: Issues and Possibilities*.

Keynote address to Higher Education Academy annual conference, 30 June–2 July, University of Manchester [Digital Audiovisual File], available at http://www.heacademy.ac.uk/resources/audioandvideo/annualconference2009

Beck, U. and Sznaider, N. (2006), 'Unpacking cosmopolitanism for the social sciences: A research agenda', *British Journal of Sociology*, 57, (1), 1–23.

Blackmore, J. (2002), 'Globalization and the restructuring of higher education for new knowledge economies: New dangers or old habits troubling gender equity work in universities?', *Higher Education Quarterly*, 56, (4): 419–44.

Calcutt, L., Woodward, I. and Zlatko, S. (2009), 'Conceptualising otherness: An exploration of the cosmopolitan schema', *Journal of Sociology*, 45, (2), 169–86.

Davies, I., Evans, M. and Reid, A. (2005), 'Globalising citizenship education? A critique of "global education" and "citizenship education"', *British Journal of Educational Studies*, 53, (1), 66–89.

Davies, L. (2006), 'Global citizenship: Abstraction or framework for action?' *Educational Review*, 58, (1), 5–25.

Delanty, G. (2006), 'The cosmopolitan imagination: Critical cosmopolitanism and social theory', *British Journal of Sociology*, 57, (1), 25–47.

Edwards, R. (2001), 'Making space for lifelong learning: Pedagogies of (dis)location', *Rising East: The Journal of East London Studies*, 4, (2), 22–32.

Edwards, R. and Usher, R. (2008), *Globalisation and Pedagogy: Space, Place and Identity* (2nd edn). London: Routledge.

Fairclough, N. (2001), *Language and Power* (2nd edn). London: Longman.

Falk, R. (1993), 'The making of global citizenship', in J. Brecher, J. Brown Childs and J. Cutler (eds), *Global Visions: Beyond the New World Order*. Boston: South End Press.

Freire, P. (1996), *Pedagogy of the Oppressed*. New York: Ramos Press.

Gacel-Ávila, J. (2005), 'The internationalisation of higher education: A paradigm for global citizenry', *Journal of Studies in International Education*, 9, (2), 121–36.

Giroux, H. A. and Giroux, S. S. (2006), 'Challenging neoliberalism's new world order: The promise of critical pedagogy', *Cultural Studies*, 6, (1), 21–32.

Grace, A. P. (2006), 'Creating a blueprint for a critical social pedagogy of learning for life and work: Canadian perspectives', in *Proceedings of the Australian Educational Research Conference*, available at http://www.adulterc.org/Proceedings/2006/Proceedings/Grace.pdf

Gunesch, K. (2004), 'Education for cosmopolitanism: Cosmopolitanism as a personal cultural identity model for and within international education', *Journal of Research in International Education*, 3, (3), 251–75.

Ladson-Billings, G. (2004), 'New directions in multicultural education: Complexities, boundaries, and critical race theory', in J. Banks and C. A. McGee Banks (eds), *Handbook of Research on Multicultural Education*. San Francisco: John Wiley & Sons, pp. 50–68.

Lagos, T. G. (2002), *Global Citizenship – Towards a Definition* [Internet], available at http://depts.washington.edu/gcp/pdf/globalcitizenship.pdf, accessed 12 November 2009.

Marshall, H. (2009), 'Educating the European citizen in the global age: Engaging with the post-national and identifying a research agenda', *Journal of Curriculum Studies*, 41, (2), 247–67.

Mendieta, E. (2008), *From the Abolition of Politics to a Politics of Liberation: Globalizations from Below and the Cosmopolitanism of the Other: A Discussion*. Paper presented at the American Philosophical Association's Easter Division Meeting, December, Philadelphia, available at http://www.sju.edu/~jgodfrey/MendietaCosmopolitanism.pdf

Mignolo, W. (2000), 'The many faces of cosmo-polis: Border thinking and critical cosmopolitanism', *Public Culture*, 12, (3), 721–48.

Mocombe, P. C. (2004), *Where Did Freire Go Wrong? Pedagogy in Globalization: The Grenadian Example* [Internet], available at http://www.net4dem.org/mayglobal/Events/Conference%202004/papers/PaulMocombe.pdf (accessed 12 November 2009).

Mohanty, C. T. (2003), *Feminism without Borders: Decolonizing Theory, Practicing Solidarity*. Durham and London: Duke University Press.

Naidoo, R. and Jamieson, I. (2005), 'Empowering participants or corroding learning? Towards a research agenda on the impact of student consumerism in higher education', *Journal of Education Policy*, 20, (3), 267–81.

Norris, P. (2003), *Global Governance and Cosmopolitan Citizens* [Internet], available at www.hks.harvard.edu/fs/pnorris/Acrobat/Cosmopolitans2.pdf, accessed 12 November 2009.

Nussbaum, M. (1994), 'Patriotism and cosmopolitanism', *Boston Review*, 19, (5), [Internet], available at http://bostonreview.net/BR19.5/nussbaum.html

Pavel, M. (1995), Foreword, in C. E. Sleeter and P. L. McLaren (eds), *Multicultural Education, Critical Pedagogy and the Politics of Difference*. Albany: State University of New York Press.

Philippou, S., Keating, A. and Hinderliter Ortloff, D. (2009), 'Conclusion: Citizenship education curricula: Comparing the multiple meanings of supra-national citizenship in Europe and beyond', *Journal of Curriculum Studies*, 41, (2), 291–99.

Rizvi, F. (2007), 'Postcolonialism and globalization in education', *Cultural Studies*, 7, (3), 256–63.

Rizvi, F. and Walsh, L. (1998), 'Difference, globalisation and the internationalisation of curriculum', *Australian Universities' Review*, 41, (2), 7–11.

Schattle, H. (2007), *The Practices of Global Citizenship*. Lanham, Maryland: Rowman & Littlefield.

Scott, P. (2000), 'Globalisation and higher education: Challenges for the 21st century', *Journal of Studies in International Education*, 4, (3), 3–10.

Shultz, L. and Jorgenson, S. (2008), *Global Citizenship Education in Post-Secondary Institutions: A Review of the Literature* [Internet], available at http://www.uofaweb.ualberta.ca/uai_globaleducation/pdfs/GCE_lit_review.pdf (accessed 19 November 2009).

Skirbis, Z., Kendall, G. and Woodward, I. (2004), 'Locating cosmopolitanism. Between humanist ideal and grounded social category', *Theory, Culture & Society*, 21, (6), 115–36.

Chapter 5

The Globalization and Marketization of Higher Education: Some Insights from the Standpoint of Institutional Theory

Izhar Oplatka and Jane Hemsley-Brown

Introduction

Globalization, that is, the increasing worldwide integration of economies over recent decades (King, 2004), is associated strongly with the triumph of liberal capitalism as the dominant economic mode (Walford, 1994). Additionally, governments have turned to deregulatory policies in Russia (Hare *et al.*, 1999), the Eastern Bloc (Czarniawska *et al.*, 2002), Holland (Jongbloed, 2003), Israel (Oplatka, 2002), China (Mok, 2000), Asia (Gray *et al.*, 2003) and Africa (Maringe *et al.*, 2002).

When it comes to the higher education (HE) arena, elements of globalization are widespread and multifaceted and the HE market is now well established as a global phenomenon, especially in the English-speaking nations of Canada, USA, Australia and the UK (Binsardi *et al.*, 2003; Dill, 2003; Gibbs, 2001; Taylor, 2003). In 2006, over 2.9 million students were studying outside their home countries and some estimates suggest this number will increase to eight million by 2025 (Altbach, 2008). Since 2000 the number of foreign students enrolled in tertiary education overseas has increased by 54 per cent (OECD, 2008).

The process of globalization of HE is accompanied by a process of marketization, because universities have to compete for students and resources by adopting market-like ideologies and diversity policies (Edwards, 2004). Basically, marketization includes the adoption of customer-oriented attitudes and inter-institutional diversity, and emphasizes the importance of external relations, systems of quality assurance, inter-organizational competition, and marketing-led management (Oplatka *et al.*, 2002).

In this chapter, we critically reflect upon the marketization process of HE institutions, and use the three basic concepts underlying the institutional theory of organization: conformity to institutional rules, isomorphism, and normatively based decision-making. Briefly, we develop several arguments by asking, (1) to what extent can changes conducted in HE institutions in response to globalization and internationalization be fundamental changes, rather than just image development? (2) Can HE institutions be genuinely responsive to international and local students' special needs/wants? (3) Can we expect high levels of diversity within universities following the recruitment of large numbers of students? (4) To what extent are students able to make choices based on clear and visible information about the university?

The chapter aims to challenge the basic premises underlying the processes of globalization of HE systems, and especially the continuing marketization process, from the standpoint of the institutional theory of organization originating in sociology (Hall, 2001). Using institutional theory of organization as a theoretical framework for examining the theoretical essentials of these major processes currently in evidence in many HE systems may explain the barriers to diversity, responsiveness, and improvement – all of which are assumed to be driven by the introduction of marketization policies in HE systems.

The institutional theory of organization is useful for analyzing the current marketization of HE for several reasons. First, it has become a leading approach to understanding organizations and their environments in general, and educational ones in particular (Hoy *et al.*, 2008), as it accounts for many contemporary environmental processes in compulsory and HE systems worldwide.

Second, and arising from the first reason, it provides insight into the strong influence of socially organized environments on the educational organization, and explains why many educational organizations tend to adopt symbol-like elements rather than acting rationally. In our view, marketization brings many forms of symbolic elements into the HE system.

Third, due to the uncertain nature of the education process (in terms of teaching and learning processes), coupled with the vague nature of HE purpose, we perceive colleges and universities as institutions. According to Abell (1995), the institution is a more or less agreed-upon set of rules that carry meaning for and determine the actions of some population of actors. It is composed of 'cultural, cognitive, normative, and regulative elements that, together with associated activities and resources, provide stability and meaning to social life' (Scott, 2001, p. 48). The settings in which HE activities take place corroborate this definition for it is based, by and large, on cultural and normative elements due to uncertain technologies and purposes.

Major elements underlying the marketization of HE

In most countries, marketization has been viewed as a 'compromise between privatization, academic autonomy and state control' (Young, 2002, p. 79) as established leaders throughout the world call for 'freedom from all the shackles of government regulation' (Dill, 2003, p. 136). A comprehensive description of marketization is suggested by Marginson (1999):

> (Marketization) is apparent in the growing role of private costs, in the increasing inequalities between the resources and status of education in different institutions, and in the varying experiences of 'consumption' within common systems. It can be recognised also in the growing role of competition between institutions, and in the plethora of corporate activity, such as marketing, business plans . . . (p. 230)

The issues and implications of the global marketization of HE and privatization (Arimoto, 1997; Kwong, 2000) have been discussed in the context of a number of key concerns: problems of increasing competition between institutions (Mazzarol *et al.*, 1999; Ivy, 2001; Coates *et al.*, 2003; Farr, 2003), funding issues (Brookes, 2003), and widening participation or social segmentation (Ball *et al.*, 2002; Farr, 2003).

The discourse of markets and marketization in HE, though, needs further explanation and clarification if one aims to analyze its structure and characteristics. Based on previous analysis (for example, Le Grand *et al.*, 1993; Marginson, 1999), it seems that educational marketization comprises six recurring characteristics and aspects which are highly relevant for the institutional analysis of this process: rational choice decision-making; inter-institutional competition; customer-oriented attitudes; marketing-led management of HE institutions; and the importance of external relations.

Rational choice decision-making

Attempts by governments to enhance the quality of HE through the encouragement of market forces are based on an assumption that students are, or will become, informed consumers making rational choices of HE courses and institutions (Baldwin *et al.*, 2000). It is expected that prospective students will consider every institution and programme profoundly and systematically. Thus, research into HE choice, or consumer behaviour in HE markets, although not extensive, has principally been stimulated by an individual institution's need to anticipate the long-term implications of choice and to understand the key factors involved in student choice (Foskett *et al.*, 2001).

Inter-institutional competition

The marketization process further intensifies competition in which HE institutions have to respond to various stakeholder groups (Hemsley-Brown *et al.*, 2006). The competition can be quite intense and the degree of threat depends on factors such as distance to the nearest alternative, quality of product, entrance policies and marketing strategies. In this new situation all the individual HE institutions need to compete to attract and retain students, and to achieve a reputation as a successful and effective institution (Maringe *et al.*, 2009).

It is commonly premised that improvement and efficiency in HE institutions is strongly driven by competitive forces both within existing and between new HE providers. Thus, as HE becomes more privatized, with its services regarded as a source of income to replace declining public funds, internationalism is seen more in terms of overseas markets (King, 2004).

Customer-oriented attitudes

Under the marketization process it is the consumer who becomes the centre of the educational institution's attention (Foskett, 1998). The marketing concept holds that achieving organizational goals depends upon determining the needs and wants of target markets and delivering the desired outcomes more effectively and efficiently than competitors (Kotler *et al.*, 1999). The HE institution is expected to acknowledge the primacy of the marketplace and of customer needs in shaping its plans, curriculum and other educational activities to meet those needs more precisely (Gray, 1991). Universities are encouraged to be more responsive to students' needs and demands.

It is in the area of knowledge production – of research – where globalization currently most affects HE. Thus, one aspect of HE institution responsiveness is expressed by common demands of 'application' or the usability of knowledge, that are increasingly influential in determining what is researched and how, particularly through the research funding arms of government (Maringe *et al.*, 2009). Globalization is absorbing universities into a distributed knowledge production system, involving universities in many more alliances and partnerships as they seek to acquire specialized and up-to-date knowledge, including an increasing range of non-university research and development companies, and where basic and applied research are increasingly converged (King, 2004).

Marketing-led management

One major feature of educational marketization is an increased priority being given by HE institutions to the marketing of their strengths and services (Hemsley-Brown *et al.*, 2006; Maringe *et al.*, 2009). Issues of public relations and promotion, both locally and internationally, are becoming more significant because the survival of HE institutions is dependent on their capacity to maintain or increase their 'market share' of local and international students, results and resources and to market their service to external environments.

Likewise, in the context of increasing competition universities have been forced to equip themselves with the necessary marketing intelligence and information that will enable them to face the challenge of such an international market for HE (Binsardi *et al.*, 2003). Marketing is about exchange and delivery of value between those who provide the educational service and those who seek to benefit from it, and is not a means to an end but a process of building relationships based on trust that are aimed at empowering the clients or customers of HE (Maringe *et al.*, 2009).

Importance of external relations

The marketization process highlights the importance of external relations in the HE institution due to the turbulent, rapidly changing environments of HE nowadays. In order to survive in their competitive environment, HE institutions need to pay more attention to external relations; they are expected to display independent initiative and power over their environments to achieve both organizational effectiveness and efficiency (Foskett *et al.*, 2001). In King's (2004) view, as companies in the globalization era become more aggressive, they invest in certain areas and this has the consequence of turning a basic science into a more entrepreneurial form (King, 2004).

Furthermore, as part of the 'contextualization process' characterizing our time, universities and colleges are required to understand in a more intimate way both the internal and external environments in which they intend to develop their curriculum. They should devise a curriculum which not only reflects the needs and wants of potential customers, but can also make a valid claim for inclusion and incorporation in the new educational environment (Maringe *et al.*, 2009). Thus, in order to survive their competitive and uncertain environment, HE institutions need to become entrepreneurially oriented, which requires anticipating and responding to new initiatives, challenges and opportunities in their external markets. Entrepreneurship involves the identification and exploitation of an opportunity, taking risks, and adopting a new/ different perspective of creative opportunities (Hirsch *et al.*, 1998), such as the simultaneous delivery of programmes locally and overseas or transferring whole departments and programme portfolios offshore to Asia, for example.

Institutional and symbolic aspects of marketization

The institutional perspective is becoming a dominant approach to understanding organizations and their environments (Hoy *et al.*, 2008). While institutional approaches were strong in economics, in political science, and in sociology early in the twentieth century, the revival of the 'new institutionalism' in sociology is commonly attributed to the works of John W. Meyer and Richard Scott in the seventies (Rowan *et al.*, 1999). They changed the way institutions were thought about by organizational sociologists.

Although many theoretical views (for example, contingency theory, resource dependencies, and so on) have emphasized the impact of environment upon organizations, only institutional theory highlights the significance of the wider social and cultural environment as the ground in which organizations are rooted (Meyer *et al.*, 1977; Scott, 1995). In that sense, this theory reconceptualizes organizational environments, emphasizing the role of supposed forces of knowledge systems, institutional beliefs, rules and roles in affecting organizational structures and operation independent of resource flows and technical requirements (Rowan *et al.*, 1999).

This theory is much more applicable to organizations that exist in weak technical, but strong institutional environments such as educational organizations and hospitals (Meyer *et al.*, 1977). For example, educational institutions that do not possess clear technologies (that is, instruction) are especially likely to conform to institutional rules, for, by doing so, they can gain legitimacy with stakeholders in their environments (Meyer *et al.*, 1977).

However, the institutional explanation of organizational phenomena is not without criticism. Hall (2001) suggested that structural characteristics that cannot be explained by other reasons are attributed to institutional forces, and that this perspective is potentially tautological reasoning. Other critics claim that the institutional perspective has almost become 'authoritarian' as it has swept the theoretical landscape (Hirsch, 1997), and has also become institutionalized (Tolbert *et al.*, 1996), as there is very little consensus on the definition of key concepts, measures or methods.

In this chapter we define three main elements of the institutional theory of organizations which constitute the theoretical frame for the analysis of basic assumptions of marketization in HE.

1 Conformity to institutional rules. The focus here is on the organization's tendency to incorporate rationalized myth and societally agreed rules in its structure, thereby promoting survival, social legitimacy and apparent success without increasing efficiency or technical performance.
2 Isomorphism. Another central element of institutional theory is that conformity of organizations to institutional rules, over time, leads organizations in the same institutional sector to resemble one another.
3 Normatively based decision making. The decision-making process is claimed to be strongly influenced by collective norms and values that impose social obligations on them and constrain their choices. Conformity to institutional rules and rationalized myth, rather than self-interest and expedience, is likely to guide one's behaviour.

Though we find this frame useful for analysing the reform of parental choice in practice, and though the elements are discussed separately in the sections to follow, they overlap and are interconnected with one another.

Conformity to institutional rules: An emphasis on marketing-oriented changes

A major theoretical assumption of market ideology is that marketization will improve the quality of teaching, stimulate change and increase efficiency of research in HE, mainly through the introduction of competition among HE institutions (Chubb *et al.*, 1990; Tooley, 1992). Competition was initially defined as 'producers striving to attract consumers to choose their service or product instead of those of other providers' (Woods *et al.*, 1998, p. 138). Thus, it is interesting to seek to understand whether changes driven by globalization and marketization are fundamental or just marketing-oriented.

Given the institutional theory view of conformity to institutional rules, the discussion to follow questions the premise that marketization will necessarily result in fundamental changes in HE institutions and in an increase in their effectiveness and their responsiveness to students and other stakeholders (for instance, industry). In contrast, HE institutions may rather adopt marketing-based adaptations which conform to institutional rules and, in turn, promote their survival and social legitimacy.

For institutional theorists, institutionalized norms, values and technical lore play an extremely significant role in innovations and changes in educational organizations (Rowan, 1982). Innovations and activities in HE tend to gain legitimacy and acceptance on the basis of social evaluations, such as generalized cultural beliefs and the endorsement of legislatures or professional agencies (Meyer *et al.*, 1978; 1992). HE institutions are under the pressure of conformity to adopt changes and innovations that have the support and endorsement of key agencies in the institutional environment, such as the government, industry and financial agencies.

For example, policies aimed at widening the participation of students from less privileged social groups urge HE institutions to lower their entry requirements and establish special refresher courses for them even if the academic success of these students is questioned. Likewise, the drive to harness university research to wider strategic national goals and to integrate it into broader plans for economic development might urge universities to prioritize applied research at the expense of intellectual, curiosity-driven and creative basic research that has characterized many HE institutions since their foundation many centuries ago (King, 2004).

Along the same lines, educational organizations are assumed in institutional theory to incorporate into their structure 'rationalized myths', a term coined by Meyer *et al.*, (1977) to refer to rules specifying procedures to accomplish an outcome that are based on beliefs assumed to be true or just taken for granted. They are true because they are believed. Myths become rationalized when they take the form of bureaucratic or professional rules specifying procedures necessary to accomplish a given end (Scott, 2001). Arising from this point, then, is that HE institutions competing for new and current students may choose to adopt rationalized myths that maximize their image as a good institution whose structure and programmes are consistent with deeply institutionalized, rule-like understandings about the best way to produce a given end. In this regard, there are examples of procedures to measure research quality based on external criteria. These include the Research Excellence Framework (REF), used from 2008 onwards for the assessment and funding of research in England (HEFCE, 2009). The procedures are employed not because they have been proven to contribute specifically to academic growth and development, but because 'standards' are commonly perceived as an efficient way to improve performance in the global world.

The discussion to this point suggested that the need for conformity to institutional elements might induce HE institutions in the global era to implement improvements and innovations which are, in fact, a mirror of their environment's values and beliefs; otherwise, they might be perceived as failing institutions. In doing so, HE institutions are assumed to adopt marketing-led changes (that is, changes that do not necessarily contribute to their core technology, but have a symbolic power to attract prospective students) rather than fundamental changes (in teaching methods or research foci, for instance). HE institutions may present their applied researches publicly, without any reference to their 'real' contribution or their efficiency in performing these studies (in terms of cost versus benefits or time use). At the same time, they may 'conceal' basic research in Life Sciences or scholarships in the Arts that gain lesser societal respect and appreciation than those in applied sciences like Business Administration or Economics.

Another basic premise of institutional theory is that conformity to institutionalized rules can promote the long-term survival of the organization without necessarily increasing its efficiency or technical performance (Meyer *et al.*, 1977; DiMaggio *et al.*, 1991; Scott, 2001), although no clear definition or measure is suggested for these concepts (Tolbert *et al.*, 1996). This argument stands in sharp contrast to rational system models, which hold that organizational performance is the crucial determinant of organizational success.

In that sense, in order to survive the competition, HE institutions in market-like environments are assumed to go to the greatest lengths – not to accomplish improved teaching and learning quality or empirical ends, but to maintain their legitimate status as successful academic institutions. Meyer and colleagues (1992, p. 56) have suggested that 'a school succeeds if everyone agrees that it is a school; it fails if no one believes that it is a school, regardless of its success in instruction or socialization'. The same can be claimed about HE institutions. For example, in order to promote the teacher training colleges managed by the Israeli Ministry of Education, policy-makers have decided to make these colleges 'academic', that is, enlarge the number of teacher educators with a PhD and re-structure their organization to accommodate 'academic' procedures (for example, clear and rigorous regulations and more theory-oriented courses).

Yet, the contribution of this policy to the efficiency and effectiveness of teacher training programmes has never been considered profoundly 'academic' – it is widely considered as the right way to organize post-secondary education in an era of globalization and the knowledge economy. In contrast, in the name of 'enhancing academic rigour', practice-based courses have been replaced by theoretical ones, thereby minimizing the exposure of pre-service teachers to practical knowledge, a very important aspect in any vocational training.

Similarly, allocating an increasing amount of time and resources to marketing and image-building, as observed in many studies worldwide (for example, Hemsley-Brown *et al.*, 2006; Maringe *et al.*, 2009; Oplatka, 2009), seems to be crucial for apparent institutional success, more so than improving the research and teaching domain. From the institutional theory standpoint, a failure to incorporate the proper elements of structure is negligent and irrational; the continued flow of support is threatened (Rowan *et al.*, 1999). It implies that failing HE institutions in the competitive environment are those failing to conform to the socially legitimated elements formulated by the principles of a knowledge economy, such as applied research, technology-assisted learning or improved leisure and social facilities (for example, sports centres and high-quality accommodation). Absurdly, at the same time the ostensibly 'failing' institutions can be very effective in the invisible aspects of HE teaching and research – aspects not necessarily perceived to be features, but ones we would simply take for granted in a high-quality institution.

Furthermore, educational innovations tend to have high levels of technical uncertainty and, as a result, can seldom be justified on the basis of solid technical evidence. Instead, for example, HE institutions are likely to adopt new forms of programme organization, such as one-year MA programmes, or rename old titles of academic courses more attractively, rather than focusing on changing teaching approaches and beliefs; two elements considered by Fullan (1991) to be an indispensable aspect of educational change. If the 'public' can watch the 'visible, material changes', the HE institution, then, is expected to gain legitimacy as an efficient academic provider.

To this point, we have seen that advocates of HE marketization ignored the symbolic aspects of educational and academic success, which means that technical efficiency and effective teaching do not necessarily promote the HE institution's competitive edge. School success in the competitive environment appears to be influenced by the institution's capability to build an image of an organization which complies with institutional rules and expectations of how good academic construction should be (for example, an increased range of 'applied' courses available to students or the opening of new 'attractive' and programmes in demand).

But, if an HE institution's success is assumed to be connected to its capability to promote symbolic elements compatible with institutional rules in its community, then the issue of responsiveness receives a slightly different meaning. While advocates of educational marketization assumed that HE institutions, left to their own devices, would respond positively to students' preferences (Chubb *et al.*, 1990), we would like to put forward the idea that their responsiveness is symbolic in its essence. Put differently, their core technology, that is, teaching and research, would not be significantly modified in accordance with the needs of industry, the national economy and students' wants, but the contrary. Only those symbolic elements with high influence on measurable academic success and survival would be changed. Ramsden (2009) argues that although HE in the UK is taking the views of students more seriously since the National Student Survey (NSS) and universities are deploying mechanisms for responding to student feedback, this approach needs to go further, beyond simply collecting and responding directly to students' concerns. The students' perspectives should be embedded in all aspects of planning for teaching, quality enhancement and quality assurance.

Based on institutional theories, HE institutions, by responding positively to these sorts of societal and economic needs, only conform to institutional rules, values and ideologies, without changing their basic technology or increasing their technical efficiency. They adopt structural changes which have limited influence on teaching and research, but are highly significant to the image production of HE institutions operating in the new market environment.

Isomorphism and myth-making: Any possibility for diversity of providers?

A major component of the market ideology refers to existing diversity of supply, which means the amount of difference between educational institutions in terms of educational content and teaching methods (Chubb *et al.*, 1990). Competition, it is held, will enable the flowering of diversity as institutions seek niche markets that respond to the needs of special groups.

The preceding section evidenced the issue of conformity to institutional rules, which is a central idea in institutional theory. Organizational conformity, it is held, moulds the structure of organizations and, over time, it leads organizations in the same institutional environment to resemble one another (Rowan *et al.*, 1999). DiMaggio *et al.*'s works (1983; 1991) are especially insightful in illustrating the link between organizational conformity and isomorphism among organizations in the same sector. They contend that there is great pressure on organizations to engage in the same types of activities to look and act alike. Organizations within the same institutional environments tend to become homogenized. In that sense HE institutions, even in competitive arenas, are expected to resemble each other in respect to buildings, instruction and curriculum, classroom design, and similar ways of engaging in promotion processes.

Institutional theories may account for the barriers to diversity among HE institutions in competitive arenas. DiMaggio *et al.* (1991) identify three mechanisms that promote institutional conformity: coercive conformity, imitative conformity and normative conformity. These conformities are conceived of as the forces leading to isomorphism among organizations in the same sector and may shed some light upon constraints of HE marketization and diversification.

Coercive conformity stems from political influence and problems of legitimacy. HE and particularly universities have been heavily engaged with the design and development of performance measurement systems since the 1980s. In the corporate sector these systems are intended to be leading indicators of long-term financial success, and in the UK budget reductions in the public sector have created an emphasis on the measurement of the effectiveness and efficiency of universities (Tapinos *et al.*, 2005). They claim that:

> Academic institutions in the UK concentrate primarily on financial viability and growth. For this reason they found that (the) 'University of Warwick has made no significant change in its mission and vision in the last 15 years, and does not address directly the measurement of the social benefits and contribution to society'. (p. 196)

Similarly, a mandatory structure of academic programmes issued by the Israeli Council of Higher Education decreases the possibility of diversity among universities and colleges in the HE market.

Imitative conformity results from adopting standard responses from other sources to reduce uncertainty. When organizations have weak technologies and ambiguous goals, they may model themselves on other organizations that they perceive to be more legitimate and successful (Hoy *et al.*, 2008). It follows that a weak college or university may create programmes and engage in activities similar to those found in more prestigious HE institutions, not because they necessarily improve its efficiency or quality of teaching, but because it may gain legitimacy with stakeholders by being perceived to be a successful HE institution. For instance, teacher training colleges in Israel have adopted procedures and regulations that are more suitable for a research university than for a vocational training-focused institution. In so doing, they strive to win the reputation of an academic institution that is rated higher in the league tables.

Normative conformity comes primarily from professionalization. Academics have experienced the same formal education and acquired cognitive knowledge. They learn standard methods of practice and normative rules about appropriate behaviour. Those expecting diversity to emerge, then, do not seem to take this aspect into account. Thus, academics focus more on their own individual work (research and teaching) and increasingly leave organizational decision-making to administrators. Nevertheless, most academics still have administrative roles to perform (such as course directorship) (Baruch *et al.*, 2004).

Thus far we have seen how institutional theory supports those who claim there is no diversity of provision in education, and explains the sources of isomorphism among HE institutions, even in competitive environments. Advocates of HE marketization, it is suggested here, have ignored the potential impact of cultural, normative, imitative and coercive conformity upon universities and colleges. Nevertheless, consistent with the criticism against the institutional perspective (Tolbert *et al.*, 1996), there is a need to bear in mind that the isomorphism process tends to be moderate rather than total, due to disagreements among organizational decision-makers concerning institutional influences, different responses to educational policies, and internal political arrangements that make institutions more or less receptive to change processes.

Institutional elements and limited rational choices

The preceding sections discussed major concepts and assumptions underlying the institutional theory, with high relevance for analyzing the barriers to the application of market forces in HE. When these elements are combined, the limitation of a rational choice process, which is a core premise in the ideology of the educational market, is emphasized. From the institutional view, institutional elements (for example, conformity, isomorphism, and loose coupling) seem to be an obstacle to rational choice of HE institutions. Accordingly, applicants are unlikely to choose rationally, but, on the contrary, ideologically and normatively. One aspect of the assumed rational choice process is that vigilant information collection is difficult to apply due to the institutional features of the HE institution that 'hide' the core activities, that is, instructional and research activities, and display symbolic aspects. This leads prospective students to base their choice upon 'external' factors (for example, prestige and image) rather than on effective teaching and the value of research conducted in a certain institution.

Rational models of choice are based on the view that choices and decisions in the marketplace are the result of rational calculations (Foskett *et al.*, 2001). Two basic elements of this view are the focus of the forthcoming analysis: that individuals will seek to maximize the benefits they gain from the choices they make, and that they will make choices that are based entirely on self-interest.

The institutional theory, though, rejects rational actor models (DiMaggio *et al.*, 1983; Scott, 2001). As it emphasizes the normative aspects of institutions, behaviour is assumed to be guided not primarily by self-interest, but by an awareness of one's role in a social situation and a concern to behave appropriately, in accordance with others' expectations and internalized standards of conduct. Institutional theorists claim that the power of social patterns to shape individual beliefs and behaviour and to conceive of individual actions is determined more by non-rational than by rational forces (Scott, 2001).

Individuals are strongly influenced by collective norms and values that impose social obligations on them and constrain their choices.

Put differently, according to institutional theory, not only are organizations expected to be conformist with institutional rules, they are also expected to respond to individuals, that is, the prospective students. Applicants' choices are based more on normative and social elements than solely on utility maximization or self-interest. HE institutions are chosen not because they necessarily match the student's needs and desires, but rather because they are compatible with what Scott (2001) calls the cognitive conceptions of institutions, that is, the schemata and ideological formulations, taken for granted, that define appropriate structures and lend meaning and order to practical action.

The view of a process of rational choice implies also the need to consider more than one alternative in a way that maximizes one's benefits, but the institutional element of isomorphism among organizations in the same sector makes HE institutions resemble one another. To wit, a basic conjecture of a process of rational choice – considering alternatives – is limited in HE. In addition, a societally agreed model of what is a good university/college is so ingrained that it is unlikely that students have any strong desire to seek alternative kinds of organizational structure for these institutions.

Summary and conclusion

In summary, while in market theory's ideal concept of the consumer, individuals choose goods according to their preferences and self-interest (Foskett *et al.*, 2001), students' preferences, from an institutional view, are a mirror of institutional beliefs and ideologies. Student-consumers base their choice on criteria which are taken-for-granted schemata of what should be in universities or colleges, not necessarily on what is really going on in these institutions.

Theoretical and empirical implications

From the institutional analysis presented in this chapter, a number of insights can be provided. First, the implementation of many features of HE marketization in the HE environment and the HE institution is constrained by institutional elements. Thus, inter-organizational competition in the HE arena is unlikely to result either in structural, empirical and instructional improvement, or in more efficient performance, as advocates of HE marketization claim. A host of institutional characteristics of HE institutions minimize or even impede the impact of competition upon these institutions, as we argued in this chapter. In fact, these institutional elements seem to leave HE managers with only one alternative: to gain social legitimacy in the era of the knowledge economy and globalization by means of marketing and image-building. Indeed, the attention given to HE marketing has been increasing in recent years (Hemsley-Brown *et al.*, 2006; Maringe *et al.*, 2009).

Similarly, rational choice decision-making processes and customer-oriented attitudes are obstructed by institutional elements. For a wide variety of determinants discussed at length in this chapter, prospective students cannot 'see' the real activities taking place in courses, and therefore need to rely heavily on symbolic aspects of HE. The HE institution cannot be responsive to public demands and expectations due to many institutional constraints on its performance and functioning. Thus, the conjecture that responsiveness to customers' needs will lead to institutional improvement is limited to external, symbolic elements.

As the analysis discussed in this chapter is theoretical-conceptual, some implications for future research merit highlighting. Researchers may want to explore the effects of HE globalization on symbolic and ritual elements within HE institutions on one hand, and the establishment of real change on the other hand. This will provide some insight into the meaning of conformity to institutional rule, inter-organizational isomorphism, and normatively based decision-making in HE.

References

Abell, P. (1995), 'The new institutionalism and rational choice theory', in W. R. Scott and T. Christiansen (eds), *The Institutional Construction of Organizations: International and Longitudinal Studies*. Thousand Oaks, CA: Sage.

Altbach, P. G. (2008), 'Globalization and forces for change in higher education', *International Higher Education*, 50, (Winter), 2.

Arimoto, A. (1997), 'Market and higher education in Japan', *Higher Education Policy*, 10, (3–4), 199–210.

Baldwin, G. and James, R. (2000), 'The market in Australian higher education and the concept of student as informed consumer', *Journal of Higher Education Policy and Management*, 22, (2), 139–48.

Ball, S. J., Davies, J., David, M. and Reay, D. (2002), '"Classification" and "Judgement": Social class and the "cognitive structures" of choice in higher education', *British Journal of Sociology of Education*, 32, (1), 51–72.

Baruch, Y. and Hall, D. T. (2004), 'The academic career: A model for future careers in other sectors?', *Journal of Vocational Behaviour*, 64, 241–62.

Binsardi, A. and Ekwulugo, F. (2003), 'International marketing of British education: Research on the students' perception and the UK market penetration', *Marketing Intelligence and Planning*, 21, (5), 318–27.

Brookes, M. (2003), 'Higher education: Marketing in a quasi-commercial service industry', *International Journal of Non-Profit and Voluntary Sector Marketing*, 8, (2), 1465–520.

Coates, G. and Adnett, N. (2003), 'Encouraging cream-skimming and dreg-siphoning? Increasing competition between English HEIs', *British Journal of Educational Studies*, 51, (3), 202–18.

Chubb, J. E. and Moe, T. M. (1990), *Politics, Markets, and America's Schools*. Washington, DC: Brookings Institution.

Czarniawska, B. and Genell, K. (2002), 'Gone shopping? Universities on their way to the market', *Scandinavian Journal of Management*, 18, (4), 455–75.

Dill, D. D. (2003), 'Allowing the market to rule: The case of the United States', *Higher Education Quarterly*, 57, (2), 136–57.

DiMaggio, P. J. and Powell, W. W. (1983), 'The iron cage revisited: Isomorphism and collective rationality in organizational fields', *American Sociological Review*, 48, 147–60.

—— (eds) (1991), *The New Institutionalism in Organisational Analysis*. Chicago: University of Chicago Press.

Edwards, K. (2004), 'The university in Europe and the US', in R. King (ed.), *The University in the Global Age*. Houndmills, UK: Palgrave Macmillan, pp. 27–44.

Farr, M. (2003), '"Extending" participation in higher education – implications for marketing', *Journal of Targeting, Measurement and Analysis for Marketing*, 11, (4), 314–25.

Foskett, N. (1998), 'Schools and marketisation', *Educational Management and Administration*, 26, (2), 197–210.

Foskett, N. and Hemsley-Brown, J. (2001), *Choosing Futures: Young People's Decision-Making in Education, Training and Careers Markets*. London: Routledge-Falmer.

Fullan, M. (1991), *The New Meaning of Educational Change*. New York: Teachers College Press.

Gibbs, P. (2001), 'Higher education as a market: A problem or a solution?', *Studies in Higher Education*, 26, (1), 85–94.

Gray, B. J., Fam, K. S. and Llanes, V. A. (2003), 'Cross cultural values and the positioning of international education brands', *Journal of Product and Brand Management*, 12, (2), 108–19.

Gray, L. (1991), *Marketing Education*. Milton Keynes: Open University Press.

Hall, R. H. (2001), *Organizations: Structures, Processes and Outcomes*. New Jersey: Prentice Hall.

Hare, P. and Lugachev, M. (1999), 'Higher education in transition to a market economy: Two case studies', *Europe-Asia Studies*, 51, (1), 101–22.

Hemsley-Brown, J. and Oplatka, I. (2006), 'Universities in a competitive global marketplace: A systematic review of the literature on higher education marketing', *International Journal of Public Sector Management*, 19, (4), 316–38.

Higher Education Funding Council for England (HEFCE) (2009), *Research Excellence Framework*, available online at: http://www.hefce.ac.uk/research/ref/ (accessed 7 September 2009).

Hirsch, P. M. (1997), 'Sociology without social structure: Neo-institutional theory meets brave new world', *American Journal of Sociology*, 102, 1702–23.

Hisrich, R. D. and Peters, M. P. (1998), *Entrepreneurship*. Boston: Irwin McGraw-Hill.

Hoy, K. H. and Miskel, C. G. (2008), *Educational Administration: Theory, Research and Practice*. New York: Allyn and Bacon.

Ivy, J. (2001), 'Higher education institution image: A correspondence analysis approach', *The International Journal of Educational Management*, 15, (6), 276–82.

Jongbloed, B. (2003), 'Marketisation in higher education, Clarke's triangle and the essential ingredients of markets', *Higher Education Quarterly*, 57, (2), 110–35.

King, R. (2004), *The University in the Global Age*. Houndmills, UK: Palgrave Macmillan.

Kotler, P. and Armstrong, A. (1999), *Principles of Marketing*. New York: Prentice Hall.

Kwong, J. (2000), 'Introduction: Marketisation and privatisation in education', *International Journal of Educational Development*, 20, 87–92.

Le Grand, J. and Bartlett, W. (1993), *Quasi-Markets and Social Policy*. London: Palgrave Macmillan.

Marginson, S. (1999), 'Education and the trend of markets', *Australian Journal of Education*, 43, (3), 229–40.

Maringe, F. and Gibbs, P. (2009), *Marketing Higher Education: Theory and Practice*. London: Open University Press.

Maringe, F. and Foskett, N. H. (2002), 'Marketing university education: The South African experience', *Higher Education Review*, 34, (3), 35–51.

Mazzarol, T. and Soutar, G. N. (1999), 'Sustainable competitive advantage for educational institutions: A suggested model', *International Journal of Educational Management*, 12, (6), 287–300.

Meyer, J. W. and Rowan, B. (1977), 'Institutionalised organizations: Formal structure as myth and ceremony', *American Journal of Sociology*, 83, 340–63.

—— (1978), 'The structure of educational organizations', in M. W. Meyer (ed.), *Environments and Organizations*. San Francisco: Jossey-Bass, pp. 78–109.

Meyer, J. W., Scott, W. R. and Deal, T. E. (1992), 'Institutional and technical sources of organizational structure: Explaining the structure of educational organizations', in J. W. Meyer and W. R. Scott (eds), *Organizational Environments: Ritual and Rationality*. Newbury Park: Sage, pp. 45–70.

Mok, K. H. (2000), 'Marketising higher education in post-Mao China', *International Journal of Educational Development*, 20, 109–26.

OECD (2008), *Highlights from Education at a Glance*. OECD, Indicators. Paris: Secretary-General of the OECD. Available at: http://browse.oecdbookshop.org/oecd/pdfs/browseit/9609011E.PDF (accessed 7 September 2009).

Oplatka, I. (2002), 'Implicit contradictions in public messages of "low-stratified" HE institutions: The case of Israeli teacher training colleges', *The International Journal of Educational Management*, 16, (5), 248–56.

—— (2009), 'Marketing the university: The subjective perceptions of Israeli academics of their role in attracting new students to their institution', *Journal of Higher Education Management and Policy*, 31, (3), 207–17.

Oplatka, I., Foskett, N. H. and Hemsley-Brown, J. (2002). 'Educational marketisation and the headteacher's psychological well-being: A speculative conceptualisation', *British Journal of Educational Studies*, 50, (4), 419–41.

Ramsden, P. (2009), 'The future of higher education teaching and the student experience', *Times Higher Education* (THE) online. Available at http://www.timeshighereducation.co.uk/Journals/THE/THE/13_November_2008/attachments/teaching_and_student_experience_Ramsden.pdf (accessed 7 September 2009).

Rowan, B. (1982), 'Organizational structure and the institutional environment: The case of public schools', *Administrative Science Quarterly*, 27, 259–79.

Rowan, B. and Miskel, C. G. (1999), 'Institutional theory and the study of educational organizations', in J. Murphy and K. Seashore-Louis (eds), *Handbook of Research on Educational Administration*. San Francisco: Jossey-Bass, pp. 359–84.

Scott, W. R. (1995), 'Introduction: Institutional theory and organization', in W. R. Scott and S. Christnesne (eds), *The Institutional Construction of Organizations*. Thousand Oaks, CA: Sage.

—— (2001), *Institutions and Organizations*. Thousand Oaks, CA: Sage.

Tapinos, E., Dyson, R. G. and Meadows, M. (2005), 'The impact of the performance measurement systems in setting the "direction" in the University of Warwick', *Production, Planning and Control*, 16, (2), 189–98.

Taylor, J. (2003), 'Institutional diversity in UK higher education: Policy and outcomes since the end of the binary divide', *Higher Education Quarterly*, 57, (3), 266–93.

Tolbert, P. S. and Zucker, L. G. (1996), 'The institutionalisation of institutional theory', in S. R. Clegg, C. Hardy, and W. R. Nord (eds), *Handbook of Organization Studies*. London: Sage, pp. 175–90.

Tooley, J. (1992), 'The pink tank on the Education Reform Act', *British Journal of Educational Studies*, 40, (4), 335–49.

Walford, G. (1994), *Choice and Equity in Education*. London: Cassell.

Woods, P., Bagley, C. and Glatter, R. (1998), *School Choice and Competition: Markets in the Public Interest?* London: Routledge.

Young, S. (2002), 'The use of market mechanisms in higher education finance and state control: Ontario considered', *The Canadian Journal of Higher Education*, xxxii, (2), 79–102.

PART II

Management and Empirical Perspectives

Chapter 6

The Response of Governments and Universities to Globalization and Internationalization in Higher Education

John Taylor

Introduction

Globalization is widely recognized as one of the most powerful forces for change in higher education. The term 'globalization' is commonly used by politicians keen to encourage ideas of competition and perceptions of international excellence, and by university leaders looking to foster new approaches to teaching and research. Yet there is no universally accepted definition of the term and it is widely used as a shorthand collective for a wide range of different forms of economic and social change. One of the first scholars to discuss the impact of globalization, Giddens described globalization as 'the intensification of worldwide social relations which link distant locations in such a way that local happenings are shaped by events occurring many miles away and *vice versa*' (Giddens, 1990, p. 64). Here, therefore, are concepts of distance and geography. However, other scholars have taken the understanding of globalization further. Held *et al.* refer to an increase in the pace of change and to the importance of cross-boundary linkages in their definition of globalization as 'the widening, deepening and speeding up of world interconnectedness' (1999, p. 2). Subsequently, Held *et al.* defined globalization as:

> a process (or a set of processes) which embodies a transformation in the spatial organisation of social relations and transactions – assessed in terms of their extensity, intensity, velocity and impact – generating transcontinental or interregional flows and networks of activity, interaction and the exercise of power. (Held *et al.*, 2003, p. 68)

Castells identifies the emergence of a new world economy, free from local and territorial roots. He writes that:

> productivity and competitiveness are, by and large, a function of knowledge generation and information processing; forms and territories are organised in networks of production, management and distribution; the core economic activities are global – that is, they have the capacity to work as a unit in real time, or chosen time, on a planetary scale. (Castells, 2001, p. 52)

Here it is immediately possible to identify trends familiar to modern higher education, including the emphasis on knowledge creation and communication, and the emergence of new, international forms of delivery. Ideas of globalization and the knowledge economy are inextricably interconnected. Similarly, globalization also conjures up notions of the decline of the nation state and the emergence of multinational organizations of governance and multinational corporations. Ohmae refers to the reduction in the ability of states to control their own affairs when faced by the growth of transnational organizations and, especially interesting in the context of higher education, to the increasing focus of consumers on international markets (Ohmae, 1995).

The impact of globalization on higher education has been considered by many authors. Scott described globalization as perhaps 'the most fundamental challenge faced by the university in its long history' (Scott, 1999, p. 35) and, in particular, he emphasized that universities were active leaders in the process of globalization, not just passive recipients of change (Scott, 1998). Scott subsequently made two more key points: that globalization not only transcends national boundaries but ignores them, and that globalization is part of the move from modernity to post-modernity, a movement within which universities not only represent an embodiment of modernity, but a major catalyst for and an instrument of change (Scott, 2000). Other authors have linked globalization with the emerging ideas of academic capitalism (Slaughter *et al.*, 1997), the entrepreneurial university (Clark, 1998) and the enterprise university (Marginson *et al.*, 2000). Here the forces of globalization are seen to foster competition between universities, for students, for academic staff and for research. Similarly, globalization is often associated with new forms of national and institutional management, especially the adoption of 'new public management' (Marginson *et al.*, 2000; Musselin 2005). As far as the conduct of teaching and research is concerned, new technology, especially the emergence of the Internet and the widespread use of information and communication technology (ICT), is both a cause and effect of globalization. For universities, it is impossible now to conceive of a working environment without regular access and exchange of information at high speed around the world (Smeby *et al.*, 2005). At the same time, the perceived decline in the nation state can be seen as a special challenge to the role of the public university; Kwiek argues that 'in the globalizing world of today, references made to national culture as the *raison d'etre* of the university sound less and less convincing' (Kwiek, 2001, p. 33).

Globalization, therefore, is a key social and economic trend and force for change, impacting on society in its broadest sense, and on higher education as part of that society. It may be viewed as inevitable and irreversible. Van Damme identified four key tendencies in higher education related to globalization: the creation of 'new and tremendously important demands and exigencies towards universities as knowledge centres'; 'an increase in demand for higher education worldwide'; 'an erosion of national regulatory and policy frameworks'; and the emerging borderless higher education market (Van Damme, 2001, pp. 2–4).

By contrast, internationalization forms part of the response and is made up of the many different strategies, policies and activities put in place by governments, universities and academic staff. Earlier understandings of internationalization emphasized the context of study programmes, the movement of students between countries and the introduction of programmes spanning more than one country (Pickert *et al.*, 1992). Harari referred to the process of campus internationalization, characterized as follows: 'it is faculty with an internal commitment striving to internationalize its own course offerings. It is the presence of an obvious institution-wide positive attitude toward understanding better other cultures and societies' (Harari, 1992, p. 75). However, the definition rapidly broadened to encompass all aspects of university life. De Wit described internationalization as 'the complex of processes whose combined effect, whether planned or not, enhances the international dimension of the experience of higher education in universities (de Wit, 1995, p. 28). Similarly, Knight emphasized the all-embracing nature of internationalization, arguing that internationalization was a 'process of integrating an international dimension into the teaching/training, research and service functions of a university or college or technical institution' (Knight, 1997, p. 29). More recently, Knight has revised her definition to offer a comprehensive definition of internationalization in higher education. This definition of internationalization is now widely accepted: 'Internationalization at the national, sector, and institutional levels is defined as the process of integrating an international, intercultural or global dimension into the purpose, functions or delivery of post-secondary education (Knight, 2004, p. 11).

Globalization and internationalization are therefore key concepts for higher education today; their impact and consequences are widely discussed and analysed. In this paper, however, a different approach will be adopted, looking primarily at the response of governments and universities to these pressures and, in particular, aiming to identify the underlying motivations and rationales that influence such responses. This approach will also highlight some of the contradictions apparent in the response of both governments and institutions.

Seizing the opportunities

Globalization has rapidly established higher education as a commodity within international trade. For the 2007–08 academic year, it is estimated that international students contributed about US\$15.54 billion to the US economy, based on fees paid and the costs met by the students in supporting themselves and their families (GlobalHigherEd, May 2009). In practice, if multiplier effects for service industries were also taken into account, the figure would be much larger. In Australia, in 2007–08, education services ranked as the third largest export earner, behind coal and iron ore. Each international student, with their family, contributed A\$28,921 to the Australian economy, worth 0.29 of a full-time worker. Overall, it is estimated that over 122,000 jobs in Australia are dependent upon the recruitment of international students. Education represents 27 per cent of total exports by value, compared with only 1 per cent in the early 1970s (GlobalHigherEd, April, 2009). In the US, Australia and other countries, higher education now represents a crucial part of the national economic profile. The economic significance of world trade in higher education is massive overall and is now critical for many countries. With such dependence comes strong political interest.

The expansion of activity and recognition of the economic significance of higher education, especially for certain cities and regions, has prompted some governments to offer incentives to universities. Thus, in the UK the Prime Minister's Initiative (PMI), originally launched by Tony Blair, aims to secure the UK's position as a leader in international higher education. Dedicated funding was made available with the aim to enhance the UK's competitive position, increase the number of international students in the UK; ensure that international students have a high quality experience; build strategic partnerships and alliances; and maintain the UK's position in major education markets, while achieving growth in student numbers from a wider range of countries. Here, it is possible to see government concerned to expand the recruitment of international students and interested in both the emergence of new markets and the maintenance of quality to ensure that such objectives are fulfilled. A further example of such a government initiative is the Erasmus Mundus programme funded by the European Union, offering substantial financial support for international students to come to Europe. Other European governments, including the Netherlands, Germany and Spain, have also taken steps to encourage recruitment of international students.

For governments, therefore, international students offer direct financial benefits to the economy; however, the perceived benefits are much wider, with such students often filling skills gaps in local or national labour markets and also offering the long-term prospect of closer trading links with the country concerned. International students, and the links they maintain with the countries where they obtain their higher education, offer governments a route by which to extend their international influence. Such benefits are, of course, vulnerable within competitive markets. New providers are a constant threat, and countries are seeking to develop their own provision. Hence, the concern of governments is to maintain quality and to enhance national attractiveness. In other cases, governments have had to move quickly to offset threats to demand, as when the Australian federal and state governments were forced in July 2009 to develop a new strategy for international students following a series of well-publicized attacks on international students.

With the recognition by governments of the opportunities offered by the trade in higher education, and the associated link between globalization and the application of market forces, higher education has also formed part of discussions on international regulation through the General Agreement on Trade in Services (GATS). To date, negotiations on the GATS have not been resolved, but issues to be addressed include cross-border supply (including online delivery), student mobility, physical presence (including branch campuses and joint ventures with local institutions) and movement of academic staff to provide educational services.

For governments, therefore, globalization and internationalization offer some clear economic opportunities. However, the motivation for governments can be much wider and deeper than simply direct economic gain. Internationalization may be presented 'as a positive process encountered and engaged in by the universities and individuals, as well as a set of activities by individuals, universities and national and international level actors' (Nokkala, 2007, p. 207). These views see internationalization as a necessary response, both social and economic, to a changing world; at the same time, such ideas also draw upon wider traditions of the university as a driver of science and scholarship. Governments may also see further benefits of value to society as a whole, through the personal growth of individuals and the advantages gained from international experience, including tolerance, multicultural acceptance, wider understandings and tacit knowledge, as well as the usefulness of international awareness for subsequent employment. In this way, internationalization of higher education may be viewed as a 'public good', something to be encouraged with a view to wider social and economic benefits.

Overall, however, Nokkala argues that it is ideas of competition and competitiveness that dominate the thinking of higher education policy-makers. This view emphasizes the contribution of higher education to national competitiveness, based on 'the functioning of the universities in the innovation system, the contribution of internationalization to the competitiveness of the country and the national higher education system, the role of the university in educating future knowledge workers and the importance of internationalization in the context of competition for international knowledge workers' (Nokkala, 2007, p. 208). Globalization has changed the nature of the world economy. Altbach *et al.* note that 'global capital has, for the first time, heavily invested in knowledge industries worldwide, including higher education and advanced training', reflecting 'the emergence of the 'knowledge society', the rise of the service sector, and the dependence of many societies on knowledge products and highly educated personnel for economic growth' (Altbach *et al.*, 2007, p. 290).

In some cases, globalization and internationalization in higher education can serve a wider political purpose for countries, and this is of direct relevance to governments. For some small countries, the development of international networks of teaching and research allow participation in large-scale projects that would otherwise be impossible. Similarly, some developing countries have grasped the opportunities offered by globalization to expand higher education alongside domestic provision. Thus Malaysia, for example, has welcomed outside providers as a means of increasing the supply of higher education and responding to growing demand without excessive pressure on national funding. At another level, within the European Union steps towards internationalization, such as student exchanges and the creation of the European Research Area, may be viewed as steps contributing not only towards greater economic cohesion, but towards political integration.

For governments, therefore, globalization and the internationalization of higher education have provided new opportunities, prompting a response motivated by income and employment, skills requirements, quality of life and wider social values, and international competitiveness. Many of the same rationales apply at institutional level. In many countries, international students are required to pay higher fees than local or home students; recruitment, therefore, becomes financially attractive for both private and public universities. From a financial perspective, recruitment of international students may help to diversify the funding base of institutions, making public universities less dependent on government sources, and is clearly attractive for universities facing financial problems. For private universities, fee-paying international students offer a similarly lucrative source of income. Interestingly, the emergence of global markets and the application of new technology, both characteristics of globalization, are features of the emergence of private, 'for profit' providers of higher education, such as Laureate and the Apollo Group, both major US companies now offering higher education around the world, either directly or in partnership with local providers. For universities of all kinds, therefore, globalization has created opportunities to develop and exploit new markets in order to raise revenue. The result has been the emergence of courses targeted at international student recruitment and the development of proactive, sometimes aggressive, marketing and competitive practice.

Globalization has also provided opportunities to enrich the university experience. Internationalization may be seen to help in the preparation of students for the workplace through increased international awareness, and can encourage the achievement of high international standards. Recruitment of international students provides an attractive cultural diversity, and may help to sustain key subject areas where home student recruitment is failing. Knight has concluded that the main motivations for universities to engage in internationalization are to enhance research and knowledge capacity, and to increase cultural understanding (Knight, 2006).

However, the institutional motivation is often more complex. Faced by an increasingly competitive environment that includes both existing providers and new competitors, universities are often keen to present themselves as possessing an international profile. Most universities are to some extent 'international', not least because knowledge has traditionally permeated national boundaries with ease. Now, modern technology has created almost perfect permeability, subject to access to necessary equipment and to familiarity with the English language. Nevertheless, the presence of international students and staff and the existence of international research programmes are still seen as vital for the standing of any leading university. Universities around the world are swift to claim 'international excellence' in many forms of teaching and research, often without any clear definitions or criteria. For universities, therefore, internationalization is motivated not just by financial gain, but also by notions of excellence and quality, and assumptions of competitive strength that are conveyed by international activities. These ideas are readily transmitted to academic staff members, for whom personal status and career progression may also be linked to ideas of international reputation, normally measured by publishing in the leading international journals, invitations to participate in prestigious international conferences and research projects, and receipt of international funding.

The drive to be 'international' has stimulated massive changes in higher education. Recruitment of international students has stimulated different forms of marketing and competition, and has placed a new emphasis in many countries on student welfare and support services. New models of delivery have emerged, such as pre-university courses for international students (sometimes leading to entrance qualifications), induction programmes, language support and pastoral guidance. The movement of academic staff has also increased, with universities battling to attract the leading researchers from around the world. New forms of cross-border delivery have developed, including franchising and licensing arrangements with local providers. Some universities have created international campuses; Monash University in Australia, with campuses in South Africa and Malaysia, and the University of Nottingham in the UK, with campuses in China and Malaysia, are just two of many examples of such initiatives. The impetus towards internationalization has also prompted widespread adoption of the English language as the primary means of delivery. Thus, in the Netherlands and in the Nordic countries, English is in common usage for teaching, allowing the recruitment of international students with no knowledge of the native language. The process of internationalization also impacts upon the curriculum, with widespread opportunities for international study options and placements, and increasing use of international content within degree programmes.

It is easy to be cynical about the motivation of universities in their response to globalization. New markets and new technology have created opportunities for much-needed income generation, and the clamour for international status has been a driving force in many institutions, stimulated in part by the emergence of international rankings of universities such as those produced by *Times Higher Education* and by Shanghai Jiaotong University. However, globalization has also created new opportunities to broaden student experience, to extend cultural awareness and to offer students more choice and breadth of curriculum.

Globalization has also helped to transform research practice within higher education. New, international collaborations are possible, facilitated by opportunities for sharing of data and conferencing. In practice, research can take place 24 hours each day. Expertise can be shared between leading universities. Interestingly, universities can often be both partners and competitors at the same time, one of the apparent contradictions to emerge from globalization. Building on the new opportunities for international collaboration in research, universities have participated actively in transnational collaborative initiatives such as the European Union Framework programmes; research collaboration also lies at the heart of international networks such as Worldwide Universities Network. Publications involving authors from more than one country have increased; the opportunities for academic staff and research students to spend research time in different countries have multiplied; and universities now proactively seek out potential international partners among their perceived peer group of institutions in order to enhance their combined competitive research power.

To a certain extent, research has always been international and both knowledge and researchers have always moved across international boundaries. However, globalization has shifted the internationalization of research to a different, much higher level. Wider access to knowledge and research, a new awareness of the importance of international standing and an active sensitivity to the demands of international competition have pushed universities and their academic staff to adopt new ways of working. Many themes of research groups are now common. In some of these areas of work, the role of the single researcher working on his or her own has been significantly reduced. The impact of globalization on research and the response of universities may therefore be seen as part of the shift from 'mode one' to 'mode two' research (Gibbons *et al.*, 1994). In some cases this may be true, but much of the new globalized research is also traditional, pure research and certainly subject to traditional forms of peer review and publication. Thus, globalization has helped to change the nature of research, but to view this as simply a move from 'mode one' to 'mode two' is over-simplified. Rather, universities have sought to encourage an international approach to research of all forms and across all disciplines and subject areas.

Universities, like governments, have responded positively and often enthusiastically to the opportunities arising from globalization and internationalization. This reaction may be driven by a desire to secure additional income or tdiversify income dependence, or to enhance status and increase competitive advantage, but it also reflects a genuine desire to promote an international academic and cultural awareness among staff and students and to enhance quality in both teaching and research.

Responding to the threats

Closely associated with the emergence of globalization and internationalization in higher education is a discourse of free trade, with both students and providers of higher education free to move around the globe. For many governments, this trade represents an opportunity, but for others it can represent a threat. Thus, the emergence of international providers and the delivery of cross-border higher education in its diverse forms may undermine the position of local institutions within a particular country and may challenge national cultures; moreover, the emergence of new providers may be seen to represent a threat to the quality of higher education.

Governments seeking to develop their own national higher education institutions in order to meet national needs for skills and knowledge, and to make a national impact on the knowledge economy, may be concerned by the 'brain drain'. Students leave to study abroad, many of whom may not return, and new providers emerge, motivated by profit rather than by the wider, public benefits of higher education. These issues have been much debated in the context of African higher education. In South Africa, for example, the emergence of external providers and the potential response by South African institutions, encouraged to engage in possibly harmful and wasteful market-based competition, has been seen as contrary to national interests and possibly detrimental to the new democratic government (Waghid, 2001). The response of the government has been to emphasize national needs in terms of its strategy for higher education and in the funding for higher education. The South African government has also voiced concerns about the quality of some external providers, in particular the emergence of so-called diploma mills. As a result, very strict procedures are now in place before outside universities are allowed to deliver programmes directly in the country.

More generally, the perceived threats arising from globalization of higher education are often presented as a tension between the developed world (the 'exporters') and the developing world (the 'importers'). In 2009, speaking at the UNESCO Higher Education Conference, the South African Minister of Higher Education, Blade Nzimande, argued that there had been no significant break in the mechanism of knowledge production between the colonial and post-colonial eras, and that African universities were consumers of knowledge produced in developed countries. Concerns about the preservation of indigenous knowledge and knowledge production are closely related to anxieties about the erosion of national identity and culture. As a result, governments in many developing countries seek to protect their higher education from international competition. In 2005, as part of the International Association of Universities (IAU) survey of universities, 81 per cent of African universities identified risks associated with internationalization, primarily associated with commercialization, commodification and marketization (Knight, 2007).

However, the 'developed' versus 'developing' world argument is much too simple. Many governments around the world face a threat from globalization as institutions become 'disembedded' from their national context and from national governance, and become less responsive to national needs through the transnational flows of people, information and resources (Beerkens, 2004). Diversity of funding reduces reliance on national government and therefore can induce reduced policy compliance; similarly, research activities may focus on international rather than national priorities and the importance of new forms of international accreditation has grown, potentially to replace national controls. Furthermore, the ability of universities to engage in international activities, which may or may not reflect well on the country as a whole, represents a further danger in the eyes of the national government. The response of some governments has been to seek new mechanisms of control. In Australia, in response to concerns voiced about the quality of 'offshore' activities undertaken by some universities, the government made available additional funds to the Australian Universities Quality Agency (AUQA) to allow for additional quality audits. In the UK, similarly, the international activities of universities have received growing attention from the Quality Assurance Agency (QAA). More generally, the *UNESCO/OECD Guidelines for Quality Provisions in Cross-Border Higher Education* have sought to provide some regulation of the higher education market. However, imposing controls on the delivery of borderless higher education is difficult for both importing and exporting countries, and the threat to quality and to the traditional university remains. Marginson *et al.* conclude that 'in the wake of the trends to more extensive and intensive cross-border initiatives, the very notion of 'public' education and, related to that, notions of priority, responsibility and accountability are in question' (Marginson *et al.*, 2006, p. 24).

For governments in countries active in supplying higher education, a major threat is the growth of new national providers that challenge provision for existing markets. While countries such as the US, UK and Australia have established high profiles for recruitment, the competition and the search for new markets are relentless. Countries in the European Union are increasingly active. Moreover, many countries in the developing world are becoming significant competitors, such as China, Malaysia and India. A further threat is the growth of domestic capacity within countries, especially if this represents a cheaper option for students. Governments are forced to determine their own strategies and to assess their own strengths and weaknesses.

Another threat to arise from globalization and internationalization of higher education identified by some governments relates to the international students themselves, including access to social and health services, and employment rights. However, in recent years, the most significant threat perceived by governments concerns international security and the possibility of terrorists entering a country under the guise of students. As a result, governments such as the US and the UK have new restrictions on access and visa controls and new monitoring arrangements for international students in the country.

One view of globalization is that it is an inevitable process, a social and economic phenomenon that sweeps all before it. It is clear, however, that national priorities and political imperatives have encouraged many governments to respond to perceived threats, usually by means of legislative and voluntary control mechanisms.

For universities, there are also threats to be countered. Concerns about the erosion of quality have alerted universities to the threat to their reputation from internationalization. Universities must maintain quality and standards, but this may mean rejecting potential high fee-paying students, or making clear strategic decisions to favour certain disciplines, postgraduates rather than undergraduates, or students from certain countries; the application of strict entrance requirements, especially regarding language proficiency, has also occurred. High fees have also created high student expectations, and universities now compete openly not only on the basis of academic provision and reputation, but on the basis of support services and infrastructure. In the same way, the internationalization of research has created new demands and expectations in terms of institutional support, and new challenges have emerged, such as the management of intellectual property.

The response of universities has taken various forms. On the one hand, new forms of central direction and control have been exerted in order to influence the range and form of international collaborations. Thus, activities with certain countries or with certain institutions may be prioritized within a centrally driven institutional strategy. On the other hand, the opportunities, but perhaps especially the risks attached to globalization and the internationalization of higher education, have also stimulated an increasingly professional approach to the management of international activities. Internationalization can no longer be left purely to the initiative of individual members of the academic staff. Universities have responded by developing formal strategies and project planning, dedicated leadership (such as a vice-president international or a deputy vice-chancellor international) and specialized international offices; increasingly, leading universities also have overseas branch offices in countries of importance for recruitment or research.

While globalization and internationalization have offered huge new possibilities for universities, another form of threat has also emerged: that of being left behind or left out. While most universities have some claim to international activity, even if this is marked simply by an awareness of international affairs within the curriculum, the reality is that, in practice, the true benefits of globalization are shared by a relatively small number of leading universities, mainly research-based institutions, with high levels of international presence.

The risk, therefore, is that globalization results in widening gaps between universities. This poses a challenge for many institutions. The response of some teaching-based universities, especially some American community colleges and Australian technical colleges, has been to market themselves aggressively, especially in the delivery of English language programmes in vocational subjects. Nevertheless, the risks remain. Within the competitive world of international higher education, some universities will inevitably be more successful than others; the rewards of success are high, but so are the costs of failure.

Reflecting on motivation

This paper has sought to argue that the response of governments and of institutions to globalization and internationalization of higher education is the outcome of a complex mixture of motivations based around opportunities and threats. The balance will vary between different countries and for different universities; paradoxically, the interpretation and effects of globalization can be very local in practice. Moreover, the policy response of governments and universities can be riddled with contradictions and inconsistencies. Thus, countries that advocate free trade in higher education may also impose controls and restrictions; similarly, universities that compete vigorously to recruit international students may also be in collaborative networks with their main competitor institutions. Moreover, research has also shown that motivation within institutions may vary at different levels within the organization, with leaders and senior managers driven more by the status and prestige of internationalization, deans or heads of departments driven mainly by financial opportunities, and academic staff mainly focused on the academic advantages to be gained through recruitment of international students or the pursuit of international research (Liang *et al.*, forthcoming).

Globalization is widely seen to be an inevitable process. However, by placing the emphasis on motivation as the key driver of national and institutional responses, this paper also suggests that globalization and internationalization raise issues of choice and prioritization; the response reflects the outcome of a complex interaction of ideas and interests, often with unforeseen consequences and outcomes.

The table below aims to summarize the different responses emerging from perceptions of globalization as an opportunity or a threat. Not surprisingly, in some cases there may be opposite responses from different governments or from different universities arising from their different starting points. However, equally interesting are some of the similarities that also emerge. Thus, a concern about quality emerges whether globalization is seen in a positive or negative light. Another significant point emerging from both sides of the debate is recognition of the public benefits from higher education. Thus, globalization, often seen as a force linked with private economic gain, may actually work to reinforce the role of the public university. Both in a positive sense, though an appreciation of the benefits and opportunities of internationalization for society as a whole, and in a negative way, in defence against perceived threats, the public university may gain from the mixture of motives at play. Also of significance is the range of government interventions in response to both opportunities and threats that suggests that the decoupling of the university and the nation state is by no means a foregone conclusion. If this argument is accepted, the impact of globalization is less about the substitution of national perspectives by international ones as about an extension of local and national interests to embrace a wider international view. This discourse is openly observed in many higher education institutions that parade their international credentials alongside, not instead of, their local, regional and national obligations. Finally, what is also clear is that globalization will foster innovative forms of teaching and research, regardless of whether globalization is seen as an opportunity or a threat.

Summary and conclusion

Table 6.1 Summary of the policy response of governments and universities to globalization and internationalization of higher education

	Seizing the opportunities	*Responding to the threats*
Government	Policy response: Free trade promoted Competition advocated Financial incentives introduced Quality assurance enhanced New markets developed Cultural diversity welcomed Both public and private benefits appreciated Broad view of value of teaching and research	Policy response: Protection introduced Quality controls applied Emphasis on national interest and public role of universities Narrow view of value of teaching and research Protection of national culture Restrictions to movement applied
Universities	Policy Response: New courses developed New forms of management introduced Professionalization of services Research networks established Cultural diversity promoted New methods of delivery encouraged Quality assurance enhanced Use of new technology encouraged	Policy Response: Entrance barriers established Movement to innovative forms of delivery Institutional partnerships promoted Separation of teaching and research Expansion of new technology

Many contradictions also become clear. Thus, while globalization may be openly associated with free trade and movement, it is noticeable how the government response is often towards control, whether to take full advantage of opportunities or to fight off threats. Similarly, within universities, the response of leaders and managers is commonly towards control and direction. The response to globalization is, in practice, too important for governments or university leaders to allow a laissez-faire approach. Overall, it is clear that globalization and internationalization provoke a range of responses; sometimes complementary, sometimes contrasting and conflicting. It is the resolution of these tensions by different governments and different institutions that will ultimately shape the response of higher education to the challenge of globalization and internationalization.

References

Altbach, P. and Knight, J. (2007), 'The internationalisation of higher education: Motivation and realities', *Journal of Studies in International Education*, 11, (3/4), 290–305.

Beerkens, H. J. J. G. (2004), *Global Opportunities and Institutional Embeddedness: Higher Education Consortia in Europe and South East Asia*. University of Twente: Centre for Higher Education Policy Studies.

Castells, M. (2001), 'Information technology and global capitalism', in W. Hutton and A. Giddons (eds), *On the Edge, Living with Global Capitalism*. London: Vintage.

Clark, B. R. (1998), *Creating Entrepreneurial Universities: Organisational Pathways of Transformation*. Oxford: Pergamon Press.

Gibbons, M., Limoges, C., Nowotny, H., Schwartzman. S., Scott, P. and Trow, M. (1994), *The New Production of Knowledge: The Dynamics of Science and Research in Contemporary Societies*. London: Sage.

Giddens, A. (1990), *The Consequences of Modernity*. Stanford: Stanford University Press.

GlobalHigherEd (2009, 4 April and 13 May), at http://globalhighered.wordpress. com

Harari, M. (1992), 'The internationalisation of the curriculum', in C. B. Klasek (ed.) *Bridges to the Future: Strategies for Internationalising Higher Education*. Pullman, WA: Washington State University, Centre for International Development.

Held, D. and McGrew, A. (2003), *The Global Transformation Reader: An Introduction to the Globalisation Debate*. Cambridge: Polity Press.

Held, D., McGrew, A., Goldblatt, D. and Perraton, J. (1999), *Global Transformations: Politics, Economics and Culture*, Stanford: Stanford University Press.

Knight, J. (1997), 'A shared vision? Stakeholders' perspectives on the internationalisation of higher education in Canada', *Journal of Studies in International Education*, 1, (i), 27–44.

—— (2004), 'Internationalisation remodelled: Definition, approaches and rationales', *Studies in International Education*, 8, 5–31.

—— (2006), *Internationalisation of Higher Education: New Directions, New Challenges. The 2005 IAU global survey report*. Paris: International Association of Universities.

—— (2007), 'Internationalization brings important benefits as well as risks', *International Higher Education*, 46, (Winter), accessed at http://www.bc.edu/ bc_org/avp/soe/cihe/newsletter/Number46/p. 8_Knight.htm

Kwiek, M. (2001), 'Globalisation and higher education', *Higher Education in Europe*, 26, (1), 27–38.

Liang, Z. and Taylor, J. (forthcoming), *UK Universities in China: Questions of Motivation*.

Marginson, S. and Considine, M. (2000), *The Enterprise University. Power, Governance and Reinvention in Australia*. Cambridge: Cambridge University Press.

Marginson, S. and van de Wende, M. (2006), *Globalisation and Higher Education*. Paris: OECD.

Musselin, C. (2005), 'European academic labour markets in transition', *Higher Education*, 49, 135–54.

Nokkala, T. (2007), *Constructing the Ideal University. The Internationalisation of Higher Education in the Competitive Knowledge Society*. Tampere: Tampere University Press.

Ohmae, K. (1995), *The End of the Nation State: The Rise of Regional Economies*. The Free Press: New York.

Pickert, S. and Tarlington, B. (1992), *Internationalising the Undergraduate Curriculum: A Handbook for Campus Leaders*. Washington, DC: American Council on Education.

Scott, P. (ed.) (1998), *The Globalisation of Higher Education*. Buckingham: Open University Press.

Scott, P. (1999), *Globalisation and the University*. CRE-Action, 115.

—— (2000), 'Globalisation and higher education: Challenges for the 21st century', *Journal of Studies in Higher Education*, 4, (1), 3–10.

Slaughter, S. and Leslie, L. (1997), *Academic Capitalism. Politics, Policies and the Entrepreneurial University*. Baltimore: Johns Hopkins University Press.

Smeby, J. and Trondal, J. (2005), 'Globalisation or Europeanisation? International contact among university staff', *Higher Education*, 49, 449–66.

Van Damme, D. (2001), *Higher Education in the Age of Globalisation: The Need for a New Regulatory Framework for Recognition, Quality Assurance and Accreditation*. Paris: UNESCO.

Waghid, Y. (2001), 'Globalisation and higher education restructuring in South Africa: Is democracy under threat?', *Journal of Education Policy*, 16, (5), 455–64.

de Wit, H. (1995), *Strategies for Internationalisation of Higher Education: A Comparative Study of Australia, Canada, Europe and the USA*. Amsterdam: EAIE.

Chapter 7

The Management of Internationalization in Higher Education

John Taylor

Introduction

In 1973, Fielden and Lockwood wrote their groundbreaking book *Planning and Management in Universities*, the first comprehensive, practical account of higher education management in the UK. Their book offers an overview of the key management functions within higher education. It presents a picture of hierarchical structures, with very formal decision-making structures dominated by powerful committee machinery. A theoretical presentation of the organizational structure for a university is put forward. Interestingly, in their book there is no mention of internationalization as a key function within universities; none of the committees discussed carry internationalization as a central element within their terms of reference and no senior officer in the university has internationalization within his or her remit. It is apparent that, in the early 1970s, internationalization was barely recognized as an area of activity requiring leadership and management within higher education institutions in the UK; and a similar position would have been found in many other countries.

This is not to say that internationalization was not present in higher education. Knowledge has always moved easily between countries and some academic staff and students have always travelled between countries. However, three things have changed. First, as universities seek to respond to globalization and strive to establish their position within an increasingly market-driven, competitive world, the perceived importance of internationalization as a factor influencing the status of a particular university has increased. From being part of a 'normal' working life, internationalization has been elevated to a key strategic objective for many universities around the world. Second, the sheer scale of activity has changed, with increasing numbers of students moving between countries for all or part of their studies, new forms of international collaborative research activity and a new emphasis on internationalization within the curriculum. Third, the nature of university organization and management has changed. Universities have moved towards new forms of executive management, flatter decision-making structures, devolved responsibilities and enhanced professionalism within services and support. As a result, a new approach to the management of internationalization has emerged within higher education institutions.

University management has been transformed in recent years. This transformation has been driven by the complementary ideas of 'new managerialism' and 'new public management' that emerged in the 1980s and has been widely considered within higher education (Marginson *et al.*, 2001; Henkel *et al.*, 1999; Kogan *et al.*, 2000). These approaches to institutional management are characterized by new approaches to control and organization, with consequent changes in academic cultures and working practice (Deem *et al.*, 2007). A new emphasis has emerged on efficiency, performance and the achievement of targets; the significance of income generation and the diversification of sources of income has increased; and more devolved management has emerged that is linked to new forms of accountability. Within these changes, a number of important themes emerge. One is the significance now attached to leadership. Clark (1998) identified the 'strengthened steering core' as one of the key factors in the transformation of universities, and Shattock also emphasizes the importance of leadership in the management of successful universities: 'Leadership is essential, but distributed, rather than charismatic or personal, leadership will be the most likely to produce sustainable high institutional performance' (Shattock, 2003, p. 176). A second area of change is the changing role of the professional manager. Whitchurch discusses the increasing professionalization of staff and, in particular, highlights how such managers can move into new positions between academic and professional domains (Whitchurch, 2008).

This chapter aims to consider a range of management issues arising from globalization and internationalization, and to relate these issues to overall changes in higher education management. At the same time, it aims to offer an overview of the key functions relating to internationalization now undertaken within higher education institutions.

Strategy

The emergence of globalization and internationalization as major forces for change within higher education has prompted a significant management response from universities. In particular, universities have moved to develop formal strategies for internationalization in order to coordinate the institutional response (Taylor, 2004). Early strategies tended to be written by 'enthusiasts' and were concerned more with activities rather than the process of internationalization (Knight, 2004). Middlehurst *et al.* identify three stages in the development of activated strategy:

Phase 1	Internal Activity	Disparate and unconnected activities
Phase 2	International Strategy	Coordination and some alignment
Phase 3	Internationalization Process	Efforts to integrate, achieve leverage and added value

(Middlehurst *et al.*, 2007)

There is no single format for an international strategy. Typically, a strategy document will begin with a statement of institutional missions and objectives relating to internationalization. Commonly, an emphasis is placed on the role of the particular university in teaching and research, and on the contribution made to wider society; in some universities, there will be a further emphasis on ideals of world peace and international understanding. Most universities will then undertake some level of self-review, examining the present levels of internationalization, and environment scanning. The detailed content may vary widely, but the following are among the topics often covered:

- International students – recruitment, welfare, student experience, new degree programmes, student analysis, student exchanges.
- Home students – interaction with international students, international experience within degree programmes.
- Cross-border programmes – international delivery of programmes, partnerships, franchising, online delivery.
- Language skills – international students, home students, staff.
- Curriculum – pedagogy, content of programmes, degree structures, credit transfer.
- Research and knowledge exchange – networks, partnerships, international funding.
- Staff development – training, increasing staff awareness, motivation, skills, travel opportunities.
- Support services – organization, advice and guidance, cultural diversity, support of families.
- Staff appointments – recruitment of international staff.
- Partnerships – key partners, special projects.
- Governance – control of activities.
- Organization – coordination, leadership, role of the international office.

While a strategy for internationalization may be comprehensive, universities have also become more selective in their approach, often concentrating their efforts on a limited number of high-profile initiatives. In this respect, the strategy documents show characteristics of planning, target setting and central direction, all features of new managerialism. They have also been associated with new forms of organization and leadership.

Organization

Thirty or forty years ago, internationalization was barely recognized as a key task of leadership and management in higher education. It was essentially an 'amateur' activity, normally pursued by academic staff, free from institutional direction and oversight. Thus, links were forged with international institutions that might come and go, based around personal contacts by single members of staff or small groups. International students might also come or go, again often based on personal contacts or the initiatives and interests of the particular student. Internationalization was not an unfamiliar concept. Academic staff might travel, but to a limited degree; most universities had a range – often a very wide range – of memoranda of agreement for staff and student exchanges and other forms of partnership, but many of these agreements were 'paper' exercises, based around an enthusiastic member of staff and his or her inter-ests. Internationalization at this time can, in fact, be seen as an embodiment of academic freedom, based upon the initiative of the individual and relatively free from institutional control.

However, the pressures of globalization, both in terms of the opportun-ities offered and the threats posed, have forced a new form of international response with increasing levels of control and regulation. It can be argued that internationalization has become too important to be left to the keen enthusi-astic 'amateur'. New forms of organization have emerged. Many universities now have a vice-president, deputy rector, deputy or pro vice-chancellor with responsibility for institutional leadership and management in this area. These individuals are commonly responsible for strategy formation and implementa-tion, for the development of substantial international partnerships and for overall coordination of international activities. In these appointments, a level of central control and direction begins to emerge with policy and activity driven from the centre of the institution, as part of overall institutional strategy, and not dependent upon local initiatives. A second key development has been the emergence of central international offices, established to lead, encourage and coordinate international activities. These offices now form a distinctive element within professional services, not just in support of senior officers but in taking forward the international agendum. This may include negotiation of important links and partnerships, maintenance of existing links, international student recruitment and coordination of all activities linked to international-ization. The work of such offices has become highly professional, illustrated for example by the work of the European Association for International Education (EAIE), the second largest professional body in education in Europe, and offering a range of publications, conferences and courses to support the professional development of its members. In the work of the international office it is easy to see the new forms of manager identified by Whitchurch; professional, sometimes highly specialized and acting at a high level. Many international offices have dedicated specialists for certain geographical areas (such as the Middle East or Latin America) or for particular areas of activity (such as research funding). Significantly, in terms of the analysis of institutional governance, such offices are often free to make offers of admission or to enter new international partnerships; the balance of initiative has shifted from local, in departments and faculties, to central direction.

To supplement central officers and central leadership, many universi-ties now also have a network of advisors working at faculty or departmental level. Some academic staff in departments will be charged with leading the departmental response. The overall result is more formalized structures of organization. Universities look to partner a smaller number of institutions believed to be of the same or better peer status; conversely, links with institu-tions believed to be of lower status may be discouraged. Targets for student recruitment, for home students travelling abroad, for research activity and for international staff recruitment may be set within the context of overall strategies. A culture of targets, incentives and rewards has been established. Professionalization has developed rapidly in this area of professional services, but so have the pressures to succeed and the controls exerted. As the risks of failure have increased in the minds of institutions, so the forms of organization and governance have changed.

Financial management

The emergence of internationalization has had a very significant impact on the financial management of many universities. On the one hand, new sources of income have opened up, including international student fees, cross-border provision, and international research and consultancy. Potentially, for some universities, there are rich pickings to be had and universities have not been slow to see the opportunities. Such activities can be seen to grow and diversify the business; alternatively, they may be a response to reductions in income at home or from other activities. On the other hand, the risks in internationalization may be high. Competition is tough and new competitors are emerging all the time; for diverse, public sector universities, competition from more specialized, private sector, sometimes 'for profit' providers may be intense. Competition may also emerge from home countries as they seek to establish their higher education. Political changes and threats to quality also make internationalization a risky business. For some universities, over-dependence on international activities may be a serious problem, especially if their market position is relatively weak.

Internationalization also often requires a level of investment before returns are forthcoming. This may take the form of new course development or new forms of marketing. At the other extreme, universities engaging in the establishment of an international campus or in major online delivery of academic programmes may need to raise substantial capital and form complex business partnerships with other bodies. New skills of business planning are necessary. In this sense, many of the activities associated with internationalization are not just academic decisions; an appropriate business and financial case must be forthcoming, with associated risk analysis. Within the institution there may be further implications for financial management. Schemes may be required to distribute fee income, to cover central costs of student services or research support and to recover initial investment costs, to meet direct costs of teaching and research, and to provide incentives for the departments or even individual members of staff concerned. Arguments about the additional effort required to teach international students, and the need to provide incentives and compensation are familiar in many universities. Further issues may also arise because the opportunities for internationalization are commonly unequal within the institution. As far as international student movements are concerned, Business and Management and Engineering and Technology are often the main areas of demand. This is not to say that there are not wider opportunities for especially entrepreneurial universities, often in niche markets, but most universities display a spectrum of involvement in international activities. An important tension emerges for institutional managers regarding the extent to which the rewards and costs of internationalization should be evenly distributed across the institution or should be attributed to those departments and faculties most concerned. Further issues and dangers arise in the case of departments able to generate high levels of international funding. To what extent is it legitimate for the institution to accept the existence of a 'cash cow', bringing financial benefits possibly at the expense of a more balanced academic and financial portfolio?

Internationalization has introduced new demands for skilled financial acumen within higher education management. The stakes are potentially high. The response of institutions has been to turn to more dedicated forms of professional management and to increase levels of control within the system. Engaging in large-scale international activities, such as an international campus, can bring massive rewards, but the risks are high and the scale of investment is massive. Strong qualities of leadership are required, coupled with specialist management. Academic leaders and professional services must work in partnership. Universities must be fully aware of their costs before entering such initiatives, including the opportunity costs involved; a vice-chancellor sidetracked by a major international initiative is, in effect, foregoing other opportunities or loosening the reins of control elsewhere. This may be totally justified, but it needs to be consciously planned and appropriate arrangements put in place. In effect, internationalization has an impact on an institution much wider and deeper than is often initially understood.

Marketing

One of the activities within higher education management that has been transformed by internationalization is marketing. International student recruitment is a fiercely competitive activity, both between countries and between institutions. Much of this is a competition based on fees, but many other factors are influential in student decision-making, especially brand and reputation. Understanding existing markets and, often especially important, identifying new markets ahead of the competition, have become vital aspects of activity for many universities. International student recruitment fairs are now commonplace all over the world, but these only represent the tip of the iceberg. New practices have emerged, including 'special deals' for overseas countries sending large groups of students, initial discounting in order to establish a market and the use of international recruitment agents who identify potential students in return for a share of the fee. Branding has become crucial and high fees can be maintained by leading universities based on their perceived reputations.

Good market research has become crucial and has come to influence course design and delivery. Thus, new programmes may be approved not only for their academic merit but for their potential for recruitment of international students. Targeted recruitment activities are undertaken, within particular countries and using particular media, including multilingual websites and specially designed literature. International students themselves are actively involved in further recruitment on their return to their home countries.

Universities depend heavily on their reputation, and techniques such as customer experience marketing are now widely applied in order to understand the needs of international students more fully. Increasingly, however, reputation is often equated with position in international rankings of universities such as those produced by Times Higher Education and by Shanghai Jiaotong

University. Some international governments will only sponsor students to attend universities placed highly in these rankings; for many students they provide a vital source of comparative information. These rankings are highly contested, especially in methodological terms. Most are based primarily on research reputation and say little or nothing about the likely experience of international students. Nevertheless, they are highly significant in marketing and recruitment. Marketing extends beyond just student recruitment and is central to the development and implementation of an internationalization strategy in other ways. The establishment of 'an international reputation' is a fundamental driver of internationalization for many universities. Thus, the promotion of international research, the organization of international travel and international events and the facilitation of contracts and introduction of potential value all become crucial. International marketing can be expensive and carries high risks, but the returns in terms of reputation and recruitment can be spectacular. Here again, therefore, it is possible to see the impact of new managerialism applied forcefully within higher education institutions.

Student services

There is no question that internationalization has been a factor contributing to the increasing profile attached to student services in many universities. International students in most countries pay premium fees and there is vigorous competition among universities to recruit these students. With high fees often come higher expectations about the quality of residential accommodation, language support and welfare provision. Universities themselves compete openly to offer the best services. In international student recruitment, word of mouth is a key factor and universities recognize that one of their best marketing tools is a positive recommendation from happy students. Much educational theory also suggests that the wider university environment has a significant impact on student happiness and on academic achievement. This is, perhaps, especially apparent in the case of international students working in an unfamiliar country, and often working in an unfamiliar language. Universities are therefore driven by genuine concern for student welfare and a strong element of self-interest to develop effective support services for their international students. A wide range of examples may be cited, including 'meet and greet' arrangements for new students arriving in the country, special induction programmes, specialist advisory, consultancy, pastoral and tutorial arrangements, language support, cultural assimilation (often alongside parallel arrangements to encourage international students to share and maintain their own cultures), support for families and financial advice. The range of provision is impressive and continues to increase; a response to competition and to market accountability, but also a reflection of the sincere care and concern felt by many institutions and by institutional staff members. It is too easy to be cynical about the motivations of universities and their staff towards internationalization.

A further important aspect of student support relates to forms of academic advice and guidance. In this respect, universities are, perhaps, rather less successful. International students entering higher education in a different country must cope with a wide range of different practices and expectations. New learning skills must be developed. There is a strong responsibility on universities, especially bearing in mind the fees being charged, to provide guidance for their new students, especially in their first year. Libraries and computing services must be introduced, and expectations about workload and assessment require careful explanation. For example, there are significant cultural differences experienced by many students in undertaking the requirements for an assignment; similarly, for many students, debate and discussion is unfamiliar in the teaching environment and questioning a teacher may be seen not as part of a constructive dialogue but as a sign of disrespect. A crucial issue currently facing universities in many countries concerns academic misconduct such as cheating, plagiarism and falsification of data. Such practices are widely condemned, yet it is important to realize that many international students come from cultures where there are different expectations and where, for example, sharing of assignments and answers to problems is commonplace. In many countries, international students appear disproportionately in cases of misconduct, especially for plagiarism or for submitting work that they have not in reality authored. Such practices cannot be condoned, but it can be understood if universities have not adequately explained their expectations or given necessary advice and support. There are particular issues here for universities recruiting for one- or two-year Master's degrees or other programmes where the period of student assimilation within a new culture is shorter than for other programmes. Moreover, it is important that such support is effectively grounded throughout the institution, across all academic staff and professional services, and is not left solely as a 'problem' to be dealt with by specialist educational development professionals.

Here, therefore, are some of the tensions facing universities as they take forward their internationalization. Recruitment of international students is attractive for many reasons, but it also imposes additional costs and responsibilities on institutions that must also be recognized. Student services are often at the sharp end of this tension. For universities, the response has involved the emergence of new areas of activity – such as international student counsellors, financial advisors and specialists in visa and residential regulations – and increasing professionalization more generally. However, the emergence of such services offering specialist support does not shift total responsibility away from the wider staff base in the institution. University leaders and managers must also ensure that all staff are equipped and sensitive to the particular needs and requirements of international students.

Staff development

One of the key developments of university management that has emerged strongly in recent years has been the organization and delivery of staff development programmes. Such programmes are now found in most universities, especially in Europe, North America, Australia and New Zealand. Among the issues driving this trend has been a growing recognition of the need to equip staff at all levels with the awareness and skills necessary for effective internationalization within higher education. For academic staff, this might include issues of new forms of course delivery, especially in cross-border provision, or better understanding of different approaches to student learning. In some countries, there may be issues related to language proficiency; for example, universities in the Netherlands and in many Scandinavian countries now expect high levels of competence in the English language. For all staff, training is now often provided in cultural awareness and in equal opportunities; more generally, programmes directed at raising levels of customer care often originate with issues relating to international students.

However, the management implications of internationalization on staff development go wider still. There are now increasing opportunities for staff to travel abroad within their careers and this is strongly encouraged by many universities and may be assisted by the availability of dedicated funding. When recruiting new members of the academic staff, many universities now actively seek appointees with international work experience or particularly relevant skills, such as language ability. For academic staff, many of the same issues apply as at institutional level. Thus, gaining 'an international reputation' is crucial to career advancement and this requires international awareness and orientation, travel for research and networking, publication in international journals and books, attendance at international conferences and involvement in international partnerships. To succeed in this way requires a combination of motivation, perceived rewards and acquired skills.

Management of quality

Internationalization has prompted important concerns about quality. At one level a tension may be perceived between the desire to optimize income and the need to maintain standards. Thus, a temptation may arise for the university or department facing financial difficulties in delivery to accept a marginal student, and there are often suspicions that normal requirements have been eased in such circumstances. On the other hand, a reputation for quality is essential for the long-term successful pursuit of internationalization; once a reputation has been tarnished, it is very difficult to restore it.

Quality impacts upon all aspects of the student experience. Accurate, informative course information and swift decisions may help to make the prospective international student feel wanted. Effective induction programmes and ongoing support services are also vital. Concerning the recruitment of international students, a crucial debate facing many successful universities-concerning relates to the numbers of international students to accept as a proportion of the total class size, especially if drawn predominantly from the same country. International students come expecting to benefit from the experience of their host country; if the class is dominated by students from their own country, possibly representing 80 per cent or more of the cohort, this experience may be compromised, leading to dissatisfaction. Resolving this tension is a major challenge for university managers; capping student recruitment at times of financial strain may be difficult to accept, but may be necessary in order to maintain reputation.

Further issues relating to quality occur in student progress and assessment. International students are often working in a language other than their own; is it therefore acceptable to make some allowance for this in marking and grading? The answer in terms of quality and standards is 'no', but there are pressures, both financial and from human sympathy, to be more generous and understanding. Again, effective management controls are important.

Where universities engage in cross-border activities, often outside normal arrangements for quality assurance, particular measures may be needed. New degree architectures have emerged, such as 2+2 degrees where the first two years are spent in the home country and the second two years spent abroad, often entering at the second year stage. The 'split PhD' is a similar initiative, involving research in two institutions in different countries. In Europe, Erasmus Mundus programmes involve the student studying in three or more countries. While such programmes are often highly attractive, they have compelled careful consideration of quality, as well as challenging traditional funding arrangements. Questions of mutual recognition can be contentious. For European countries the Bologna Process, aiming at the achievement of a common degree framework and common credit transfer system, offers one response to these issues. Partnerships with local providers, franchising arrangements and the employment of locally based staff are also fraught with potential problems that require careful management and strict controls. Similarly, where universities are sending their students abroad on placements or to gain international experience, it is vital to maintain effective oversight and quality control; basic health and safety requirements must also be maintained. The management of quality is often seen as bureaucratic. It is a vital function that must be balanced with the desire to move ahead with entrepreneurial internationalization. There is not necessarily a conflict, but the two processes require coordination and management in order to ensure effective delivery.

Another aspect of quality highly relevant in the agenda for internationalization concerns curriculum design and management. Internationalization increasingly involves the adaptation of curriculum to ensure that it provides international awareness. This may include the delivery of options in international topics, the use of international course materials and the development of case studies on international topics. For academic staff and for course approval and review procedures, such requirements present a new task, less associated with income generation and more related to ensuring that all students receive some form of international experience.

Summary and conclusions

This chapter has aimed to show first the emergence of internationalization as a key area of activity within higher education management and, second, how the forces of new managerialism and new public management have impacted upon the management of internationalization. The response of universities has been, on the one hand, to encourage enterprise and innovative activity, as seen by new programmes, new forms of delivery and new approaches to cross-border provision, but on the other to impose new forms of control and organization and new approaches to strategic direction. The response to internationalization, possibly because it is a relatively new form of management function in higher education, is almost the epitome of new public management, characterized by strong central leadership and direction coupled with devolved delivery and accountability. For higher education, the emergence of internationalization as a management function is also associated with new forms of professionalism and new approaches to administration; while responsibility for delivery clearly rests with academic staff, internationalization has also encouraged new forms of centralized control and oversight. Indeed, some of those involved might feel that internationalization has become too important to be entrusted to the diverse motivations and less predictable notions of academic staff. In this respect, internationalization has become a major force for change in how the modern university is managed.

References

Clark, B. R. (1998), *Creating Entrepreneurial Universities*. Oxford: Pergamon Press.

Deem, R., Hillyard, S. and Reed, M. (2007), *Knowledge, Higher Education and the New Managerialism: The Changing Management of UK Universities*. Oxford: Oxford University Press.

Fielden, J. and Lockwood, G. (1973), *Planning and Management in Universities: A Study of British Universities*. London: Chatto & Windus.

Henkel, M. and Little, B. (eds) (1999), *Changing Relationships Between Higher Education and the State*. London: Jessica Kingsley.

Knight, J. (2004), 'Internationalization remodelled: Definition, approaches and rationales', *Studies in International Education*, 8, 5–31.

Kogan, M. and Hanney, S. (2000), *Referring Higher Education*. London: Jessica Kingsley.

Marginson, S. and Considine, M. (2001), *The Enterprise University in Australia: Governance, Strategy and Reinvention*. Cambridge: Cambridge University Press.

Middlehurst, R. and Woodfield, S. (2007), *Responding to the Internationalisation Agenda: Implications for Institutional Strategy*. York: Higher Education Academy.

Shattock, M. (2003), *Managing Successful Universities*. Maidenhead: Open University Press.

Taylor, J. (2004), 'Towards a strategy of internationalisation: Lessons and practice from four universities', *Journal of Studies in International Education*, 8, (2), 149–71.

Whitchurch, C. (2008), *Professional Managers in UK Higher Education: Preparing for Complex Functions*. London: Leadership Foundation for Higher Education.

Chapter 8

Key Trends and Emerging Issues in International Student Mobility (ISM)

Steve Woodfield

Introduction

The extent of international student mobility (ISM) is one of the key indicators of the globalization and internationalization of higher education. The number of students enrolled in higher education outside their country of citizenship has risen dramatically from 0.6 million worldwide in 1975 to three million in 2007 (OECD, 2009), and the number of international students is estimated to reach eight million by 2025 (Bohm *et al.*, 2004). This rapid expansion has changed the extent, forms and structures of international student mobility, which is constantly evolving and becoming increasingly closely related to other types of cross-border education (CBE) such as transnational education (TNE).

The changing nature of ISM can be viewed in two ways – growth and diversity. First, there has been an observable and continuing growth in both demand for overseas educational opportunities and capacity in higher education institutions (HEIs) worldwide. This increase is actively encouraged by the major stakeholders in higher education – governments, HEIs), employers and students (and their families) – who recognize the personal and socio-economic benefits of mobility (OECD, 2004; Altbach, 2004). Increasing ISM is also a policy objective at supranational level, where national governments recognize the importance of inter-governmental and regional agreements to facilitate and encourage the mobility of students, researchers and academics (for example, via Europe's Bologna Process). This growth has also been accompanied by intensified competition between countries and between providers in the recruitment of internationally mobile students, and an increase in the volatility of international student mobility, and thus the predictability of overseas student flows.

Secondly, there is a noticeable trend towards increased diversity in international higher education, in terms of types of provision (or delivery modes), host countries, the types of students and providers. For example, HEIs are now able to offer educational programmes outside of their home states and regions (TNE), either through a physical presence overseas, or via distance education or e-learning. In many cases this programme mobility (OECD, 2004) requires significant cooperation with overseas partners and many universities are diversifying their overseas activities and linkages. For those countries heavily engaged in the 'export' of cross-border provision (such as the USA, Germany, the UK and Australia), this diversification into TNE represents part of a strategy to avoid over-reliance on traditional international student recruitment in an increasingly competitive global market which also includes diversifying the source countries for international students. For 'importing' countries, developing a range of overseas linkages (particularly with institutions with more advanced HE systems) offers an opportunity to help meet demand; to develop local capacity through collaborative partnerships and support student and faculty exchange schemes; to research links and curriculum development; and to utilize this newly developed capacity to attract international students to local programmes.

This chapter seeks to explore the impact of this increasing growth and diversity in ISM through critical analysis of existing literature and recent research findings (OBHE and Kingston University, 2009; Woodfield *et al.*, 2009), to highlight some emerging trends and issues, and to assess how these are addressed within national internationalization strategies (focused on Europe, Australia and the USA). By discussing the prospects for future development of ISM, this chapter seeks to inform current thinking and practice at both policy and institutional level on this important topic.

Emerging models and types of student mobility

ISM is typically associated with the second of the four WTO General Agreement on Trade in Services (GATS) modes for supplying services, 'cross-border consumption', where students physically 'cross' national borders for the purpose of study. However, in an increasingly globalized world, students can be 'mobile' before, during and after their studies. In an age of relatively low-cost travel (in advanced economies) students are able to travel for holidays, charity work and volunteering, work placements, and as part of their studies.

Physical mobility

However, although all types of mobility are clearly important in providing an experience of different cultures and contexts, the main focus of ISM is on mobility to another country for the purpose of study. The most common forms of ISM are full-programme or 'diploma' mobility and short-term (typically up to a year) or 'credit' mobility (for example study abroad and student exchange programmes). Diploma mobility comprises the majority of all student mobility worldwide (Verbik *et al.*, 2007), mostly involving students travelling abroad to study for full-degree programmes to countries with a perceived higher quality HE system than in their home country. Teichler (2008) describes this hierarchically oriented mobility as 'vertical' in contrast to 'horizontal' mobility between similarly developed HE systems (for example within Europe or between Europe and the USA). The term 'vertical' can also be used to describe mobility at the end of a particular cycle of education (for example Bachelor's or Master's degrees) and the term 'horizontal' to cover mobility within a cycle.

Diploma mobility is the simplest type of mobility since it usually only requires a relationship between a student and a university, while short-term mobility requires a partnership between an organization in one country (a university or a study abroad agency) and a university in another – although in some cases institutions establish their own study abroad locations overseas. Credit mobility is more common as a form of 'horizontal' mobility, largely because it requires the often complex transfer of credits between two institutions to count towards a qualification, necessitating a high degree of comparability between institutions and HE systems. In most cases there is an exchange agreement between institutions in different countries. In Europe this is generally part of the EU's Lifelong Learning scheme, in which partner institutions have reciprocal arrangements to receive agreed numbers of students, but non-European exchange programmes are usually arranged bilaterally between institutions, in some cases as part of a broader strategic alliance. In some types of credit mobility the period of study is integrated into the curriculum (for example in language or area studies courses).

Transnational education and 'virtual' mobility

Beyond this traditional typology of ISM the situation becomes considerably more complex, particularly in the case of transnational education (TNE), sometimes called 'offshore' education or Institution and Programme Mobility (IPM) (OECD, 2004). This type of provision covers the GATS modes of 'cross-border supply' and 'commercial presence' and covers four main types of activity: traditional distance education or e-learning; commercial presence abroad; overseas presence of teachers or support staff; and satellite or branch campuses. In some cases, such as in the case of twinning and some supported distance learning programmes, TNE programmes can cover both of the GATS modes, and more than one of the TNE types. TNE is described by the OECD (2004, p. 3) as 'taking a degree or other post-secondary course offered by a foreign university without leaving their home country' and is often discussed separately from other types of mobility.

However, in practice, student mobility (credit and diploma) is often now an integral part of TNE programmes. For example, under an overseas progression arrangement, a student completes a period of study at an institution in one country and then, following successful completion, is admitted to an overseas partner institution (with advanced standing). Student mobility is also facilitated by other forms of bilateral partnerships such as twinning agreements, or joint degrees, where a student is enrolled at a foreign institution but will complete part of their studies at a partner institution in the home country. Usually the student must travel abroad in order to complete their studies. Even where they do not physically travel abroad, students on TNE programmes could still be described as 'virtually' mobile. This concept suggests that a person does not need to leave their home country to be mobile and can gain some of the benefits from international education or experience either at their home institution as part of an 'internationalization at home' agenda (de Wit, 2002), or when enrolled in a TNE programme delivered wholly abroad by an 'overseas' institution (for example a distance learning or a franchise programme). Technological developments have facilitated the practicality of such mobility (for example high speed internet connections and videoconferencing facilities) and are popular for those less willing or able to study abroad.

Patterns and flows of international student mobility

The rapid growth of international student mobility and its increasing diversity and complexity makes understanding and predicting the worldwide flows of students studying with overseas providers increasingly difficult. Most experts suggest that relatively little is known about the true nature, extent and impact of ISM (Santiago *et al.*, 2008; Verbik *et al.*, 2007; Teichler, 2008). There is a lack of accurate, internationally comparable and comprehensive data in many countries (for example, countries use different criteria such as nationality and citizenship to identify international students and many students studying in the private sector are excluded), and a limited number of large-scale international comparative research studies on this topic (Kelo *et al.*, 2006).

Although official statistics on international enrolments are collected by UNESCO, OECD and EUROSTAT, these do not cover 'credit mobility' (although some study abroad is covered), are incomplete at doctoral level, and often do not distinguish between Bachelor's and Master's students. The main reason for this is that data are collected by national agencies for their own purposes using different criteria. The data problems are more pronounced when TNE is considered. Australia, Canada and the UK are the only 'exporter' countries that currently monitor the transnational activities of their institutions. TNE, due to the very nature of the fact that it crosses borders, has problems with the availability of accurate data. TNE may be too 'young' in its stage of development for data collection to become important and sophisticated enough for research purposes. Although there have been some reports that have sought to analyze data on TNE and have made some very optimistic projections regarding the future demand for TNE (Bohm *et al.*, 2004), the robustness of the data has been questioned (Garrett *et al.*, 2004).

Supply and demand for CBE have increased dramatically in recent years, and are projected to increase dramatically over the next twenty years (Bohm *et al.*, 2004). Analysts suggest that the rapid increase in demand has largely been driven by the high levels of unmet demand for higher education in many parts of the world, particularly in India and China, but also in other parts of Asia and there are significant pockets of demand in other regions. However, evidence suggests that this growth in demand is predominantly limited to diploma mobility, while credit mobility has enjoyed only steady growth. Trend data also show that international student numbers in different countries can vary from year to year, meaning that the market is volatile and relatively soft, making projections related to ISM difficult.

Analyses of international student mobility are also closely integrated with debates around whether student mobility acts as a subset of highly skilled migration. ISM could be described as 'brain circulation' but is often described as 'brain gain' or 'brain drain' for importing and exporting countries, depending on their national context and socio-economic development strategies. Countries tend to recruit international students depending on their perceived research strengths and reputations, for example Germany and the USA are strong recruiters in the scientific subjects and Australia and the Netherlands recruit significant numbers of students in business subjects and the humanities (OECD, 2009). In recent years the term 'circulation' or 'exchange' has been used to signify that flows are becoming more complex and multi-directional (de Wit, 2008).

It is becoming increasingly important to understand where internationally mobile students are going and coming from and to compare the balance of 'inward' and 'outward' mobility in different countries. Historically, the main flows have been in diploma mobility from 'East to West' or from developing to advanced economies (particularly from East Asia to English-speaking destinations), and there is some evidence of different 'tiers' of destinations for international students. The main English-speaking destination countries (the UK, the USA and Australia) and France and Germany represent top tier countries and account for 70 per cent of all internationally mobile students, although other countries may increase their market share as the international HE marketplace becomes more competitive. Intra-regional flows are also of growing importance (for example, within Europe and within the Asia-Pacific Region), as is the relative lack of outward mobility of students in English-speaking countries (Fielden *et al.*, 2007). Around half of the internationally mobile students in Europe are from other European countries; including the UK (Kelo *et al.*, 2006). It would also be useful to undertake an analysis that compares host and source countries in terms of economic size and shape, distance, and psychological and cultural links.

There is also increased competition between countries and providers in the international student recruitment market, largely because students now have a greater choice of destination countries beyond the traditional 'major English-speaking destination countries'. Other Western European nations, such as France, Germany, Denmark, Sweden and the Netherlands, are beginning to increase their efforts to attract more non-European students and offer courses in English (Wächter *et al.*, 2008). Traditional importing countries, such as Singapore, China, Hong Kong and Malaysia, are also beginning to both improve and diversify their education systems and recruit significant numbers of international students themselves, challenging the market share of traditional international recruiters (particularly the USA). This increasingly competitive context is likely to increase the volatility on student flows in the future as potential students reformulate quality/cost equations based on the wider range of options available. Other factors include changing economic and political relationships between countries, fluctuating exchange rates, changing student quality and value perceptions, immigration requirements, and crime and safety issues. In recent years, some importing countries have seen 'slumps' in recruitment from particular countries and regions as a result of individual factors such as terrorist attacks, economic crises, health scares, and immigration policy changes. However, these seem to occur as temporary changes rather than as the beginning of trends, although this could change in the future.

National, institutional and supranational rationales driving international student mobility

In recent years there has been a growth in the development of international or 'internationalization' (Knight, 2005) strategies at both national and institutional levels (Fielden, 2007). The motivations for such strategies are partly cultural and partly economic, although most now focus on the role of HEIs in developing human resources to promote national (and international) socio-economic development through recruiting the best students and staff, enabling students to pursue valuable overseas study and work experience opportunities, and supporting research collaboration with high-quality overseas partners (OECD, 2004). International student recruitment (and mobility in particular) is becoming more important strategically in terms of the economic and social benefits that it provides for both importing and exporting countries (OECD, 2008; OECD, 2009).

National-level rationales for international student mobility

Although the strategic approach followed in each country or institution is contextually defined, international strategies (at both national and institutional level) tend to focus on the following areas in relation to international student mobility:

Marketing and recruitment strategies

Both governments and HEIs are investing in marketing and recruitment strategies to help attract overseas students (both credit and diploma). This includes developing national branding and marketing initiatives, analyzing marketing intelligence on student profiles and decision-making, developing an overseas presence in selected locations, and fostering collaborative relationships within key countries at both national and institutional levels. Australia and the UK have been particularly active in this area, and there are some signs that US institutions, as well as those in Europe, are beginning to step up their marketing activities. In many European countries there is also a national policy to support and encourage institutions to develop English-language provision (and in some cases provision in other languages) designed to help recruit international students and to provide home students with the language skills to help encourage more outward mobility in both study and employment. Countries such as the Netherlands and Denmark have also begun to provide recruitment incentives to international students, such as scholarships and grants, and have modified immigration and visa regulations to provide international students with the ability to work during and after study.

Student finance and tuition fees for international students

In most countries worldwide there has been a reduction in the amount of public funding for higher education combined with government encouragement for institutions to generate additional sources of income, usually via student fee income. In Europe, national governments are becoming less willing to subsidize students from outside the EU/EEA, and the introduction of tuition fees for such students is a relatively new and sometimes controversial development (for example, in Germany and the Nordic countries). The fee income from international students in most European countries is usually intended to cover the cost of recruiting, teaching and supporting students rather than generating surplus revenue through differentiated fees for non-EU/EEA students (as is the case in the UK or Australia). National governments expect institutions to use this additional income to improve the quality of their education provision, facilities and student support services, all of which have been identified as key factors in attracting international students and developing institutions' reputations internationally.

Educational capacity building and quality enhancement

Institutions and national governments worldwide are seeking to enhance the quality of their higher education provision and view ISM as a key element in achieving this goal. For emerging countries, CBE (both ISM and TNE) can play a key role in capacity building in terms of skills development, widening access, building research capacity and a broader contribution to socio-economic development (for example in the Middle East and Asia). For institutions in more developed countries international strategies which focus on international student recruitment and engaging in collaborative projects and programmes (in teaching, research and knowledge transfer) can help improve academic and research capacity, and help support a wider 'internationalization' agenda in terms of developing globally relevant curricula, facilitating student and faculty exchange, and improving campus diversity and fostering cultural understanding.

Regulation and quality assurance

National governments are increasingly emphasizing the importance of regulation and quality assurance related to ISM and there is considerable scope for innovative practice in this area to help gain competitive advantage. There is usually a marketing rationale for such policies, which often seek to ensure that the quality perceptions of a national education system overseas are not damaged by low quality and substandard provision, and inadequate entry standards.

Some countries (for example the UK) have developed guidance on quality assurance in this area and others have focused on consumer protection as a means of ensuring minimum standards of support for international students (for example, the Netherlands and Australia). Individual institutions are also participating in benchmarking activities to gain an insight into the quality of their academic and administrative services to international students. From an importing country perspective there is a desire to ensure that CBE works towards educational capacity building and economic development. Importing countries, particularly in East Asia have used regulation and quality assurance requirements in an attempt to ensure that cross-border provision is developmental as well as revenue-generating in its impact.

International collaboration and cooperation that supports international student mobility

Although there is a trend towards intensified competition in ISM (at both national and institutional levels), mutually beneficial collaborative and cooperative partnerships remain a major a feature of international education, particularly within different regions but also inter-regionally (OECD, 2004). Within Europe, there are a significant number of government to government, or multilateral partnership agreements related to student mobility that are designed to foster collaboration and achieve mutual benefit for both partners – for example, through promoting student or researcher exchange and joint degree programmes. In addition, many European countries are also pursuing strategic national-level alliances with key countries outside Europe, such as the USA, China and India, which they hope will foster student, researcher and staff mobility and other types of collaboration in areas such as research and collaborative teaching provision. There are an increasing number of offshore or transnational offices or bases in Asia and the Middle East and these are often intended to act as regional hubs, which can help to support student recruitment and other types of international engagement (for example with the business sector) in key countries and regions.

At the regional level, the Bologna Process in Europe and other examples of regional interaction elsewhere in the world, such as the ASEAN region, are focused on removing barriers to student mobility. At the supranational or international level, there is growing policy level contact within organizations such as UNESCO and the OECD related to issues such as quality assurance, trade in educational services and TNE. Quality assurance issues, particularly with regard to TNE, are becoming more complicated and fluid, and require constant monitoring as quality assurance arrangements in importing countries are growing and becoming more sophisticated, enabling inter-country comparisons of quality to become more feasible. In addition, international education agendas come under the auspices of the GATS/WTO, and the impacts of deregulation are increasingly being monitored at a supranational level.

At the institutional level, there are also many examples of bilateral partnerships between institutions which often have a focus on facilitating student mobility (and also faculty and researcher mobility) as part of a broader range of collaborative international activities. In many cases, these are envisaged as a complement to diploma mobility, both to create new and reliable channels of international recruitment, and to provide different study options for students overseas without the need to leave their home country. There is also a growing trend towards either self-funded or externally funded dual or joint degree pro-grammes, which are emerging as a new type of mobility (usually not captured by mobility statistics). This type of provision includes the Erasmus Mundus programme, which supports multi-institutional partnerships within Europe, and the Atlantis/FIPSE (a joint European–US programme), which involves US institutions in partnership with institutions in Europe and other parts of the world. These programmes generally require students to study in more than one of the partner institutions. An interesting model which facilitates short-term student mobility is the multilateral partnership approach (for example networks, alliances and consortia), where groups of like-minded institutions work together for mutual advantage (for example, the Worldwide Universities Network [WUN], the International Association of Research Universities [IARU] and Universitas 21). These often also support collaborative teaching provision and mobility between member institutions.

Student motivations and decision-making for international student mobility

The motivations and rationales for ISM are constantly evolving, both for students and for their funders and supporters. Given the diversity of student backgrounds, national origins, abilities and ambitions, internationally mobile students' motivations for mobility and their decision-making about what and where to study are likely to differ significantly.

Any decision to study abroad is influenced by both 'push' and 'pull' factors – terms used as an analogy to global trade flows (de Wit, 2008; Altbach *et al.*, 1985). In general, push factors influence a decision whether or not to study abroad, and pull factors influence where a student decides to go – although in some cases the factors are intertwined. Push and pull factors often involve a combination of personal, national and global drivers such as personal ambi-tion, increasing globalization, global finance and exchange rates, and foreign and socio-economic policies in a student's country of origin and destination.

Student decision-making: studying abroad (push factors)

From a student perspective, push factors include their own desires to study or travel abroad for personal development (to experience a different culture or learning context, enhance their language skills, pursue high-quality study or research options unavailable at home); to enhance their employability (CIHE, 2008); or to eventually migrate to their chosen study destination.

From a governmental perspective push factors can include a desire to improve the country's educational and research capacity through students' application of the skills and experiences gained abroad to support national socio-economic development, or a desire to help foster connections and build relationships in other countries to help meet foreign policy goals. This often means that students are encouraged to study abroad via scholarships and other student support packages, especially at postgraduate level. International initiatives such as the Bologna Process and the Brisbane Communiqué are also significant drivers in encouraging greater mobility. Teichler (2008) suggests that the growing movement towards 'internationalization at home' may have reduced the attractiveness of the cultural side of mobility, citing 'the declining exceptionality of mobility', and argues that the value of study mobility could be overstated especially as some of its benefits, such as improved intercultural understanding and interaction with people from other countries, can easily be achieved through travel or work. There are concerns that short-term mobility schemes, such as Erasmus, are not significantly increasing in size, and may in fact contract as a result of other Bologna reforms which have stimulated the growth of shorter, more tightly packed, university programmes. Although the reforms make credit mobility simpler, they leave less room for mobility and may ultimately make studying abroad for short periods less attractive.

In the UK (Fielden *et al.*, 2007) and in some other English-speaking countries (for example Australia and New Zealand) there has been concern about students' lack of outward mobility. From a student perspective, limited language skills, high-quality study options at home and the lack of mobility culture are cited as the main factors in these countries. There is also a lack of consensus over whether an overseas study experience provides significant benefits to students from advanced economies compared with those from developing countries.

Student decision-making: deciding where and what to study (pull factors)

Once students have decided to study abroad, they then make a decision about which country to study in, which institution to study at, and which study programme to follow. There is currently little systematic research related to international students' study choices, although evidence suggests that students choose their destination country before selecting an institution and programme (Santiago *et al.*, 2008).

At national level, there are a number of 'pull' factors that focus on the relative attractiveness of the study destination related to the motivations described above and that can act as enablers, or barriers, in student decision-making. Such factors can be inherent to a country as a whole (for example, language, shared culture or religion, cultural diversity, climate, location, safety, or living costs) or be directly related to its educational reputation. Recent studies focused on student decision-making related to studying abroad (i-graduate, 2008; JWT Education, 2007; and Sussex Centre for Migration Research and Centre for Applied Population Research, 2004) and how students form perceptions of potential study destinations (ACA, 2006) have produced interesting findings on the differing impact factors, such as language, study level, national policies, cost, institutional reputation, and nationality, on mobility choices. In some cases, students also receive government guidance on preferred countries and institutions, often related to international ranking systems and tied to scholarships and recognition of study abroad. Students' motivations for mobility are also heavily influenced by the types of mobility that are available (credit or diploma), and the length and mode of study. For example, postgraduate students are more likely to be influenced by institutional reputation issues, whereas undergraduates are more focused on lifestyle issues and the country of study as an attractive destination to spend three or four years.

Educational reputation can be influenced by national government policy, such as internationalization strategies, quality assurance initiatives, the level of tuition fees, scholarships, immigration and visa regulations for study and work, and consumer protection legislation. Recent studies (Middlehurst *et al.*, 2007; OECD, 2004; Middlehurst, 2008) have highlighted the crucial importance of ensuring that there is policy coherence between the sections of government responsible for areas of relevance to CBE such as education, culture, trade, immigration, foreign affairs, economics and finance, and international development. The range of information and guidance available to students is growing rapidly, from sources such as the Internet, recruitment agents, and national and institutional marketing materials (for example, prospectuses, national branded websites and word-of-mouth through friends, family or alumni).

At the institutional level, there are other pull factors which can be based on quality perceptions, credit transfer regulations, location, institutional marketing and internationalization strategies, financial incentives, and the student support infrastructure that institutions are able to provide. In particular subject areas and for certain delivery modes, for example professional and vocational subjects and distance learning, there has been a growth of 'new providers' in the HE market. New providers include private universities, for-profit universities (for example Phoenix, Sylvan, and the Apollo Group) and local private colleges and universities in markets abroad, as the HE market becomes increasingly 'borderless' and cuts across conventional geographical, temporal and spatial boundaries (CVCP, 2000). In terms of distance learning and e-learning, international organizations (such as the Commonwealth of Learning, UNESCO, and the World Bank) are supporting the development of open and virtual universities in developing regions (for example, the Commonwealth, Asia, Africa and the Arab states) and the use of 'open source' materials to help build sustainable capacity in these regions (Daniel, 2004).

The characteristics of students engaged in cross-border education

Although there is limited research into the characteristics of internationally mobile students, recent consumer insight research in the UK has identified a range of 'learning tribes' (Shepherd, 2008) within the broad category of internationally mobile students, which highlights the heterogeneity of internationally mobile students depending on their different needs and circumstances, and their different national HE contexts. This research suggests that mobile students are in fact highly heterogeneous and that both nationality and family background are important factors in diploma mobility.

Other reports suggest that students engaged in diploma mobility are generally seeking access to a high-quality education unavailable at home (Santiago *et al.*, 2008). The majority of these students are from less advanced countries that lack sufficient education capacity to meet the demand from highly qualified students, although some – particularly within Europe – are students who travel to pursue opportunities in specialist programmes in a neighbouring country or a country with which there are particular linguistic or cultural ties. Credit mobility appears to attract a different type of student, who can be motivated by a desire for personal development, to develop language proficiency, or whose study programme requires a period of study abroad. For some students, a period of study abroad may be an integral dimension of youth mobility culture which values time spent abroad.

However, although on the surface the types of students engaged in diploma and credit mobility may appear to be very different, in fact they often share some characteristics. Recent reports describe the emergence of different 'tiers' of mobile students (Lasanowski, 2009, Santiago *et al.*, 2008). The 'top' tier would consist of a globally mobile 'elite' of the most able (and affluent) students, who have the confidence, ability and resources to travel (for study, work and other reasons) to the most attractive destinations worldwide, and who are largely unaffected by factors such as tuition fees, culture, distance, living costs, and language, and are driven by perceptions of quality. In emerging countries, students with this kind of 'mobility capital' are generally engaged in diploma mobility, and in more advanced economies they usually participate in credit mobility and to a lesser degree in full-programme mobility, for example within Europe.

Below this top tier of globally mobile students are students who are motivated by the employment benefits of study abroad and are seeking a direct return on their investment by studying in one of the most attractive destination countries or, failing this, in one of the second-tier countries. Such mobility is likely to be highly expensive and, even if students have access to scholarship funding, they are likely to require significant funds to finance a period of study abroad. Students may be self-financed, or supported by their families, and are thus highly sensitive to trade-offs between the key factors that influence student decision-making. In some cases, these students may not seek an overseas experience and may be attracted by more flexible modes of cross-border learning that combine different delivery modes, such as face-to-face and distance or online learning in their home countries, and study periods at both foreign and local providers, provided they are of sufficient quality and status. Such mobility is often linked with opportunities for migration abroad after studying, and has implications for brain drain and capacity building in developing countries.

Beyond these top two tiers are students with more limited or no mobility capital. Such students are more likely to travel to neighbouring countries, those with historical links where they may pay no fees or where they may receive scholarship support. However, in many cases they are not mobile at all and this is likely to have significant equity implications.

Summary and conclusion: future prospects for international student mobility

Although there are clearly issues with quality and comparability of data on cross-border education flows, evidence suggests that both demand and supply for international student mobility are growing worldwide and will continue to do so for the foreseeable future. Even in countries that are rapidly developing their HE capacity, such as China and India, there is still significant unmet demand which can only be satisfied through cross-border education (both ISM and TNE). Among the major importing countries, only Australia could be said to be anywhere near saturation in terms of inward mobility and many countries, and individual HEIs, have developed a strategic focus on increasing the inward flows of talented students that can contribute to national socio-economic development.

Although there has been a rapid growth in ISM in recent years, its nature has been constantly evolving. Therefore it is very unlikely that future developments will involve the same kind of mobility; with the same kind of students, travelling for the same reasons, going to the same destinations, studying the same subjects, and studying in the same ways. It is also difficult to predict whether there will be a 'massification' (Scott, 1998) of mobility that will increase the number of mobility options, and provide opportunities for a wider a range of students to study, or work, abroad or whether ISM will continue to benefit the more able and affluent students. Although there may now be more evidence of increased 'brain circulation' or 'brain exchange' (Bhandari *et al.*, 2009), there is still a sense that ISM plays a major role in helping more developed countries to recruit the 'top tier' of talented students and researchers at the expense of the developing world. However, this may change and CBE may become more democratized as it evolves.

The factors influencing student flows are becoming more complex and interconnected as the nature of CBE changes rapidly. There is greater competition at national and institutional level for the recruitment of students and cross-border flows are becoming increasingly volatile, as increasingly knowledgeable students consider an expanding range of accessible and affordable options to engage with CBE. Collaborations between institutions in different countries via TNE are blurring the boundaries between home and overseas study, and the growth of strategic alliances between institutions is providing increased opportunities for short-term mobility either for short courses or as part of a progression arrangement for a longer programme. This has been developed in response to a trend towards shorter, more intense study programmes, and may reduce the feasibility and attractiveness of long-term mobility. Private and for-profit providers are also becoming more prominent in facilitating mobility at all levels.

National governments and institutions respond to these changes as they redefine their approaches to CBE to take into account the need to balance intensified marketing activity and improved services to students, increased competition and collaboration, and the encouragement of skilled migration with capacity building. There is a trend towards collaboration and partnership at both national and institutional levels, encouraged by regional initiatives such as the Bologna Process and the Brisbane Communiqué, and also increased engagement with a wider internationalization agenda in many countries that encompasses both internationalization 'at home' and abroad. National governments recognize that what is required to successfully address global challenges such as economic crises, terrorist threats, climate change and poverty is international collaboration in which ISM can play an important capacity-building role in the development of a highly skilled global workforce and help to promote increased intercultural knowledge and understanding.

References

Academic Cooperation Association (ACA) (2006), *Perceptions of European Higher Education in Third Countries*. Brussels: European Commission.

Altbach, P. (2004), 'Higher education crosses borders', *Change*, 36, (2), 18–24.

Altbach, P. G., Kelly, D. and Lulat, Y. G. M. (1985), *Research on Foreign Students and International Study: An Overview and Bibliography*. New York: Praeger.

Bhandari, R. and Blumenthal, P. (2009), 'Global student mobility: Moving towards brain exchange', in R. Bhandari and S. Laughlin (eds), *Higher Education on the Move: New Developments in Global Mobility*. New York: IIE.

Bohm, A., Follari, M., Hewett, A., Jones, S., Kemp, N., Meares, D., Pearce, D. and Van Cauter, K. (2004), *Vision 2020: Forecasting International Student Mobility – A UK Perspective*. London: British Council.

Committee of Vice-Chancellors and Principals (UK) (CVCP) (2000), *The Business of Borderless Education: UK Perspectives*. London: CVCP.

Council for Industry and Higher Education (CIHE) (2008), *Global Horizons and the Role of Employers*. London: CIHE.

Daniel, J. (2004), *Education Across Borders: What is Appropriate?* Presented at the 1st UK International Education Conference, Going Global: The Internationalization of Education, Edinburgh, United Kingdom, 9 December 2004. Available at http://www.col.org/resources/speeches/2004presentations/Pages/2004-12-09.aspx.

de Wit, H. (2002), *Internationalization of Higher Education in the United States of America and Europe: A Historical, Comparative, and Conceptual Analysis*. London: Greenwood Press.

—— (2008), 'Changing dynamics in international student circulation: Meanings, push and pull factors, trends and data' in H. de Wit, *et al.* (eds), *The Dynamics of International Student Circulation in a Global Context*. Rotterdam: Sense Publishers.

Fielden, J. (2007), *Global Horizons for UK Universities*. London: CIHE.

Fielden, J., Middlehurst, R. and Woodfield, S. (2007), *Global Horizons for UK Students: A Guide for Universities*. London: CIHE.

Garrett, R. and Verbik, L. (2004), *Transnational Delivery by UK Higher Education, Part 1: Data and Missing Data*. London: OBHE.

International Graduate Insight Group (i-graduate) (2008), *StudentPulse 2008*. London: i-graduate.

JWT Education (2007), 'Promoting what we've got – encouraging people to study in the UK', Presentation at the 4th Annual International Student Conference, March.

Kelo, M., Teichler, U. and Wächter, B. (eds) (2006), *EURODATA: Student Mobility In European Higher Education*. Bonn: Lemmens.

Knight, J. (2005), *Borderless, Offshore, Transnational and Cross-Border Education: Definition and Data Dilemmas*. OBHE Report No. 34. London: OBHE.

Lasanowski, V. (2009), *International Student Mobility: Status Report 2009*. London: OBHE, June.

Middlehurst, R. (2008), 'Leadership and internationalisation', in C. Shiel and A. McKenzie, *The Global University: The Role of Senior Managers*. Poole: Bournemouth University.

Middlehurst, R. and Woodfield, S. (2007), *Responding to the Internationalisation Agenda: Implications for Institutional Strategy*. York: Higher Education Academy.

The Observatory on Borderless Higher Education (OBHE) and Kingston University (2009), *An Analysis of National and Institutional Approaches for Attracting International Students and Facilitating Internationalisation in the United Kingdom and Selected European Countries*. Research Series Number 3, London: UK Higher Education Europe and International Units.

OECD (2004), *Internationalisation and Trade of Higher Education: Opportunities and Challenges*. Paris: OECD.

—— (2008), *Education at a Glance 2008*. Paris: OECD.

—— (2009), *Education at a Glance 2009*. Paris: OECD.

Santiago, P., Tremblay, K., Basri, E. and Arnal, E. (2008) 'Internationalisation: Shaping strategies in the national context', in P. Santiago, K. Tremblay, E. Basri and E. Arnal, *Tertiary Education for the Knowledge Society*, vol. 2, ch. 10. Paris: OECD.

Scott, P. (1998), 'Massification, internationalization and globalization', in P. Scott (ed.), *The Globalization of Higher Education*. Buckingham, UK: Society for Research into Higher Education/Open University Press.

Shepherd, J. (2008), 'The new seekers', *Guardian*, 18 March.

Sussex Centre for Migration Research and Centre for Applied Population Research (2004), *International Student Mobility*. Report commissioned by the HEFCE, SHEFC, HEFCW, DEL, DfES, UK Socrates Erasmus Council, HEURO, BUTEX and the British Council. Bristol: HEFCE.

Teichler, U. (2008), 'Student mobility: Where do we come from? Where are we? Where are we going to inside the EHEA?' Presentation at the ACA Annual Conference 2008, Tallinn, 16–17 June.

Verbik, L. and Lasanowski, V. (2007), *International Student Mobility: Patterns and Trends*. London: OBHE.

Wächter, B. and Maiworm, F. (2008), *English-Taught Programmes in European Higher Education: The Picture in 2007*. Bonn: Lemmens.

Woodfield, S., Middlehurst, R. and Fielden, J. (2009), *Universities and International Higher Education Partnerships: Making a Difference*. London: Million+.

Chapter 9

Higher Education Reforms and Problems in China: Challenges from Globalization

Hongshia Zhang

Acknowledgement: This research is sponsored by the Educational Science Planning Committee of Jiangsu Province under the core project: A12006103.

Introduction

Under the imperative of globalization, Chinese higher education (HE) has experienced great reforms since the launching of the well-known 'reform and open-door policy' in 1978. Along with general development and progress in the past decades, many challenges of Chinese HE become more striking as the reform goes deeper. Rooted deeply in thousands of years of Chinese history, and entangled with the recent so-called Chinese-styled socialist political and economical systems, these problems are difficult to handle. This paper adopts an historical perspective to trace their origin and to investigate their nature in order to identify some principles and measures to promote reform in the future.

Reforms in past decades

Generally speaking, the reform of Chinese HE conducted in recent decades can be summarized as covering six areas. First, education aims and goals has been re-oriented to meet the needs of modernization and globalization. Second, the leadership of the Chinese HE system has to some extent been decentralized and devolved. Third, the scale of HE has expanded and reached the massification stage. Fourth, market economy principles have been employed in some domains and fields of the HE sector. Fifth, quality control policies and measures have been introduced and implemented. Finally, international cooperation in higher education practice has become more active and productive.

As early as 1983, Deng Xiaoping delivered the famous 'three facings' idea that 'Chinese education must face modernization, must face the world, and must face the future'. This notion was written into the historical document *The Decisions on Reform of the Educational System*, which was issued by the CCPCC

(Chinese Communist Party Central Committee) in 1985. (In the past two decades, there were three important documents which guided the reforms: *The Decisions on Reform of the Educational System*, which serves as the foundation of all later documents since it concerns important issues such as education aims, structure, leadership and ownership of education institutions at all levels; *The Programme for Education Reform and Development in China*, issued by the CCPCC and the State Council in 1993; and *The Action Plan for Revitalizing Education in the 21st Century*, issued by the Ministry of Education (MoE) in 1999. The three documents will be termed in short as *The Decisions*, *The Programme*, and *The Action Plan* respectively in this text.) Deng Xiaoping's proposal implied that Chinese education would no longer act solely as either a political or a cultural tool to implement an insular cultural legacy. It must take part in the process of globalized education development. This idea was different in principle from those in any documents issued by the government before, and it constituted the ideological foundation and leading principles for later reforms.

Coordinated with the new education aims and the emerging market economy system which started to penetrate the HE sector, the highly centralized educational system established in the 1950s was eventually rectified by *The Programme* in 1993. The central government, which once controlled strategic planning, finance funding, resource allocation, subject structure, curriculum development and even textbook selection, was subsequently assigned responsibility only for guiding and carrying out accreditation and evaluation undertakings.

Before 1999, the Chinese HEIs (higher education institutions) were divided into three main streams according to their funding sources and administrative authorities: those affiliated to the MoE (about forty institutions); those affiliated to other ministries of the state government such as agriculture (about one hundred); and those affiliated to local governments at provincial and municipal levels (more than eight hundred). According to *The Programme*, this fragmented 'blocks and strips' system was gradually reconstructed. Today, only the MoE and local governments in particular can administer HEIs independently, at state and provincial levels respectively. Other ministries can only cooperate with the MoE regarding special colleges such as agricultural colleges. Local governments are granted more authority and responsibilities than before.

Along with the amalgamation and devolution movement, access to universities and colleges was expanded. In order to accelerate the development of HE, the MoE issued *The Action Plan* in 1999. The specific goals postulated by the document include: first, to popularize senior high school education in urban and economically advanced areas; second, to enlarge the scale of HE so that the gross enrolment rate reaches 15 per cent, held to be the participation level at which mass education is achieved, by the year 2010 (Trow, 1973); and finally, to set up more technical and vocational schools and colleges in addition to ordinary institutions.

In 2002, the gross enrolment rate goal was reached, eight years ahead of schedule. In 2004, the enrolment rate rose to 19 per cent; in 2007, the rate reached 23 per cent (Figure 9.1). By 2008 there were 2,239 HEIs in China, compared to 1,000 in 1999, and the number of undergraduates grew over the same period from 6.43 million to more than 27 million. (MoE, 2009.)

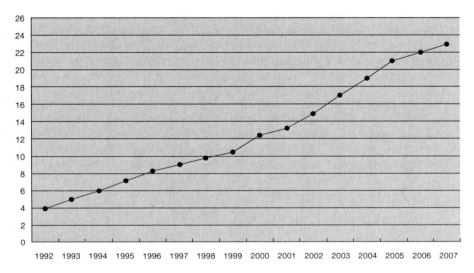

Figure 9.1 Gross entrance rate in China in millions, 1992–2007 (based on the statistics of the MoE website)

Besides increasing enrolment in ordinary HEIs, the Chinese government, following the experience of many developed countries, extended the technical and vocational education (TVE) sector in order to fulfil the task of the massification of HE. In addition, privately-run HEIs boomed at the same time (Figure 9.2); another approach to massification which is taken by developed countries. By 2006, the number of TVE institutions (TVEIs) at HE level reached 1,147, among which 994 were private, while the total number of four-year state-run ordinary institutions was just 720. In 2007, TVE enrolment was 2,812,800, 9.6 times that of 1990; and the total number of students was 8,544,500, 11.5 times that of 1990 (Yu, 2009). In terms of TVE at secondary education level, there were more than 14,000 institutions with a total of 5,660,000 students in 2007.

In order to maintain and support so large a HE system, the supply and demand principle of a market economy was employed in accordance with leadership devolution from the central government to individual institutions. One of the fundamental tasks of HE marketization was to change the founding system. *The Action Plan* advocated a multiple-source funding system for public HEIs instead of the previous single, central government allocation mode. The new funding sources included government funding, tuition fees from students, private sector endowment, earnings from social services and consultancy by faculty, and earnings from technology innovation and commercialization. Next, a policy of tuition fees was tried out in 1994 for some popular majors, and extended to all majors in all HEIs by 2000, just one year after the issuing of *The Action Plan*.

Meanwhile, the Higher Education Law, which approved the legal status of private sector HE, was issued in 1998. The law states: 'The state encourages all sectors of society including enterprises, social organizations or groups as

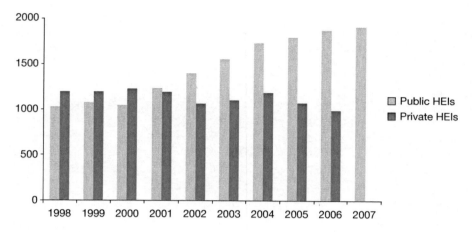

Figure 9.2 Growth of HEIs in China, 1998–2007 (based on the statistics of the MoE website)

well as individual citizens to run higher education institutions in accordance with the law, and to participate in and support the reform and development of higher education.'

In addition to the changes in the funding system, the graduate job assignment system has also been abolished, according to the supply and demand principle. Meanwhile, the lifelong employment system for faculty is being reformed in the shape of the US model characterized by 'publish or perish'.

In accordance with the goals of devolution and increased access, a shift from a central to a multiple funding system, and a move from a state exclusive to a social and individual inclusive system of ownership, the university internal administration and management mode is being switched to the marketization track. Many institutions have adopted Western-style organizations, for instance a board of trustees, senate, or academic committee, and so on. Nevertheless, the unique Chinese double-leadership system of a president and a party secretary in a single university has been preserved.

In order to solve the problems of decreasing standards directly caused by the rapid increase in the enrolment rate, and the time-consuming task for university administrators of institutional amalgamation and marketization, the Third National Conference of Education was held in 1993 by the MoE. At this conference the global trends of education objectives, disciplinary structure and curricula were reviewed, and a series of measures were proposed for action: (1) to build world-class universities; (2) to update curriculum and instruction methods; and (3) to initiate a nationwide undergraduate education quality evaluation policy.

It is widely recognized that HE is central to a country's development in the globalized world of the twenty-first century. The skills war between developed countries is vigorous, since it is viewed as the decisive strategy for a country's competitiveness. With limited educational resources, the Chinese government allocates funds by initiating various programmes such as the latest 'one thousand talents' programme for attracting overseas academic leaders. The government has also divided HEIs into different groups according to their status and geographical positions. The most prominent groups are 'Project 985' and 'Project 211' universities. Project 985 was set up in May 1998 to build world-class universities. It originally embraced nine top Chinese universities; now it has more than 43. Project 211, set up in 1995, aims to build up about a hundred quality HEIs with hundreds of key subject areas as a national priority for HE development in the twenty-first century.

The Action Plan for Revitalizing Education in 2003–2007, issued in 2004 as the new version of *The Action Plan*, codifies and further develops this policy of world-class university construction. The first phase input from the state to each of the '985 universities' was 14 billion Chinese yuan, and the second phase was similar. It is now in its third phase.

The executive targets of Projects 985 and 211 are to promote overall institutional capacities in the quality of teaching and research through: recruiting and nurturing academic leaders and competitive staff worldwide; upgrading the structure of academic programmes; enhancing the infrastructure and laboratory facilities for teaching and research; enhancing scientific research and technological innovation; accelerating the pace of transferring scientific findings into productivity; and strengthening international exchange and cooperation.

In order to enhance the training capacity of high-level experts and keep pace with the cutting-edge standards of the international community in the key fields of science and technology, some traditional subjects and majors have been integrated into the unified Key Subject Bases in the top 985 universities. These bases are intended not only to focus on academic excellence, but on the application of the subject, in order to optimize the workforce structure and achieve win-win relationships between university, local government and economic entities.

In term of university curricula, the Third National Conference of Education also agreed several reform objectives. The first was to integrate science and humanities knowledge to ensure a general education which helps students to be broadly prepared to adapt to a fast-changing society. The second was to give special weight to foreign languages and computer skills in the curricula. The third was to pay more attention to practical skills and the employability of students. The final objective was to encourage faculty to use imported advanced texts and materials from developed countries in teaching. To reach these objectives, the MoE initiated a project in 2003 to select and reward 1,500 'model courses' from various universities and upload them online. So far, over 1,300 model courses have been selected and distributed online.

In order to construct a quality insurance system of HE, it was decided that all institutions of higher learning be assessed every five years by the government. This policy was implemented in 2002, and was completed in May of 2008 for all public HEIs with four-year academic programmes.

In recent years, international cooperation projects in the Chinese HE sector have boomed. For instance, the number of state government-approved projects for setting up internationally cooperative institutions or academic programmes with postgraduate degrees increased from 219 in 2005 to 509 in 2006 (see

MoE, website). Nanjing University (where the author currently works) as one of the '985 universities' of the first phase, has established collaborative relationships with 29 countries and regions, and assigned 294 collaboration agreements since 1979. It has accepted 5,400 foreign students to study at all levels in the university, and invited 1,800 visiting scholars and dozens of contract academic staff from abroad to its campus since 1979. (Office of International Cooperation and Exchanges, 2007).

Problems to solve

From the above description of the reform process, we can see that in recent decades there has been a series of guiding official documents at different stages of the reform. By comparing the contents of these documents it is not difficult to find that some reform tasks and targets remain a theme. This means that the underlying problems of Chinese HE have not yet been resolved and form a legacy from one document to another throughout the decades. These problems seem generally connected with the issues of education quality, education equity, and administration mechanisms.

Education quality can be used as an integrated indicator of the achievement or effectiveness of the whole reform. According to a recent national survey of student satisfaction with undergraduate teaching in China (Zhang and Qu, 2007), the degree of student satisfaction was very low in comparison with the findings of a USA survey conducted by the Carnegie Foundation for the Advancement of Teaching in 1984. Ironically, the lowest degree of student satisfaction was found in the '985 universities'.

After many universities and colleges amalgamated and changed their leadership in 1999 and afterwards, the effectiveness of resource utilization is believed to have somehow improved. But this is not the general situation. As Qingshi Zhu, President of the Chinese Science and Technology University, sarcastically noted in response to a journalist's question: 'My greatest contribution in my ten-year office term was just to not make any contribution, thus I did not bring about any damage to my university' (Stone, 2009).

The main factor connected with student satisfaction, as identified by the survey, was the low standard of faculty in the '985 universities'. It is not surprising, given that of the 600,000 Chinese students who studied abroad in the past thirty years, only a quarter returned. Another important factor was the pressure on faculty in these universities to carry out research tasks in order to catch up with the level of publishing at world class universities, which has forced faculty to devote more time and energy to research than to teaching (Zhang, 2006).

Moreover, the quality evaluation mechanism is absolutely ineffective. In fact, it has triggered a flood of criticisms on websites from both faculty and students. The targets of this criticism were not only the application of government-centred mechanisms instead of peer review of the evaluation, but also the pervasive corruption on the central government evaluation panel.

With regard to the issue of equity, the first national conference especially for rural education since the founding of the Peoples' Republic of China

(PRC) was held by the State Council in 2003. It explicitly declared the strategic status of education in rural areas as 'the priority of priorities' in building a harmonious society. In many subsequent documents, such as *The Action Plan for Revitalizing Education in 2003–2007* and the report for the 17th Congress of the CCP in 2007, the importance of rural education was also emphasized. However, there is a long way to go to accomplish the task in terms of both quotas and quality. For example, in 2005 only 80 per cent of families in rural areas of China met the criteria for the lowest education tuition fees (He, 2007).

In addition, many scholars from ordinary universities have criticized Projects 985 and 211 as being unfair. Similarly, the gap between regions and institutions has widened. In terms of the model course selection mechanism, criticism has also been levelled at its unfairness and opacity. In fact, this situation exists not only at the institutional level, but at individual faculty level. Almost all administrative areas in a university, such as staff recruitment and promotion, academic programme evaluation and research achievement evaluation, are manipulated to a large extent by a few giants, rather than rules being adhered to. This may be the most serious type of equity problem in the Chinese HE sector.

With regard to institutional stratification and differentiation undertakings, the process is very slow. The data in Table 9.1 show that the majority of private institutions are vocational colleges, and vice versa, so the fate of the private sector is related to the significant fluctuations in the numbers of TVEIs in recent years. The cause of these fluctuations is unstable government policy, together with traditionally held values where labouring vocations are looked down upon. According to a survey (Han, 2007), 38.18 per cent of the participants chose 'low salary' and 21.18 per cent chose 'low social status' as the reasons for their dislike of being a worker. Moreover, 20.15 per cent of the participants expressed the opinion that they did not think they would like to be a blue-collar worker, even if the salary were attractive.

Table 9.1 Development of private HEIs and TVEIs in China

Year	2000	2001	2002	2003	2004	2005	2006	2007
Total private HEIs*	1282	1291	1202	1277	1415	1329	1272	1203
State**	43	89	133	173	226	252	278	297
Four-year institutions among State	2	2	4	8	9	24	25	30
Private TVEIs	1239	1202	1069	1104	1189	1077	994	906

*   Non-TVEIs. Calculated on the data from the MoE website.

**   From Pan and Lin (2005), 'The development of private HEIs in China to 2020', *Journal of Zhejiang Shuren University*, 3.

Regarding university internal administration and management reform, although Western-style organization has been adopted, for instance boards of trustees, and senate and academic committees, the way of running them is largely Chinese. Hence, the processes of selection, resolution, evaluation of academic programmes or research projects and so on can hardly take place fairly and effectively and the 'brain drain' and widespread academic corruption in HE persist.

In summary, while more resources have been input into the Chinese HE sector from both inside China and abroad and the infrastructure of the education administration system has been improved at both state and institutional levels through adopting the model of developed countries, the output of the achievements is less positive from the point of view of both faculty and students.

The challenges of globalization

Despite most of the problems described being found to a greater or a lesser degree in other countries, their extent and causes are different. There must be numerous elements behind the causes of the Chinese education system's persistent problems, but one of the most critical is the understanding and treatment of the relationship between globalization trends and unique Chinese traditions. In fact, this challenge did not emerge in modern times. It has deep cultural roots and has accumulated throughout the history of Chinese education. The following section elaborates some aspects of this challenge in terms of the inconsistency in education aims, education content, and the management mechanism of the HE system.

Inconsistency in education aims

As stated earlier, Deng Xiaoping's 'three facings' notion, together with other official documents, set up new educational aims in the early 1980s. However, this issue remains controversial in the current literature and this is reflected in educational practice. The root of this conflict can be traced back to the time of the Opium Wars (1840–42), when Western education began to emerge in China. Conflict was rife between Confucianists and open-minded officials for decades afterwards. The famous compromise between the two sides at the end of the nineteenth century was to let 'Confucian classics constitute the national ideology, whereas Western technologies serve as utilities'; which sowed the seeds of contradiction in the aims of Chinese education. During the famous 'May Fourth Movement' from 1919 to 1920, which primarily appealed for the introduction of democracy and science to China, the debate became more intense. Moreover, this debate was vigorously revived in 2009 at the time of the sixtieth anniversary of this great movement.

Like all civilizations, Chinese education in ancient times was the privilege of the elite. However, until the nineteenth century it was unique in that it aimed exclusively to produce government officials. The difference in curricular content between the West and China helps this to be understood. The ancient Chinese curriculum in Confucius' time (551–479 BCE) focused on the Six Arts, that is, rites, music, archery, chariot-riding, history, and arithmetic; whereas the curriculum in ancient Greece concentrated on the Seven Arts, which consisted of grammar, rhetoric, dialectic, arithmetic, geometry, astronomy, and music. It is evident that the former is politics-centred, while the latter is rather more knowledge-centred. Take, for example, the study of music: the content differed in that the Chinese approach was concerned with political ritual whereas the Greeks were interested in the science of sound. After the Han Dynasty (202 BCE–220 AD), the Six Arts curriculum was gradually replaced by one even worse: the Four Books and Five Classics, which eliminated arithmetic, music, archery and chariot-riding (which featured elements of primary mechanics). The new curriculum outlined the principles of feudal society, as well as its moral codes for personal conduct. The guiding principle of the society was conceived as a rigid feudal stratum, and the aim of education was its maintenance. If we think of moral education as the heart of the education enterprise of a society, we find that Confucian teaching excluded any concept of justice. In contrast, this idea possessed special importance in Aristotle's *Nicomachean Ethics*. This absence of a sense of justice in traditional Chinese educational content presents special obstacles to the ongoing reform of citizenship education aroused by the trend of globalization. For instance, at all levels of Chinese education, while modern concepts of moral education as citizenship have been implemented, traditional Chinese moral teachings are simultaneously emphasized. Many generations of Chinese educators influenced by Confucius attach great importance to the Chinese sense of collectivism as a central value, which is fundamentally incompatible with the key concept of justice in citizenship education.

The ancient Chinese civil service examination (1300s–1905) has also had an enormous impact on the present practice of educational reform. This consisted of essay questions to test candidates' understanding of the Four Books and the Five Classics, determined whether candidates could be appointed as officials. Students could prepare for these examinations by enrolling in the feudal institutions of higher learning called 'Shuyuan', whose main function was to prepare students for the examinations. This ancient phenomenon was transformed into 'examination-preparing education', which has been the target of reform over recent decades to establish a new paradigm called 'competence education' or 'whole person education', in line with modern educational aims. However, the reform has so far proved difficult and ineffective.

Even in *The Decisions*, issued in 1985, as in former documents there was still an exhortation to keep everything in accordance with the so-called 'four fundamental principles' while conducting education reforms. The 'four fundamental principles' were meant to insist on going the socialist road, on the people's democratic dictatorship, on CCP leadership, and on Marxism-Leninism-Mao Zedong's thought. As a result, almost all of the articles listed for reform in *The Decisions* were not effectively implemented until the late 1990s. For instance, due to the '6.4' democracy movement in Tiananmen Square in 1989 and the collapse of the Soviet Union, some anti-reform arguments emerged in defence of the old socialism. Some people criticized Deng's 'three facings' theory for having 'no place left for Chinese traditions'. At this vital time, Deng Xiaoping announced his well-known saying: 'Go reform with bigger paces; do not care too much about our surname being Socialism or Capitalism'; 'We must adhere to reform for at least 100 years without hesitation.' *The Programme* then was able to be launched in 1993, and the education law was soon promulgated which confirmed that: 'Education is the basis of modernization of the country, and the state shall ensure priority to the development of educational undertakings.

The whole (of) society should (be) concern(ed.) with and support it.' More recently, facing accelerated challenge from globalization, the report for the 17th National Congress of the CCP in 2007 declared that we need to learn from all nations for the sake of modernization. However, when the lesson is put into practice, tremendous obstacles appear.

The debate on education aims dates from the dawn of modernization in this country and has not yet reached a unified resolution. Though public arguments on education aims are seldom witnessed in China, this ambiguous state of affairs is evident in the inconsistencies and contradictions of government policy and practice respectively.

Inconsistency in education contents

Given the kind of educational aims stated above, it is inevitable there are many contradictions within Chinese university curricula. On the one hand, the natural science subjects in universities' curricula have been structured in line with Western standards; on the other hand, humanities and social sciences haved stayed very Chinese. As a result, students are living in an atmosphere full of contradictions, especially those who study natural sciences. These students sometimes have to face courses that are run totally against the scientific principle that arguments should based on facts rather than assumptions and ideology. For students in humanistic and social science majors, it is extremely difficult to learn modern research methods which are widely applied in Western universities. After reciting so many Chinese humanistic classics, these students find it difficult to see the significance of distinguishing fact from perception, and scientific theory from personal argument. They hardly even appreciate the role of fact collection in verifying an argument. Those subjects required by the MoE to use imported foreign textbooks in teaching, as mentioned before, are mainly confined to the fields of natural sciences and technology (Zhang *et al.*, 2006).

This inconsistency can also be found in the subject development policies from the government. Even as the CCPCC and the government call for philosophy and the social sciences to catch up with international standards, the subject of Marxist philosophy is legitimated to be the top priority above all other branches of social sciences and philosophy. In terms of the academic assessment and rewards system, there are no rewards in the humanities and social sciences which take account of publication in English, although government policies encourage the recruitment of overseas Chinese students, including those in the field of social science. This inconsistency helps us to understand the reason for the ineffectiveness of the policy to construct world-class universities and the low level of satisfaction among both students and faculty. More fundamentally, this also gives a clue to Joseph Lee's famous question on why modern science did not emerge in China, despite its long, prosperous civilization.

Inconsistency in management mechanisms

Contradictions also exist in the administration sector between superficial reform activities and the hidden assumptions underlying them. All the reforms, as stated above, have been carried out under the 'hidden assumption', using the term invented by Schein (1985), that the CCPCC should hold the power to direct the reform in both scope and amplitude. This assumption substantially goes against the principles and practices employed by institutions in the environment of globalization. While economic principles have been introduced, the associated law and order has not been established. So corruption in the processes of student enrolment, infrastructure construction projects, and even international cooperation projects remains and is incurable. That is why, as pointed out earlier, although universities have adopted the Western-style administrative and managerial organization, the methods are largely Chinese, and the outcomes are negative and ineffective.

These phenomena cannot be explained without referring back to the long history of the autocratic feudal system in China. Specifically, it is not the government itself which is to blame; these circumstances have wide and deep foundations. Some university faculty members and academic leaders, especially those in the field of Chinese humanities, seem pledged to bring the historical motto, to let 'traditional Chinese values constitute the national ideology, while Western technologies serve as utilities' into the twenty-first century.

In terms of developing of private institutions of HE as a means to enlarge the system, extreme vicissitudes have been encountered in recent decades. If we look back into the fate of Shuyuans, the ancient institutions of higher learning described above, it becomes more understandable. Almost all of those Shuyuans were originally private institutions and experienced rising prosperity, only to be taken over by the government at their peak and turned to the track of corruption (Cao, 2005).

Summary and conclusion

Robertson's world culture theory can be applied here to help to form a conclusion. He frames the key features of globalization:

> As a process that both connects and stimulates awareness of connection, globalization dissolves the autonomy of actors and practices in the contemporary world order. In this process of relativization, all units engaged in globalization are constrained to assume a position and define an identity relative to the emerging global whole. (Robertson, 1992, p. 29)

Unfortunately, the Chinese have not yet developed an adequate awareness of this connection and, far from assuming a correct position and defining an identity relative to the emerging global whole, it is obvious that almost all of the international cooperative projects and programmes in Chinese universities are conducted in a passive, instrumentalism-oriented way without clear objectives for cultural interaction. The majority of Chinese officials, most ordinary people and even a significant number of intellectuals still pay attention solely to the technical side of Western civilization, with a strong belief that Chinese culture, in the mental domain at least, is absolutely superior than its Western counterpart.

Given the complex historical background and the trend of globalization, it is imperative for the Chinese government and scholars to answer some fundamental questions before initiating further reforms in education enterprise. The most fundamental question seems to be how to join the globalization track without losing Chinese identity in terms of education aims.

There are, indeed, some elements of merit in Chinese culture. For example, the virtue of thrift is, in principle, congruent with modern environmentalism, and the virtue of tolerance benefits the process of building a harmonious global society with diverse beliefs and cultures. Even with a sense of collectivism, if rooted in a rational mind rather than something akin to clan-based spirit, it is worthy of being given blessing. These virtues can be preserved for Chinese identity and passed down to future generations. However, they are more appropriate to cure the diseases attributed to some Western cultures, than those of China.

We Chinese need to change some aspects of our character, for the sake of our own nation and the whole human race. The spirit of the May Fourth Movement, with appeal for science and democracy, still needs to be popularized. In terms of integrating the educational aims and contents of the cultures of the West and China, we should be confident there is a possibility of educating students to be at the same time responsible and critical in thinking, as practiced by those from nations such as Japan. At present, educators in China should be able to help students distinguish temporary social problems, such as the imperfections of the legal system, as either an attribute of a social-transition period or as being influenced by traditional culture, rather than emanating solely from the intrinsic defects of modernity.

It is evident that the Western route of HE development is evolutionary: from democracy to marketization, then to economic prosperity, and finally to massification. In China, however, due to the long-established segregation of ideology and utility, the crucial triangular relationship between government, society and universities for maintaining a healthy education system, according to Clark (1983), has not been established. As a result, there has been no balance between the economy, the market, gross entrance rates, education aims, curricula, and so on. These constitute the fundamental causes of the quality problem and other challenges presented earlier. It has been pointed out by P. G. Altbach that three necessities are needed for China to become a country with a strong HE enterprise: Academic freedom; a just and fair competitive environment; and willingness to serve society (Chen *et al.*, 2009). In fact, the critical proviso is obviously a fair and efficient management system for attracting top scientists and scholars to create world-class universities and, finally, to solve the phenomenon of brain drain. Culture matters, indeed (Harrison *et al.*, 2000).

References

Boyer, E. L. (1987), Carnegie Foundation for the Advancement of Teaching. *College: The Undergraduate Experience in America*. New York: Harper & Row.

Cao, H. B. (2005), 'Thousands of years of fluctuation: An interpretation of Shuyuan's spirit', *Chinese News Weekly*, 43 (in Chinese).

Chen, T. and Jang, C. (2009), 'Professor Altbach on China's target to become a powerful higher education country', *University Education Science*, 2 (in Chinese).

Clark, B. R. (1983), *The Higher Education System: Academic Organization in Cross-National Perspective*. Los Angeles: University of California Press.

Han, Q. L. (2007), 'A study of the factors influencing TVE development in China: The Chinese culture', *The Journal of Adult Education College of Hebei University*, 9, (3), 31–2 (in Chinese).

Harrison, L. E. and Huntington, S. P. (2000), *Culture Matters: How Values Shape Human Progress*. New York: Basic Books.

He, Z. (2007), 'Higher education tuition fee endurance of the families in rural area of China', *Rural Economic Issues*, 6 (in Chinese).

Ministry of Education (2009), 'Higher Education in 2009 with general higher education enrollment eligibility list', at http://www.moe.edu.cn/edoas/website18/28/info1242788474781628.htm (in Chinese).

Ministry of Education, Chinese Ministry of Education of the People's Republic of China website, at http://www.MoE.edu.cn/edoas (in English).

Office of International Cooperation and Exchanges (2007), The Office of International Cooperation and Exchanges and the Office of Taiwan, Hong Kong and Macao Affairs at Nanjing University website, at: http://wb.nju.edu.cn/foreground/sub.php?catid=16.

Pan, M. and Lin, L. (2005), 'The development of private HEIs in China from the present to 2020', *Journal of Zhejian Shuren University*, 3 (in Chinese).

Robertson, R. (1992), *Globalization: Social Theory and Global Culture*. London: Sage.

Schein, E. (1985), *Organizational Culture and Leadership: A Dynamic View*. San Francisco: Jossey-Bass.

Stone, R. (2009) 'University head Zhu Qingshi challenges old academic ways', *Science*, 326, (5956), 1050, at http://www.sciencenet.cn/m/user_content.aspx?id=272452

Surowski, D. B. (ed.) (2000), 'History of the educational system of China', in *PIER World Education Series*, at www.math.ksu.edu/

Trow, M. (1973), 'Problems in the transition from elite to mass higher education', paper presented to the Conference on Future Structures of Post-Secondary Education, Paris, 26–9 June, 63–71.

Yu, Z. W. (2009), 'The reform of the technical and vocational education development in the past 30 years: Experience and implications', *Higher Education Research*, 1 (in Chinese).

Zhang, H., Feng, Z., Rao, Y. and Shao, J. (2006), 'A comprehensive survey on the uses of imported textbooks in universities', *Higher Education in Jiangsu Province*, 6 (in Chinese).

Zhang, H. and Qu, M. (2007), 'Disparity in student satisfaction of Chinese undergraduate teaching between research and common institutions: A national survey of 73 institutions', *Chinese University Teaching*, 4 (in Chinese).

Zhang, Y. (2006), 'New solutions to new problems: Director Raoxue Zhang talks about how to improve higher education quality', *Guangming Daily*, 19 October (in Chinese).

Chapter 10

Capacity Building for Demography in Southern Africa: International Collaboration in Action

Rosalind Foskett

Introduction

Globalization is having a major impact on how universities seek to work together to address the issues facing people, societies and the environment. Institutions are increasingly seeking to work with partners to ensure that students gain an international perspective to their studies. In addition, higher education institutions (HEIs) need to work with global partners in order to access funding for research and development. It is increasingly recognized that internationalization of universities is not just about recruiting students from different countries, but is about working with international partners on a range of issues involving teaching, research and knowledge transfer.

Partnership and the issues associated with setting up and maintaining successful relationships is, therefore, an important aspect of internationalization. Institutions cannot have global reach without maintaining strategic and operational links with a range of other institutions and businesses. Working in partnership requires skilful leadership and management and the partnership relationship itself needs maintaining alongside the research, education or knowledge transfer activity which is being pursued. Universities must, therefore, develop these skill sets in their staff in order to become major international players.

This chapter will examine the processes involved in setting up a major international research and development project funded through the Edulink programme of the European Union. The programme, Strengthening Training and Regional Networks in Demography (STARND) is a collaborative partnership between HEIs in the Southern African Development Community (SADC) and in the United Kingdom (UK). The partners include universities in five participating African countries (Botswana, Malawi, Namibia, South Africa and Zambia) and a research-intensive university in the UK. While the partnership reflects bilateral and multilateral links which were already in existence, the STARND project was the first where all the members had worked together jointly. The aims of the programme are threefold: to strengthen the capacity for academic leadership in demography and population studies in the partner universities; to improve the quality of demography teaching; and to review the contents of demography and population studies programmes to align them more closely with development in the SADC region and emerging global priorities.

From the beginning the participants agreed to adopt a partnership approach and the aim was to ensure that all partners were involved fully. The objectives are being achieved through a phased approach with the research project being broken down into twelve work-streams. The intention is to make the partnership sustainable beyond the length of the initial funding. To this end the approach adopted has been participatory, with each partner fulfilling a specific role in the research and development process.

The socio-political context is the increasing need for qualified demography graduates to work in African countries. Sub-Saharan Africa is faced by a number of serious challenges closely related to high population growth. In many of the participant countries population growth rates exceed 2 per cent (Table 10.1). For many people poverty, food insecurity and poor health are a daily reality and societies are beset with problems associated with an increasing burden of communicable and non-communicable disease including HIV/AIDS, obesity and malnutrition. HEIs play an important part through their research and teaching in establishing effective programmes to tackle health and population problems, and in informing public policy.

Table 10.1 Average Annual Rate of Population Change by SADC Country (%)

Country	2000–2005	2005–2010
World	1.26	1.18
Angola	3.03	2.67
Botswana	1.31	1.45
Comoros	2.21	2.29
D.R. Congo	2.37	1.91
Lesotho	1.10	0.87
Madagascar	2.85	2.69
Malawi	2.87	2.78
Mauritius	0.94	0.70
Mozambique	2.65	2.33
Namibia	1.93	1.93
Seychelles	0.37	0.47
South Africa	1.38	0.98
Swaziland	0.81	1.33
U.R. Tanzania	2.67	2.88
Zambia	2.29	2.43
Zimbabwe	0.03	0.27

Source: Population Division of the Department of Economic and Social Affairs of the United Nations (2009) World Population Prospects: The 2008 Revision. Highlights. New York: UN.

However, universities themselves are in need of development. They often find themselves under-resourced and under-skilled in comparison to others within the global higher education arena. The reality of teaching large numbers of students with small numbers of academic and support staff means that it is often difficult for research-active staff to involve themselves in bidding for grants large enough to address the demographic challenges that face the region. The support in the universities may be poorly developed, such that researchers are lacking the help they need in systems such as finance, human resources and staff development. In order to make a difference, therefore, it is not just academic development that needs to take place but capacity building for management and leadership within the departments and their universities which needs to be addressed. This case study is an example of a partnership adopting this approach, an example of synergy between academic development and institutional capacity building.

A partnership model

International collaboration and partnership as a mode of working is common in universities and there are many examples of success in both research and teaching. It is part of the current political scene, with many governments and funding agencies seeking to gain the greatest impact from research and development, believing that partnership spreads the benefits and increases global reach. In developing the curriculum, partnership between universities and employers and specialist organizations such as non-governmental organizations (NGOs) is seen as a way of increasing the relevance of the programmes, which in turn will increase the competitiveness of the economy.

A definition of what constitutes partnership has not been universally agreed upon (for example, IPHI, 2001; Tett *et al.*, 2003; Wildridge *et al.*, 2004). In many countries such as the UK and the United States of America (USA), the seeds of current education/business partnerships can be traced back to the belief, prevalent in the 1980s, in the capacity of the private sector to show public sector organizations the way to run their operations. This was a centralized and controlling definition of partnership, in which one partner has the right answers and the other must adopt their way of working. This approach has tended to change into a view of partnership which is more democratic and participatory, and which embeds a 'social-ethical inflection' (Jones *et al.*, 2000). It is, therefore, much more common today to see partnerships as a grouping of interested and skilled people from a range of organizations which are working together to tackle major problems (mainly identified in the political agenda). Not all partners will contribute equally, but they will all participate, and the decision-making will constantly be changing to allow the partners to take account of each other.

Collaboration and partnership are both words which have at their heart the idea of cooperation and working towards a common goal. Dhillon (2005, p. 215) describes this as the 'social glue for achieving shared goals'. In this case study the shared goal is to produce more, well-trained demographers to work in the context of SADC countries. Research has shown, however, that it is important to ensure that partnership brings increased benefits. Partnership working can be disempowering if it is imposed as an approach to a perceived problem, rather than a bottom-up solution identified by the people involved (Slack, 2004). As Tett *et al.* (2003, p. 39) explain:

> Rather than create more opportunities for democratic engagement, partnerships may simply serve to incorporate communities and professionals more deeply into arrangements that they have little genuine control over and that do not really serve their best interests.

Underpinning most definitions of partnership are two key concepts. First there is the idea of mutuality of benefit. This may be overtly stated in the aims of the partnership but, even if it is not, each partner will believe that they will benefit from being part of, rather than apart from, the group (Foskett, 2005). In this case study, by working together, the partners secured funding for the project, and will be able to share curriculum solutions for demography and build capacity within their institutions for further research and development. Second, there should be 'a change in process, product or output' (Tett *et al.*, 2003, p. 39) as a result of the partnership. The partner universities, at the end of the project, will have begun to identify and address the academic and leadership needs in relation to research and teaching in demography in the partner universities. Alongside these institutional needs, the development needs of the SADC region will have been analysed and assessed in relation to current demography curricula in the partner institutions. This will help the academic leaders within the partnership to ensure that programmes embrace the needs of the region and that the curriculum is aligned with development priorities. There are many authors who have written about the benefits and pitfalls of partnership (for example, Huxham *et al.*, 2000; Wildridge *et al.*, 2004; Connolly *et al.*, 2007). Whatever the definition, there is an underpinning assumption that partnership is a good thing and that the synergy within the relationship ensures that the total is greater than the sum of the parts.

So, why did this group of institutions from countries across Southern Africa and the UK come together to work in partnership? The cynic would argue that it was a marriage of convenience, a pragmatic association to fulfil the criteria for gaining funding from the European Union Edulink program. However, we need to explore more deeply the reasons the universities and the individuals became involved. Previous research carried out on partnership and the motivations of organizations in becoming involved identified three types of aims held by potential partners: mission aims; development aims; and business aims (Foskett, 2005). Mission aims are those that are related to the underlying values of the organization. People have a deep-seated commitment to these aims and are happy to articulate and share them with other partners. As a demonstration of what the organization and the individuals believe in, they have high moral status, they tend to be quite strategic and they are very important in gaining the initial commitment to the partnership. For example, in the confidential evaluation of the first colloquium of the STARND partnership, the most common aim stated by the participants was to build capacity in demography training in the SADC region, closely followed by a wish to improve the quality of demography graduates. People are happy to share aims such as these with other partners from the start, however they are rarely the only, or the most important, reasons why partners join in.

Development aims tend to emerge as the partners get to know each other and begin to work together. Admitting them is a function of trust. As partners become more comfortable and committed to the partnership, and providing they feel valued as members of the group, they will begin to identify aims that they have which relate to other drivers. The most common of these relate to their development needs. They will believe that they will learn from being engaged with the partnerships and be able to develop personally and/or institutionally. In this case, emergent aims related to the development needs of the partners included the need to enhance the quality of teaching, develop professional networks and expose students and less experienced staff to international colleagues.

The third category of aims which exist at the start of a partnership relate to the business of the partner. In the case of universities this includes funding, research quality and building the curricula vitae of individuals. The evaluation demonstrated that this international partnership was no different. There were a number of business aims identified by the participants. In answer to a question on the main benefits of the partnership to their institution, partners' responses included the need for additional resources, enhanced reputation and strengthened capacity for research. Individuals also had personal business aims including access to teaching resources, support for PhD study in the UK, and collaboration with a high-calibre international team. In many partnerships, these business-related aims remain unspoken as they are perceived to be unworthy and of lower moral status. However, understanding them is vital to the success of the partnership and its long-term sustainability, as individuals will only remain committed and motivated if they feel that these needs are being addressed. The strongest partnerships take time to understand the motivations of the members.

A participatory approach

Another key aspect of international collaborative partnerships is developing a participatory approach. Definitions of a participatory approach differ, but often include empowerment of disadvantaged individuals or organizations. The following definition by the World Bank (1992, p. 177) is a typical example:

> [Participation is] . . . a process by which people, especially disadvantaged people, influence decisions that affect them.

A participatory approach in development is not a panacea and critical studies have shown that it can fail, particularly where conditions are not favourable for individuals to become fully involved or where there is manipulation by one of the partners or external agencies (Brett, 2003). In this case study, the partners wanted to avoid these pitfalls. Success is more likely, in this example, as the partners are all senior academics in reputable HEIs and therefore each partner is valued for the strengths they bring to the project.

All participants need to feel valued and involved. There are many studies of the barriers facing partnership. One of the critical success factors is a clear articulation of the aims of each of the partners and convergence of those aims towards a common purpose (for example Wilson *et al.*, 1997; Clegg *et al.*, 2002; Foskett, 2005). The participants need to engage in activities which will allow them to understand the motivations of other participants and how their own needs fit. Commitment will also depend on risk. Partners will make an early decision about risk. This might be through application of a risk-assessment tool such as that developed by Craft which is based on factors such as the partner's strength and expertise and their experience of partnership (Craft, 2004). However, more often than not, partners use a 'gut feeling' of the risks involved.

In developing a participatory approach, it is important that all partners feel that they have ownership of the development and that problems which result from unequal power relationships are avoided (Quicke, 2000; Milbourne *et al.*, 2003; Foskett, 2005). Trust between partners can take a long time to develop and it helps if early work is undertaken to ensure that the partners know each other (Bottery, 2003). A number of mechanisms were put in place early on in the STARND partnership to avoid the UK partner assuming undue dominance and control, and to encourage participation. Each of the partners was involved and consulted in the development of the initial bid. This went beyond obtaining a signed letter of willingness to collaborate; involving input from partners and building on existing relationships. An early event was planned to get all partners together for a colloquium in South Africa. This event, jointly planned by the host university and the UK partner, involved all partners contributing actively by leading sessions, taking part in workshops, and sharing social activities. The workshops were built around different aspects of the work and partners were encouraged to participate fully in refining the research approach. The research and development activity has been divided into twelve work packages and partners are involved to a greater or lesser extent in each. Events have been planned at regular intervals throughout the project and each will be hosted by a different partner.

In evaluating the first colloquium, the operation of a participatory approach was investigated. Participants were questioned about what, in their opinion, was having the biggest effect on promoting active partnership. Four elements were identified as being of greatest importance, particularly as it was an international partnership: the ability to meet together; the interactive workshops; participation in the development of the bid; and getting to know people. In the words of one participant, active partnership had been fostered by:

> bringing together everyone to share experiences as well as the transparency of the . . . [leaders] . . . brings a sense of ownership.

Partners may feel threatened by working with others. This may be due to a fear that the credit will reflect on one partner at the expense of the rest, or that one partner will take control and deflect the aims of the partnership. However, the complexity of an international collaborative partnership like the STARND project requires firm management. This is not at odds with a participatory approach, providing the means by which partners can have their say and influence outcomes is transparent. At its worst, collaboration can be used as a vehicle of control over individuals or institutions. The meetings can become a means of disseminating decisions taken elsewhere or imposing conformity. There is a big difference between this and a truly participatory partnership.

An analysis of need

The STARND Project is unusual in that it involves work in two complementary strands. Each part of the project is being managed through one of twelve planned work packages (Table 10.2). One strand of the work is to identify the development needs of the academic leadership in relation to research and teaching in demography (work packages 3, 7 and 10). This will involve the identification of the constraints both internal to the institution and externally. The second strand is to identify the demographic development priorities within the SADC region and to ensure that these are mirrored in the demography curricula offered in the institutions (work packages 4, 5, 6, 8, 9 and 10). Each of these strands will now be discussed in more detail.

(a) Strand 1: Institutional needs assessment

The overall vision for this strand of the project is to build capacity in higher education institutions in the management and leadership of teaching and research. All institutions, and all individual academics, have strengths and development needs in aspects of their work. By identifying these, the partnership will work together to build centres of excellence producing highly-qualified graduates able to serve the development priorities in respect of research and the teaching of demography and population science. Universities and their academic departments have four broad areas of knowledge and expertise: academic disciplinary knowledge (in this case, in demography); pedagogical knowledge (how to teach and foster learning); leadership expertise (providing vision and direction); and management expertise (for example in finance, human resources or external relations). In order to continue to grow and develop, higher education institutions need to be continually building capacity in each of these to survive in an increasingly globalized environment (Stephens, 2007).

What is meant by capacity building in the context of this case study in Southern Africa? Capacity building relates to all dimensions of the development of teaching and research in the partner institutions. It is about *going further*, that is, taking the science of demography and its impact to higher levels and to greater breadth. It is also about *moving faster*, that is, being more efficient, responsive and effective in research, education and enterprise. And it is about *sustainability*, that is, achieving permanent and persistent impacts of what we do. The academic capacity-building activity of the project is discussed below in Strand 2. In Strand 1 the partners developed a needs assessment tool

Table 10.2 The twelve work packages comprising the STARND project

Work package	Title	Brief description
1	Project management	Preparing a project management tool. Coordination of project partners.
2	Project planning	Administering the project plan.
3	Institutional needs assessment	Developing and applying an assessment tool to identify institutional needs in the management and leadership of research and teaching.
4	Evidence review	Review of evidence on obesity, malnutrition and non-communicable diseases in the SADC region and development of research-led teaching interventions.
5	Semi-structured interviews with key experts	Interviews with key regional officers involved in demography, population studies and human, social and economic development.
6	Review of documents	Desk review of existing curricula, population policies and development strategies.
7	Institutional development activities	Development and delivery of a programme of activities to build institutional management and leadership capacity.
8	Teaching and research colloquia	Development and delivery of activities to inform research-led teaching, develop pedagogy and support research capacity.
9	Development of teaching material	Production of teaching materials and curriculum resources for use in class and online.
10	Evaluation	Evaluation of the teaching materials and training activities.
11	Dissemination	Dissemination of outputs to partners and stakeholders in the SADC region.
12	Sustainable futures	Planning for future initiatives.

which would allow identification of the development needs of each institution with respect to pedagogy, leadership and management.

By using a participatory approach, the partnership identified a number of objectives for this strand of the project:

- Improved teaching and learning in demography and population studies
- Enhanced institutional support for the academic staff
- Enhanced academic leadership
- Partnership development
- Enhanced research-led teaching
- Improved internal and external networks
- Improvements in the quality and impact of research
- Increased success in future funding bids.

We employed a development model which would drive the activity (Figure 10.1). All partners were actively involved in each of the stages. By focusing on the academic unit (or department, school or division), the partners identified the activities they shared in common (Figure 10.2). Working together, the partners identified needs in terms of academic unit leadership and delivery of teaching, research and enterprise. They also identified the evidence that would be sought on the strengths or weaknesses in each area, and developed specific questions to be included in the needs assessment instrument. For example, in terms of *managing people*, one of the contributory processes is providing induction for new staff. Evidence of successful management in this area could be an online induction programme and evidence of weakness might be the

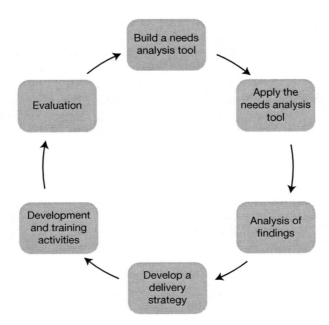

Figure 10.1 The needs assessment development model

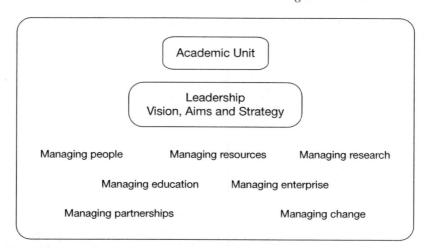

Figure 10.2   The academic unit

lack of an induction policy. Questions which would then appear on the needs assessment instrument might include:

- Do you have a written induction policy?
- How has the induction policy been made available?
- Do you have an induction event?
- What mechanisms are employed to evaluate the success of induction?

Using this participatory approach, the needs assessment questionnaire was developed and owned by all participants.

Referring to Figure 10.1, the questionnaire covering all the areas of activity in the academic unit was applied. In each of the partner universities, five respondents were chosen to complete it by the institutional link researcher: three members of academic staff working in the unit, the academic unit leader, and a senior member of staff in the institution with responsibility for staff development. For each partner institution the link researcher was asked to complete a summary report of the institutional needs, including a list of five priorities for action and five features of good practice (strengths). This, together with the overall analysis of the findings, allowed the partnership to develop, deliver and evaluate a training and development plan to build capacity in the universities involved. Partners were involved both in the delivery (of their strengths) and in development activities (on their needs). By involving people both as trainers and trainees, the partnership was strengthened by the mutuality of outcome.

(b) Strand 2: Needs assessment for demography curricula

The methodology employed for this element of the project is based on the use of several tools. At the initial colloquium, demography and population scientists reviewed the existing academic curricula which form the basis of training in the region. They also developed a semi-structured questionnaire for use in the field. The aim of this questionnaire was to gather evidence in a systematic way from interviews conducted with key personnel involved in social and human development in the SADC countries. Interviewees would include SADC personnel involved with work in the following areas:

- The Social and Human Development Programme
- Poverty Eradication
- Environment and Sustainable Development
- Education, Skill Development and Capacity Building
- Health (HIV/AIDS and non-communicable diseases)
- Statistics
- Gender, Equality and Development.

All partners would be involved in interviewing officers in government departments (for example, the Ministry of Economic Development), the director of a national research institute aligned with demographic issues, and members of multilateral and bilateral development partners (for example, the World Bank and Oxfam).

Analysis of these interviews, together with a desk-based analysis of key policy documents, will provide the team with a deeper understanding of the development priorities and challenges facing populations in the SADC region. This information will form the basis of an assessment of the current curricula for training demographers and population scientists and to produce new courses and programmes to better meet current and future needs.

Another work-stream is a review of the evidence on the burden of non-communicable disease and the levels of weight problems and obesity among adults and under-nutrition among mothers and children in the region. This review will include secondary analysis of existing demographic and health data. Resources for teaching will be developed to accompany the outputs of the research and the case study will be used by the partners as an example of research-led teaching. This research-led teaching is part of the pedagogical development in demography, which is one of the review's intended outcomes. Further teaching materials will be developed by the team for wider dissemination among the partners and the SADC countries.

Delivering sustainable change

One of the principal outcomes of any international partnership should be sustainability, which is about delivering a product that will endure beyond the life of any project funding. Partnerships can become long-lasting, providing they have been set up well in the first place. Successful partnership development has four components (Foskett, 2006). The first is defining the *purpose* of the partnership so that everyone is clear about what is to be achieved and how. Time is needed for the partners to get to know each other and to explore the aims of the partnership in full; not just relying on an understanding of the overarching aims, but drilling down into what individuals want to achieve. This will underpin the second stage of partnership development, which is about *commitment* to the project in practice. This stage may include securing senior management support, ensuring that the right people are involved, budgeting sufficient time and other resources and developing trust between the partners. These first two stages (purpose and commitment) can take a long time, but it is time well spent. In international partnerships, distance may be a barrier to effective working relationships unless excellent communication pathways are developed.

The third phase, *management*, relates to moving the partnership forward by putting in place the systems which will facilitate the work to be done and bind the partners together. It will require the right model of leadership to be put in place as well as developing strong management of the work processes. The fourth phase is *development*. Once the partnership is in place it needs nurturing and developing. This is best envisaged as a circular process of implementation, evaluation and further change as necessary, as the partners work on successive projects together.

Continued and sustained involvement in the partnership will depend on the partners achieving their aims for the partnership both institutionally and individually. By this final stage, the hope is that the partners have grown closer together, are engaged in a range of activities, and have been formed into a true partnership with a high degree of mutual trust.

Conclusion

Partnership work is both problematical and rewarding at the same time, and for an institution to be involved as an international player it is essential. There are many challenges facing international partnerships, such as communication, leadership, development of trust and manageability. In this case study, developing a clarity of purpose across such a diverse partnership was necessary and, as I have explored in this chapter, building up a productive working relationship took time in the early stages.

Although this project is not yet completed, the aim is for the partnership to continue in the future and become sustainable. The existing project will end with a final colloquium to explore future networking and further initiatives within the SADC region. The nature of international collaborations such as this is that there are natural multiplier effects as scholars are trained and gain employment with partner organizations and beyond. By addressing education and research needs, the capacity for further successful action is secured and international networks established. From this, benefits accrue to the partner universities. However, the advantages extend beyond this: to the students who follow more appropriate programmes; to the employers who can employ people trained to meet their needs using a curriculum in which they have had input; and to the people of the SADC region, whose everyday challenges are better understood and whose lives will be improved.

Summary

1 Institutions are increasingly seeking to work with global partners to engage in research and to ensure that students gain an international perspective to their work.
2 Institutions must understand the processes involved in partnership to be able to form effective international links. Successful partnership has four components: defining the purpose; securing commitment; managing the processes; and developing sustainability.
3 This chapter illustrates the use of a participatory approach to partnership development and examines some of the benefits and pitfalls.
4 Capacity building in international institutions involves the development of four areas: developing the academic capacity in research and teaching, in this example, in demography and population studies; developing pedagogy and innovating in teaching and learning; developing the leadership capability within institutions at different levels; and building capacity in management of processes, systems and people.

References

Bottery, M. (2003), 'The management and mismanagement of trust', *Education Management and Administration*, 31, (3), 245–61.

Brett, E. A. (2003), 'Participation and accountability in development management', *Journal of Development Studies*, 40, (2), 1–29.

Clegg, S. and McNulty, K. (2002), 'Partnerships working in delivering social inclusion: Organizational and gender dynamics', *Journal of Educational Policy*, 15, (5), 587–601.

Connolly, M., Jones, C. and Jones, N. (2007), 'Managing collaboration across further and higher education: A case in practice', *Journal of Further and Higher Education*, 31, (2), 159–69.

Craft, A. (2004), 'The assessment of quality risks in collaborative provision', *Quality in Higher Education*, 10, (1), 25–9.

Dhillon, J. K. (2005), 'The rhetoric and reality of partnership working', *Journal of Further and Higher Education*, 29, (3), 211–19.

Foskett, R. (2005), 'Collaborative partnership between HE and employers: A study of workforce development', *Journal of Further and Higher Education*, 29, (3), 251–64.

—— (2006), 'Collaborative partnerships for curriculum development: An analysis of the critical factors in the development of policy-led undergraduate programmes', unpublished PhD thesis, University of Southampton.

Huxham, C. and Vangen, S. (2000), 'What makes partnerships work?', in S. P. Osbourne (ed.), *Public–Private Partnerships: Theory and Practice in International Perspective*. London: Routledge, pp. 294–310.

Institute of Public Health in Ireland (IPHI) (2001), *Partnership Framework: A Model of Partnership for Health*. Dublin: IPHI.

Jones, K. and Bird, K. (2000), '"Partnership" as strategy: Public-private relations in Education Action Zones', *British Educational Research Journal*, 26, (4), 491–506.

Milbourne, L., Macrae, S. and Maguire, M. (2003), 'Collaborative solutions or new policy problems: Exploring multi-agency partnerships in education and health work', *Journal of Education Policy*, 18, (1), 19–35.

Quicke, J. (2000), 'A new professionalism for a collaborative culture of organizational learning in contemporary society', *Educational Management and Administration*, 28, (3), 299–315.

Slack, K. (2004), 'Collaboration with the community to widen participation: "Partners" without power or absent "Friends"', *Higher Education Quarterly*, 58, (2–3), 136–50.

Stephens, D. (ed.) (2007), *Higher Education and International Capacity Building: Twenty-five Years of Higher Education Links*. Oxford: Symposium Books.

Tett, L., Crowther, J. and O'Hara, P. (2003), 'Collaborative partnerships in community education', *Journal of Education Policy*, 18, (1), 37–51.

Wildridge, V., Childs, S., Cawthra, L. and Madge, B. (2004), 'How to create successful partnerships – a review of the literature', *Health Information and Libraries Journal*, 21, 3–19.

Wilson, A. and Charlton, K. (1997), *Making Partnerships Work: A Practical Guide for the Public, Private, Voluntary and Community Sectors*. York: Joseph Rowntree Foundation/York Publishing Services.

World Bank (1992), *Participatory Development and the World Bank*, B. Bhatnagar and A. Williams (eds), Washington, DC: World Bank Discussion Papers, 183.

PART III

Case Studies in Higher Education Internationalization

Chapter 11

Student Experience in the Globalized Higher Education Market: Challenges and Research Imperatives

Rodney Arambewela

Introduction

Student experience is highly topical in the current globalized higher education (HE) market, and has attracted considerable attention in the recent past among researchers, administrators and other stakeholders in HE systems around the world (Ryan *et al.*, 2005). This has been due to the strong relationship that exists between student experience and student satisfaction and the challenges faced by institutions to provide students with a positive educational experience in an environment of increasing student mobility and diversity, rising student expectations of service quality and value for money. In addition, recognition of the significant economic, social and cultural benefits accruing from the internationalization of higher education and the presence of a large number of culturally diverse international students with different academic and social backgrounds on university campuses have also highlighted the importance of student experience in higher education institutions (HEIs) all over the world.

Student experience is how a student views student life in a learning institution. It reflects the perceptions of students of the academic and non-academic services offered by the institution to help them successfully navigate their educational pursuits. These perceptions are based on students' prior expectations of the services and facilities associated with their academic life and manifest themselves either as positive or negative experiences impacting on their satisfaction with the learning environment. The problem is that expectations are volatile and subject to change as students continue to review them based on the experience they accumulate over time. These are then reflected in changed perceptions and levels of satisfaction with the learning environment.

Early research studies on satisfaction defined it as a post-choice evaluative judgement concerning a specific purchase decision (Oliver *et al.*, 1988). The dominant conceptual model used in the satisfaction literature is the disconfirmation of expectations paradigm. This paradigm postulates that customer satisfaction is related to the size and direction of disconfirmation, which is defined as the difference between an individual's pre-purchase expectations (or some other comparison standard) and post-purchase performance of the product or service (Anderson, 1973). When expectations are not fulfilled, the level of satisfaction decreases.

Research indicates that satisfaction is positively related to customer loyalty and future purchase decisions and, in the context of HE, student satisfaction therefore becomes a critical factor in sustaining continued allegiance towards the institution with prospects for promoting new students and undertaking further studies in the same institution (Townley, 2001; Guolla, 1999). As providers of professional services, institutions are aware of the value of student loyalty, goodwill, and the need to maximize student achievement and retention which are positive outcomes of student satisfaction (Blodgett *et al.*, 1997). It is therefore imperative for HE institutions to ensure that their service delivery initiatives are well targeted and directed to enhance student experience. While teaching and learning remains an important aspect of students' experience, it is argued that HEIs should endeavour to improve the total experience of students' learning environments, given that the enhancement of both the social and intellectual development of students are the primary goals of these institutions (Tinto, 1989).

This chapter will focus on current discourses, themes and issues identified in the literature on student experience and discuss future research opportunities that would promote strategic responses to common challenges in the internationalization agenda. It will discuss the limitations in current literature, which is based on a narrow view of internationalization focused primarily on social and psychological issues related to tertiary students, and those initiatives designed to address the needs of these students. It has barely touched on the experience of postgraduate students and changes in graduate identities as a result of transnational experiences (Rizvi, 2005). The focus of most of the literature has been the first-year experience of university students, as it is considered most critical in influencing student attitudes and perceptions of the learning and support environment in later years (Tinto, 1996, McInnis *et al.*, 2000, Blythman *et al.*, 2003).

The chapter is presented in three parts. It will begin with a brief outline of how student experience is viewed in the current globalized HE market. It will then discuss the current discourses, themes and issues which are directly relevant to the understanding of student experience. The final section will provide concluding remarks, with a discussion on the limitations of the current literature on student experience and future research imperatives. While HE refers to a number of tertiary education sectors, the discussion in this chapter is primarily focused on the university sector.

Student experience in the globalized higher education market

Much has been written about globalization and its effects on HE policy and practice and how universities respond to the challenges and opportunities presented by the globalized educational environment. These responses are characterized by divergent views about the effects of globalization; some positive and some negative, but with a broader agreement that globalization has transformed HE across the world with far-reaching effects on university policies and practices. It has also strongly influenced the international orientation of universities to become competitive in a changing global marketing environment. All these developments have had a significant impact on the learning environment and as a result on the experience of students on campus.

The impact of globalization on nation states and the resultant effects on HE policy have been associated with conflicting discourses on modernity and the rise of neo-liberalism, where concepts such as deregulation, market efficiency and competition are seen as vital to the political, economic, cultural and technological progress of nation states. In this scenario, the nation states are expected to play by a set of global rules to remain active players in the global knowledge economy. A major contention is that neo-liberalism promotes a vocationalist agenda in HE to suit the workforce needs of the global economy, in preference to a more liberal and enlightenment-oriented education which focuses on an education that promotes social responsibility, global citizenship and intercultural competencies. The popularity of Business and Management courses in universities is cited as an example of the vocationalist agenda, though such trends are not always universal in character. For example, statistics from the US Department of Education (2008) suggest that while Business and Management degrees conferred in the US continued to grow by 45 per cent during 1996–97, the number of Social Science and History degrees awarded also grew by 32 per cent during the same period, contradicting the argument for a pure vocationalist orientation of the universities.

Some globalization theorists (Strange, 1996) argue that the forces of globalization represented by transnational capital, global media and supranational political systems around the world have strengthened cross-border affiliations to the extent that their national cultures and political systems have been made insignificant. Some others (Yang, 2003) contend that globalization, driven by a culture of consumerism and individualism, has perpetuated global inequality and has made the rich–poor gap much wider, manifested by a disproportionate distribution of wealth and opportunities in life. These types of positive and negative aspects of globalization are present in the discourses on the role of HE, access and equity, student mobility, student diversity, internationalization, and teaching and learning, all of which have a direct influence on HE policy development, institutional governance and ultimately on student experience.

The above background illustrates the complexity of the HE environment, the policy drivers and the likely impact on the experience of students. It has been argued that the growing interest in student experience is largely an outcome of marketization and commodification of HE within the globalization and internationalization agenda. The creation of a global market, based on the discourse of global competition, motivated primarily by economic and political interests, has encouraged institutions to embrace the marketplace and become customer-focused business enterprises (Currie, 1998, p. 15). This process has been supported by the neo-liberal ideology that has become the dominant paradigm over the last three decades of the twentieth century (Yang, 2003). Universities are therefore driven by 'student consumerism', where students are treated as customers whose satisfaction with the services offered is of paramount importance to the viability of the institutions (Cain *et al.*, 2004). While this is a dominant discourse in relation to the effects of globalization and internationalization on HE policy and practice, some argue that globalization is a reality that needs to be accepted, and condemning the process is futile. What is proposed therefore is to engage in an education that is responsive to the imperatives of contemporary globalization (Apple *et al.*, 2005).

It is, however, clear that the main purpose of university education policy has now shifted towards providing students with knowledge and skills to operate in a global labour market driven by the knowledge economy. This policy shift is supported and encouraged not only by universities but by world organizations such as the OECD, which has declared that international education is a cause, consequence and symptom of globalization. Furthermore, the OECD proactively promotes the new liberal assumptions and their preference for a global trend towards commodification, privatization and commercialization of education. In this process the social-efficiency goals of education take precedence over the traditional social and cultural development of the individual and the needs of the community (Rizvi, 2005). The policy shifts also demand changes in the university curricula to produce a new kind of worker with the ability to adapt to a changing labour market.

Current discourses, themes and issues regarding student experience

The aim of this section is to provide an overall perspective of how student experience is viewed and positioned in the discourses, themes and issues highlighted in the current literature. Four main discourses and associated themes and issues are discussed in this section: massification of HE; international student mobility and changing identities; growth of information and communication technologies (ICT); and teaching and learning.

Massification of higher education

The presence of a socially and culturally diverse student population in the HE sector, with different educational backgrounds and learning styles, is now a reality. It is estimated that the global demand for HE will reach 120 million by 2020 (Altbach *et al.*, 2001) with a continued increase in student diversity. For example, reports indicate that, by 2015, 80 per cent of US HE students will be non-white, of which half will be Hispanic, most of whose parents would not have had any education in American schools (Gürüz, 2008). This is a result of increased access, equity and widening participation in HE, a policy encouraged by respective governments and implemented by universities worldwide, based on the premise that education is a force for opportunity and social justice and not for the entrenchment of privilege. It is argued that massification of HE has been influenced by conservative ideology, which considers education a public good to be shared for the benefit of all members of society. In the US the process of massification started in the 1930s and in Europe in the late

1960s and 1970s, almost three decades later (Trow, 1972). Once confined to elite students, universities thus became learning institutions for students of different socio-economic and cultural backgrounds and this trend started to be replicated in other countries.

This widening participation in HE has made universities no longer restricted to 18- to 21-year-olds from privileged elite or middle-class families studying full-time. The profile of the student body is now complex, with an increasing number of 'earning and learning' students (Van der Wende, 2002), part-time, off-campus and distance education students. This trend is more visible in developed countries with the growth of knowledge economies. This has resulted in the rise of lifelong learners of all ages in the population, proactively encouraged by respective governments. The demographic shift and increased enrolment of non-traditional students have made and will continue to make an enormous impact on the university environment and student life and experience on campus.

A key challenge of this student diversity is coping with differences in the expectations of students in terms of their educational, social and economic goals, which appear to change with time and as a result of the changing environment. Scott (2005, p. 298) explains that 'students represent multifarious histories, expectations and responses; and these are continually being shaped and reshaped in an interaction of student agency with socio-culturally and politically formed pedagogic imperatives'. Other research has indicated that a lack of preparation for academic life and unrealistic student expectations, largely due to misleading or inadequate information on university courses, campus facilities and the social environment, are major barriers in the development of a positive student experience (Fearn, 2008). Managing student expectations with a provision of information on university life that fairly reflects what students can expect is considered critical in these circumstances.

The success of access and equity policies has been criticized by many researchers (see Jones *et al.* (2005) on UK Government policies) on the basis that the expansion of student enrolments has not been matched by corresponding increases in government funding and resources in universities, which then have been under pressure to seek finances from alternate sources. Private sector funding and international student recruitment, spurred by global demand for international HE which is expected to grow from 2.173 million students in 2005 to 3.720 million students in 2025, have become alternate sources of income for universities to bridge the financial gap. The reduction of government funding has also put pressure on students (and parents) to share some of the costs of their education, as reflected in the introduction of and increase in tuition fees, withdrawal of subsidies and introduction of student loans. As a consequence, students feel themselves to be 'customers' and demand 'value for money', and exert pressure on universities to deliver services to their satisfaction. These factors will have a significance influence on the mission of HE systems and institutions as well as on student experience.

International student mobility and changing identities

International student mobility is a direct response to globalization and the creation of the global knowledge economy. It is inextricably linked to the internationalization agenda and the growth of transnational HE. It could be argued that international student mobility is driven by neo-liberal ideology, which has promoted the global trend towards commodification, privatization, and commercialization of HE (Rizvi *et al.*, 2005). The dominant feature in student mobility is the movement towards 'knowledge producers' led by the West, particularly the US, from 'knowledge users' comprising the developing countries, particularly Asia, with major implications for the skilled labour market. This movement was supported by the migration policies of the 'knowledge-producing' countries, which were linked to skilled labour; hence the asymmetric flow of skilled labour from knowledge-user to knowledge-producer countries resulting in skill shortage in knowledge-user countries. This was in concert with neo-liberal ideology, and the competencies produced by student mobility and internationally oriented qualifications helped promote a professional labour market with huge benefits to knowledge-producing nations.

It is argued that internationalization of HE and student mobility have created opportunities for students to develop cosmopolitan experiences, intercultural skills and an international outlook which will serve them well for employment in the global knowledge economy. With exposure to new forms of learning and cultural environments, students are likely to reshape their self-identity and become 'travelling cultures' (Clifford, 1997) with the ability to adapt themselves to new cultural and economic environments. Rizvi (2005, p. 79) calls them mobile identities, 'linked more to their strategic interests within the emergent global economy and culture than to any broader moral conception'. In a recent article, Rizvi (forthcoming) argues that international students operate in transnational spaces of their own making, negotiating the spaces they inhabit in order to become transnational subjects and professional identities who are responsive to both the constraints and the possibilities of transnational flows and networks. This is an area of student experience that has not attracted much academic interest, resulting in a major gap in the international student experience literature.

Growth of Information and Communication Technologies (ICT)

The impact of advanced ICT on HE has been significant in changing the HE environment worldwide. This has had wide-ranging implications for teaching and learning, and the delivery of other support services to students. Equipping graduates to compete in the global knowledge economy is hailed as one of the major benefits of the use of advanced technology in teaching and learning. It is, however, acknowledged that there are significant challenges, as technology remains a disruptive innovation which requires large investments of time and money. Oblinger *et al.* (2001) provide a detailed account of the impact of technology on teaching and learning, as well as the challenges it presents to

HEIs. According to this research the emergence of hybrid environments blurs the line between classroom and online instructions. Similarly, 'distributed learning' and its subset, 'distance learning', has enabled the faculty and students to interact anywhere and anytime on or off campus. This has separated students in time and space from their peers and instructors, presenting a new and challenging learning experience for both staff and students, and resource implications for universities. Currently, more than half of the programmes offered in US HEIs are hybrid, and there has been a significant increase (up to 80 per cent) in students using mobile technology as a tool for learning (Zastrocky *et al.*, 2004). The younger generation of students is seen as e-literate, with higher computer skills and the ability to benefit from the ICT revolution. The concern, however, is whether the advances of ICT will be able to create a level playing field for all students, given the increasing diversity of the student population and their varying capabilities. This would be especially relevant to international students from developing countries where the use of ICT may be in its infancy. The application of ICT is also considered a cost-intensive proposition, given the investment required on a range of development activities such as website development, database management, graphic design, licensing of content, and student support services, which are increasingly being outsourced to private providers who use new ICT (GUNI, 2009).

There is also an ongoing debate as to whether the importance of traditional campuses will diminish over time, though the majority of educators worldwide seem to believe that pedagogically nothing can replace the 'human touch' or face-to-face interaction with students. (Oblinger *et al.*, 2001). It is clear, however, that ICT will continue to have an enormous impact on teaching and learning in universities and will also remain as a major driver of internationalization of HE.

Teaching and learning

There is a large volume of literature on teaching and learning in higher education, as academic quality is considered critical to the enhancement of student experiences in higher education. The discourses vary from student learning styles, teaching quality, curriculum, assessments and feedback to language skills.

The role of university teachers in enhancing the experience of international students is widely accepted and supported by many research findings (Trotter *et al.*, 2006; Tran, 2008). It has been argued that teachers remain the first port of call for international students in general and that the development of trust and confidence between students and teachers helps students connect with their university. Tran (2008) and Lacina (2002) have found lecturers play a significant role in enhancing the student experience through their close interaction and continuous dialogue with students. Biggs and Tang (2007) contend that teachers should focus on outcome-based approaches to student learning through constructive alignment and the development of assessment tasks aimed at the intended learning outcomes of students. With increasing workloads and demands for research outputs, higher education institutions must ensure that teachers are provided with adequate support and staff development opportunities to enable them to fulfil these responsibilities.

MacLean and Ransom (2006, p. 60) summarize the position succinctly:

> Academics have 'insider' knowledge; they are familiar with and understand academic conventions that few students new to university life do. In a culturally inclusive classroom, academics are aware of their culturally influenced teaching and learning styles and 'value add' their teaching by explicitly sharing this 'insider' knowledge with their students. Culturally aware teaching is also about observing and understanding students as individuals and exploring their responses rather than judging them by ethnocentric standards.

Understanding how students learn is critical to the improvement of student learning and teaching in an environment of increasing diversity of the student population in HEIs all over the world. This student diversity is manifested in the demographic, cultural and educational backgrounds and also the changing expectations of students. One of the major pedagogical challenges is the diversity in learning styles and study approaches of students influenced by prior learning backgrounds (Prosser *et al.*, 1999; Ramsden, 2003; Biggs *et al.*, 2007). The literature makes it quite clear that teachers and university administrators must have a good understanding of the learning background, expectations and aspirations of all of their students in order to implement successful strategies in this respect. Many universities have developed research programmes and tools to measure student experience, and engagement and satisfaction in teaching and learning, in order seek insights into strategies to enhance student experience among students. A major concern, however, in these research programmes is that the methodologies adopted are primarily quantitative. While they are suitable for comparing and evaluating different benchmarks and performances of teaching and learning, it is debatable whether quantitative methods are able to capture the feelings and complexities of student experience better than qualitative research approaches.

Two major discourses in relation to teaching and learning concern the feasibility of adapting teaching to suit different audiences and the learning experiences of international students, both of which have their origins in student diversity. The debate centres on the extent to which adaptation should occur, though there is consensus among researchers that a strong alignment with different learning approaches is necessary and that it could be achieved through changes to curricula and how they are delivered (Smith, 2002). It is neither realistic nor necessary to accommodate a customer-oriented model to suit all learning styles (Egege *et al.*, 2008), but some other researchers suggest that there are opportunities for 'congruent customization', where a range of teaching styles is used to address variation in learning approaches (De Vita, 2001). Biggs *et al.* (2007) suggest that the curricula should be adaptive in their structure to allow students to negotiate their learning objectives, preferred learning styles and methods of assessment. This validates the notion that there are no differences in the cognitive capacity of the individual, irrespective of the culture to which the individual belongs.

This approach demands a high degree of integration across subjects within a course and a better understanding of how cultural background influences the development of individual learning style preferences and how educational institutions utilize this information to diversify delivery methods (De Vita, 2001). The question, therefore, is how much do we know about students and how do current recruitment strategies in HEIs enable such enlightened approaches?

The second discourse in teaching and learning is in relation to international students of Asian origin, who are the major drivers of demand for international education worldwide. The debate has centred on the cultural deficiency approach and cultural proficiency approach. The basic premise of the cultural deficiency approach is that many international students come with learning experiences which favour rote, reproductive, surface, teacher-centred and dependent approaches which are inappropriate in Western education systems. This has given rise to negative stereotypes (see Samuelowicz, 1987; Ballard *et al.*, 1997) which have been challenged by more recent research (Tran, 2008; Ninnes *et al.*, 1999). A major criticism is that the cultural deficit approach misrepresents the learning background of international students and also makes the mistake of treating all international students from Asia as a homogeneous group, ignoring differences among individual students and the education systems in different Asian countries (Chalmers *et al.*, 1997). The cultural proficiency approach is an upshot of these perceptions, supported by the works of researchers like Biggs (1987) and Chalmers *et al.* (1997), who argue that learners from Confucian cultures are not passive or rote learners, but are active and strive to achieve a deep understanding of the course content. For example, it has been argued that repetition is a learning strategy (incorrectly interpreted as rote learning) adopted by students from Chinese heritage cultures to internalize well-understood material and to enable accurate recall of such material. Biggs (1996) contends that in this case repetition becomes a deep learning strategy. The problems with the cultural deficit approach have also been confirmed in a study of Indian students (Ninnes *et al.*, 1999).

Stereotyping can be avoided by a good understanding of who your students are. Osland and Bird (2000) argue that, while sophisticated stereotyping is helpful to a certain degree (such as Hofstede's five dimensions of cultures), 'generalization' should be treated with 'scepticism'. Culture is not a static reality; rather it is a dynamic and multifaceted phenomenon and in an era of constant change, generalization has limited utility (Putnis *et al.*, 1996, p. 74). Wang (2008, p. 11) recommends that Western academics, instead of 'regarding themselves as the privileged holders of Western ideas who can impose radical prescriptions for the situations in developing countries', should develop their intercultural competence and intercultural learning to become flexible reflectors and commit themselves to catering to the needs of learners from different cultures.

Summary and conclusion

Student experience in the current globalized HE market continues to be of a significant focus for universities. Increasing student mobility, student diversity, emergence of ICT, the lack of public funding and the trend towards massification and commodification of education have placed HE institutions under enormous pressure to deliver services to the satisfaction of their stakeholders. Students remain the main stakeholders and student satisfaction is a critical link to competitive advantage for these institutions. With the pressure for increasing student enrolments and decreasing student attrition, the emphasis placed on positive student experience has become much greater.

This chapter discussed four main discourses, themes and issues identified in the literature on student experience. It also highlighted future research imperatives, having established several gaps in current literature to ensure a better understanding of the expectations and aspirations of students to optimize their experiences in the globalized HE environment.

A major issue discussed in this chapter is the importance of understanding our students better in order to provide them with a positive student experience. Student experience varies depending on students' background, degree of engagement with learning activities and other social and cultural factors. Therefore there is an urgent need for a better understanding of their cultural, social and prior educational backgrounds, expectations and aspirations without 'generalizations' or stereotyping of their abilities and behaviour. Ensuring a positive student experience is a responsibility of all stakeholders in HE: senior administrators, academic and non-academic staff, the media, local community and also students themselves. It is necessary that university staff and students are trained in cross-cultural awareness and understanding to operate successfully in this highly diverse and dynamic HE environment.

An understanding of student expectations before and after they enter HE and how these expectations change over time and influence their perceptions of the learning environment is also critical. Undertaking such longitudinal studies will provide insights into the dynamics of student experience and enable these experiences to be viewed in a holistic manner, linking to other aspects of student life. This has relevance to the strategic interest of universities to allocate more resources to enhance the first year experience of university students. While such a focus on the early stages of the student life cycle is considered logical, the fragmentary attention given to student services in the latter stages of student life is extremely risky. This is because student experience is subject to constant change, given the changing expectations and priorities of students coupled with the transformation of student identity over time. University strategies therefore need to be more comprehensive and progressive.

Research has also indicated that lack of preparation for academic life and unrealistic student expectations, influenced largely by either misleading or inadequate information on academic courses, campus facilities and the social environment, are major barriers to the development of positive student experience (Fearn, 2008). Student satisfaction is the barometer of service quality in education and contributes to benefits such as student retention, positive word-of-mouth communication and competitive advantage. It is incumbent, therefore, on universities to manage student expectations through the provision of timely information on academic life that accurately reflects what students may expect.

It is clear that the extant literature is focused narrowly on the social and psychological concerns of the student body, and teaching and learning in formal settings. Little or no attention is paid to other support services or experience constructed in informal settings that would be critical to a greater understanding of student experience. For example, an extensive literature review undertaken by the UK Higher Education Academy on student experience since 1992 has confirmed that only 14 out of 278 studies dealt with student experience related to non-academic support services (Ertl *et al.*, 2008). An analysis of the most recent literature on student experience, based on research papers in major journals published since 2006, has also indicated that this trend seems to be continuing as less than 2 per cent of these studies made any reference to non-academic support services. This highlights that it is a neglected area in contemporary research (see Table 11.1).

Another area addressed in this chapter focused on the dominance of quantitative methodologies used in research studies related to student experience. While quantitative research approaches are useful in testing hypotheses and making statistical evaluations, it is debatable whether they can provide the best insights into students' feelings. Qualitative research approaches, on the other hand, are considered more appropriate in these circumstances because they can capture the nuances and complexities of student experiences. It will therefore be necessary to review the existing methodological frameworks with greater emphasis on qualitative analysis of student experience and make use of methods that are able to explain the mediated and contextualized nature of learning, as well as social and organizational aspects of learning from a qualitative angle.

As highlighted in this chapter, a gap in student experience literature also exists in relation to the experience of postgraduate students, as most research studies on student experience focus on undergraduate students, and particularly on their first-year experience. Postgraduate students are different from undergraduates; more mature, older and educated, with greater life experience. Their experiences are embedded in different academic traditions, such as training in research. Their expectations of university life are vastly different from those of undergraduates. Given the upsurge in enrolments of postgraduate students in universities in recent years, direction of more research into the postgraduate sector of HE is therefore required.

Another major gap in literature addressed in this chapter was related to student experience beyond graduation, such as changing student identities, cosmopolitan experiences and the development of intercultural skills needed to function effectively in the global knowledge economy. Current HE systems are based on training competitive human resources, but this objective falls short of the purpose of university education to prepare students to develop resources of courage, resilience and empathy that would allow them to negotiate the challenges of becoming a global citizen with a strong sense of social responsibility. In this context, universities need to provide an experience that

Table 11.1 Recent literature on student experience (from 2006 to the present)

Author/date	Study area	Research design	Sampling strategy	Sample frame	Sample size	Key findings	Limitations of the study
Henderson (2009)	Learning environment and student experience	Exploratory semi-structured interviews	Non-probability Purposive	Students in a UK University	52	Internationalization of curricula Use of English	Single university
Turner (2009)	Cross-cultural teaching	Case study approach Students' commentaries	Non-probability	International students in a UK university	66	Challenges affecting group work in a cross-cultural setting Cultural stereotyping English language issue Teaching redesign options	Business school students only
Nieto *et al.* (2009)	Cultural competence	Survey approach Interviews	Probability (Stratified sampling)	International students taking ESL classes in a Midwest US university	112	Cultural competence on teaching and learning process Cross-cultural competence Significant differences in language and culture	International students in ESL classes only Sample is gender imbalanced

Author/date	Study area	Research design	Sampling strategy	Sample frame	Sample size	Key findings	Limitations of the study
Brown *et al.* (2008)	Adjustment of international postgraduate students	Ethnographic approach, participant observation and depth interviews	Non-probability Purposive	International postgraduate students at a university in the south of England	150	Positive and negative feelings in the adjustment process All experienced homesickness Inability to cope with challenges of adjustment journey Cultural shock Growth in intercultural competence	Postgraduate students only One UK university
Merali (2008)	Attitudes and experiences of MBA students	Longitudinal survey	Non-probability	MBA students	71	Differences in attitudes and experiences	One university in UK
Grayson (2008)	Outcomes of domestic and international students	Descriptive Research Survey Approach	Census	International and domestic students at four Canadian universities	4872	Higher academic involvement of international students than domestic students International students experience less social and academic support	Canadian universities only Academic related variables only

(continued)

Table 11.1 (*cont.*)

Author/date	Study area	Research design	Sampling strategy	Sample frame	Sample size	Key findings	Limitations of the study
Johnson (2008)	An investigation into pedagogical challenges	Case study Direct observation Interviews	Convenience-sampling	Lecturers and EAL students at an NZ university	25	Perceived challenges; language, academic literacy, use of technology tools in learning, bridging linguistic and pedagogical expectations	One faculty Small sample size
Tran (2008)	Academic performance	Case study Interviews	N/A	International students	N/A	Academic expectations in writing, interaction with academics, faculty support services	Four Chinese students only One university
Campbell et al. (2008)	UG students	Qualitative Interviews	Non-probability Purposive	Business students of Asian origin in NZ	22	Positive learning experiences Gain independence Acquire new skills English language main barrier Cultural differences	Business undergraduates only Asian origin
Sawir et al. (2007)	International students	Qualitative Interviews	Probability Sampling	International students on shore in Australia	200	65 per cent experienced loneliness or isolation Personal and cultural loneliness Causes for loneliness were identified –age/gender	Nine Australian universities only

Author/date	Study area	Research design	Sampling strategy	Sample frame	Sample size	Key findings	Limitations of the study
Trice *et al.* (2007)	Academic experiences	Survey	Purposive	International Graduate students	497	Positive overall experience Negative curriculum Predictors of PG plans	One US university
Kim (2007)	Doctoral students	Exploratory Research Case study approach Interviews	Probability	Doctoral students from public university in the US	9	Need for strong and supportive academic advising relationships Difficulties in student-advisor relationships Insufficient English skills	Male Korean students
Trotter *et al.* (2006)	Enhancing the early student experience	Case study Interviews	Purposive sampling	Programme managers within a UK university	20	Maximizing student retention and optimizing achievement Student experience and retention	One UK university
Deardorff (2006)	Assessment of Intercultural Competence	Two stages Survey Delphi technique	Cluster sampling	Post-secondary institutions Administrators Scholars	100	Identified 22 elements of intercultural competence Two models of intercultural competence	Sample size and selection
Robertson *et al.* (2006)	Students' experiences of learning in a research environment	Exploratory Research Interviews	Non-probability	Students studying at an NZ university	34	Satisfaction in studying in a research environment.	One NZ university One aspect of student experience

will enable students to successfully interact with society, build intercultural relationships and give them the ability to deal with new technology. More research
is therefore required to investigate how student experiences of mobility, transition and travel, as well as formal learning, shift perceptions of their identity,
and of their own cultures, on the one hand, and the emergent global culture
on the other. This would entail research into cross-cultural pedagogy, cultural
sensitivity and awareness, and cultural dissonance (Tsolidis, 2001; Allan, 2003,
Rizvi, 2005). This area of research will be of great value to universities, enabling
them to understand their student bodies better and to formulate appropriate
policies to make university experiences more memorable for students.

References

Allan, M. (2003), 'Frontier crossings: Cultural dissonance, intercultural learning and
    the multicultural personality', *Journal of Research in International Education*, 2, (1),
    83–110.

Altbach, P. G. and Teichler, U. (2001), 'Internationalization and exchanges in a
    globalized university', *Journal of Studies in International Education*, 5, (1), 5–25.

Anderson, R. E. (1973), 'Consumer dissatisfaction: The effect of disconfirmed
    expectancy on perceived product performance', *Journal of Marketing Research*, 10
    (February), 38–44.

Apple, M. W., Kenway, J. and Singh, M. (eds) (2005), *Globalizing Education: Policies,
    Pedagogies and Politics*, New York, Peter Lang.

Ballard, B. and Clanchy, J. (1997), *Teaching International Students*. Canberra: IDP
    Education.

Biggs, J. B. (1987), *Student Approaches to Learning and Studying*. Camberwell, Vic.:
    Australian Council for Educational Research.

—— (1996), 'Enhancing teaching through constructive alignment', *Higher Education*,
    32, (3), 347–64.

Biggs, J. and Tang, C. (2007), *Teaching for Quality Learning at University*, Maidenhead:
    Open University Press/McGraw Hill.

Blodgett, J. G., Hill, D. J. and Tax, S, S. (1997), 'The effects of distributive, procedural
    and interactional justice on postcomplaint behaviour', *Journal of Retailing*, 73, (2),
    185–210.

Blythman, M. and Orr, S. (2003), 'A joined-up policy approach to student
    support', in M. Peelo and T. Wareham (eds), *Failing Students in Higher Education*.
    Buckingham, UK: SRHE/Open University Press, pp. 45–55.

Brown, L and Holloway, I. (2008), The adjustment journey of international post
    graduate students at an English University, *Journal of Research in International
    Education*, 7, (2) 232–49.

Campbell, J. and Li, M. (2008), Asian Students' Voices: An Empirical Study of Asian
    Students' Learning Experience at a New Zealand University, *Journal of Studies in
    International Education*, 12, (4), 375–96

Cain, J. and Hewitt, J. (2004), *Off Course: From Public Place to Marketplace at Melbourne
    University*. Melbourne: Scribe.

Chalmers, D. and Volet, S. (1997), 'Common misconceptions about students from
    South-East Asia studying in Australia', *High Education Research and Development*, 16,
    87–98.

Clifford, J. (1997), *Routes: Travel and Translation in the Late Twentieth Century*.
    Cambridge, MA: Harvard University Press.

Currie, J. (1998), 'Globalization practices and the professoriate in Anglo-Pacific and North American universities', *Comparative Education Review*, 42, (1), 15–29.

Deardorff, D. K. (2006), 'Identification and assessment of intercultural competence as a student outcome of internationalization', *Journal of Studies in International Education*, 10, (3), 241–66.

De Vita, G. (2001), 'Learning styles, culture and inclusive instruction in the multicultural classroom: A business and management perspective', *Innovations in Education and Teaching International*, 38, (2), 165–74.

Egege, S. and Kutieleh, S. (2008) 'Dimming down difference' in Dunn, L. and Wallace M. (Eds), *Teaching in Transnational Higher Education: Enhancing Learning for Offshore International Students*. New York and London: Routledge, 67–76.

Ertl, H., Hayward, G., Wright, S., Edwards, A., Lunt, I., Mills, D. and Yu, K. (2008), *The Student Learning Experience in Higher Education: Literature Review Report for the Higher Education Academy*. Higher Education Academy, UK.

Fearn, H. (2008), 'Living the dream', *Times Higher Education*, 11–17 September, 1, (862), UK.

Global University Network for Innovation (GUNI) (2009), *Synthesis of the GUNI Higher Education in the World Reports*, Basingstoke: Palgrave MacMillan.

Grayson, J. P. (2008), 'The experiences and outcomes of domestic and international students at four Canadian Universities', *Journal of Higher Education Research and Development*, 27,(3), 215–30.

Guolla, M. (1999), 'Assessing the teaching quality to student satisfaction relationship: Applied customer satisfaction research in the classroom', *Journal of Marketing Theory and Practice*, 7, (3), 87–97.

Gürüz, K. (2008), *Higher Education and International Student Mobility in the Global Knowledge Economy*. Albany: State University of New York Press.

Henderson, J. (2009), 'It's all about give and take, or is it? Where, when and how do native and non-native uses of English shape UK university students' representations of each other and their learning experience?', *Journal of Studies in International Education*, 13, (3), 398–409.

Johnson, E. M. (2008), 'An investigation into pedagogical challenges facing international tertiary-level students in New Zealand', *Journal of Higher Education Research and Development*, 27, (3), pp. 231–43.

Jones, R. and Thomas, L. (2005), 'The 2003 UK Government Higher Education White Paper: A critical assessment of its implications for the access and widening participation agenda', *Journal of Education Policy*, 20, (5), 615–30.

Kim, Y. (2007), 'Difficulties in quality doctoral academic advising', *Journal of Research in International Education*, 6, (2), 171–93.

Lacina, J. G. (2002), 'Preparing international students for a successful social experience in higher education', *New Directions for Higher Education*, 117, (1), 21–7.

McInnis, C., James, R. and Hartley, R. (2000), *Trends in the First Year Experience in Australian Universities*. Canberra: AGPS.

MacLean, P. and Ransom, L. (2006), 'Building intercultural competencies: Implications for academic skills development', in J. Ryan, and J. Caroll (eds), *Teaching International Students: Improving Learning for All*. London: Routledge, Chapter 6.

Merali, F. (2008), Exploring the different attitudes and experiences of UK domiciled versus international MBA students towards peer assessment. Paper presented at the Higher Education Academy Annual Conference, July, Harrogate, UK.

Nieto, C. and Booth, M. Z. (2009), 'Cultural competence: Its influence on the teaching and learning of international students', *Journal of Studies in International Education*, 20, (10), 1–20.

Ninnes, P., Aitchison, C. and Kalos, S. (1999), 'Challenges to stereotypes of international students' prior educational experience: Undergraduate education in India', *Journal of Higher Education Research and Development*, 18, (3), 323–42.

Oblinger, D. G., Barone, C. A. and Hawkins, B. L. (2001), 'Distributed education and its challenges: An overview', from www.acenet.edu/AM/Template.cfm?Section= Search&section=reports2&template=/CM/ContentDisplay. cfm&ContentFileID=5066, accessed 22 September 2009.

Oliver, R. L. and DeSarbo, W. S. (1988), 'Response determinants in satisfaction judgments', *Journal of Consumer Research*, 14, (March), 495–507.

Osland, J. S. and Bird, A. (2000), 'Beyond sophisticated stereotyping: Cultural sensemaking in context', *Academy of Management Executive*, 14, (1), 65–77.

Prosser, M. and Trigwell, K. (1999), *Understanding Learning and Teaching: The Experience in Higher Education*. Buckingham, UK: Society for Research into Higher Education/Open University Press.

Putnis, P. and Petelin, R. (1996), *Professional Communication: Principles and Applications*. Sydney: Prentice Hall.

Ramsden, P. (2003), *Learning to Teach in Higher Education* (2nd edn), London: RoutledgeFalmer.

Rizvi, F. (2005), 'International education and the production of cosmopolitan identities', *RIHE International Publication Series*, 9, 77–92.

—— (forthcoming), 'International students and doctoral studies in transnational spaces' in P. Thompson and M. Walker (eds), (2010) *A Companion of Doctoral Studies*. London: Routledge.

Rizvi, F., Engel, L., Nandyala, A., Rutkowski, D. and Sparks, J. (2005), 'Globalisation and recent shifts in educational policy in the Asia Pacific: An overview of some critical issues', UNESCO, Bangkok, Occasional Paper Series APEID, Paper 4.

Robertson, J. and Blackler, G. (2006), 'Students' experiences of learning in a research environment', *Journal of Higher Education Research and Development*, 25, (3), 215–29.

Ryan, J. and Carroll, J. (eds) (2005), *Teaching International Students: Improving Learning For All*. London: Routledge.

Samuelowicz, K. (1987), 'Learning problems of overseas students: Two sides of a story', *Journal of Higher Education Research and Development*, 6, (2), 121–33.

Sawir, E., Marginson, S., Deumert, A., Nyland, C. and Ramia, G. (2007), 'Loneliness and international students: An Australian study', *Journal of Studies in International Education*, 20, (10), 1–33.

Scott, G. (2005), *Assessing the Student Voice*. Report to the Federal Government, University of Sydney.

Smith, J. (2002), 'Learning styles: Fashion fad or lever for change? The application of learning style theory to inclusive curriculum delivery', *Innovations in Education and Teaching International*, 39, (1), 63–70.

Strange, S. (1996), *The Retreat of the State: The Diffusion of Power in the World Economy*. Cambridge: Cambridge University Press.

Tinto, V. (1989), 'Dropout from higher education: A theoretical synthesis of recent research', *Review of Educational Research*, 45, (1), 89–125.

—— (1996), 'Reconstructing the first year of college', *Planning for Higher Education*, 25, (1), 1–6.

Townley, P. (2001), 'The construction of a model of qualitative evaluation to support the development of the policy and practice of raising student satisfaction in an institution in the higher education sector', Conference proceedings, Higher Education Close Up Conference 2, Lancaster University, UK, 16–18 July.

Tran, L. T. (2008), 'Unpacking academic requirements: International students in management and education disciplines', *Journal of Higher Education Research and Development*, 27, (3), 245–56.

Trice, A. G. and Yoo, J. E. (2007), 'International graduate students' perceptions of their academic experience', *Journal of Research in International Education*, 6, (1), 41–66.

Trotter, E. and Roberts, C. A. (2006), 'Enhancing the early student experience', *Journal of Higher Education Research and Development*, 25, (4), 371–86.

Trow, M. (1972), 'The expansion and transformation of higher education', *International Review of Education*, 18, (1), 61–3.

Tsolidis, G. (2001), 'New cultures, new classrooms: International education and the possibility of radical pedagogies', *Pedagogy, Culture and Society*, 9, (1), 97–110.

Turner, Y. (2009), '"Knowing me, knowing you, is there nothing we can do?" Pedagogic challenges in using group work to create an intercultural learning', *Journal of Studies in International Education*, 13, (2), (Summer), 240–55.

US Department of Education (2008), *Digest of Educational Statistics 2008: Post Secondary Education*, from http://nces.ed.gov/programs/digest/d08, accessed 26 October 2009.

Van der Wende, M. C. (2002), 'The role of US higher education in the global e-learning market', Research and Occasional Paper Series, CSHE, at http://cshe.berkeley.edu/Publications/Papers/ROP.WendePaper1.02.pdf.

Wang, T. (2008), 'Intercultural dialogue and understanding: Implications for teachers' in L. Dunn and M. Wallace (eds), *Teaching in Transnational Higher Education: Enhancing Learning for Offshore International Students*. New York and London: Routledge, 7–65.

Yang, R. (2003), 'Globalisation and higher education development: A critical analysis', *International Review of Education*, 49, (3–4), 269–91.

Zastrocky, M., Yanosky, R. and Harris, M. (2004), 'E-learning in higher education: A quiet revolution', at http:www.gartner.com (accessed 26 October 2009).

Chapter 12

Course Reorientation to Enhance Chinese Students' International Awareness

Dianmin Wang

Introduction

This chapter presents a case study of a graduate English course designed to offer selected readings of classical works from both Eastern and Western civilizations, with a view to helping students to recognize cultural differences and enhance international awareness by comparative study. While it was reported that '[t]he international dimension of higher education is a topic of intense interest and debate in this first decade of the twenty-first century' (Knight, 2003, p. 1), discussion of curricular development is rare. Nanjing University, a Chinese research university, has explicitly set out to become a first rate institution by means of internationalization of its education. Currently, one important part of its endeavour is to redesign general education by internationalizing the curriculum and to prepare the students to work competently in the international context. In response to the new international dimension, the graduate English course, a compulsory course which has always concentrated on linguistic knowledge, needs to be reconstructed to be geared to both the call of the institution and the demand of the state. Under such circumstances the selected reading of classic works is offered to try it out on a small scale. Our aim is to find out whether the course can make a difference to students' recognition of East-West cultural roots or origins that underlie the divergence in thinking and ideology, thereby forming international awareness and shedding any provincialism they might have. The chapter describes action research into what happens on the one-semester course – the decision to offer the course, students' initial reactions, modifications of the pedagogical methods, results and conclusions.

Background of the curricular reform

There is a national consensus among the Chinese that globalization is an irreversible and sweeping trend, independent of the will of any individual man. The state leaders were wise and far-sighted enough to view it as an opportunity for China to catch up with developed countries and uplift the nation, and therefore in the late 1970s instituted the Open Door Policy and the economic reform which has since continuously added momentum to English learning.

The impact of globalization on education made itself felt as early as 1983, when Deng Xiaoping wrote: 'Orient education towards modernization, the outside world and the future' (Adamson, 2004, p. 156). In the mid-1990s the Ministry of Education of the People's Republic of China (MEPRC) issued 'The 9th 5-Year Plan for China's Educational Development and the Development Outline by 2010' which made clear 'the strategy of developing China through science, technology and education to accelerate economic and social progress' (MEPRC, 1995). In terms of higher education, curriculum in the 1990s changed from having emphasis on reading and translation, which aimed to 'prepare an educated elite to play a pioneering role in economic modernization in the context of the Open Door Policy' (Adamson, 2004, p. 150), to improvement in communication skills and cross-cultural awareness. For example, the Education Law of the People's Republic of China (ELPRC) passed in 1995 stipulates that '[e]ducation shall be carried out in the spirit of inheriting and expanding the fine historical and cultural traditions of the Chinese nation and assimilating all the fine achievements of the civilization progress of human beings' (ELPRC, 1995). Both the state and the institutions encourage, at least in principle, diverse international academic cooperation, including joint research projects as well as mobility and exchange of scholars and students, and even support financially, if conditions permit, bilingual education using the latest foreign textbooks.

Against this background, at Nanjing University the issue was raised of transforming the graduate English course from a linguistic to a cultural focus. Several factors account for the decision. From the broader national perspective, the Chinese economy, which depends to a large extent upon transactions and cooperation with foreigners, is demanding an increasing amount of manpower able to work in cross-cultural contexts. English therefore has assumed almost the same status as that of the mother tongue, Chinese, and is taught in China from primary school all the way to doctoral education. The direct consequence is that students have learned English for over a decade by the time they start their postgraduate study, unlike their predecessors, who had little formal learning back in the late 1970s when graduate English was made a compulsory course. Although much weight is given to English, students feel less motivated to continue learning and hope to spend more time and effort on more marketable knowledge and skills so that they can secure better paid jobs. As Zhao and Campbell observe, most Chinese learners of English are motivated not by 'international communication', but by the desire 'for social and economic mobility' (Bolton, 2003, p. 250). They even openly complain that one more semester of English study is a waste of time for the class; it seems to them they are simply repeating what they have done for years. The predominant language orientation in the English class must change if it is to appeal to students. In brief, the booming economy, growing interaction with the international academic community and handsomely paid jobs at multinational corporations necessitate a reorientation of tertiary English towards communicative competence and cross-cultural knowledge.

The local reality helps shape the pathway of curricular reform. In their efforts to build a world-class higher education institution, the strategy planners at Nanjing University understand that a global view of its mission – aimed at placing the institution at the forefront of international academic research and training qualified talent competent to work in the international context – is crucial if its education set-up is to adapt to the demands of a new era characterized by irresistible globalization. It follows that internationalization should be implemented as an effective and reasonable strategy to achieve this goal, and both faculty and students be encouraged to participate in international academic activities.

Formulation of the course

Culture, as a broad concept, has more than a hundred definitions and its functions, especially in language learning, have been adequately discussed (Samovar *et al.*, 1998; Scollon *et al.*, 1995; Hall, 2002; Gudykunst, 2003). 'The teaching of pragmatic conventions tied to the grammatical and lexical structures of communicative acts such as greetings, requests, refusals, apologies, complaints, and so on, became an important feature of the teaching of culture' (Kumaravadivelu, 2008, p. 176). But it is obviously improper to teach this so-called superficial culture to graduate students, for today's ever-increasing cultural exchange and widespread mass media provide students with sufficient opportunities to access these aspects of foreign culture and they have also learned a good deal about them in their previous language classes. I am inclined to agree with Goodenough, who 'defines culture not as things or behavior but rather as the forms of things that people have in mind, their models for perceiving, relating, and otherwise interpreting them' (Gudykunst, 2003, p. 260). Goddard (2004) indicates that an important task of second language (L2) teaching is to 'to bring the learner to an understanding of those L2 concepts and values which form the interpretative frame within which L2 individuals negotiate meaning' (p. 146). Slattery (1995) states that:

> Curriculum development in the postmodern era emphasizes discourses that promote understanding of the cultural, historical, political, ecological, aesthetic, theological, and autobiographical impact of the curriculum on the human condition, social structures, and the ecosphere rather than the planning, design, implementation, and evaluation of context-free and value-neutral schooling events and trivial information. (p. 152)

On the students' side, poor language competence on one hand and lack of motivation on the other make it necessary to redesign the English class. Surveys shows that they are in favour of learning more about Western culture, which coincides with our intention to reorient the English class from purely linguistic-focused learning to content-based cultural study. Coleman (1998) states that '[s]tudies of the motivation of university language learners invariably show the importance of an interest in the foreign people and their culture' (p. 46).

It was then decided that classic works should be the source of course material for the new class. The underlying reason was that the thinking and behaviour of Chinese is in a large part determined by 'Chinese traditional cultural beliefs' (Lixian *et al.*, 1998, p. 107); for the West, the great classic works are also thought of as being the foundation of Western culture and providing a practical guide for students' lives and to the issues of the present time (Bloom, 2007; Ford, 1994; Levin, 2004). Since this was a novel attempt that transcended traditional English learning, I decided to adopt action research because we were 'in continual need of revision, in their [our] thoughts and actions' (Noffke *et al.*, 1995, p. 4). A major part of the research was to steer the students towards concentrating on the course objectives by means of arousing their interest and motivation.

Initial planning of the course

As the traditional graduate English course is just a one-semester course and there is no consensus as to the exact works that are regarded as the great books or the canon (Ford, 1994, p. 13), I could not be too ambitious and provide students with a complete list of works. Rather, what I could strive to achieve was to help them gain some insight into the differences between the Eastern and Western traditions in order to develop their cross-cultural awareness and cultivate a critical mind. It was therefore clear that I had to be highly selective in deciding on the works to be included. With the help of the programme's leading researcher, Professor Hongshia Zhang, it was decided to single out certain topics of interest to students and choose books that dwell upon those topics. The topics included were justice, friendship, education, religion and social evolution; the relevant sections containing these topics were extracted from both Chinese and Western works that included *The Republic, Nicomachean Ethics, Emile, The Protestant Ethic and the Spirit of Capitalism, Democracy* and *Education* from the Western canon, and *The Analects, Mencius, Great Learning, Zhong Yong* or *The Great Mean, Dao Te Jing* from the Chinese classics. The Chinese extracts contain both the English versions and the original Chinese texts, for the sake of facilitating references to the original, since the highly condensed and obscure classical Chinese often permits different interpretations and translations.

The participant students were deliberately chosen from a variety of disciplines ranging from Chinese, law and information management, to medical science, electronics and physics, representing humanities, social sciences and science. We wanted to see if there would be any disciplinary difference in terms of the effect of the course on the students.

First cycle: implementation of the course

As cultural transformation is not to be realized 'by passively receiving and accepting cultural information that emanates from various vested interests' (Kumaravadivelu, 2008, p. 181), one of the primary concerns was the motivation of the students. Stipek states 'that decision about the nature of the tasks, how performance is evaluated, how rewards are used, how much autonomy students have, and myriad other variables under a teacher's control largely determine student motivation' (Dornyei, 2005, p. 106). The shift from a conventional English class to a cultural orientation made it necessary to inform students of the course objectives and requirements with a view to stimulating them and eliminating any possible resistance. In the first class, therefore, I gave the following introduction.

Course description: This course looks at some topics – justice, friendship, education, religion and capitalism – with a contrastive and critical view. The course will explore the East-West difference on those issues and encourage students to apply the ideas to analyzing certain aspects of our life and the modern world. The course aims at not only improving students' English proficiency, but at developing their analytical ability as well as cultural awareness for a better intellectual life.

Course requirement: As the class is designed to be student-centred and encourages cooperative learning, students are supposed to be active participants.

1   They should be well prepared when they attend the class. By reading beforehand, they need to show, in the classroom, their understanding and evaluation of the ideas in the text. The class will take the form of presentation, discussion, and debate. The teacher provides necessary information, raises questions and provides help if need be.
2   Everyone must have delivered at least four in-class speeches and written assignments respectively. The final score is divided into two parts, one is the student's overall performance during the semester; the second is the final exam at the end of the semester. The final exam is made up of two parts – presentation and term paper.
3   Their performance will be recorded as part of their final score. Students must follow their tutor's instructions. They must take class oral activities seriously and hand in written homework on time, as these will make a difference in their score.

Although it might have been expected to be a recondite philosophy class, I expected students to play a major role and set forth student-centredness. As Slattery (1995) states, 'Postmodern hermeneutics affirms the primacy of subjective understanding over objective knowledge and conceives of understanding as an ontological (study of being) problem rather than an epistemological (study of knowledge) problem' (p. 106). I thus required them to work hard and actively participate in class discussions if they desired to achieve substantive intellectual gains in addition to improving their English; to which there was no objection. In fact, the students predictably applauded the reorientation and showed willingness to do what was demanded of them. Indeed, they came to the class with anticipation of this 'fresh air' sweeping away the stale smell of the dull repetition of what they had done for so long. Even so, I still had worries in the beginning, the major one being their inadequate English competence to deal with the difficult task of reading obscure philosophical texts.

As mentioned above, the class was planned to be student-centred through a communicative approach; that is, the students should be prepared to discuss the content of the texts and offer their opinions about the issues raised by the teacher, whereas the teacher conducts the class discussion and helps students with their English if necessary. The first couple of weeks went on as normal. Students dutifully read the texts and prepared for their class speech. But their speeches were mostly simple lists of the ideas found in the texts, with skin-deep comments. There was no telling whether or not they had contemplated what they had read and come to a personal understanding. This was less than what I had hoped for. Before I made any improvements, however, more serious problems were to arise.

Problems and resistance

Not surprisingly, none of the students had previously read the works and most of them had hardly thought seriously on the issues pertaining to the course topics. Their excitement soon waned as both the language and the content were more than what they could manage with ease. They complained that the language was hard to understand and that they felt nervous to speak in class, knowing that their speeches and performance would be recorded and counted as part of the final score. As each class was made up of approximately fifty students from varying departments, they felt under pressure to speak yet reluctant to volunteer. To play safe, they used in their speeches quotations from the original with superficial comment – the 'Yes, I agree to it' or 'No, I disagree with it' sort of response. Worse still, they felt rather humiliated when they had to inform the teacher of their name after their speech for the teacher to keep a record. The written homework, which I had assumed would be well thought out, turned out to be mostly quotations from the original with minor personal comments or assessments, just as their speeches had been. Inquiry revealed that they were overwhelmed by the sheer amount of reading and the formidable nature of the texts; besides, as they all had a full schedule interspersed with experiments and off-class talks in other courses, it was virtually impossible for them to find sufficient time to make an in-depth study of the material. It came as no surprise that they carried out the assignment in an expeditious fashion and simply gave superficial comments.

Three weeks later I made a major pedagogical change, devoting most of the class hour to textual explanation, leaving presentations to off-class discussions. My intention was to allow them to spend more time 'digesting' what they 'devoured' in class by arriving at a personal understanding and applying the ideas to an analysis of the real world. To ease their tension during presentations, they proposed to work in groups and deliver speeches collectively instead of individually, to which I readily agreed. This arrangement had an added advantage; namely the brainstorm provided opportunities for them to pool their thinking and produce better results than previously expected.

The following discussion session, however, did not turn out as I anticipated. One reason was that the groups were poorly organized; group members were not explicitly assigned specific tasks and they had met hastily before the discussion seminar, with the result that they were unable to produce a well-prepared presentation. I stopped the discussion after two speeches and solicited their further suggestions to improve the class. The following was what they offered:

- Each group should have a specific question and each member should have a specific task. The contributions of all members make team work and cooperative study possible.

- The profound philosophical reading material is too formidable for them to take in. Having little philosophical training, they would prefer to focus on literal meanings and textual understanding as well as text-related questions.
- The language is difficult and the meaning tricky. The sentence structure is depressingly complicated and the ideas are abstract and elusive. Students feel so entangled in unravelling the meaning that they find themselves none the wiser.
- Most students, accustomed to traditional lecture classes in which they are passive listeners, cannot adapt to student-centred classes in which they have to think for themselves and speak their minds. This, coupled with their poor oral English, causes them to be very tense in speaking.
- To stimulate them to take active part in discussion, they should not be worried about how well they talk and their speeches should not be recorded as the basis for marking.
- Some students asserted that prescribed literary and/or Bible reading materials are dull and hardly relevant to their lives.

I explained that I did not mean to offer a philosophy class, nor did I harbour any hope of training them to be philosophers. What they needed to do, as I maintained, was to draw upon the ideas from these classic works to help them critically assess the society in which they live. This meant they must learn to have their own interpretation of the material and be able to employ the ideas to understand the world around them. I emphasized that I was interested in their personal views rather than orthodox authoritative ones. I also reassured them that their final score would have more to do with what they said than how they said it.

My observations confirmed their lack of interest in reading long, drab texts. In my diary I wrote:

> My efforts to arouse their enthusiasm in the classic works do not seem to have produced the desired result. Their talks are, as before, short of in-depth thinking, or, as I put it, dry and superficial. Perhaps I am overambitious to require them to look at the world with an enlightened view. These busy graduates are so preoccupied with their studies that they do not have time or the inclination to direct their attention to what is happening around them; or, they have never been encouraged to think for themselves and do not know how. The ideas in the books are inaccessible to them. Anyway, it hardly works if I simply ask them to associate the ideas from their readings with the real world. I have to do something to make the class 'useful' to them and let them know it pays to take the course seriously by really getting into it.

Second cycle: course readjustment and execution

Mindful of their troubles, I adopted a pragmatic attitude and worked out, for the benefit of the students, a modified pedagogical scheme: I would read aloud the material in class, analyse complicated sentence structures and meanings, and stop to make some explanatory comments when the ideas had realistic significance that cast light on current social issues and political policies. These issues and policies or catch-phrases, which made good discussion topics, were assigned to them in such a way that each group had one specific question, rather than having to consider them all. To help them apply the ideas, I gave a demonstration of one example. While reading Plato's justice section, we found the following concept of justice in *The Republic:* 'helping our friends and damaging those against us' (Plato, 2006, p. 8). Although no one would admit to this sort of justice, people, including nations, act on the words of John F. Kennedy when he said: 'Support any friend, oppose any foe' (Pei, 2003, p. 11). Are we wiser than the ancient philosopher? The question naturally led students to examine critically the practices of individuals and states, discussing the absurdities and working out solutions. My brief explanation and questions functioned as a guide, steering students to productive contemplation. In this way, students found themselves capable of viewing matters in light of the ideas derived from the material, and they came to agree that it was fun to read such works.

It dawned on me that I should not have depended on the students' initiative, for they were used to being instructed and the heavy reading task left them little time to think over what they had read. They apparently expected my instruction and inspiration. This meant that the class had to be somewhat teacher-centred, or teacher-and-student-centred. Admittedly, the change accorded with the reality of the class. I interspersed the reading material with brief suggestions and relevant, realistic questions. The approach proved effective in setting students thinking. For example, by asking students to consider such social phenomena as prohibitive house prices and excessive rewards for executives of state-owned companies in the light of Aristotle's concept of justice, that 'the just is proportional and intermediate' and that rewards should be 'according to merits' (Aristotle, Book V), I found myself actually exposing them to broader social issues, including justice and equalitarianism, which still persist in Chinese minds, the distinction between 'the unlawful' and 'the unfair', and human nature – good or evil – to name just a few. Consequently, their presentations and the subsequent discussion were both extensive and insightful.

Of course, students were always welcome to contribute their own questions. The medical groups, in particular, were active. Some of them had previous working experience in hospitals and brought up interesting issues concerning medical practice, giving rise to heated discussion. Other students also prepared thought-provoking speeches that integrated ideas derived from reading materials with realistic issues. Furthermore, they began to make creative comparisons of Eastern and Western ideologies concerning topics covered in the materials. Later extracurricular discussions, marked by evident enthusiasm and earnestness, turned out to be as successful as I had hoped. Some students told me that they thought I was knowledgeable; one student, in particular, emailed to say that he was my faithful fan. I take this as recognition of my endeavours and their endorsement of the course.

The extracurricular seminar in which each group had a specific question to discuss effectively relieved students' anxiety and enlivened the atmosphere. One student wrote in her homework that '[d]uring the time of the discussion, which was held every Thursday evening, we had a very free but meaningful time, we expressed our opinions, no matter what we thought about the topics, we just say [spoke] it out'. In their effort to produce collective presentation, all members had specific tasks and discussed what they each had prepared before the presentation, thus making it possible for fresh ideas to come out. Contending with opposing ideas proved to be, as the students said, an effective way to 'promote their critical thinking and make them more confident and more logical when they deal with problems'.

Results

Given the course description, I set to measure the outcomes of the course from three perspectives, namely English competence, cross-cultural awareness, and critical thinking. I kept the manuscript and/or Powerpoint demonstration of the students' speeches and written essays, as the data enabled me to make a longitudinal study of their English. Despite occasional mistakes and poor expressions, there was obvious improvement in their written English. The most palpable improvement was the increasing use of complicated sentence structures and phrases of what Swales calls 'qualifications and strength of claim' (Swales *et al.*, 2004, p. 125). In their emails and my interviews with some of them, they explicitly expressed that their English was much better than before. One student said that he felt proud to be able to read abstruse philosophical works, the accomplishment of which he even boasted to the English majors. Both their subjective reflection and my objective assessment confirmed that they had made progress with their English, especially in reading and writing.

The investigation of cross-cultural awareness was somewhat complicated but fascinating. First, I examined if students were aware of East-West contrasting ideas concerning the topics covered in the course. Then, I wanted to see if they had assumed, based on what they had learned in the course, an unbiased attitude towards different cultures which shapes their own critical outlook. The data include the written manuscripts of their speeches, essays, personal emails, and interviews. Through my analysis of this data, I am able to summarize the major points of each topic as follows.

Justice

Although it is scarcely a concept which corresponds to Western justice Chinese *yi* (variously translated as justice, loyalty, righteousness), among the five virtues of *ren* (humanity or benevolence), *yi* (righteousness), *li* (propriety or courtesy), *zhi* (wisdom), and *xin* (faithfulness or credit), overlaps with justice. While both Platonic and Confucian theories are concerned with the ideal society, one student wrote, 'in the traditional Chinese culture, order and harmony stood for the highest legal value, or the highest value of justice'. Confucian philosophy therefore emphasizes 'family relationships and individual self-cultivation and perfection' as the core for building a harmonious world. *Yi*, in this context, signifies one's obligation and dedication to the state, as distinguished from Plato's state justice, which is analogous to individual justice.

All the students agree that both Plato and Aristotle's accounts of justice throw new light on social issues and significantly expand their horizons. The ideas that 'the just is intermediate' and 'the reward should be "according to merits" in some sense' (Aristotle, Book V) are especially appealing when students use them to think critically about economic activities. The law students draw on equality to explore the different legislative and judicial grounds of Chinese and Western legal systems. Nevertheless, some are unexpectedly supportive of the idea that 'justice is nothing but the interest of the stronger man' (Plato, 2006, p. 14). If one man is stronger than others, he is able to 'make them agree on the faith of justice in his mind'. However fallacious this may sound, these students find this is the real situation in our lives and therefore the idea is, in a sense, justified.

Capitalism

This part turns out to be the most controversial. Max Weber attributes, in his *The Protestant Ethic and the Spirit of Capitalism*, the evolution of capitalism to the Protestant ethos of credit, thrift, industriousness and time sense; that is, 'time is money'. He further claims that the absence of this ethos made it unlikely that capitalism would evolve in the oriental countries. This is refuted as simplistic and biased. Chinese people also possess these qualities, and religious beliefs alone cannot account for why China has pursued, in the course of history, a different path of social development.

It happens that the world is now undergoing a severe economic recession. The cause of the current economic crisis, as far as the students are concerned, can be traced to the avarice of the capitalist. Taoism, with its emphasis on human-nature harmony and resignation of lust, is reckoned as a good cure for this money grasping. By learning to restrain man's undue desire for wealth, the students further resort to the wisdom of Taoism as a remedy for current environmental deterioration and global warming.

In addition, one student takes a critical view of Weber from the viewpoint of Max' class ideology. Weber, according to the student, fails to recognize brutal class exploitation as a result of ruthless avarice for money in capitalist society. Ascribing the spirit of capitalism to Protestant ethics, in his words, 'covers up the essence of capitalist exploitation'. Nevertheless, this same student also writes that Weber tends to be idealistic and his 'outlook has a great saving grace, which deeply touches me'.

Friendship

Although certain attributes of friendship can be found in both Chinese and Western patterns of interpersonal relations, an important distinction between Chinese and Western conceptions of friendship made itself apparent as students were asked to find idioms and proverbs on friendship. For the Chinese, popular sayings and historical anecdotes about friendship, if anything, refer to the true friend as *zhiji*, literally one who understands you, or another self.

Once a person finds such a *zhiji* friend, which is not often, he regards the friend as his intimate and calls him his brother. He may, if need be, give up everything, even his life, for his friend without demanding anything. This, the students argue, differs fundamentally from Aristotle's account of three kinds of friendship characterized by utilitarian purposes. The Chinese concept of mutual understanding, which transcends time and space, creates an emotional bond that is by far more lasting than Western friendship, whichis prone to fade away as friends do not see each other anymore, or they are no longer useful or pleasing. The students further conclude that Chinese friendship is altruistic, whereas its Western counterpart is egotistic. This knowledge, be it not completely accurate, will help them, they believe, better approach friendship with Westerners.

Education

Most group presentations and essays make a contrasting analysis of education. The three masters, namely nature, human education and experience, which Rousseau expounded in *Emile*, are employed to condemn Chinese education. The educational role of experience is largely neglected by Chinese parents and teachers. The students share with Rousseau the view that educational institutions 'turn out double men, always seeming to relate everything to others while actually relating nothing to anyone but themselves' (Rousseau, Book I, p. 33). Most Chinese parents, however, ready to spend large sums of money on educating their offspring, are preoccupied with knowledge and skills that lead to good schools and colleges, and fail to acknowledge the educational value of nature and experience. Likewise, at schools and even colleges, with the examination-oriented and so-called spoon-feeding mode of teaching, teachers care little about students' well-being, instead focusing onrote memorization and mastery of facts and information – most of which is trivial – to pass various examinations. Children, under the heavy burden of homework and the pressure to score high in exams, find themselves lacking both time and energy to observe nature and learn from the contact. The students in the study made an appeal to return to the basics of education, that is, the cultivation of all-rounded development of the individual rather than a preoccupation solely with information cramming.

Dewey's educational philosophy is particularly welcomed by the students, who deem that 'the idea of preparing for the present rather than future is illuminating'. Reflecting on their own schooling, the students find that such a conception is largely absent in the Chinese educational system, which is characterized by an instrumentalist philosophy. As one student wrote in her essay: 'China's current education just pays much attention to intellectual development and little to the moral education; besides, it overlooks how to shape human's [human] character, which has caused a serious departure from the orginal [original] purpose of education.' Too much weight, in this view, is given to so-called practical knowledge and skills that enable students to find jobs in the increasingly competitive job market. The same mentality diverts elementary and secondary education from caring about children's present life to accentuating the subjects that help them pass examinations to get access to better schools and colleges; students thus are forced to focus on rote learning and passing examinations instead of maintaining their curiosity and interest. Much of the 'dead knowledge', as they name it, is soon forgotten, which is a regrettable waste of time and effort. They conclude, in the light of Dewey's view, that 'the biggest failure is more and more students lose interest in learning . . . If education is growth, it must progressively realize present possibilities, and thus make individuals better fitted to cope with later requirements'.

By comparing Dewey's educational philosophy with Confucians', students perceive similarities. One wrote, '[b]ecause experience plays such [an] important role in [the] educational process, the new education system, proposed by Dewey's theory, is [a] student-driven system against [as opposed to] the old knowledge-driven system. [The] student becomes the central focus of [the] education system. Dewey argued that an educator must take into account the unique differences between each student. This idea is similar with [to] the education[al] idea of Confucius, who is the most famous philosopher in China'.

Follow-up interviews

About six months later I randomly selected some students from liberal arts and science departments and interviewed them in groups of four or five in order to find out, among other things, the long-range effects of the course on students' critical thinking and cross-cultural awareness. The questions fell into three categories, namely their overall assessment of the course, their achievement, and their views on social issues and public opinions. To elicit authentic responses I asked general questions, avoiding specific ones that might remind them of what they had learned or show a certain bias which might influence their reply.

They all lent support to the course, saying that it was both inspiring and refreshing. In retrospect, they felt it was 'miraculous' that they were able to read philosophical works in English, an accomplishment that is itself a reward for their assiduous efforts. Nonetheless, they hesitated when asked to tell specifically what they remembered about the details. In fact, no one could give a complete account of the topics and the relevant ideas. Through mutual reminding they were able to provide the complete picture, which I take as a normal response, but a limited success for the course.

The investigation of critical thinking was carefully carried out. I hoped to see their critical thinking on a more general level rather than on explicit issues relating to the course topics, so I first asked them to offer their views on the idea of Chinese rejuvenation. First they responded that this notion was rather indistinct and fuzzy. Despite the booming Chinese economy, they held a dim view of Chinese rejuvenation as they were convinced that, from what they knew about their respective disciplines, China still has a long way to go before it can confidently proclaim its 'renaissance'. When it came to Chinese culture, they had mixed feelings. As globally influential philosophies, Confucianism and Taoism can still provide individuals with moral guidance; however, they definitely need transformation and evolution to keep pace with the times. What was comforting was that they did not show blind complacency or chauvinism with regard to Chinese culture. It seems that they are sober in making judgement, a sign of a critical mind, but it remained to be further determined how much they gained from this particular course.

Summary and conclusion

Previous surveys show that students look forward to shifting the focus of English courses from linguistic to cultural competence. At the graduate level, this cultural competence is understood as knowledge of deeply rooted culture, the underlying ideology that shapes the characters of different cultural communities. Given that the great canon, the preferred source of cultural origins to be used in such a class, is generally assumed to be a challenge to both teachers and students, this pilot project was illuminating and rewarding. In the first place, a teacher's commitment and enthusiasm is essential to the course. In addition to the normal one-hour class, I regularly met four times a week with different groups of students and encouraged them to offer meaningful ideas and discussion, which, as the students acknowledged, effectively banished their fears. Secondly, the great works must in one way or another find their way into students' lives if they are to be enlightening and useful. This can be achieved by highlighting the ideas and applying them to our present life and society in a way that allows students to realize that these ideas are, after thousands of years, still fresh and illuminating. By allowing students to think for themselves, the great works can be shown to be conducive to their ethical and ideological well-being and therefore nourish their souls, so that they enjoy reading them rather than reject them as dull and dead. Once they are interested in such works, they are naturally motivated to overcome difficulty in reading and make progress. In other words, arousing students' interest and confidence, which play an important role in any course, is particularly crucial to the success of a course for the obvious reason that the course offering will be unappealing if it is 'not relevant to the concerns of today's students' (Ford, 1994, p. 7).

At the beginning of the project, it was hoped that the course would enhance students' cross-cultural awareness and critical thinking. It should be pointed out that, due to the short duration of the project – one semester – and the varying degrees of intellectual maturity among the students, it is difficult to measure quantitatively the difference the course made to the students with regard to the two capabilities mentioned above. As mental development requires time, it is recommended that the course offering be extended to at least one academic year in order to discern its efficacy. The content of the course – the topics or themes – needs to be expanded and carefully selected. Indeed, it is an issue of debate what concepts should be included as representative of either Eastern or Western culture (for instance, individualism–collectivism, which is thought to be a characteristic cultural difference) and whether it is possible to provide students with a systematic and overall appreciation of the different cultures with a view to enhancing their international awareness. In addition, better qualitative and quantitative measurement must be designed to accurately assess the result.

References

Adamson, B. (2004), *China's English: A History of English in Chinese Education*. Hong Kong: Hong Kong University Press.

Aristotle (350 BCE), *Nicomachean Ethics*. W. D. Ross. (trans.), at http://classics.mit.edu/Aristotle/nicomachaen.html (accessed 13 November 2009).

Bloom, A. (2007), *The Closing of the American Mind*, Zhan Xunying (trans.). Nanjing, China: Yilin Press.

Bolton, K. (2003), *Chinese Englishes: A Sociolinguistic History*. Cambridge: Cambridge University Press.

Coleman, J. A. (1998), 'Evolving intercultural perceptions among university language learners in Europe', in M. Byram and M. Fleming (eds), *Language Learning in Intercultural Perspective: Approaches through Drama and Ethnography*. Cambridge: Cambridge University Press.

Dornyei, Z. (2001), *Teaching and Researching Motivation*. Pearson Education (2005), Beijing: Foreign Language Teaching and Research Press.

Education Law of the People's Republic of China (ELPRC) (1995), at http://www.moe.edu.cn/edoas/website18/en/laws_e.htm (accessed 13 November 2009).

Ford, L. C. (1994), *Liberal Education and the Canon: Five Great Texts Speak to Contemporary Social Issues*. Columbia, South Carolina: Camden House.

Goddard, C. (2004), '"Cultural scripts": A new medium for ethnopragmatic instruction', in M. Achard and S. Niemeier (eds) *Cognitive Linguistics, Second Language Acquisition, and Foreign Language Teaching*. Berlin: Mouton de Gruyter.

Gudykunst, W. B. (ed.) (2003), *Cross-Cultural and Intercultural Communication*. Thousand Oaks, California: Sage Publications.

Hall, J. K. (2002), *Teaching and Researching Language and Culture*. Pearson Education. (2005), Beijing: Foreign Language Teaching and Research Press.

Knight, J. (2003), *Internationalisation of Higher Education Practices and Priorities: 2003 IAU Survey Report*. International Association of Universities, at http://www.unesco.org/iau (accessed 13 November 2009).

Kumaravadivelu, B. (2008), *Cultural Globalization and Language Education*. New Haven: Yale University Press.

Levin, R. (2004), *The Work of the University*, F. Wang (trans.). Beijing: Foreign Language Teaching and Research Press.

Lixian J. and Martin, C. (1998), 'The culture the learner brings: A bridge or a barrier?', in M. Byram and M. Fleming (eds), *Language Learning in Intercultural Perspective: Approaches through Drama and Ethnography*. Cambridge: Cambridge University Press.

Ministry of Education of the People's Republic of China (MEPRC) (1995), The 9th 5-year plan for China's educational development and the development outline by 2010, at http://www.moe.edu.cn/edoas/website18/en/planning_n.htm (accessed 13 November 2009).

Noffke, S. E. and Stevenson, R. B. (eds) (1995), *Educational Action Research: Becoming Practically Critical*. Columbia University, New York: Teachers College Press.

Pei, N. (2003), *Famous Speeches of the Twentieth-Century*. Beijing: Chinese Foreign Translation Publication Company.

Plato (2006) *The Republic*, I. A. Richards (English trans.) and Z. Duan (Chinese trans.). Beijing: Chinese Foreign Translation Publication Company.

Rousseau, J. (1762). *Emile, or On Education*, G. Roosevelt (trans.), at www.ilt.columbia.edu/pedagogies/rousseau/index.html (accessed 13 November 2009).

Samovar, L. A., Porter, R. E. and Stefani, L. A. (1998), *Communication Between Cultures*

(3rd edn.). Boston, MA: Wadsworth Publishing (2000), Beijing: Foreign Language Teaching and Research Press.

Scollon, R. and Scollon, S. W. (1995), *Intercultural Communication: A Discourse Approach*. Blackwell Publishers (2000), Beijing: Foreign Language Teaching and Research Press.

Slattery, P. (1995), *Curriculum Development in the Postmodern Era*. New York and London: Garland Publishing.

Swales, J. M. and Feak, C. B. (2004), *Academic Writing for Graduate Students* (2nd edn.) Ann Arbor: University of Michigan Press.

Chapter 13

Challenges to Institutionalizing Internationalization in a UK University

Joanna Al-Youssef

Introduction

Internationalization has been a buzz-word at policy level in different contexts including businesses, universities and governments. Its meanings and inter-pretations have largely been associated with competition and markets (Haigh, 2008; Toyoshima, 2007). However, these rather teleological views of inter-nationalization, which have a propensity to see it in terms of its instrumental value alone, have not yet succeeded in capturing its complexity. By capturing this, more effective international strategies may be devised. 'Every time I say it, I'm thinking of it in a different way', is how an individual holding a position at an international office in a UK higher education institution (HEI) chooses to construe internationalization, seeing it as a fluid, non-graspable term.

The growth in the number of international students in the UK and the pres-sure from the UK Government in the form of Prime Minister Initiatives (PMIs) 1 and 2 – which aimed at increasing the number of international students in British HEIs (PMI1) and at further developing UK universities' international activities (PMI2) – together with the increased competitiveness among HEIs for a higher ranking, has forced many UK HEIs to move towards more strate-gic thinking about internationalization. Internationalization has, therefore, become a target as well as a tool for system development and planning for many of these HEIs. Thus, within higher education (HE) contexts in the UK, internationalization has somehow materialized into institutional strategies dictating not only perceptions of internationalization in HEIs, but how it is to be used as a tool to exalt those HEIs onto a higher rank and to increase profit generated through international activities in a highly competitive global world (Bolsmann *et al.*, 2008). Internationalization strategies have become a priority for many HEIs in the UK, whose agendas have been mostly pushed by external factors such as government initiatives (Stier, 2002). As mentioned above, these agendas include those of certain parties in the university featured in the case study presented in this chapter. Main findings of the study include a multiplic-ity of interpretations of internationalization, which possibly reflect individuals' roles and their world views. Although a priority, the international strategy is also found to be a response to internal and external factors. Implications of the strategy are thought to be in terms of recruitment, profile, visibility, and harmonizing individual and department initiatives.

This chapter will present a study carried out to explore thoroughly meanings of internationalization in relation to an international strategy. The research is a case study of a single UK university where an international strategy is centrally created and promoted. With its empirical base in in-depth interviews, the case study research described is unusual for challenging interpretations of internationalization that have previously been largely researched through surveys and questionnaires. The research and its findings take the concept of internationalization away from the practices of the institution and into the accounts of the individuals who manage it. The chapter aims to contribute to the debate on internationalization meanings and practices by providing insight into how the term internationalization is understood in relation to a university's internationalization strategy from diverse positions within university management, and how these interpretations influence approaches to the implementation of the strategy.

Summary of prior research

Prior research in the field of internationalization of HE has focused mainly on international students' experiences or patterns of their mobility (Marginson, 2006). As far as policy is concerned, there has been an emphasis on the commercial and diplomatic values of the 'education export industry' (Elliott, 1998). More recently, Kehm *et al.* (2007) identified seven themes in publications on the internationalization of higher education. These include student and staff mobility, the internationalization of learning, teaching and research, internationalization strategies, knowledge transfer, the mutual influence of HE systems on each other, cooperation and competition, and national and supranational policies regarding the international dimension of HE.

Research on internationalization and international strategies in particular has largely been descriptive of and confined within the contexts where research was conducted. Earlier attempts to map internationalization in a model within HEIs in various contexts, such as Davies (1992), Rudzki (1995a, 1995b), Knight (1995), and Van Dijk *et al.* (1997), resulted in a prescriptive approach that did not seem to account for the multiplicity of interpretations of internationalization, but approached it as a single entity and a target. Davies' (1992) study aims at examining the organizational consequences of internationalization, with a focus on strategy and delivery. Rudzki's (1995b) study aims to describe and examine internationalization strategic policies and success factors, resources, obstacles, and future trends. The study carried out by Van Dijk *et al.* (1997) examines how internationalization is organized in HEIs' internal processes, and Knight's (1995) survey examines the rationale, priority and meanings of internationalization, and organizational factors affecting the integration of an international dimension into HEIs.

Key findings of these studies are represented in models of internationalization developed in the studies' conclusions. Davies' (1992) model proposes that the implementation of an international strategy depends on its importance to the

HEI concerned (central vs. marginal), and on the style by which the strategy is introduced (ad hoc vs. systematic). Rudzki's (1995b) model presents two modes of internationalization. The reactive mode starts with academic staff making contacts in other institutions. Management then seeks control of the growing activity, resulting in possible conflict between management and staff. Finally, a shift towards a more proactive mode may follow. The proactive mode, on the other hand, begins by exploring the understanding of internationalization in the HEI. The choice of a strategy and policy plan follows. The next stage is the implementation of the strategy, followed by measurement of the performance against the policy, and a re-evaluation of the policy. Van Dijk *et al.*'s (1997) model presents three dimensions of internationalization policy associated with policy (priority or marginal), support (interactive support from all departments, or one-sided support from a single department) and implementation (structural or ad hoc). Van Dijk *et al.* (1997) argue that if an institution's internationalization policy is a priority, systematically implemented and with interactive support, this is an indication that the institution is aiming to be highly internationalized. Finally, Knight's (1995) model represents internationalization as a cycle, ideally starting with awareness of the importance of internationalization, followed by commitment, planning, reviewing and reinforcement.

Ambiguity surrounding meanings of internationalization is still present, despite attempts such as those made in the studies mentioned above to provide insight into the term. A more recent example of such attempts is a pilot study of a UK institution investigating the changing of its strategy and practice (Middlehurst *et al.*, 2007). The study reveals that, at that institution, there are two perceived broad aspects of internationalization: the first is in relation to the institution's international activities at home and abroad, and the second is described as 'structural' or 'cultural'.

In what follows, a description of the case study is provided in more detail, identifying a multiplicity of opinions and interpretations of an internationalization strategy and referring to the challenges this poses to implementation, even when a strategy has been developed through consultation.

Internationalization case study

The study reported here is inspired by a concern with the confusion over what internationalization means. The aim is to explore the issues further within the context of an HEI that is in the process of developing an international strategy. It was a timely and valuable opportunity to investigate the participants' perceptions of the process and of internationalization while the institution was moving towards strategic thinking about its international activities and internationalization.

The context

The institution in which the case study was conducted reflects the trend for internationalization to become a strategic goal, as mentioned above, in the sense that it is at the stage of developing its international strategy. It is a medium-sized university, with a bias towards science, engineering and management courses and ranking quite highly in the various university league tables that have been published. About 25 per cent of its students may be classified as 'international', with around 70 per cent of these being from outside the European Union. It is of a specific type of institution; a research-led, campus-based university with a wide variety of international activities steered by its central management (that is, the vice-chancellor's office) and also by its relatively autonomous individual departments. Participants in this interpretive, inductive study are individuals in various middle and senior management positions across the university's departments. These are individuals who are directly or indirectly involved in the making of the strategy or in the university's international activities. The aim of the study is to explore their understandings of internationalization with reference to the newly formulated international strategy.

A note on the methodology

The theoretical claims made in the body of literature on internationalization overlook certain types of information that can only be gathered through an in-depth study of individuals who are in direct contact with the process, and their perceptions of it. Thus, the data which this research produces are of special significance in addressing the shortcomings of the literature. As stated earlier, the aim of the research is to explore participants' interpretations of internationalization. This aim is achieved through in-depth interviewing, and inductive analysis.

The data are of two types: interviews were organized with middle and senior management staff in the university's different divisions involved in the process of internationalization, such as the International Office, to explore how they understood the process. As supplementary data, university documents related to internationalization policy and implementation, such as the newly created international strategy, were analysed. Due to their importance for informing the interviews, and being the policy context point of reference, the documents were analysed before conducting the interviews.

There were five documents used in this case study: the university's international strategy document, a discussion paper leading to the formulation of that international strategy, an international operational plan to follow the international strategy, the university's mission statement, and a document reporting on a study of international students' experiences at that university. These documents were chosen because they all included the concept of internationalization. Basic content analysis was the method used in analysing these documents both to examine their 'manifest content', which refers, for example, to word counts; and to explore their 'latent content' or the underlying values and meanings, in this case meanings surrounding internationalization as viewed in the documents, and looking at words as 'indicators' (Sarantakos, 2005). Documents were mainly used to direct the research question and research focus. The international strategy document in particular also provided a tool to use in the interviews by asking the interviewees to comment on it. The questions emerging from the documents regarding internationalization were further investigated in the interviews that followed. After analysing the documents, 21 in-depth semi-structured interviews were planned and conducted with individuals in diverse management positions at the university in order to understand their views on internationalization.

The international strategy

The international strategy document is divided into a University Vision Statement, University Mission Statement, International Strategy Vision, Strategic Goals, and International Strategy Aims and Objectives. From the start, the university's vision as an internationally-recognized research institution would seem to demand that high quality teaching and learning is offered. Being international is seen in relation to the academic aspects of the university's life, first and foremost, and it is linked to notions of standards and esteem.

The central focus on academic success, research and teaching and its importance for the university is further emphasized in the Mission Statement of its international strategy. It is, however, not clear how this is to be achieved. The Mission Statement refers rather ambiguously to the university's role in an international context that is itself not defined.

Globally significant and valuable research appears once more, to be the core mission of the university and its international community, as stated above. If the word 'global' is taken to refer to the labour market for which students are prepared, the focus appears to be on work, which implies a rather instrumental view of education.

Although one cannot expect much detail from a vision statement, it does raise questions about how the research referred to in the statement is to be of importance to varying contexts around the globe. It also raises questions about the nature of those 'skills for life and work' referred to in the document and whether they are part of the teaching/learning/research goals mentioned in the section on strategic goals in the strategy document.

There are two broad aims of the international strategy, under which there are more specific objectives. The first aim looks at increasing the numbers of international staff and students and the number of international research activities, whether it is this particular university's staff engaging with research internationally, or visiting scholars from abroad participating in its academic activities. On the other hand, the main themes in the second aim are international profile and reputation 'as a leading research university', international communications and marketing, links with alumni and sporting excellence.

In sum, the international strategy vision in the document shows the university to be a world-class institution, with an international community and with a focus on international research. The strategic goals also revolve around international research, an international curriculum, an international student body, international partnerships, and unspecified facilities and services. In the first aim of the international strategy, 'international' is still seen in terms of the academic life of the institution. Through the second aim, to raise the university's international profile, there is an emphasis on international ranking.

According to the strategy plan outlined in the international strategy document, what makes the university international is having more international students, staff and links, a higher international profile, a curriculum that takes into consideration home and overseas students, and excellence in research at an international level. The emphasis in the document is on academic activity, placing it at the centre of the strategy plan, around which a culture and ethos are assumed to be created.

The international strategy document's goals and aims in particular reflect a desired end-state. The document reflects a linear image of internationalization, moving from 'here' to 'there' through certain strategies. The question of how this is to be achieved remains unanswered in this document alone. The word 'international' seems to refer to the arena within which a standard is set.

What appears to be encouraged in the international strategy document is an increase in the level of activity, rather than any fundamental changes in the university's culture, although there is reference to the development of an international culture, which, presumably, the university did not have in the past, or does not now have. It might be argued that a strategy document does not need to include much detail, and that it is by nature a brief document laying out broad aims and objectives. However, a critical reading of the document is important, as the issues raised above represent areas investigated further in the interviews.

Individual responses to the strategy

On the plus side

Views and interpretations of the strategy varied considerably. To begin with, a senior manager says that the strategy aims to encourage departments to try to be specific, and the university to be explicit, about what they do and how they do it. The strategy is seen to be important for the university's identity and how the university views itself as a competitor in the international marketplace. It is seen as a reflection of the image the university wishes to project to potential international students. It is being enhanced in practice by a support system for those international students studying at the university, although possibly suffering from a stereotyping approach to these students; as one senior manager states, 'We have encouraged every department to have one person who will have had some training in the different [. . .] possible presenting characteristics of students' (senior manager in the university central management).

Another view is that the international strategy is important in the sense that it provides a 'high-level overview' of the university's successful international activities and the increase in the numbers of international students. The strategy is seen to be the result of a recognition that for international student numbers to be maintained, a formal document reflecting an understanding of the international student market is needed (Head of the International Office). The Head of Marketing thinks that the strategy is a long-term commitment and is not a temporary 'trend' or 'brand'. It is a major statement in terms of the university's brand and its position. It is also 'top level stuff' that is more than just recruitment of international students. There is also the view that the strategy comes with a cost that the university needs to be able to afford, and there is a need for a more 'world[-oriented] frame of mind to think outside the UK news media' (Head of Marketing), and be able to sell the university to the world; reflecting a tension in the internationalization imperative and the national function or orientation of the university.

The strategy is also seen as important in increasing the university's visibility and so raising its profile to increase international students' recruitment. This in turn is thought to contribute positively to the university's image; a view of HE as a competitive business in which a strategy is the means to remain at the top.

Being competitive and following the steps of other universities that focus on their internationalization agenda is the other side of the same coin of being globally recognized and belonging to a 'global club', and not being left behind in terms of strategic partnerships. However, competitiveness is not seen as the only motive. Some external factors or pressures, such as the HEFCE (Higher Education Funding Council for England), appear to push the international strategy agenda, but it is to be hoped they are not the only drivers. According to a university senior manager, the external drivers of the international strategy affect the internal affairs of the institution, and the process of formulating the international strategy is not as proactive as is thought.

> The national policy . . . the pursuit of privatization, the obvious internationaliza-
> tion of Higher Education, the collaborative agreements that have been made,
> the obvious financial need to recruit overseas students and generate external
> research, so it's the changing context which is driving a lot of this. (faculty
> dean)

Increasing the numbers of international students at the university is encouraged by outside influences. However, maintaining those numbers is a difficult task, due to the very same influences. An example given by a participant from the university's International Office is the pressure from the UK Government to recruit more international students, yet strict immigration rules do not allow such recruitment.

The international strategy at the university is also seen to be bringing together and harmonizing initiatives that would otherwise be going in different directions. The strategy according to this view 'is providing a reinforcement of what has been separate practice' (faculty dean). The international strategy is also believed to be a way to justify certain university activities, such as international exchange programmes or recruiting international students. This view could be interpreted in terms of Rudzki's (1995b) reactive or ad hoc internationalization path, as being at the point where the central administration decides it needs to regularize activities. It may be argued that creating the strategy is about extending power and control over what is already happening in the university. There is reference to the decentralized character of the university and the hope that the strategy would have a harmonizing effect after years of growth in terms of size and identity, and of fragmented departmental efforts and initiatives. However, the strategy is also thought to be enlightening in terms of the understanding of whether those initiatives need to be brought together in the first place:

Even more positively, one middle manager believes that the international strategy is about having a different mental model and a new way of thinking about internationalization and about partnerships – in short, a policy shift. The strategy is a way forward by a means other than merely raising the university's academic profile, and that is understood in terms of recruiting international students and providing the services to support them, as well as recruiting international staff to meet the needs of overseas students. Moreover, the international strategy is important for the university, as strategic thinking is needed, especially in the way support is given to improve international students' experience, 'otherwise we might lose international students coming to the UK because there are lots of other competitors they can go to' (middle manager at the International Office). Being competitive is again the underlying principle for providing services to the groups labelled as 'international' at the university.

On the minus side

On the other hand, a centre director and senior academic sees the strategy as an incomplete document, in the sense that it does not prescribe instruments for action; and no follow-up seems to be indicated:

> [The strategy] is still very abstract, and it's not instrumentalized [. . .] Most people say 'yeah I accept that', but I think it's more important to make something of the strategy, challenge those in charge of the strategy to put instruments in place [. . .] There's no reference at all to a follow-up. (centre director and senior academic)

The above, rather negative view of the strategy is also shared by another senior academic lecturer who is involved in international students' recruitment and who thinks that some items on the strategy document, such as recruiting international students and staff, are already taking place. This participant also believes that the document itself is not going to change anything at the university. The fact that the strategy outlines what is already taking place means that it might be considered a burden for some people at the university and an extra demand on their time, and so it may be resisted. The Head of Security thinks that the strategy document itself, in the way that it is worded, does not mean much, although it is acknowledged to be important for an institution to have such a document listing the goals it is working for, in terms of the recruitment of international students and ranking. It is, however, 'detached from the real message that perhaps ought to be getting across, this is the ground, the grassroots of what we should be doing' (Head of Security). The international strategy is seen to be less intended for aspects of the university that are not academic. Implicit in the view of internationalization as an 'academic thing' is a feeling of exclusion and reality sense that this internationalization strategy does not see the university in its totality.

The Head of the university's International Office sees the international strategy as 'very much a framework [. . .] and what it needs is fleshing out in certain areas'. Although, according to this participant, the meaning of internationalization is not yet fully established at the university, the international strategy document provides direction for its internationalization activities, the allocation of resources into the most effective channels, the bringing together of isolated academic efforts, and adherence to regulations and restrictions, as 'we mustn't have people going off and doing things without proper reference to our corporate planning or quality assurance mechanisms' (Head of the International Office). This view could be seen to imply a view of the university as a monolithic, bureaucratic, corporate being.

Some participants refer to limited resources and competition as potential issues in relation to implementing the international strategy. One senior manager thinks that the biggest issue facing the international strategy is at 'grassroots' level, referring to the individual departments and individuals who need to be genuinely interested in the strategy in order to interact with it and understand it. The participant believes this can be achieved through strong communication between the senior management and departments, and thinks of implementing the strategy as a process that requires monitoring and reflection to ensure the goals are achieved as desired by the senior management. The participant emphasizes the importance of communication between the centre and departments. This view may, however, also indicate a top-down approach where senior management 'tells' departments what is intended and what the agenda is, and encourages them to take it on board.

The Head of Student Services' concern regarding the university's international strategy is to do with it not recognizing certain aspects of university life as points of strength; it focuses on raising the university's profile and ranking using sports, for example, as a tool, but within an approach that is fundamentally market-oriented. The strategy document does not address many issues that are important in relation to the student experience, and it is described as 'an institutional response to internationalization' in which student experience is 'not [. . .] as prominent as some of the other aspects of the policy or strategy' (Head of Student Services). Although accepting what the university's strategy is all about, the view that student experience is not yet prominent in the strategy could possibly be an implied – though mild – criticism of the university's 'promotional' strategy within a market discourse. Another participant thinks that culture is the main issue in the way of implementing the strategy, and believes that culture in the sense of people's attitudes to the international strategy and to internationalization is a key element in making it happen. This might be seen to indicate a view of internationalization not only in terms of institutional activities, but also as a collective deep and fundamental change.

At the central management level, it is thought that implementation of the international strategy might come up against an Anglocentric view on the part of some academic staff who do not see the need to internationalize, and who think that if international students and staff choose to come to the UK, they will have to adapt. It is also thought that there might be a view among some people at the university that the strategy is driven by financial factors alone, and this would stand in the way of its implementation.

Another senior manager and faculty leader thinks that the work of academics is already international and the strategy might be seen as restricting their choice of research partnerships, as they might feel pulled away from their core mission and comfort zone. The strategy might be resisted because it could interrupt the routine some people are used to and present an uncomfortable change for them. This view seems to favour a more bottom-up approach, together with a strong element of an ad hoc approach. This might be seen as a classic clash between the bureaucracy of management and the independence of academics/academic freedom. This is a wider cultural clash that is manifested here in relation to internationalization.

Looking at the issues surrounding internationalization and the international strategy at the conceptual level, a senior manager and academic distinguishes between a purely academic or educational approach to internationalization and the university's economic strategy of internationalization. The result may be tension between the two rationales. This tension is the result of a clear divide at the institution with regard to priorities and interpretations of internationalization.

A senior manager believes that the main issue with the strategy concerns the university's 'conservative' management structure and a leadership that does not explicitly reveal a way of engaging internationally worldwide. Another senior manager thinks that the 'devolved' structure of the university means that the strategy would be considered to different degrees by different departments, the reason being that there are competing priorities due to the lack of any real model of centralization.

Implications for implementation

As can be seen in the views above, the international strategy is interpreted differently and is seen to be of different degrees of importance depending on the individual. Underlying the participants' views may be differences in individuals' roles and positions at the university, as well as their worldviews.

Views on the implications of the international strategy vary from it providing an opportunity to recruit more international students, to giving the university more visibility and raising its profile, to being a policy shift and bringing together the otherwise dispersed initiatives. The international strategy can be said to have implications in two broad areas. The first area is the university's external activities, which include student and staff recruitment, and research links and partnerships, and related to this is its external image, reputation and ranking. The second area is the university's internal culture, which includes its sense of community, departments' and individuals' work, and, at a deeper level, the university's identity, and degree of centralization and control.

The model that emerges from the above views, as far as the international strategy is concerned, is, therefore, reactive moving on to proactive; and ad hoc moving on to systematic (Figure 13.1). The university appears to be somewhere down the line of Rudzki's (1995b) reactive model, at or below the stage of central management taking control (as implied by management respondents describing it as 'pulling together initiatives going in different directions') before reaching the stage of conflict, with perhaps a jump to the first step in Rudzki's (1995b) proactive model, that is, 'Analysis', then going along this path to implementation. The non-emergence of conflict might be attributed to strong central management control, or to the relatively high level of autonomy of departments who do not see internationalization as a priority to pursue at an institutional strategic level. This might be seen to reflect a structuralist view of internationalization where the focus is on activities rather than individuals as agents in a policy process (Trowler, 2002) in which individual actors and their perceptions play an important role. Ignoring individuals' input and perceptions, Trowler (2002) argues, could lead to a gap in the implementation of policy. In the case of this university, the international strategy seems to be considered the 'responsibility' of the central management and so it is not clear to some interviewees how it is to be implemented.

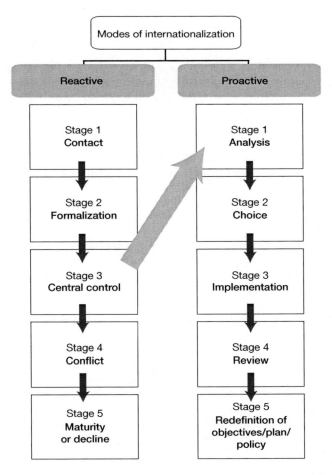

Figure 13.1 The university's mode of internationalization (adapted from Rudzki, 1995b)

By focusing on activities, and responding mainly to external or internal factors, the internationalization being promoted at the university is weak (Appadurai, 2001; Sanderson, 2004) and symbolic (Turner *et al.*, 2008). The data, however, reveal some indications of strong and transformative internationalization in what some interviewees refer to as an international community and an internationalization culture. These, however, do not appear to be main aims in themselves and are more a by-product of increasing international student and staff numbers, and international activities.

What the participants' views also reflect is some individuals' frustrations and uncertainty when it comes to the international strategy and internationalization. The barriers mentioned by the interviewees are related to individual and institutional practices, and can be seen to fall into seven broad categories: individuals' resistance, the university's management structure, limited human and financial resources, lack of a culture supporting the strategy and internationalization, lack of agreement on what internationalization means, lack of integration between different nationality groups, and lack of a university-wide implementation plan. Many of these areas reflect an understanding of internationalization in terms of activities (for instance, support and marketing through resources), university population, and culture. However, the reference to individuals' resistance as a barrier implies that the respondents place emphasis on the importance and centrality of individuals' commitment to internationalization.

Another element that emerges from the data is the possible 'tension' between individuals as agents, and the university's management and structure. When talking about the barriers to the international strategy, many of the respondents talk about individuals: individual academics, individual departments, and so on. This may be seen to contrast with their views regarding internationalizing as a university, generating income as a university, the central management and the rest of the university, students as a group, staff as a group, and so on. It seems that while internationalization is thought of as a good thing for all, the problems are seen to lie mostly with the individual. It is the individual resisting, feeling burdened, feeling restricted or not committing. There is a tension between the individual academics' 'educational rationale' of internationalization, and the university's 'economic rationale', putting the two in opposition. This corresponds to the tension between the agentic and the structuralist views of internationalization (Trowler, 2002). The data suggest that this tension is thought to go unnoticed at the central management level, which again reinforces the idea that the approach preferred at this level of the university is top-down. This approach is evident in the data in individuals' accounts of looking for some indication of what the 'university' wants to do, and what they are told or not told in relation to the strategy; the uncertainty which comes from the centre, and their expectation of an institution-wide move towards internationalization. Moreover, the very fact that resistance to the international strategy by individuals is considered a barrier reveals that those individuals did not have any bottom-up input in the strategy.

Discussion

Two views of internationalization seem to be expressed by the respondents. The first sees the world as a global economy, and so internationalization becomes more of a 'financial strategy' where marketing, branding, international reputation and ranking in the league tables are vital for the survival of a business-like institution. The second view of internationalization, on the other hand, perceives the world as a multicultural community in which cooperation, partnerships and mutual understanding, as well as a multicultural campus, are core elements of a truly internationalized university.

However, although the second view is not said to be prompted by financial imperatives, the interview data show that soft marketing is an aim of such an approach. This is illustrated through some respondents' emphasis on the importance of research collaborations and the recruitment of international students, for example, where this is thought to contribute to income generation. The first view of internationalization can be described as statistical, numerical, or quantitative. The second view can be understood as a cultural or qualitative view. In the majority of the responses, internationalization is quantified: numbers of students or staff, numbers of partners and so on. This approach comes from a rather 'material', macro view of the university as a structure that contains those 'items'. On the other hand, viewing the university as a meeting point for people from diverse backgrounds and cultures leads to a more 'non-material' micro approach to internationalization. The predominant view of internationalization, however, is that it is a goal to reach, presumably through implementing appropriate strategies.

Unlike Knight's (1999) view of internationalization as, not only a response, but an agent of forces of globalization, change is thought by some respondents to be required to achieve internationalization, and there is no reference to how or whether the university can change with internationalization. The internationalization referred to in the data can be described as 'aspirational' since it is about the university's aspiration to achieve a high profile, high reputation and high ranking. It can, therefore, be said that this is a short-term internationalization since the factors it is responding to are themselves likely to change. Perhaps there is a need for a more sustainable type of internationalization, in which members of an HEI co-create and sustain internationalization in their ongoing day-to-day interactions, practices and meaning-making. By this, it provides a framework for creating the positive international community and culture referred to in the data, in the sense that it goes beyond nationality badges and into a deeper individual dialogue with the Cultural Other (Sanderson, 2004). At a strategic level, a sustainable internationalization might be much harder to achieve since strategy is about activities, targets, aims and objectives codified by the central management into a brief document. However, to achieve it, it is plausible and maybe beneficial for the implementers of the strategy to reconsider the discourse which includes references to 'us' and 'them' in the international strategy document.

Internationalization of HE, in its weak, symbolic form, can be seen as lying between macro globalization forces which give rise to the Cultural Other and the 'collective' Cultural Other, on the one hand, and the University's micro international activities on the other, while actively working with both. In its stronger form, internationalization can be seen as the catalyst for counteracting the Cultural Other by working its way through the self by constant reflexivity, and this needs to be added to the agenda of HEIs before it is fully embraced and felt in the 'total environment' of the university (Haigh, 2008).

Summary and conclusion

This chapter presented a case study exploring the meanings of internationalization as perceived by individuals in the middle and senior management at a single UK HEI. The research is important in the sense that it utilizes purely qualitative methods to investigate the perceptions, rather than the practices, of internationalization as seen by individuals who are directly involved in the process. The chapter explored the findings of the study in relation to the international strategy. Main conclusions include a multiplicity of interpretations of internationalization and opposing views of the strategy that would potentially have negative influences over its implementation.

Further research is needed into the meanings of internationalization and international strategy at all levels at the university, not only the middle and senior management level, to give a broader picture. Research is also needed into investigating ways of integrating sustainable internationalization into the university's culture, and how this is to influence and be influenced by other aspects of the university's life and identity.

References

Appadurai, A. (2001), *Globalization*. Durham: Duke University Press.

Bolsmann, C. and Miller, H. (2008), 'International student recruitment to universities in England: Discourse, rationales and globalisation'. *Globalisation, Societies and Education*, 6, (1), 75–88.

Davies, J. L. (1992), 'Developing a strategy for internationalisation in universities: Towards a conceptual framework', in C. B. Klasek (ed.), *Bridges To The Future: Strategies for Internationalizing Higher Education*. Carbondale: Association of International Education Administrators.

Elliott, D. (1998), 'Internationalizing British higher education: Policy perspectives', in P. Scott (ed.) *The Globalization of Higher Education*. Buckingham: Society for Research into Higher Education and Open University Press.

Haigh, M. (2008), 'Internationalisation, planetary citizenship and Higher Education Inc.', *Compare*, 38, (4), 427–40.

Kehm, B. M. and Teichler, U. (2007), 'Research on internationalisation in higher education', *Journal of Studies in International Education*, 11,(3/4), 260–73.

Knight, J. (1995), *Internationalisation at Canadian Universities: The Changing Landscape*. Ottawa, Canada: AUCC.

—— (1999), 'Internationalisation of higher education', in J. Knight and H. de Wit (eds), *Quality and Internationalisation in Higher Education*. Paris: Organisation for Economic Co-operation and Development, 14–29.

Marginson, S. (2006), 'National and global competition in higher education', in H. Lauder (ed.), *Education, Globalisation and Social Change*. Oxford: Oxford University Press.

Middlehurst, R. and Woodfield, S. (2007), 'International activity or internationalisation strategy: Insights from an institutional pilot study in the UK', *Tertiary Education and Management*, 13, (3), 263–79.

Rudzki, R. (1995a), 'The application of a strategic management model to the internationalization of higher education institutions', *Higher Education*, 29, (4), 421–41.

—— (1995b), 'Internationalisation of UK business schools: Findings of a national survey', in P. Blok (ed.), *Policy and Policy Implementation in Internationalisation of Higher Education*. Amsterdam: EAIE.

Sanderson, G. (2004), 'Existentialism, globalisation and the cultural other', *International Education Journal*, 4, (4), 1–20.

Sarantakos, S. (2005), *Social Research*. Basingstoke: Palgrave Macmillan.

Stier, J. (2002), *Internationalisation in Higher Education: Unexplored Possibilities and Unavoidable Challenges*. University of Lisbon: European Conference on Educational Research.

Toyoshima, M. (2007), 'International strategies of universities in England'. *London Review of Education*, 5, (3), 265–80.

Trowler, P. (2002), *Higher Education Policy and Institutional Change: Intentions and Outcomes in Turbulent Environments*. Buckingham: Society for Research into Higher Education and Open University Press.

Turner, Y. and Robson, S. (2008), *Internationalising the University*. London: Continuum International Publishing Group.

Van Dijk, H. and Meijer, K. (1997), 'The internationalisation cube: A tentative model for the study of organisational designs and the results of internationalisation in higher education', *Higher Education Management*, 9, (1), 157–67.

Chapter 14

Internationalization in the Universities of Spain: Changes and Challenges at Four Institutions

Laura E. Rumbley

Introduction

International dimensions in higher education have been recognized since the foundation of the earliest medieval universities of Europe (Altbach *et al.*, 2001; Haskins, 1923, 2002), but the late twentieth and early twenty-first centuries have witnessed an unprecedented surge of interest and new developments in internationalization in post-secondary education. Much like globalization – a distinct but related phenomenon – internationalization in recent years has moved rapidly to the top of national and institutional agendas across the globe, particularly as this phenomenon has been tightly linked to issues of quality, modernization, innovation, and relevance.

Spain provides an especially interesting and extremely current example of how internationalization has moved centre-stage in higher education, exerting an enormous influence over institutional planning and development, as well as wider national policy discussions of the current and future role of universities. In 2002, Professor Carlos Seoane, a long-time observer of the international dimension in Spanish higher education, wrote 'The internationalisation of the universities now constitutes one of their strategic objectives, and this has been one of the most notable changes in recent years' (p. 237). This assessment makes clear that the phenomenon is today a central consideration for Spanish universities. Yet, with its short history on agendas at both the national and institutional level, internationalization has not been widely or deeply studied in the Spanish context.

The need to understand how internationalization is perceived, operationalized, and sustained (to a greater or lesser degree) in the universities of Spain is becoming more and more critical, however. The country is placing great emphasis on the international recognition and relevance of its universities in a bid to achieve (and sustain) greater economic competitiveness and intellectual excellence (Warden, 2009). Notably, in 2008 the government of Spain launched the publicly sponsored Foundation for the International Promotion of Spanish Universities, known as 'Universidad.es'. That same year it unveiled *University Strategy 2015*, a policy paper outlining its objectives for quality, excellence, competitiveness, and internationalization within the Spanish university system over the next seven years.

Through an analysis of four Spanish university experiences – as well as a consideration of developments at the national level in Spain – this chapter argues that a distinct set of opportunities and imperatives have stimulated Spanish higher education to actively pursue an agenda of internationalization since Spain's accession to the European Union in 1986, and to engage the phenomenon in specific ways. The central conclusion drawn from this exercise is that Spanish higher education is both empowered and constrained by its unique history and current circumstances, but above all demonstrates an impressive and expanding commitment to the international dimension.

Meanwhile, lessons from the Spanish experience provide a window on an expanded understanding of internationalization from a conceptual standpoint, as articulated graphically in the 'delta model for internationalization'. Developed through a process of applying Knight's (1994) seminal 'internationalization cycle' to the four Spanish case study universities discussed here, the delta model highlights the importance of several key contextual factors to the understanding of internationalization within institutions of higher learning; it also brings to the fore the fundamental insight that internationalization is, at its essence, about *change*.

Internationalization in Spanish higher education: an overview

Understanding internationalization in a number of specific Spanish institutions requires a broader sense of the international dimension in the country's higher education system as a whole. Indeed, a series of rationales, strategies, and outcomes relevant to internationalization stand out quite clearly in the case of Spain, characterized by a higher education community that has moved assertively over the last two decades to engage internationally in a variety of ways.

Rationales

Spanish interest in internationalizing the university sector can be usefully distilled down to three primary sets of rationales: historical, geopolitical and strategic.

To an important degree, contemporary internationalization in Spanish higher education is rooted in a particular historical understanding of Spain's place in the world. Spain's historical ties to the European community of nations, its centuries-old political and cultural interactions with the north of Africa, and its long colonial history in Latin America, provide a clear point of entry for contemporary Spanish higher education to engage with these particular regions of the world.

On the geopolitical front, it is difficult to underestimate the importance of contemporary Spanish involvement in the political and social life of Europe, and the way that this engagement has energized the processes of internationalization in the universities of Spain. In very succinct terms Martha Peach (2001) asserts that Spain's entrance into the European Union in 1986 'breached the walls surrounding education and introduced educational internationalization' (p. 70). Since that time, Spain's participation in the European educational framework has been highly enthusiastic and steadily growing, based in large part on the compelling opportunities and imperatives presented by the climate of integration and cooperation in Europe over the last nearly 25 years, particularly as embodied by the ERASMUS student mobility programme and, more recently, the Bologna Process.

Beyond the issues of history and geopolitics, it is crucial to recognize that Spanish higher education is also motivated to internationalize for very basic strategic reasons. The effects of globalization are challenging universities everywhere to radically reassess fundamental assumptions about their missions and modes of operation, and internationalization is emerging as a primary response to the changing paradigm for higher education. Preparing graduates for work in a global economic order; facilitating access by faculty and students to key information networks; and enabling students and researchers to contribute to – and benefit from – rapid new developments in the fields of science and technology are just a few of the profoundly important challenges Spanish higher education faces in the new century.

Strategies

Spanish universities have tended to engage in strategies for internationalization that are both geographically and operationally oriented. Specifically, there has been a clear geographic focus on engagement with Europe and Latin America (with an important although quantitatively less robust interest in the United States), coupled with emphasis on several strategic lines of operational activity: student mobility, faculty activities, and cooperation for development.

Europeanization has arguably been synonymous with internationalization in the case of Spain, given the very real and pervasive way that the programmes and activities for European student mobility and inter-institutional collaboration in the European context have driven the overall process of overseas Spanish higher education engagement since Spain joined the European Union in 1986. Evidence of this can be seen most obviously in the highly dynamic and committed Spanish participation in the ERASMUS student mobility programme since its inception. The Spanish state has played an important role through its national ERASMUS agency by encouraging institutional participation, and coordinating and tracking engagement with this flagship program. Even more important, however, have been the actions of the individual universities, which have taken an enormous amount of initiative to develop their own institutional strategies for international engagement through ERASMUS. Across the board they have developed new offices, assigned new staff, drafted new policies, and crafted an extraordinary number of linkages with peer institutions across the continent.

Second only to engagement with Europe, Latin America is a primary area of interest for the Spanish higher education system. Here, the focus is on mobility – mostly in terms of graduate students from Latin America to Spain, and Spanish faculty members to Latin America – and cooperation for development.

The Spanish government has played a notable role in facilitating interaction with the region, through both policy and funding mechanisms. Meanwhile, Latin America occupies an extremely important position for many individual universities, as evidenced by the nature of their strategic orientations toward Central and South America and the Caribbean. There are also a notable number of Ibero-American links through academic networks and inter-institutional associations and ongoing (although slow-moving) progress on the development of an Ibero-American Higher Education Space (*Declaración de Salamanca*, 2005).

Spanish engagement with the United States clearly does not display a comparable degree of breadth and intensity as it does with Europe and Latin America. However, connections with the United States have been and continue to be important to the universities of Spain, if problematic in concrete operational terms. At the level of graduate education and research, much has been accomplished through individual contacts as well as such official mechanisms as the American Fulbright Program. At the undergraduate level, however, there is a significant imbalance in the numbers of Spanish students travelling to the United States for study versus American undergraduates in Spain, and less-than-ideal penetration of American students (who often study in 'island programmes') directly into Spanish university classrooms.

Within the functional areas of Spanish strategies for internationalization, without doubt, student mobility has been the lynchpin. Attracting international students to Spanish campuses and facilitating 'study abroad' experiences for domestic students have been the primary methods by which the universities of Spain have operationalized their international orientations. The opportunities presented by such early initiatives as the ERASMUS program, and to a notable but lesser extent the Programa de Cooperación Internacional of the Spanish Agency for International Cooperation (known by its Spanish acronym, AECI), have served to encourage the universities of Spain over the last two decades to build strategies for internationalization that put student mobility at the heart of the endeavour.

Although much more difficult to measure and document than student mobility, a variety of faculty activities constitute a significant area of focus for internationalization in the universities of Spain. The increasing numbers of international students in Spanish universities and Spanish students with study abroad interests have served as a catalyzing force, pushing professors to reconsider their material and their audiences. Faculty mobility through the ERASMUS programme is another indicator – in 2007–08 the European Commission estimated that some 3,004 Spanish faculty members went abroad under the auspices of the ERASMUS program, second only to Poland with 3,112 internationally mobile faculty members that year (European Commission, 2009b). In addition, the opportunities provided by the European Union for greater collaboration among Spanish and foreign professors have played a significant role in this area, not only enhancing internationalization in the universities of Spain, but also improving the quality and quantity of Spanish research output (Seoane, 2002).

Cooperation for development occupies another important position in Spain's strategic thinking about internationalization, playing out at both institutional and national levels. The agenda of international academic and technical engagement advanced by the AECI supports the assertion that cooperation for development is a key line of action for the Spanish higher education community. Furthermore, it is important to note that the language of cooperation is spread liberally throughout all manner of materials related to Spanish higher education engagement in contexts outside Europe and North America, including official government position papers and documents, mission statements of relevant non-governmental associations, and websites of individual Spanish universities' international programme offices and initiatives.

Outcomes

The process of internationalization in Spanish higher education has achieved three main outcomes over the last two decades. The first is growth – in interest, commitment, and direct participation – in the international dimension. One of the most dramatic examples of the expansion of internationalization can be seen in the ERASMUS student mobility statistics. In Spain's initial year of participation in the programme (1987–88), the country sent just 240 ERASMUS students abroad. In 2007–08, the country sent 23,107 students abroad, second only to Germany, which sent 23,553. Spain also received by far the largest number of ERASMUS students from abroad in 2007–08 – some 27,204, as opposed to second-place France, which received 19,970 (European Commission, 2009a).

A second major outcome has been a wide series of institutional changes directed at managing the international dimension and fostering its ongoing development. These adjustments – which have included the development of new offices, hiring and training of specialized staff, and creation of related policies and procedures – have been extensive and sustained, particularly in response to the profound growth in student mobility noted above.

Finally, accumulated experience with internationalization has bred a new level of confidence among Spanish universities in this area. For example, it is notable (at least symbolically) that Madrid played host to the European Association for International Education's (EAIE) annual conference in September 2009, effectively handling the largest-ever gathering of individuals for this purpose in EAIE's history.

Of course, the considerable achievements of internationalization in Spanish higher education must be set against a balanced assessment of what has not been attained during this period. Most notable here is the fact that, while huge increases in student mobility have been registered over the last two decades, in the context of the overall picture of Spanish student enrolment the proportion of participating students is still quite low. According to 2007–08 data from the European Commission, just 1.41 per cent of Spanish students studied abroad through the ERASMUS programme (which accounts for most of Spain's outward mobility) (European Commission, 2009c). Most of Europe is doing little better, but the percentage is still minimal. Room for improvement is also seen in the context of the breadth of interactions with the United States. Likewise, despite important advances, Spanish relations with Latin America have not yet been sufficiently consolidated. Here, the partners face significant funding gaps, colonial baggage, and a myriad of additional internal and external challenges in their complex web of relationships.

Case study descriptions and key findings

National-level considerations of internationalization in Spain are extremely important, but the exploration of the phenomenon within individual universities provides powerful insight into practical realities on the ground. In 2005–06, data for a doctoral dissertation were gathered from four very different Spanish universities in an effort to address the question of how these universities had responded to the opportunities and imperatives to internationalize since Spain's adhesion to the European Union in 1986. Data for the study were collected via semi-structured interviews with key actors within the administrative and academic leadership at the four participating universities. These perspectives were supplemented through multiple campus visits, as well as an examination of university documents and electronic resources (Rumbley, 2007).

The case study institutions selected were the Universidad Complutense de Madrid (UCM), the Universidad de Sevilla (US), the Universitat Pompeu Fabra (UPF), and the Universidad Alfonso X El Sabio (UAX). These universities reflect to some minor degree the considerable variation across the Spanish higher education system, which is currently comprised of 77 universities (Universidad.es, 2009) in 17 Autonomous Communities. Table 14.1 provides a snapshot of the basic variables relevant to each institution's profile.

Table 14.1 Fundamental characteristics of the case study universities

Institution	Year founded	Enrolment	Location	Legal status
UAX	1994	8,897[*]	Madrid	Private
UCM	1499	87,000	Madrid	Public
UPF	1990	8,525	Barcelona	Public
US	1505	58,343	Sevilla	Public

*   The enrolment figure for the UAX was taken from 'Estadística Alumnado Universitario', a webpage of the Spanish Ministry of Education accessible at http://www.educacion.es/educacion/universidades/estadisticas-informes/estadisticas/alumnado.html

Source: Universidad.es, accessible at http://www.universidad.es/index.php/universidades/publico/listado/idmenu.1108/idcategoria.1113/relcategoria.1137/

Individual institutional experiences

As determined from an analysis of the wide range of data collected from each institution, the case study universities share a number of tendencies with regard to internationalization, but also demonstrate distinct patterns of action as well as a variety of outcomes in this area.

Universidad Complutense de Madrid (UCM)

The UCM is one of the oldest universities in Spain, tracing its foundation back to a royal decree of 1293. During the first two centuries of its existence, the institution is reported to have shared national prominence with the well-known University of Salamanca (UCM, 2003). Today, the UCM boasts the largest enrolment of any Spanish university (Ministerio de Educación, 2009) apart from the Universidad Nacional de Educación a Distancia (UNED), Spain's large, public distance education university. The UCM's long history, large size, wide scope of intellectual and academic activities, central location in the nation's capital, and broad social, political, and cultural penetration lend credence to its assertion that it 'is the flagship university of Spain' (UCM, 2003, p. 12).

Internationalization manifests itself comprehensively at the Complutense. Efforts to internationalize have been made across academic and administrative sectors, through centralized and decentralized mechanisms, and with an eye on both internal and external manifestations of the phenomenon. The institution has for more than 35 years supported a substantial international relations unit, providing it with what most of the study participants from the UCM consider to be appropriate budgetary and decision-making independence to adequately advance the university's international agenda. The centralized Vice Rectorate for International Relations provides a meaningful hub through which to manage the large volume of information and resources running through this enormous institution. At the same time, the university also supports more localized management of many components of the international dimension at the level of individual ERASMUS offices and through the vice-deans for international relations within the various schools and faculties.

These realities speak to a real degree of willingness on the part of the university to internationalize, both because these efforts hold the potential to yield positive results for the institution and because of a sense of inevitability related to the international dimension. Although some study participants acknowledged a degree of reticence and apathy among some stakeholders, there appears to be little to no overt resistance to internationalization, broadly speaking. At the same time, there is a sense of unevenness in the way that internationalization is playing out at the UCM. For example, the UCM is somewhat challenged to reconcile the fact that international engagement has had a longer, stronger tradition in certain academic fields (such as the hard sciences) than in some of the humanities or social sciences areas, such as journalism or law.

Ultimately, the UCM is keenly aware of its status within Spain and the broader Spanish-speaking world as a leading institution of higher education. Internationalization figures heavily in the university's strategy to maintain its flagship status domestically and to further enhance its profile internationally. New initiatives in recent years – such as expanding its summer school offerings in Latin America and focusing on new collaborative programming in China, the Middle East and North Africa – speak directly to the UCM's desire to assert itself internationally in new and innovative ways.

Universidad de Sevilla (US)

The US celebrated its five-hundredth anniversary in 2005 and is the country's second largest institution in terms of enrolment (again, excluding UNED). It plays an important role in the economy, culture, and society of the southern-most – and most populous (Instituto Nacional de Estadística, 2009) – region of Spain, Andalucía.

The US has a strong sense of its own history and place within the regional context of Andalucía, and this sensibility has clearly influenced developments within the international dimension. The history of Andalucía – as a crossroads of cultures across the centuries and as a key link between Europe and the Americas from the fifteenth century – is frequently invoked as a fundamental reason for why the university does (and should) orient itself internationally. Historical perspectives infuse contemporary thinking about the relevance of internationalization in general for the US, and provide a powerful guiding principle for strategies to advance this work.

As a result of its unique history, the US is expressly interested in develop-ing an extensive network of linkages with Latin American universities. The willingness expressed by interviewees to incorporate non-native individuals, ideas, and methods into the university's teaching and research activities is often expressed as a natural outgrowth of the Andalucian experience of conquest, immigration, and cultural absorption and adaptation. The regional orientation is also evident in the way that the university consults and collaborates with other universities in Andalucía, in an attempt to address common policy concerns in a coherent fashion, and maximize benefits through joint ventures (such as shared international student recruitment activities).

There is a purposefulness in the US's internationalization efforts, which can be considered fairly comprehensive in the way that they stretch across the insti-tution and are guided centrally by an annual plan, supported by a dedicated budget line, and overseen by an administrator at the vice-rector level. At the same time, when this study was conducted in 2005–06, the US gave the impres-sion that it was not living up to its full potential in this area. The university's international relations during the study period were overseen by a vice-rector who was also equally responsible for institutional relations and cultural exten-sion. Likewise, the international programming department was admittedly understaffed for an institution of this size and complexity, with aspirations for growth in terms of both quality and quantity of initiatives. There was also a lack of clear vision or hierarchy of priorities articulated by the vice-rector responsible for international relations during the study period. Fundamentally, study participants pointed to a disconnection between aspirations and reality on the ground at the US, ostensibly caused by political, administrative, and financial shortcomings.

Universitat Pompeu Fabra (UPF)

The UPF was established in Barcelona in 1990 and was the first public university in Catalunya to be created following the end of the Franco dictatorship in 1975. Hosting an initial cohort of some 300 students, the UPF has grown considerably over the last nearly twenty years and enrolled nearly 8,500 students in 2008–09. The UPF is especially strong in the areas of business and economics, with one of the top-ranked university libraries in the country (UPF, n.d.). Overall, the university is considered something of a phenomenon in Spanish HE circles, given its rapid development as an institution of high academic quality and considerable international renown.

Context means everything when analyzing the UPF's approach to internationalization, in view of its conscious effort to develop a sophisticated identity that is at once local and international in nature, and very much a product of late twentieth century/early twenty-first century Europe. The UPF is clearly committed to elevating itself to a distinctly international level of activity, while still retaining a deep connection to its local roots. Its faculty is heavily Catalán, but in many cases trained abroad. Its students are drawn in great numbers from Catalunya, but study abroad in significant numbers and share classrooms – especially at the doctoral level – with many peers from outside the country. Indeed, more than 31 per cent of the graduating class in 2006–07 had international study experience and 47 per cent of the doctoral students that year were internationals. Meanwhile, the UPF provides instruction and substantive portions of its key materials not only in Catalán, but also in Spanish as well as English. On many levels, the local and the international are thus uniquely intertwined at the Pompeu Fabra.

Context is also important in terms of the UPF's age. Established in 1990, the institution is a young public university that, as one study participant pointed out, was 'practically born at the same time' as the ERASMUS student mobility program. 'Starting from zero' in the early 1990s and unencumbered by a significant incidence of endogamy, the Pompeu Fabra has evolved during a decade and a half of profound social and political change in Catalunya, Spain, and Europe.

The UPF is characterized by an expansive vision for internationalization that transcends most levels and dimensions of the institution, addressing issues in both quantitative and qualitative terms. Perhaps the most dramatic evidence of the pervasiveness of the phenomenon is the existence of a vice-rector's position (during the study period, 2005–06) that combined responsibilities for graduate education and international relations, which placed internationalization at the heart of the academic enterprise at the UPF. Furthermore, the study participants articulated a very clear understanding that the academic and administrative sides of the house must work closely and effectively together in order to achieve their goals for internationalization, and have already demonstrated a real ability to synchronize these efforts to achieve wide-reaching objectives for internationalization.

Finally, while openly recognizing limitations and challenges for the Pompeu Fabra in its ongoing efforts to internationalize, the study participants from this university overwhelmingly provide an image of an institution supremely confident in its vision for internationalization, both in terms of its appropriateness for the UPF and its achievability. There is real political momentum at the Pompeu Fabra around this issue, as well as an effective operational structure that is primed to carry the institution forward significantly in this area.

Universidad Alfonso Décimo El Sabio (UAX)

At the UAX, a newer, private institution in a publicly dominated higher education system, the data indicated an overt willingness to internationalize. As a group, the UAX study participants expressed a notable sense of personal and professional engagement with the phenomenon of internationalization, and recognized a critical connection between this work and the university's overall relevance and dynamism. However, as with the UCM and US, there is unevenness in terms of the university's international engagement. For example, the UAX's high levels of awareness and commitment (made manifest by a centrally situated and competently administered international relations office, which has existed virtually since the university's founding) are not matched by a well-developed and central role for faculty in the development of the UAX's international policies, programmes, and overall orientation.

The UAX has also opted for 'safety' as it internationalizes. Where the university has committed its energy and resources to internationalization, it has elected to engage in a somewhat narrow band of activities. The focus is on student mobility, and the somewhat limited incursions into the fields of faculty mobility and joint degree programmes represent fairly traditional, low-risk approaches to internationalization. Finally, although the study respondents at the UAX were all disposed to believe in the importance of the international dimension on its own terms, in practice the institution appears to be motivated to act principally in order to respond to a set of externally imposed circumstances. Of primary importance here is the fact that there was little evidence at the time of data collection of any internally generated initiatives for the university's internationalization.

Rationales, strategies and outcomes

Although internationalization at the four case study universities has played out differently over the last two decades, some patterns emerge that hold for the group as a whole. Just as it is possible to identify a set of rationales, strategies, and outcomes that characterize internationalization at a national level in Spain, so too is it possible to frame these concepts in general terms across the case study institutions.

In terms of rationales, there are three main constants at the case study universities. First, it is clear that context matters. More specifically, such factors as the era of the universities' foundation and maturation, their geographic location, and their unique institutional characteristics can serve as strong motivating factors in relation to internationalization. To some appreciable degree, the understanding within each institution that the university and the academic profession are inherently international enterprises is another key rationale for internationalization shared by this small group of Spanish institutions, as is the tendency for key stakeholders to be personally committed to the international dimension.

The strategies for internationalization at the case study institutions are dominated by a two-pronged approach consistent with trends at the national level. These universities pursue geographically focused strategies that place Europe and Latin America at the centre of attention. There is also limited but serious engagement with the United States, as well as a growing interest in Asia. Operationally focused strategies are also key. These are mostly centred on student and faculty mobility and faculty research, with an expanding consideration of other academic activities, such as curriculum reform and pedagogical innovation.

In terms of outcomes, there is another set of trends discernible across the case study universities. First, there have been dramatic increases in the numbers of international programmes offered and participants involved at each institution. Second, there has been a considerable maturing of administrative structures and operational behaviour in the international area. Finally, there is clear and measurable evidence of institutional change at all of the universities as a result of engagement with the phenomenon of internationalization, in terms of both mission and modes of operating.

The case study experiences and the internationalization cycle (Knight, 1994)

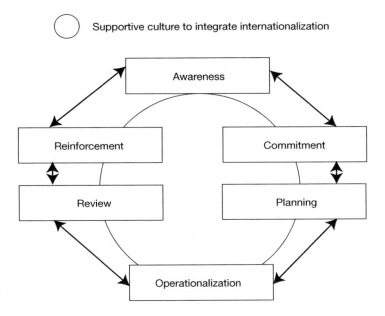

Figure 14.1 Internationalization cycle (Knight, 1994)

Another way to make sense of internationalization at the case study institutions is to consider an analysis set against the conceptual framework known as the 'internationalization cycle' (Knight, 1994). This model (see Figure 14.1) offers an elegantly simple visual representation of internationalization as a process involving six key dimensions: awareness, commitment, planning, operationalization, review, and reinforcement. When applied to the four case study institutions, two key findings emerge. The first is that, among the four universities, the UPF stands out as the most comprehensive and consistent across all six areas. Perhaps more significantly, however, among the other three institutions there is a very clear pattern of unevenness across the six dimensions. This also holds true for the UPF, but in much less stark terms. Specifically, there are high levels of awareness about commitment to and operationalization of the international dimension, but considerably less dynamism and development in the areas of planning, review, and reinforcement.

Figure 14.2 takes Knight's (1994) original model and adjusts it slightly to account for the trends identified in the Spanish universities considered here. In this modified version, the boxes representing awareness, commitment, and operationalization are enlarged to reflect their prominence within the case study universities' experience of internationalization. The boxes representing the less dynamic dimensions of planning, review, and reinforcement remain

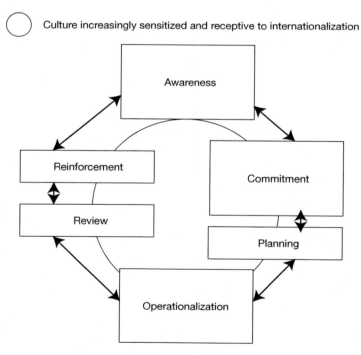

Figure 14.2 Internationalization cycle (Knight, 1994), reflecting findings at the UCM, US, UPF, and UAX (Rumbley, 2007)

smaller, symbolizing the lower profile of these areas as demonstrated by the cases. Furthermore, while the original cycle also indicates that, ideally, there should be a 'supportive culture to integrate internationalization' (Knight, 1994), the modified version in Figure 14.2 adjusts this assumption to capture the idea that the universities in this study, as a group, are operating in contexts in which there is a growing appreciation for the international dimension, if not fully supportive organizational cultures at this time.

The perception of a fundamental unevenness in the way that the case study institutions have engaged the phenomenon of internationalization is important. On the one hand, it speaks to the fact that there is significant momentum behind the movement to broaden and deepen the international dimensions at the institutions involved in this study. However, the levels of energy, resources, and strategic activity applied are clearly not equally distributed across the board, either in terms of approaches or beneficiaries. This is not to say that there is anything inherently wrong with an 'asymmetrical cycle' – a differentiated approach to internationalization may make sense for a particular institution at a given moment in time. What is troublesome in the case of the four case study institutions is that the uneven approach to internationalization appears to be more of an unintended consequence born of underdeveloped planning, review, and reinforcement activities than a result of purposeful strategies for internationalization.

The delta cycle: a new model for internationalization

Knight's (1994) internationalization cycle is eminently serviceable for a consideration of the process of internationalization. However, the application of this conceptual model to the Spanish case study institutions' experience does reveal some missing elements. These include:

a   the broader perspectives of rationale, strategies, and outcomes for internationalization, which address the questions of why universities internationalize, how and in what ways they do this, and to what ends;
b   the recognition and articulation of notable environmental factors – opportunities, imperatives, obstacles, and resources – that play a critical role in shaping institutions' experiences of internationalization;
c   the clear and unequivocal representation of the notion of change, which captures the reality of a fluid external environment as well as the transformational nature of internationalization itself, as evidenced by the adaptive responses of the case study universities.

The delta cycle for internationalization (see Figure 14.3) puts forward a revised and expanded graphic representation of Knight's (1994) original interpretation, and attempts to fill in the gaps noted above. One of the most important implications of this work is the idea that a meaningful analysis of the international dimension at a given institution must move beyond the discrete categories of interest laid out by the original internationalization cycle (Knight, 1994). The exploration of internationalization must get at the underlying questions of why universities are motivated to internationalize,

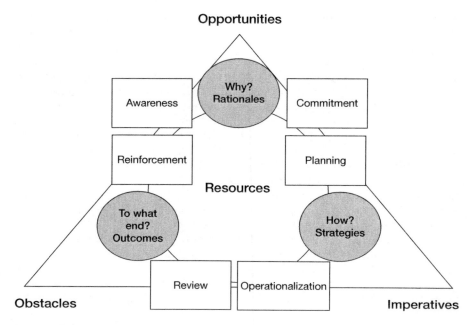

Figure 14.3 Delta cycle for internationalization

how and in what ways they choose to act on these interests, and what the end results of these efforts turn out to be, as well their impacts on the institution and its international interests.

The determination that there are four key contextual factors – opportunities, imperatives, obstacles, and resources – that serve to shape institutional engagement with the international dimension opens the door on a variety of significant implications for the study and practice of university internationalization. To fully understand and develop the phenomenon, the four environmental factors identified above ideally should be monitored and assessed on a regular basis. For many institutions, this may seem a daunting proposition. However, concerns about the ability to adequately monitor the environment may lessen as internationalization becomes more mainstream, and it becomes a much more commonplace activity at many universities for all kinds of stakeholders to think and act internationally. Similarly, while some institutions may feel decidedly acted upon by these environmental factors, others may draw strength from having developed a clearer understanding of these elements, and be spurred to develop their international dimensions in much more proactive ways. These more assertive universities may develop better planning mechanisms that will assist them in responding to the vagaries of their environments; they may even develop strategies, alone or in cooperation with other organizations, in an attempt to alter their environments in ways that are more favourable to their international interests.

Finally, the finding that change is a fundamental element of internationalization at the case study institutions means that policy-makers and practitioners at these institutions must think about the phenomenon in non-static terms. The delta cycle for internationalization asserts that change is the critical backdrop for all other components of internationalization. In order to make sense of internationalization, relevant institutional decision-makers must recognize the changeable nature of the external environment. They must also be cognizant of the ways in which the phenomenon has already, or may yet, transform the institution itself. Proactive and creative strategic planning emerges as a crucially important activity in this context.

Understanding and managing internationalization as a function of change also requires committing and sustaining adequate resources. This is critically important, given the ongoing and fundamental need to review progress, reinforce successes, and potentially change course in the face of new developments.

Summary and conclusions

Through the exploration of experiences at four Spanish universities, this chapter has attempted to shed light on the characteristics of internationalization in Spanish higher education over the last two decades. What hopefully emerges is a reasonably clear picture of institutions and people acting in ways that make sense for the time and place in which they are (or have been, or will soon be) situated; relating logically to their environments, as best they understand these; registering results that represent reasonable outcomes in light of these circumstances; and facing one overarching constant: change.

Seen in this light, the stories of internationalization at the UCM, the US, the UPF, and the UAX provide meaningful examples for other institutions around the world seeking greater insight into their own experiences with the international dimension. They draw attention to the fact that internationalization can be understood through both functional and more theoretical components, is driven and shaped by both internal and external factors, and is anything but a static phenomenon.

Two final thoughts deserve special consideration. First, opportunities and imperatives for internationalization can be extremely powerful forces. Over the last two decades, the case study institutions in this project have arguably faced a healthy and normal range of internal and external obstacles, as well as resource limitations, that have served to complicate their efforts to internationalize. At the same time, they have found themselves in an extremely fortuitous position to benefit from a confluence of compelling and unprecedented opportunities and imperatives to internationalize that have propelled their international agendas forward in highly dynamic ways. The European Union initiatives such as ERASMUS, the Bologna Process, and the commitment of the Spanish government to support and encourage these areas of interest as well as broad engagement across Latin America, represent a short list of some of the factors most relevant to this discussion. As other countries and regions of the world look at their own environments, they would be wise to consider the ways in which opportunities and imperatives have played out in Spain over the last two decades, and to explore how and if lessons may be drawn from this undeniably positive series of developments in the Spanish context. The combination of carrots and sticks, if meaningful and well conceived, can clearly produce dramatic results.

The second concluding consideration here is the fact that the universities of Spain – and arguably those higher education institutions anywhere interested in solid, sustainable internationalization – can no longer avoid engaging in relevant, comprehensive, and well-managed planning, review, and reinforcement activities. The international dimension in higher education globally has reached a degree of complexity and maturity that cannot adequately be sustained through amateurish and/or ad hoc planning and evaluation exercises. Most institutions are operating in a highly competitive environment and must engage in strategic planning processes seriously and consistently in order to advance an agenda of quality, relevance, and sustainability for internationalization. Constantly checking progress through meaningful review activities and rewarding outstanding performance and commitment will be critically important to the international agenda at the most competitive institutions.

To an important degree, the internationalization of higher education in Spain, and elsewhere, hinges on the belief of individuals that the phenomenon matters and provides positive benefits to the institutions to which they are committed. In an increasingly complex and competitive world, however, these personal passions must be hitched to solid intellectual constructs that guide clear thinking, as well as meaningful strategic planning mechanisms that drive workable lines of action. The demands of internationalization are changing and the rewards for its successful elaboration are considerable. The universities of Spain – and their colleagues elsewhere – must move forward with creative visions for the future, as well as purposeful, sustainable plans for achieving their internationalization goals.

References

Altbach, P. G. and Teichler, U. (2001), 'Internationalization and exchanges in a globalized university', *Journal of Studies in International Education*, 5, (1), 5–25.

Declaración de Salamanca (2005), 'Ibero-American summit of heads of state and government. Salamanca, Spain. October 14–15, 2005'. Accessed 18 November 2005 from http://www.cumbre-iberoamericana.org/cumbreIberoamericana/ES/Prensa/comunicadosPrensa/15-10-2005-60.htm.

European Commission (2009a), *Annex 2a: Outgoing and Incoming ERASMUS Student Mobility for Studies in 2007/2008*. Accessed 30 October 2009 from http://ec.europa.eu/education/erasmus/doc920_en.htm.

—— (2009b), *Annex 3: Outgoing and Incoming ERASMUS Staff Mobility for Teaching Assignments and Staff Training Combined in 2007/2008*. Accessed 30 October 2009 from http://ec.europa.eu/education/erasmus/doc920_en.htm.

—— (2009c), *Annex 4: Outgoing ERASMUS Students as a Share of Student Population in 2007/2008 by Country*. Accessed 30 October 2009 from http://ec.europa.eu/education/erasmus/doc920_en.htm.

Haskins, C. (1923, 2002), *The Rise of Universities*. New Brunswick, NJ: Transaction.

Instituto Nacional de Estadística (2009). *Estimaciones de la Población Actual de*

España. Accessed 28 October 2009 from http://www.ine.es/jaxiBD/menu.
do?L=0&divi=EPOB&his=0&type=db.

Knight, J. (1994), *Internationalization: Elements and Checkpoints*. CBIE Research Paper
No. 7. Ottawa, Canada: Canadian Bureau for International Education.

Ministerio de Educación (2009), 'Avance de la estadística de estudiantes
universitarios (curso 2008–09)'. Accessed 28 October 2009 from http://www.
educacion.es/educacion/universidades/estadisticas-informes/estadisticas/
alumnado.html.

Peach, M. (2001), 'Globalization of education in Spain: From isolation to
internationalization to globalization'. *Higher Education in Europe*, 26, (1), 69–76.

Rumbley, L. E. (2007), *Internationalization in the Universities of Spain: Opportunities,
Imperatives, and Outcomes*. Unpublished PhD dissertatation, Boston College (USA).

Seoane, C. (2002), 'Los vínculos interuniversitarios en un mundo global', in R. Puyol
(eds), *La Educación en España: Los Desafíos de las Nuevas Necesidades*. Madrid, Spain:
PricewaterhouseCoopers, 237–54.

Universidad.es (2009), accessed 23 October 2009 from http://www.universidad.
es/index.php/pags/publico/detalle/idpag.94/idmenu.1108/relcategoria.600/
idcategoria.1108.

Universidad Complutense de Madrid (2003), 'Vicerrectorado de Relaciones
Internacionales', *Actividades internacionales en la UCM: Guía práctica para profesores y
estudiantes*. Madrid: S. A. Lavel.

Universitat Pompeu Fabra (2009), *Internacionalización*. Accessed 30 October 2009
from http://upf.edu/international/es/about/internalisation.html

Universitat Pompeu Fabra (n.d.), News. Accessed 17 February 2007 from http://upf.
edu/enoticies/home_upf_en/0504.html.

Warden, R. (2009), 'Spain: Universities race for excellence', *University World News*.
Accessed 4 October 2009 from http://www.universityworldnews.com/article.
php?story=20091001183321358.

Chapter 15

The Role of English Language Teaching in University Internationalization in China

Jiang Yumei

Introduction

The internationalization of higher education (HE) has made its presence felt in nearly every country in the world. As a result, many universities are searching for ways to internationalize themselves by integrating intercultural and multicultural dimensions into teaching, research, and student services (Haigh, 2002). China has witnessed dramatic changes in its higher education system with the influence of the open-door policy, its entry into the WTO in 2000, and trends toward internationalization and globalization. China accelerated the pace of the transition to a market economy (with Chinese characteristics) at the beginning of the 1990s, and the changes undergone by China over the past three decades are so fundamental that virtually no aspect of social life has remained unaffected. HE is no exception. At the system level, Chinese HE has experienced changes with respect to expansion, diversification, massification and commercialization. National projects such as Project 211 and Project 985 have accelerated the pace of HE internationalization and encouraged institutional initiatives. At the institutional level, universities integrate international perspectives into their development, with a focus on student mobility, teaching staff mobility, internationalization of curricula (IOC), establishing branch campuses, institutional cooperation and mutual recognition, international joint programmes and so on.

Internationalization in HE has been a consequence of both national and global economic, political and social drivers. Universities cannot prosper without taking into account their national political, economic and cultural framework or national or local development needs:

> Even the first significant forms of internationalization, characterized by the exportation of university systems in the context of colonization or, nowadays, development aid and international trade in education, are still situated within the national frame of reference of the domestic nation state. (Van Damme, 2000, p. 2)

HE internationalization in China has Chinese characteristics. China is far from being internationalized as a developing country, and so are its institutions.

According to the classification by Huang (2007), China has the import and export-oriented type of internationalization of HE, characterized by 'importing English-language products to enhance the quality of learning and research' and 'exporting educational programmes with distinctive characteristics'. Prior to the late 1990s, dispatching Chinese students abroad constituted the most important part of HE internationalization and, since then, the internationalization of the university curriculum and importation of foreign educational programmes have come to play a central role.

The roles college English curricula play in HE internationalization

The status of language is an important factor influencing the internationalization of HE, in addition to universities' and other institutions' economic level and stage of development. English has become a dominant language in international arenas. As Altbach pointed out, 'the role of English affects HE policy and the work of individual students and scholars . . . English-language products of all kinds dominate the international academic marketplace' (Altbach, 2004). English is more than a language: it has become a passport to the international world.

China, like many other non-English-speaking countries, has attached great importance to English teaching and learning. It is widely recognized in China that foreign language learning, especially English learning, is vital to internationalization and it is not only an important part of the content of IOC but also a strategy to achieve it (Chen, 1997; Wang, 2000). Many institutions in China have put great emphasis on English teaching, and have introduced original textbooks from abroad in recent years as part of their curriculum reform (Huang, 2003). Zhang *et al.* (2006) assert that research universities in particular should promote IOC in several aspects, integrating an international perspective into the existing curricula, developing new internationalized curricula, introducing original teaching material from abroad, and emphasizing English teaching and learning so as to improve students' understanding of foreign cultures and help their adaptation to the international environment.

English proficiency is regarded as a necessary quality in modern citizens. Prior to the late 1980s, students did not learn English until they entered junior middle school in most regions of China, but today nearly all children begin English courses in primary school. In many urban areas, pupils start their English classes from the first year of their elementary education. English is one of the most important subjects all through compulsory education and senior middle school. It is also a compulsory subject in the College Entrance Examination, which is of extreme significance to most Chinese families.

College English has become a required basic course in most higher education institutions since the end of the Cultural Revolution, and the craze for learning English has become increasingly prevalent among college students. The government takes initiatives to promote English learning. Since the 1980s, the central government has implemented three reforms of College English teaching, which have been characterized by the promulgation of three generations of the College English syllabus to improve the quality of College English teaching. The College English Test (CET), administered by the Ministry of Education (MoE) since 1987, is the only nationwide official CET with widespread recognition in China. There are over 10 million people taking this test annually (Zhang, 2008a). Universities used to require CET Band 4 certificates as a prerequisite for a Bachelor's degree, which was not abolished by the MoE until 2004. However, it remains a necessity for college students to achieve at least Band 4 certificates for their future professions, since most employers require job applicants to have CET Band 4 or even Band 6 certificate. Besides, English learning is even more important to students hoping to study abroad as they have to achieve a satisfactory score in international English tests such as TOEFL or IELTS.

College English curriculum reform has been an important aspect of HE quality control in China. Higher education has witnessed a switch from quantity growth to quality enhancement. In 1998, the MoE issued the *Action Plan of Education Promotion for the Twenty-first Century* (*Guangming Daily*, 1999), which stated the policy and objectives of expanding HE enrolment. HE institutions in China have increased enrolment since 1999. According to government statistics, the total enrolment figure for HE in 2003 increased to nearly 17 per cent of the cohort aged from 18 to 21 years (China Youth Daily, 2004). This percentage shows that China has achieved mass HE as defined by Martin Trow. Due to the pace of the development, problems have arisen, with quality of HE, employment of graduates and fairness of HE topping the list. Under such circumstances, the MoE and the Ministry of Finance issued a milestone document *Undergraduate Teaching Quality and Reform Project of Higher Education Institutions* to improve the quality of HE in 2003 (http://cetr.org/ReadNews. asp?NewsID=1094, accessed 16 September 2009). College English curriculum reform is an important aspect of this project: the fourth of the nine goals of the project is to 'teach English with the assistance of information technology so that within four years, over 60 per cent of the undergraduates won't have problems listening and speaking in English' (Gao, 2007, p. 28). The document calls for the establishment of bilingual courses and the application of effective teaching methods and modes to improve college students' discipline-related English proficiency as well as their ability to conduct research in English. It also states the necessity to develop a secure, convenient and efficient online testing system of College English (Department of Higher Education, 2007). This project is a very important step to improve the quality of HE on the basis of expanding and to bring Chinese universities closer to international standards.

Case study: the reform of the College English curriculum at Nanjing University

Nanjing University, established in 1902 and known as one of the oldest and most prestigious universities in China, is a top research university in Nanjing, Jiangsu Province, which is located in eastern China. It has attracted strong policy and financial support from the central government and has been involved in nearly every national strategic higher education project. In 1993, the central government disseminated *The Outline for Reform and Development of Education in China* (Communist Party of China Central Committee, 1993), which emphasized the necessity of building up approximately a hundred key universities, a few key disciplines and specifications, and ensuring selected universities reach a high world ranking in the quality of their education, research activities, and administration and management. With the promotion of this document, Project 211 was implemented in 1995 by the central government to make an attempt to establish a hundred key universities in China by the twenty-first century. It is considered to be the first key national project in higher education that has been funded intensively by the government since the establishment of the People's Republic of China in 1949. In 1998, Project 985, initiated at the speech made by former chairman Jiang Zemin on the one hundredth anniversary of Peking University, aimed at establishing some first-rank and world-class universities in China within the next ten to 20 years. Nine universities, including Tsinghua University, Beijing University, Fudan University and Nanjing University, were selected to be funded intensively by the central government as well as local authorities. Nanjing University was a member of the first group of universities involved in these strategic projects.

Internationalization has been an important strategy to improve the international profile of Nanjing University. As indicated in its mission statement, it aims at 'cultivating top leaders of international horizons, high standards, and innovative ability' (Nanjing University, 2009). It has undertaken the task of the establishment of internationalization in four aspects (Luo, 2008). First, it emphasizes the internationalization of disciplines. It has established joint programmes with many countries and regions such as the US, Germany, Japan, the UK, Canada, Holland and France. The Hopkins-Nanjing Center, jointly established by Nanjing University and Johns Hopkins University in 1986, started Master's degree-conferring programmes in 2006 and had nearly 2,000 graduates by 2008. Second, Nanjing University has made efforts to internationalize its academic research. It successfully held over 130 international conferences from 2001 to 2007 and ten joint conferences with Taiwan from 2004 to 2006. Third, the development of its teaching staff has been aiming at an internationalized level. Around a thousand teachers annually attend international conferences, or study and research aboard.

There are nearly a thousand overseas scholars attending teaching or joint research programmes at Nanjing University each year. Since 2003, the university has started to employ professors from all around the world. Fourth, the student body has become more internationalized. Over 10,000 international students had studied at Nanjing University by 2008 and the annual number exceeded a thousand between 2002 and 2008, with over a third taking degree-conferring programmes. There are around 500 domestic students who have been dispatched overseas for study or research by the university.

Though leading the way in China, Nanjing University has a long way to go in achieving internationalization. Take the student body as an example. The enrolment number of domestic students was 3,200 in 2006, 3,250 in 2007, 3,400 in 2008 and 3,600 in 2009, which totals 13,450 (Nanjing University, 2010). International students, comparatively speaking, are far fewer in number than domestic students. Furthermore, the majority of international students pursue Chinese language and culture-related programmes and study in the Institute for International Students on Gulou, the main campus. The majority of domestic undergraduate students study on Xianlin Campus, which is 18 kilometres away from Gulou campus. Therefore, the campuses are far from internationalized in terms of the student body.

As far as curriculum creation is concerned, Nanjing University has also made great progress. The statistics quoted by administrative officials of Nanjing University in 2006 (Zhang and Li, 2006) show that Nanjing University employs over 200 foreign teachers every year; more than 150 courses have used original textbooks introduced from overseas; nine of the total of 74 undergraduate majors are related to research on international issues and there have been over 350 internationally related courses; a systematic comparison was conducted between 2,000 courses within the Nanjing University curriculum and over 4,000 courses in institutions of more than 20 countries and regions, which paved the way for developing or updating a thousand courses and creating over 300 bilingual courses.

The College English curriculum plays a supportive role in developing an internationalized curriculum. It helps in overcoming language barriers, introducing cultural and social knowledge from English-speaking countries, and facilitating students' professional development in the international environment. The College English curriculum at Nanjing University is renowned as one of the best in China. Nanjing University was elected one of 180 'pilot universities' of College English in China in 2004 and its College English curriculum was the national 'quality curriculum' in 2006. The Department of Applied Foreign Language Studies, which is responsible for College English teaching, was included in the first batch of exemplary units of College English reform.

What is the background of the College English reform?

The latest nationwide reform of College English teaching started in 2002, aiming at improving students' listening and speaking abilities so as to enhance their overall English ability (Zhang, 2008a). The MoE has designated three goals for the reform. The first is the reform of the syllabus; the second is reform of the teaching methods and contents, including textbooks, software, teaching methods and modes; and the third is reform of CET.

The MoE is determined to reform the College English curriculum for several reasons. First, College English teaching cannot satisfy the needs of both students and employers any longer. In spite of the fact that Chinese students study English for around ten years, their English competence is not developed enough for them to accomplish tasks after graduation. There are an increasing number of criticisms of the 'deaf and dumb English' style of English education, where students study English, but are still unable to understand or speak it properly by the end of their educational programme. Second, the policy of HE internationalization calls attention to the need to improve language competence. Mastering at least one foreign language, especially English, is vital to internationalization because language is the media of communication in economics, politics and culture. IOC also makes it important to master foreign languages. With more original textbooks, bilingual or English-taught causes, exchange programmes and international research opportunities, both teachers and students are urged to improve their English proficiency. Third, the reform aims at improving students' listening and speaking abilities so as to enhance their 'ability to use English in a well-rounded way' (Zhang, 2008b), which goes beyond simple linguistic competence and will have far-reaching effects on their life and career.

Under such circumstances, the MoE issued the latest *College English Curriculum Requirements* (*Requirements* for short) in 2003 and in 2007 it released the official version, which is no longer prescriptive for every institution, but is understood to be the reference document directing institutional reform on various aspects of College English teaching. According to the document, institutions have more freedom and autonomy to make their own decisions on their own curriculum:

> The requirements for undergraduate College English teaching are set at three levels, i.e., basic requirements, intermediate requirements, and higher requirements. The basic requirements are the minimum level that all non-English majors have to reach before graduation. Intermediate and advanced requirements are recommended for those colleges and universities which have more favourable conditions; they should select their levels according to the school's status, type and education goals. (Department of Higher Education, 2007, p. 23)

As a top research university, Nanjing University designed its own syllabus of College English in accordance with advanced requirements, which underlie the course design, teaching models, evaluation and teaching administration.

What are the changes taking place in the English curriculum?

CHARACTER AND OBJECTIVES OF COLLEGE ENGLISH

Before the promulgation of *Requirements* in 2004, the curriculum objective of College English was defined as 'to develop students' considerable existing reading ability and that of listening, speaking, writing and translation to enable them to communicate in English' (Revision Group of College English Syllabus, 1999, p. 1). College English teaching should help students to 'set solid linguistic foundations, master good language learning methods and improve cultural awareness so as to meet the needs of social development and economic construction' (cf.). The new objective set in *Requirements* is:

> . . . to develop students' ability to use English in a well-rounded way, especially in listening and speaking, so that in their future studies and careers as well as social interactions they will be able to communicate effectively, and at the same time enhance their ability to study independently and improve their general

cultural awareness so as to meet the needs of China's social development and intercultural exchanges. (Department of Higher Education, 2007, p. 23)

Comparatively speaking, the objectives stated in the two syllabi are different in three aspects. First, there is a transition of focus in terms of competency. The teaching objective switches from a priority on writing ability, to 'students' ability to use English in a well-rounded way', especially in listening and speaking. According to the definition of user/learner competence provided by the Common European Framework of Reference for Languages (Council of Europe, 2001), two types of competencies are distinguished: general and linguistic. General competencies are considered to comprise declarative knowledge (knowledge of the world, socio-cultural knowledge and intercultural awareness), skills and know-how (practical skills and know-how, intercultural skills and know-how), existential competence (attitudes, motivations, values, beliefs, cognitive styles and personality types), and ability to learn (Council of Europe, 2001), which are as important as communicative language competencies. Communicative competence in this narrower sense has the following components: linguistic competencies, socio-linguistic competencies and pragmatic competencies. *Requirements* has shifted the focus from linguistic competencies to a broader category of competency, incorporating both communicative competence and general competence. The notion of 'ability to use English in a well-rounded way' seems ambiguous, and an explanation of this ability is illustrated in Figure 15.1 and Table 15.1 (Wang and Chen, 2004).

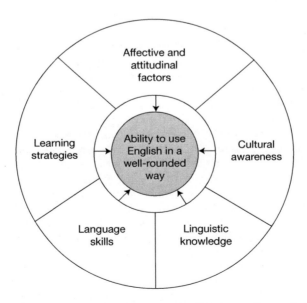

Figure 15.1 Factors influencing 'Ability to use English in a well-rounded way'

Table 15.1 Components of influencing factors

Ability to use English in a well-rounded way	Affective and attitudinal factors	International horizons, homeland awareness, team spirit, self-confidence, interest and motivation
	Cultural awareness	Cultural knowledge, cultural understanding, cross-cultural communication, awareness and competence
	Language knowledge	Phonetics, vocabulary, grammar, function, topic
	Language skills	Listening, speaking, reading, writing
	Learning strategies	Cognitive strategies, coordination strategies, resource strategies, communication strategies

Adapted from Wang (2009)

Ability is influenced by such factors as affective and attitudinal factors, cultural awareness and learning strategies as well as language skills and language knowledge. Compared with the former syllabus, the curriculum objective in *Requirements* adds a new dimension: affective and attitudinal factors (international horizons, homeland awareness, team spirit, self-confidence, interest and motivation). This new dimension belongs to the general competence category and is apparently related to internationalization.

Second, it merits attention that the character of College English is defined as 'a required basic course for undergraduate students' and 'an integral part of higher learning' (Department of Higher Education, 2007, p. 22). The character of College English is 'not only a language course that provides basic knowledge about English, but also a capacity enhancement course that helps students to broaden their horizons and learn about different cultures in the world'. In addition, 'it not only serves as an instrument, but also has humanistic values' (Department of Higher Education, 2007, p. 29). This definition enlarges College English's content coverage and enhances its status in HE.

Thirdly, the ultimate goals of learning English have been changed from 'to meet the needs of social development and economic construction' (Revision Group of College English Syllabus, 1999, p. 1) to 'to meet the needs of China's social development and intercultural exchanges' (Department of Higher Education, 2007, p. 23). Tremendous importance has been attached to intercultural exchanges in English learning, which are also a manifestation of the important role played by English courses in China's internationalization.

Nanjing University has its own syllabi of listening, speaking, reading, and writing. As stated in *Requirements*, 'taking into account the school's circumstances, colleges and universities should follow the guidelines of the *Requirements* and their College English teaching goals in designing their College English course system' (Department of Higher Education, 2007, p. 29). College English, as stated in the College English syllabi of Nanjing University, is a teaching system applying a variety of teaching modes and methods and focusing on language knowledge and skills, learning strategies and cross-cultural communication; it not only provides students with a language tool but also serves as an indispensable part of a comprehensive curriculum; therefore, it aims at developing students' applied language ability and enhancing their ability to study independently and improving their all-round English skills to prepare them for international communication and lifelong learning (Wang, 2009). The College English curriculum at Nanjing University, keeping pace with *Requirements*, is undergoing a transition in teaching objectives, which will result in changes in course content, application and administration, and testing and assessment.

According to the College English syllabus of Nanjing University, the teaching system is classified into three parts, classroom-based teaching, extracurricular teaching, and testing and assessment. The mechanism of this system is illustrated in Figure 15.2 (Wang and Chen, 2004). Classroom-based teaching is at the core of the whole teaching mechanism; extracurricular teaching and learning is an extension of the classroom; testing and assessment not only helps teachers obtain feedback, improve the administration of teaching, and ensure teaching quality but also provides students with an effective means to adjust their learning strategies and methods, improve their learning efficiency and achieve the desired learning effects.

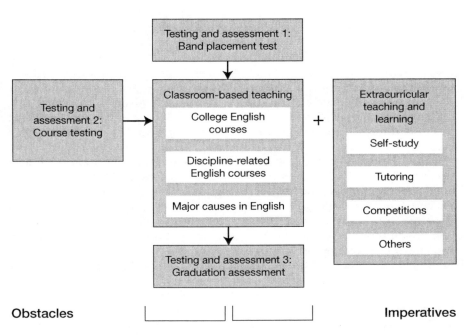

Figure 15.2 The College English teaching system (from Wang and Chen, 2004)

Course Content

The College English course system is defined in *Requirements* as 'a combination of required and elective courses in comprehensive English, language skills, English for practical uses, language and culture, and English for Special Purposes' (Department of Higher Education, 2007, p. 29). It demonstrates that the course content includes not only language knowledge and skills, but some components of general competencies. For example, English content for practical uses may involve both language knowledge and declarative knowledge in professional or academic contexts. According to the Council of Europe Framework (CEF), language activities are generally contextualized within domains which may be broadly classified as fourfold: the public domain, the personal domain, the educational domain and the occupational domain (Council of Europe, 2001, p. 14). Such content usually sets 'special purposes' as either professional or academic ones. All human communication depends on a shared knowledge of the world. In language use and learning, part of the knowledge involved is directly related to language and culture. At the same time, 'academic knowledge in a scientific or technical educational field, and academic or empirical knowledge in a professional field clearly have an important part to play in the reception and understanding of texts in a foreign language relating to those fields' (Council of Europe, 2001, p. 11). Therefore, in the reformed College English course, components of general competence such as academic and professional knowledge, intercultural skills and know-how, learning attitudes, motivations and learning strategies have been integrated into course content and acquired more importance, because the development of general competencies is indispensable to the that of communicative competences and has become increasingly important to higher learning.

The course content in this case has been undergoing considerable changes from exclusively language and culture-related knowledge and from skills to more complex and multi-dimensional knowledge and skills. Up to the turn of the century, the College English courses at Nanjing University mainly focused on language knowledge and skills. Since the beginning of this century, there have been more and more courses integrating both language and other competences.

Courses involved in the College English teaching system are classified into three categories, College English courses, discipline-related English courses and major courses in English. College English courses are designed to improve students' mastery of English language and culture, and are categorized into comprehensive basic courses and specified elective courses. Students should first obtain required credits for basic courses and then take specialized elective courses, including discipline-related English courses and major courses in English, to meet their needs. A detailed mapping of the course content is illustrated in Table 15.2.

Discipline-related English courses cater for the needs of students in different disciplines. They take language acquisition as the principal objective, with professional background and needs taken into account. For example, the Physics undergraduate programme involves an elective course named

Table 15.2 Course content of the College English curriculum

Comprehensive basic courses	Specialized elective courses		
Comprehensive English	Language knowledge and skills	Literature and culture	Academic research and application
Band 1	Vocabulary	British and American society and culture	Practical English writing
Band 2	Grammar	Cross-cultural communication	Academic English
Band 3	Speaking	English newspaper and magazine reading	Thesis writing
Band 4	Listening	British and American novels	English learning strategies
Band 5	Interpretation	English films and television	
Band 6	Viewing, listening and speaking		
Band 7	Public speaking and debating		
Band 8	Writing Reading Translation		

From Wang *et al.*, 2004

'Physics English Reading'. Major courses in English focus on major-related knowledge or skills, with English used as the teaching language. In the major of Public Administration, 'New Public Administration', taught in English, is a core course of the undergraduate programme.

Teaching administration

Administration is vital to the success of a reform. Nanjing University set up a committee in 1998 to supervise College English teaching and reinforced it in 2003. That committee, in the charge of a vice-president of Nanjing University, operates at the institutional level so that various disciplines and administrative departments can cooperate and coordinate effectively to facilitate the reform of College English teaching.

To achieve more student-centredness and individualization, this university has reduced the number of required English courses from 12 credits to eight and encouraged a larger number and variety of elective English courses from September 2009. Elective courses are not limited to language knowledge and skills and serve to improve students' overall attainment. Students are faced with more varieties and choices and their needs may be more accurately met.

College English teachers have more opportunities for professional development. A larger percentage of them pursue improvement either by means of further education or overseas training. Among the 91 College English teachers at Nanjing University, 11 have a Doctor's degree and 16 are taking doctoral programmes. Between 2003 and 2006, 52 teachers went to English-speaking countries such as the US, Canada and Australia either to further their education or receive professional training.

Teaching model

In view of the marked increase in student enrolments and the relatively limited resources, it is necessary to remould the existing unitary teacher-centred pattern of language teaching by introducing computer/classroom-based teaching models. The new model is built on modern information technology, particularly network technology, so that English language teaching and learning is, to a certain extent, free from the constraints of time or place and geared towards students' individualized and autonomous learning.

Nanjing University has invested much in applying information technology to College English teaching. It has successfully established a web-based teaching model. An online teaching platform, Skyclass, was built in 2000 and has been updated regularly ever since. The platform provides online teaching materials with video-taped lectures, web-based reference material, and a self-testing database, all of which facilitate students' autonomous learning and assessment. In addition, it has a large database of text, audio and video College English material covering a large variety of topics, such as politics, economy, history, literature, culture, technology, entertainment and so on. This platform can not only provide students with rich resources in their classroom-based and autonomous learning, but enrich their after-class life and improve their ability to use English in a well-rounded way. The College English Learning Centre, built in 2002, was the most advanced nationwide at that time, with three multimedia classrooms catering for more than three hundred students free of charge. In 2004, two multi-functional language laboratories, each with 55 seats, were built. On the new Xianlin campus, more language laboratories, pronunciation laboratories, web classrooms and student language-practice classrooms are available.

Evaluation

As mentioned above, there are three forms of evaluation: the band placement test at the start, a class test for progression and a graduation test at the end. These three types work together to ensure the quality control of College English teaching and graduate quality of students.

There have been two changes in the course testing system. One is that more emphasis has been placed on formative assessment in addition to summative assessment. A higher percentage of the total score has been given to mid-term exams and class performance, such as homework, quizzes or participation in classroom activities. Take oral English courses as an example: class performance takes up 40 per cent of the total score, the mid-term exam takes up 30 per cent, and the final exam takes up the rest.

The other change is assessment in both written and oral forms. Twenty per cent of every credit students are awarded in English comprises oral performance, and there are both written and oral tests in most of the English classes.

Summary and conclusion

To sum up, the English curriculum, to a certain extent, owes its reform to and also facilitates HE internationalization in China. There have been dramatic changes in the course character and objectives, course content, teaching administration, teaching model and evaluation. The reforms of the College English curriculum have kept up with new developments in HE in China, have improved teaching quality and meet the needs of the country for qualified personnel in the new era. With the enhanced degree of internationalization in China and its institutions of HE, College English teaching will continue to play an important role and the deepening of teaching reform will be characterized by individualized and autonomous learning facilitated with information technology.

References

Altbach, P. G. (2004), 'Globalization and the university: Myths and realities in an unequal world', *Tertiary Education and Management*, 1, 3–25.

Chen, X. (1997), 'Internationalization of higher education: From history to theories and strategies', *Shanghai Higher Education Research*, 11, 57–61 (in Chinese).

China Youth Daily (2 February 2004), 'Shanghai took the lead into the stage of popularization of higher education', accessed online at http://www.edu.cn/ 20040202/3098144.shtml, 20 May 2010.

Communist Party of China Central Committee [CPCCC] (1993), *Outline for Reform and Development of Education in China*, Beijing: People's Press.

Council of Europe (2001), *Common European Framework of Reference for Language: Learning, Teaching, Assessment.* Cambridge: Cambridge University Press.

Department of Higher Education, Ministry of Education (2007), *College English Curriculum Requirements.* Beijing: Higher Education Press (in Chinese).

Gao, S. (2007), 'Major measures to improve undergraduate teaching quality in higher education institutions', *Higher Education*, 3, 26–32 (in Chinese).

Guangming Daily newspaper, 25 February 2009.

Haigh, M. J. (2002), 'Internationalization of the curriculum: Designing inclusive education for a small world', *Journal of Geography in Higher Education*, 26, 49–66.

Huang, F. (2003), 'Internationalization of higher education in a globalization era: A historic and comparative perspective', *Peking University Education Review*, 1, (2), 93–8 (in Chinese).

—— (2007), 'Internationalization of higher education in the era of globalisation:

What have been its implications in China and Japan?', *Higher Education Management and Policy*, 19, (1), 35–50.

Luo, J. (2008), 'Dance with the world: Internationalization of Nanjing University', from the Nanjing University website: http://ndyp.nju.edu.cn/index. php?option=com_content&task=view&id=320&Itemid=2) (in Chinese), http:// bkzs.nju.edu.cn/plan.htm (accessed 10 September 2009).

Nanjing University (2009), Mission Statement, accessed at www.nju.edu.cn/cps/site/ newweb/foreground/sub.php?catid=45, 10 September 2009.

Revision Group of College English Syllabus (1999), *College English syllabus* (Rev. edn.). Shanghai: Shanghai Foreign Language Press (in Chinese).

Van Damme, D. (2000), 'Internationalization and quality assurance: Towards worldwide accreditation?' *European Journal for Education Law and Policy*, 4, 1–20.

Wang, H. and Chen, H. (2004), 'Individualized syllabus: Guarantee of successful teaching reform', *Chinese Foreign Language*, 2. http://www.cflo.com.cn/w/wznr. aspx?tag=l6&id=1649&items=47 (accessed 25 September 2009) (in Chinese).

Wang, S. (2009), 'On-line training of College English teachers in Chinese higher institutions', March 21, 2009, http://english.enetedu.com/.

Wang, Y. (2000), 'Internationalization of the curriculum in universities', *Liaoning Education Research*, 10, 44–6 (in Chinese).

Zhang, D. and Li, L. (2006), 'Characteristics and strategies of internationalization of the curriculum in research universities', *Higher Education of Science*, 2, 4–8 (in Chinese).

Zhang, A. and Jin, M. (2006), 'Internationalization: The way to high-level research universities in China', *Higher Education Development and Evaluation*, 6, 15–19 (in Chinese).

Zhang, Y. (2008a), 'An overall plan for the reform on CET', *Chinese Higher Education*, 18, 26–7 (in Chinese).

—— (2008b), 'More efforts to improve College English teaching', *Chinese Higher Education*, 17, 17–20 (in Chinese).

PART IV

Emerging Themes, Issues and Challenges

Chapter 16

The Commoditization and Standardization of Higher Education

Paul Gibbs

Introduction

In the past 20 years or so, higher education's role in the knowledge economy has undergone major transformation. Throughout Europe there has been a general tendency to erode the social contract and substitute one based on more explicit financial and economic imperatives. The underlying trend has been towards greater efficiency, driven by competitive forces within existing and between new providers of higher education. Technological change, institutional avarice for revenue and ideological dominance have fuelled the globalization of higher education, and the General Agreement on Trade in Services (GATS) is likely to accelerate these trends.

Thus transformed, higher education institutions have tended to dismiss a mission of 'common good' and embrace the fetishism of a Marxist commodity. The purpose of the shift seems clear. In an age of consumerism, institutions have embraced a business model and supplied consumables to a wider range of customers; and, like many other industries, they have sought to expand their market to attract international customers and private investment in order to compete on a global scale. Along the way, higher education redefines itself and, I suggest, risks sacrificing the diversity of its national and cultural vitality to standardization, comparability and cost effectiveness. This is evident structurally, as control has been eased away from and, indeed, often willingly relinquished by, the state, privatizing knowledge production. This homogenization of product and standardization of delivery come at a cost, both in terms of the power passed to those who determine curriculum and can afford to offer its delivery, and the risk of standardizing thought, language, innovation and notions of employability.

One example is the convergence of culture. Are global values designed to satisfy international ranking of universities worth the cost of local characteristics? According to Marginson (2005), one such ranking system, the Shanghai Ranking, shows that it is possible to create a hegemonic global-standard research university, but at the price of global standardization, subordination of most universities and countries, and the washing away of cultural and educational diversity. Indeed, the GMAT examination is now taken in a hundred countries, standardizing the level and form of acceptable knowledge for those seeking to enter prestigious schools. More widespread, moreover, is the use of the International Standard Classification of Education (ISCED), which is designed as an instrument for assembling, compiling and presenting comparable indicators and statistics of education, both within individual countries and internationally. Also, the Bologna Agreement is intended to create a common European higher education area, based on a common qualification framework. Finally, there is now even a prize, the Higher Education in Standardization award, offered by the International Organization for Standardization (ISO), won in its inaugural year by China's Jiliang University in 2008. According to the 2009 flyer, the aims of this award are to:

> . . . raise awareness of the importance of standardization worldwide by supporting institutions of higher education that have developed and implemented successful programmes related to standardization as a tool to access world markets, transfer technology and promote good business practice and sustainable development. (International Organization for Standardization, 2009)

We thus might assume that, in a complex globalized world, to be successful we need standards to understand, intervene, compare, communicate and evaluate. In doing so, we are performing something worthy; worthy, that is, of recognition from a logic that sees simple comparability, common standards and quality as a good, manageable goal and a common basis for cooperation. In this chapter, I want to consider on whose terms this is carried out and whether the consequences turn learning into a financial commodity, and diversity into commonality.

Commodification or commodity?

I shall begin by defining what is meant by commodification and non-commodification. Here, commodification refers to the production and delivery of goods and services for monetized exchange by capitalist firms in pursuit of profit. In Marxist political economy, commodification takes place when economic value is assigned to something that traditionally would not be considered in economic terms, for example an idea, identity or gender. Such 'commodity fetishism' (Ball, 2004) goes beyond the notion of consumption which typifies our everyday lives and, again, as Ball (2004, p. 2) states, we are 'denying the primacy of human relationships in the production of value, in effect erasing the social'.

As such, commodification has three constituent components, all of which must be present for it to be defined as commodified: goods and services are produced for exchange, exchanges are monetized and monetary transactions take place for the purpose of profit (surplus). For exponents of the commodification discourse, therefore, contemporary economies are characterized by one mode of exchange replacing all others. In this view of an increasingly hegemonic capitalism, the commodity economy becomes the economic institution rather than one form, among others, of producing and delivering goods and services. Does this sound like higher education to you? To commentators such as Willmott (1995; 2003), it certainly raises issues about the essential values of higher education in the development of the student as a person and as a carrier of culturally valued knowledge. It seems to him that this development is being replaced by activities devised to increase the exchange value in terms of resources that will flow to form external metrics such as research assessment exercises.

The term 'commodity', however, when used in management literature does not assume the tightly defined notion of the economist, but is used more freely to mean a packaged, consumable product capable of being considered a component of the market mechanism. It has become part of the corporate discourse of the academy as it finds its place in the knowledge industry, where the university is a revenue generator; where its intellectual capital is a resource, an asset to be leveraged, and knowledge itself becomes a commodity to be produced and traded in a market where academic endeavour and students are the merchandise. But this use is ever more dangerous in an educational context, for it seduces educationalists into devising marketing-orientated offerings in place of education. The use confirms the transformation of education into business and reveals the concept's commercial origins

Knowledge economies

The notion of a knowledge economy is widespread, so I shall limit comments here to key points relevant to the argument regarding higher education. The notion of a knowledge economy has emerged to account for the transformation from industrial to post-industrial economies among Organization for Economic Co-operation and Development (OECD) countries. Rather than focusing on the production and transformation of raw materials, as was the case in the past, new information and communication technologies and increasing globalization allow 'knowledge economies' to target knowledge-intensive activities: production, processing and transfer of knowledge and information (Nowotny *et al.*, 2001). The currency of knowledge economies is novelty, or innovation; the emergence of new ideas and new ways of doing things. As a consequence, knowledge, once considered a scarce resource, has proliferated into 'information' and into a marketable product. In a knowledge economy, knowledge is valued for its potential to generate economic development and prosperity through innovation. This instrumentalization of knowledge has meant that the kind of knowledge that is particularly prized in a knowledge economy is that which may be readily transformed into marketable products and services. This re-situating of knowledge as a tradable product radically changes the role of university research (Lincoln, 1998). A new set of demands is being made of universities, Nowotny and colleagues argue, such that knowledge is increasingly being produced for, and in the context of, application.

The notion of 'mode 2 knowledge', a term coined by Gibbons *et al.* (1994), points to a blurring of the division between knowledge 'creators' and knowledge 'consumers' in the past, when the academy was equated with the former, and industry and the professions with the latter. As Nowotny and colleagues point out, this has created a context where a university's research is increasingly contextualized and packaged for trade.

The demands of 'application', or the usability of knowledge, are increasingly influential in determining what is researched and how, particularly through the research funding arms of government. Policy initiatives on the part of governments are increasingly aimed at promoting education and research in the 'key innovation areas' of information and communications technologies, mathematics and science. This creates tensions in university environments where, traditionally, knowledge has been pursued for its own sake (Readings, 1997).

The OECD sees universities as playing a key role in strategies for building a national innovation system. The logic of economic growth through the creation and transfer of knowledge is both persuasive and pervasive. But are other benefits of a renewed emphasis on 'applied knowledge' being overlooked? What other reasons might there be for reasserting the value of knowledge that emerges through and is relevant to practices that are not reducible to economic value? I consider this as a form of de-commoditization, where I turn the instrument of the market – marketing – onto itself, to work against the dominance of the marketing and realize the liberating notion of education of which I spoke in my introduction.

Seeking to turn education into a commodity, framing it in market terms and encouraging the entry of commercial concerns could be seen as simply an expression of neo-liberal politics in a particular country. However, we need to understand the nature of the forces that have pushed governments into adopting such policies – and it is here that we can see the process of globalization directly at work. This might be conceptualized as a fundamental attack on the notion of public goods, and upon more liberal ideas of education. Learning is increasingly seen as a commodity or as an investment, rather than as a way of exploring what might help lives flourish.

Doti (2004) has described colleges and universities in the USA using price as a discriminator of their product, and he claims that price is the attribute that distinguishes the higher education market from a commodity market. He argues that this distinction is being lost and, if this is the case, that higher education is becoming more like a commodity. His empirical study suggests that the practice of balancing fees and rebates to attract students is declining, while at different rates. Thus, the more selective universities retain a greater edge of discrimination values in financial terms than the majority, which cannot aspire to such a policy and decrease fees and increase discounts when they see their returns decline over time. This represents a financial argument to resist the market forces of commoditization – and there are others.

Furthermore, the operating principle of the market tends to hand over moral responsibility to the market-making educational services for more attributes than are appropriate. Should the attributes of tolerance, justice and protection of the vulnerable be mediated through a market mechanism? Moreover, the market's speed of reaction should surely be different to that of a commodity market; time to contemplate, reason and deliberate, rather than simply assemble information, draw the most obvious self-interested conclusion, then act.

In this sense I envision the commodification of higher education somewhat as Standish (1997) does in his reflection on the use by Heidegger of the concept of 'ready-at-hand' and 'present-at-hand'. He comments that, when functioning correctly, things become what they are when used, not when they are observed. It is only when they malfunction that their contribution is really perceived. This awareness allows us the possibility of re-relating to things and seeing their wider potential. The point is that, if education becomes no more than a taken-for-granted, instrumental service which is ready-at-hand, personal engagement is limited to its perceived use. The educative process can reveal the potential of what is ready-at-hand through allowing us to become involved in ways beyond treating that which is encountered as mere equipment for something. There is a danger that students may 'come to think of themselves in terms of sets of competencies aptly summed up in standardized records of achievement, and to see education in these limited terms'. Further, the 'supposed priority of the student's autonomy is emphasized through the principles of the negotiated curriculum and the students' ownership of learning . . . where the student selects from a variety of prepared packages and where learning is, in fact, resource-driven' (Standish, 1997, pp. 453–4).

This reduction of the students' learning experience from a holistic one, where they form their future from the decisions they are able to make, to one of training students to fit into one predominant role, is paramount in the shift from Sartrian learning-for-itself to learning-for-others. It is the production model of education best suited to central control and planning. Accompanying this shift is the real risk of students facing the angst of their existence while being alienated from their authentic being.

If this reflection is to be genuine, however, it requires an authentic and self-assured confrontation with the anxieties arising from our fear of personal finitude. This can pose the threat of rejection to the social world, and it is the management of this process, with inappropriate loss of neither self-concern nor being-with-others that is, I propose, an aim of education about which all involved must surely agree. This communal involvement in the self-authentication of members of the community assists one to find meaning in the everydayness of its existence: students feel sufficiently at home to be prepared to risk reflection on themselves as becoming, rather than being. As Bonnett proposes, 'A concern for authenticity would lead to a shift of emphasis in which education is regarded as a process in which the expression and development of the individual through the acquisition of authentic understanding is central' (2003, p. 60).

Many universities are now responding to the demands of professional people at work. In the last ten years there has been a steady growth of professional doctorates (Scott *et al.*, 2004) and Master's degrees that focus on professional areas of learning. Universities have embraced the ways of managerialism in many respects and under the influence of technology (see Heidegger, 1977, 2002) have distanced themselves from a paideia, a rounded education of culture and conduct towards the instrumentality of securing work. This has been argued in many places (for example, Bok, 2003; Aronowitz, 2000; Readings, 1997) and could, as predicted, lead to the self-destruction of the university as it competes in a knowledge economy with commercial research institutions and proprietary training organizations (for example, Microsoft). In this respect it could be argued that work-based professional studies ought to offer a route to the revitalization of the university's research considerations. This is needed because of a decline in the focus of universities due to the fragmentation of their endeavour as a consequence of the specialized ground-plans of the disciplines and the objectification of beings into entities of research.

Globalization and commoditization

Shaw (2005) claims that trade in higher education has been intensified by the rapid growth of newly established universities and colleges in the Middle East and North African region and in South East Asia, both state financed and private. Many of these are strongly oriented to the provision of specific courses, notably in vocationally related areas such as English language, management, paramedical services, media and information technology. Yet globalization has different impacts on those at its core and those low incomes countries that are on its periphery. Here the expensive infrastructure is not available or in the hands of those whose sovereign nation is being 'globalized'. This has led to the role of the state and the private sector changing to that of development of the capacity to deliver skills in a global competitive sense, rather than development of social and economic inclusion. Trading in knowledge, is big business: organized, thoroughly commercial and part of the global capitalist market. Indeed, Koźmiński goes so far as to say that globalization 'implies a unification of the norms and standards that regulate almost all aspects of social life' (2002, p. 365).

Higher education is a valued international commodity and the idea that higher education is a commercial product, to be bought and sold like bananas or airplanes, has reached the global marketplace. The World Trade Organization (WTO) will be considering a series of proposals to make the importing and exporting of higher education subject to the complex WTO protocols. This would free international education from most current restrictions, many of which are designed to ensure its quality and to maintain national control over higher education. As a practical matter, WTO accreditation excludes some providers from offering higher education services, and it involves a somewhat arbitrary application of a constantly evolving set of regional standards. Vanlathem (2003) also expresses concern about the commodification and its marketization through the channels of the WTO.

It is against this background of changes and developments that one must consider the GATS and its implications for the world of higher education. Adopted in 1995 under the WTO, the GATS clearly identifies education as a service to be liberalized and regulated by trade rules. While its supporters see the GATS as an opportunity, others view it more as a threat. For some, the notion of higher education as a tradable commodity is a challenge to the traditional values of higher education – especially the idea of higher education as a public good and a public responsibility.

More universities and new for-profit companies will export academic and professional programmes as a commodity to a variety of student populations. There are already some noticeable differences among national policies in this domain. Australia, the UK and Canada are more oriented to the international market (Ryan, 2002). Many of their universities try to export their higher education as a commodity to third-world countries. American universities are more directed inwards, generally preferring campus-based integration of digital technologies, with a few examples of purchases and partnerships in physical campuses overseas.

The inclusion of education in free trade agreements has given rise to a major controversy in the world of education, as is apparent from the numerous campaigns – and other institutional responses – that have been organized in recent years to demand that education be left out of the free trade agreements. At the same time, a large number of empirical studies and theoretical analyses have been carried out on the problems associated with the commercialization of education services. These studies have addressed a wide range of issues, such as the inclusion of trade agreements in the concept of 'global governance of education' (Robertson *et al.*, 2002); the fact that trade agreements have acquired formal sovereignty over certain aspects of national education policies (Dale *et al.*, 2002); and the reasons why such agreements deepen the existing inequalities between Northern and Southern countries (Altbach, 2004).

Sir John Daniels' view (2005) is supportive of the globalization commodity argument. He argues that when products become commodities there is fierce price competition between manufacturers and profit margins are squeezed. Producers dislike this and industries often have to restructure, but consumers benefit greatly. Specifically, when querying the implications for education and asking whether the commoditization of learning materials is a way to bring education to all, Sir John's answer is:

> Yes it is, and 'open' universities in a number of countries have shown the way. By developing courseware for large numbers of students they can justify the investment required to produce high quality learning materials at low unit cost. Such materials can be used successfully outside their country of origin after local adaptation and translation. Commoditizing education need not mean commercializing education. The educational community should adopt the model of the open source software movement. We can imagine a future in which teachers and institutions make their courseware and learning materials freely available on the web. Anyone else can translate and adapt them for local use provided they make their new version freely available too. (Daniels, 2005)

Sir Daniels' views are supported by Czinkota (2004), who claims that there are a number of reasons why higher education should be liberalized in the GATS:
- Knowledge is crucial to advancement anywhere around the world.
- In spite of much support and goodwill, higher education remains a privilege or is entirely elusive for a large proportion of the global population.
- The key constraint to progress is not the availability of knowledge but its distribution, absorption and application. In its role as a global channel of distribution, higher education has become a bottleneck.
- Major funding and productivity enhancements are required.
- International competition offers the key opportunity to boost productivity and attract resources.

- Institution and program mobility will be particularly instrumental in global capacity building.

Pierre Sauvé of UNESCO, on the other hand, recognizes that there is a danger of 'McDonaldization' of higher education with the spread of a single formula on the Western model. He suggests that, when

> ... faced with increased competition, universities are tempted to invest in subjects that are going to be most profitable for them, to the detriment of less profitable ones such as human sciences. They will also be tempted to move more and more towards doing research that pleases their funding sources. In the future, parents will have to spend a greater part of their income on their children's education and that will only increase social inequality. (Sauvé, 2002)

Resisting commoditization for the sake of education

The idea behind the concepts of commodification and de-commodification is that the development of modern capitalism transferred 'labour' into a commodity so that income and survival depended on labour market participation. The establishment of such a context which can both match and confront expectations is, however, a dangerous business. Particularly for those new to the discourse of higher education within higher education institutions, the danger lies in society's value-laden practices, which have invaded the truth-seeking ethos of Jasper's ideal university. Higher education institutions owe a responsibility of critical self-scrutiny both to themselves and to their present and future communities, whose adults are, or will be, entrusted to them. In this project they will need to accept that their students are vulnerable to the reality defined for them. That reality imposes an obligation upon higher education institutions to reflect on the values of their host communities and, through their own autonomy, offer students the choices associated with the development of authentic, autonomous decision-makers. As Wilcox and Ebbs state: 'The relationship between students' attitudes and values and the environment that supports or challenges them stands as a dynamic dialectic of confirmation or rejection that affects the ethical positions and choices of both the individual and the institution' (1995).

Nentwich (2001) raises some very interesting issues regarding the commoditization of academic knowledge through the issue of copyright and academic journals. Basically the argument is whether specialized academic information should be understood as a commodity intended to generate revenues, or whether access to scholarly information is a social good that must be freely available. Contextualized in the educational arena, the argument is at the core of what commoditization is and why there can be a case for de-commoditization. Essentially it concerns the loss of the social good in the valuing of production. Returning to the Nentwich example, the case for de-commoditization of academic work involves removing those whose primary interest is in the revenue value of knowledge. If the work that is being conducted is the production of academic articles for dissemination, what actually does the publisher do to transmute the academic work into one that has an exchange value never intended in its product? Nentwich believes not a great deal and argues for open and free distribution through the universities themselves of the knowledge created by their academics as one way of de-commoditizing the process.

Useful as this strategy may be, it will fail if the institutions are themselves intent on commodifying for their own benefit. The answer seems to be to view the problem from a perspective other than the market, from where value is more intrinsic and education offers both an economic and social good made manifest in the freedom of ideas.

Prior to 1992, undergraduate and postgraduate degrees were built into strong brands by a small group of universities whose influence was beneficially reflected in the other members of the university sector. This halo effect has now been diluted to such a point that its original value is being questioned. Global positioning is not possible for all or even for a large minority of UK universities. Once the link of the ubiquitous Honours degree has been re-positioned as a thing of value only from certain universities, many new and mass institutions are rapidly left without a concept to offer their publics. Indeed this change would happen more rapidly if universities were able to charge their own levels of fees.

The marketing of higher education ought to be about de-commoditizing its offerings, not commoditizing. It should seek to integrate product and service, and combine both in an inclusive package to encourage future growth by de-commoditizing current offerings. A precedent is seen in banking, a service traditionally based on complex structures which have been commoditized to make them plainer to the consumer. The result is a commitment to serving customers' needs by providing superior service and niche products. Yet many banks are decoupling the complexities of their products to reveal the costs. They earn profit by making what they actually do seem clear, but not simple, to the customer. Similarly, higher education services could become an internationally tradable commodity within an increasingly competitive global market. The process of de-commodification of higher education should borrow from marketing knowledge without being seduced by its non-critical discourse. Whether or not communication should be totally transparent needs careful development and theorization.

Marketing synthesizes a notion of value beyond that of an experiential world and this makes us overseers rather than participants in knowledge creation. A consequence is to displace experiential meaning, as technology leads us to discard value and behaviour becomes a means to an end, losing its potential to hold intrinsic meaning. This clearly has ramifications for the world of being: as we abstract ourselves from our world, our notion of being becomes world-less. We behave as we think scholars should, and induct students into a learning community where neither they nor we know what scholarship is.

Standardization

Standardization, as both a consequence and the driver of globalization, may be seen in many forms of neo-liberal and neo-conservative policies. These emphasize accountability, choice and privatization in a global convergence of the policies and ideologies advocated by the World Bank towards the good practice advocated in predominantly English-language pedagogical journals. The standardization of a national system of higher education to embrace competitive markets involves league tables, mass education, tuition fees and close alignment with business dominant higher education systems. Standardization is manifest through credit transfer and qualification recognition, intellectual property rights, franchising and open courseware.

These bring with them a universal skills agenda, delivered in a format to suit Internet transmission and Microsoft teaching software. Research publication and the ascendancy of standard English as the sole global language is at the cost of other languages large enough to become alternatives, such as Mandarin, Hindi, Arabic and Spanish, is also a manifestation. Another is the franchising of programmes. Rather than increasing surveillance of the curriculum, what needs to be done is to examine the extent to which standardization threatens to reduce the scope for local knowledge in the curriculum.

In the global environment arguments can be made for and against a common framework for professional standards. Such a framework may enhance professionalism by providing the means to engage in dialogue across professions, promoting professional learning and developing mobility of skilled labour, regional arenas for research, and international competition between universities and between universities and other commercial research institutions and companies. Institutions already acknowledge this and are developing partnerships, consortia and networks to strengthen their position in the global arena. Increasing mobility of students demands more standardization. Examples include the programmes of the European Union; ERASMUS/ SOCRATES, and the European credit transfer system. These have tried to stimulate internationalization in higher education by the development of a trans European framework. While this has been built up, it does require compromise within the individual national frameworks.

Globalization challenges national and even regional educational and qualification policies and seeks more thorough harmonization of policy frameworks, higher education structures and management philosophies, degree systems and standardization. The process started in Europe with the Bologna-Declaration (1999) in Europe is a clear example of this. Similar tendencies of international harmonization of higher education systems exist in other parts of the world.

The Bologna Process and the Lisbon Strategy are the main vehicles or frameworks guiding the European response to globalization in higher education. The Bologna Process represents the totality of commitments freely taken by each signatory country to reform its own higher education system in order to create overall convergence at the European level, as a way to enhance international/global competitiveness. Its non-binding character was a crucial facilitator, given the need to overcome reluctance in Europe towards standardization and harmonization, despite acceptance that these were necessary.

In the longer run the need for standardization and compatibility will lead to the generalization of the Bachelor's/Master's-degree structure, the hegemony of English as the lingua franca in higher education and scientific research, the development of compatible credit transfer and accumulation systems to recognize, transport and validate teaching and learning experiences, the international recognition of degrees and diplomas, and a negotiated consensus on core knowledge and competencies and their place in curricula, especially in specific professional fields. Closely connected with the market ideology and its concomitant drive for productivity and efficiency is a growing interest in measuring educational outcome, both within societies and cross-nationally. Globalization in higher education does not necessarily imply international standardization and uniformity, but asks for policies balancing the global and the local. Our challenge is to become 'standardized thinkers' and not to lose sight of our cultural uniqueness, institutional traditions and social identity as we embrace the opportunities that the standardization of higher education can bring.

Summary and conclusion

The challenge that we face is to de-commoditize higher education. I believe that a marketing concept that respects the benefits of social and economic capital offers such an opportunity. In marketing theory, the commodity is an indistinct product, for which there are many suppliers and many buyers, which is traded in a market where the price is variable and supply and demand are elastic. In this simplification the market behaves in a way that will balance supply and demand, although it is accepted that this is not typical behaviour. Markets are distorted by supplier intervention to build and support brands which are differentiated in consumers' minds and which attract prime prices over generic products by offering perceived value. The idea of selling the commodity of higher education is thus a little over-worked, as brands already exist. I am not against brands but feel that distinct forms of higher education have become homogenized in a collusion of mediocrity based on immediacy, hedonism and financial return. The position of higher education is such that it does not encourage institutions to resist the scrutiny of the market, to confront the model and overcome commodification.

First I discuss the roles of the main actors engaged in the creation of education and what they might do to resist commodification. What can they do and how should we conceptualize their contribution to education? Quite simply, I ask whether students should be defined as customers and academics as service providers. Do these labels sit comfortably with the values and ethos of higher education?

References

Altbach, P. G. (2004), 'Globalization and the university: Myths and realities in an unequal world', *Tertiary Education and Management*, 10, (1), 3–25.

Aronowitz, A. (2000), *The Knowledge Factory, Dismantling the Corporate University and Creating True Higher Learning*. Boston: Beacon Press.

Ball, S. J. (2004), 'Education for sale: The commodification of everything!', at http://firgoa.usc.es/drupal/node/43424 (accessed 20 May 2010).

Bok, D. (2003), *Universities in the Market Place.* Princeton: Princeton University Press.

Bologna Declaration (1999), available online at http://ec.europa.eu/education/policies/educ/bologna/bologna.pdf (accessed 20 May 2010).

Bonnett, M. (2003), 'Education for a post-humanist age: The question of human dwelling', *Journal of the Philosophy of Education*, 37, (4), 707–24.

Czinkota, M. R. (2004), 'Loosening the shackles: The future of global higher education', at http://www.wto.org/english/tratop_e/serv_e/sym_april05_e/czinkota_education_e.doc (accessed 13 November 2009).

Dale, R. and Robertson, S. (2002), 'The varying effects of regional organisations as subjects of globalisation of education', *Comparative Education Review*, Special Issue on Globalisation and Regionalisation, 46, (1), 37–66.

Daniels, J. (2005), 'Higher education for sale', http://www.unesco.org/education/education_today/today03.pdf (accessed 13 November 2009).

Doti, J. L. (2004). 'Is higher education becoming a commodity?', *Journal of Higher Education Policy and Management*, 26, (3), 363–9.

Gibbons, M., Limoges, C., Nowotny, H., Schwartzman, S., Scott, P. and Trow, M. (1994), *The New Production of Knowledge: The Dynamics of Science and research in Contemporary Societies.* London: Sage.

Heidegger, M. (1977), 'The question concerning technology', in *The Question Concerning Technology and Other Essays*, W. Lovitt (trans.). New York: Harper and Row.

—— (2002), 'The origins of the work of art', in J. Young and K. Haynes (trans. and eds), *Off the Beaten Track.* Cambridge: Cambridge University Press.

International Organisation for Standardization (2009), *The 2009 ISO Award for Higher Education in Standardization*, http://www.iso.org/iso/iso_award_2009.pdf (accessed 22 October 2009).

Koźmiński, A. (2002), 'Ranking and League Tables of Higher Education Institutions', *Higher Education in Europe*, 27, (4), 365–71.

Lincoln, Y. S. (1998), 'Commodification and the contradiction in academic research', *Culture and Organisation*, 4, (2), 263–78.

Marginson, S. (2005), 'Global position and position-taking: The case of Australia', at http://www.education.monash.edu.au/centres/mcrie/publications/otherpapers.html (accessed 13 November 2009).

Nentwich, M. (2001), '(Re-)de-commoditisation in academic knowledge distribution?', *Science Studies*, 14, (2), 21–42.

Nowotny, H., Scott, P. and Gibbons, M. (2001), *Rethinking Science: Knowledge in an Age of Uncertainty.* Cambridge: Polity.

Readings, B. (1997), *The University in Ruins.* Massachusetts: Harvard University Press.

Robertson, S., Bonal, X. and Dale, R. (2002), 'GATS and the education service industry', *Comparative Education Review*, 46, (4), 472–96.

Ryan, Y. (2002), 'Emerging indicators of success and failure in borderless higher education', The Observatory on Borderless Higher Education, at http://portal.unesco.org/education/en/files/7413/10342626060gf6_middlehurst_document.doc/gf6_middlehurst_document.doc (accessed 20 May 2010).

Sauvé, P. (2002), 'UNESCO in action education: Borderless education', at http://portal.unesco.org/en/ev.php-URL_ID=10402&URL_DO=DO_TOPIC&URL_SECTION=201.html (accessed 13 November 2009).

Scott, D., Brown, A., Lunt, I. and Thorne, L. (2004), *Professional Doctorates. Integrating Professional and Academic Knowledge.* Maidenhead: SRHE and Open University Press.

Shaw, K. E. (2005), 'Researching the trade in knowledge between the West and developing countries', *The International Journal of Educational Management*, 19, (6), 459–68.

Standish, P. (1997), 'Heidegger and the technology of further education', *Journal of the Philosophy of Education*, 31, 439–59.

Vanlathem, J. M. (2003), 'Education and GATS: Preserving public education is the best way to achieve the Education For All program', *Policy Futures in Education*, 1, (2), 342–50, at http://www.wwwords.co.uk/PFIE/content/pdfs/1/issue1_2.asp (accessed 26 October 2009).

Wilcox, J. R. and Ebbs, S. L. (2005), 'The leadership campus: Values and ethics in higher education', (ASHE-ERIC Higher Education Report No. 7). Washington, DC: The George Washington University, Association for Studies in Higher Education, November, Philadelphia International Forum Symposium.

Willmott, H. (1995), 'Managing the academics: Commodification and control of the development of university education in the UK', *Human Relations*, 48, (9), 993–1027.

Willmott, H. (2003), 'Commercialising higher education in the UK: The state, industry and peer review', *Studies in Higher Education*, 28, (2), 129–41.

Chapter 17

Higher Education Partnerships for Studying and Improving Leadership Preparation and Development around the World

Bruce Barnett and Stephen L. Jacobson

Introduction

Colleges and universities have a long history of international collaboration. The genesis of American universities, for instance, was influenced by European institutions, particularly the English colleges of Oxford and Cambridge and German universities (de Wit, 2002; Dolby *et al.*, 2008). In recent years, increasing numbers of students have been enrolling in universities outside their home countries, which has not only affected the competition for international students, but has focused attention on how to accommodate their social, emotional, and academic needs. In recognizing the cultural and practical needs of international students, many universities have established support centres or student unions aimed at improving student retention, raising their expectations, and attending to their overall well-being (Kelo, 2006). Universities also have created offices of international affairs to coordinate the array of cooperative programmes being offered. A multitude of international collaborative efforts have emerged, which consist of: (a) general memoranda of agreement, (b) reciprocal exchanges of faculty, (c) reciprocal exchanges of students, (d) collaborative research, (e) exchanges of publications, reports, and other academic information, (f) medical training, and (g) outreach, such as professional development, conferences, symposia, and workshops (Duke University, 2009). Of these, faculty and student exchanges and collaborative research tend to be the most prevalent forms of collaboration.

There is also a growing recognition of the importance of globalization in the education discipline. On one hand, the importance of educating global citizens has been captured by Appiah (2006), who contends that individuals and nations need to embrace 'cosmopolitanism' by being genuinely interested in non-native practices and beliefs to obtain a universal concern and respect for legitimate differences. Citizenship education is becoming more pronounced in K-12 curriculum as a way of addressing concerns about social disintegration, disorder, moral decline, and civic and political disenchantment (Morrison *et al.*, 2009). As a result of global interest in education, international comparisons of student performance, such as the Trends in International Mathematics and Science Study (TIMSS) and the Programme for International Student

Assessment (PISA) (Akiba, 2008; Dunn, 2002; Wiseman, 2008) and international learning networks (Robertson *et al.*, 2002; Walker *et al.*, 2002) are gaining widespread attention.

On the other hand, global interest in school leadership is gaining attention, as captured in the recently published handbook of research on leadership education that 'meets a growing need to identify, describe, critique, and enrich the international literature on school leaders' preparation and development' (Lumby *et al.* 2008, p. 1). For instance, in an effort to increase its international footprint, the University Council for Educational Administration, a consortium of over 80 doctoral-granting institutions, established an Associate Director of International Affairs responsible for developing international research and learning opportunities (Barnett, 2009). In addition, in his presidential address to the Commonwealth Council for Educational Administration and Management (CCEAM), Petros Pashiardis (2008) argued that understanding globalization and the context within which school leadership needs to be examined and improved requires a redefinition of relationships between individual nations and the rest of the world, between public and private institutions, and between economic prosperity and poverty. Moreover, he contends that globalization requires the formation of regional and international networks of nations, international and non-governmental organizations, and multinational companies, because the educational policies of any one nation should no longer be examined without looking at educational policy worldwide (Pashiardis, 2008).

Coupled with globalization of education has been the formation of partnerships between higher education institutions and other agencies and organizations (Saffu, 2000). Partnerships often have been referred to as networks, alliances, collaboratives, or coalitions (Bickel *et al.*, 1995), with the intent that 'partners form a mutually rewarding relationship with the purpose of improving some aspect of education' (Regional Laboratory for Educational Improvement of the Northeast and Islands, 1986, pp. 12–13).

Examples of high-profile university partnerships include:

- the Academic Cooperation Association (2009), an association of primarily European universities that coordinates international exchange programmes, research studies, and publications;
- the United Nations Educational, Scientific and Cultural Organization (UNESCO), which is devoted to meeting global workforce needs, increasing higher education opportunities for disadvantaged groups, and promoting policies that strengthen research capabilities of higher education institutions (UNESCO, 2009);
- the European Commission's (2009) Erasmus Programme, an initiative that supports professional study and work programmes for European higher education students and faculty;
- the Fulbright Foundation (2009), which funds higher education students and faculty interested in international research, study, and employment.

To better understand higher education partnerships, this chapter examines trends in the types of higher education collaborative arrangements being formed to study and improve the preparation and development of educational leaders. Special attention is devoted to the continuing involvement of the University Council for Educational Administration (UCEA), an organization of doctoral-granting universities, in supporting international research and programme development. Our investigation begins by describing three types of international higher education partnerships: organization-sponsored, university-sponsored, and faculty-driven. Examples of each partnership type are provided, with particular attention devoted to the history, advantages, and limitations of: (a) the International Intervisitation Programme (IIP), an organization-sponsored partnership conceived by UCEA, (b) a university-sponsored partnership between the University of Calgary (UC) in Canada and the University of Waikato (UW) in New Zealand, and (c) the International Successful School Principalship Project (ISSPP), a faculty-driven partnership between colleagues in eight countries. The chapter concludes with the implications for establishing and maintaining these three types of higher education partnerships.

Higher education partnerships

Over the past 30 years, university teacher and leadership preparation programmes have collaborated with external agencies, primarily businesses, local and national funding agencies, school districts, and professional associations (Grobe, 1990). In the late 1980s, for example, the United States Congress passed the Educational Partnership Act as a way of creating an infrastructure and support system for partnerships aimed at reforming schools (Bodinger-deUriarte, Tushnet *et al.*, 1995). Examples include corporate support for programme implementation and facilities construction; grants and contracts with public and private foundations and agencies; district-based professional development schools for preparing school teachers; and student and faculty workshops and exchanges funded by educational professional associations. Because of the fluid and dynamic nature of these partnerships, they tend to evolve through a series of developmental stages, ranging from initial scepticism and lack of trust to acceptance and continuing progress (Turbowitz, 1986). Key ingredients for university-based partnerships to flourish include involving the organizations' top-level decision-makers, establishing clear roles and responsibilities, creating formal written agreements, and committing adequate resources (DeBevoise, 1986; Galligani, 1987; Grobe, 1990).

Inter-organizational partnerships have been categorized in a variety of ways. Intrilligator (1992), for instance, conceptualizes the interdependency between organizations on a continuum, ranging from cooperative to coordinative to collaborative relationships. Another conceptualization by Barnett *et al.* (1999) uses four models (vendor, collaborative, symbiotic partnership, and spin-off) to capture deeper levels of interdependency between educational organizations and external agencies. In this chapter, we propose another partnership typology based on our experiences working with higher education international collaboratives as well as emerging trends in the globalization of educational leadership preparation. These partnerships – organization-sponsored, university-sponsored, and faculty-driven – will be briefly described before examining specific ways in which these collaborations are being used around the world to conduct research and prepare and develop school leaders.

Type 1: Organization-sponsored partnerships

Many large-scale organizations and agencies, such as UNESCO, the Organization for Economic Co-operation and Development (OECD), and the World Bank, are committed to providing resources to address educational, social, economic, and medical issues, especially in developing countries. UNESCO's programme to achieve Education for All (EFA) is a partnership arrangement between other United Nations agencies (for example, UNICEF, the World Bank, and non-government agencies) and corporations. The World Bank forms partnerships with foundations, trade unions, faith-based organizations, non-government agencies, and indigenous people's movements to distribute resources for various projects, such as Internet development, forest conservation, and AIDS vaccinations (World Bank, 2009).

International, organization-sponsored partnerships in educational administration have been created, which for the purpose of our analysis, began in 1963 when Jack Culbertson, then Executive Director of UCEA, concluded that, '. . . path breakers around the world lacked formal opportunities to discuss their ideas with one another. More importantly, the field of educational administration had no structures for nurturing international development' (Culbertson, 1995, p. 178). Since that time, several organization-sponsored partnerships have surfaced within the field of educational leadership. For instance, the Commonwealth Council for Educational Administration and Management (CCEAM) was formed in 1970 to improve educational administration in Commonwealth countries by studying and disseminating information about educational administration (Thomas, 1971). The CCEAM has evolved into an international network of commonwealth universities and professional associations, including 23 affiliated bodies housed in Africa, Australasia, the Americas, Europe, and India (Walker *et al.*, forthcoming), and sponsors a journal, *International Studies in Educational Administration*. A second multinational organization, the International Congress for School Effectiveness and Improvement (ICSEI), was launched in 1988 at their inaugural conference at the University of London (Chapman, 1989). Beginning in the early 1990s, a formal governance structure, including a president and international board of directors, was instituted. Similar to CCEAM, the ICSEI has created a journal, *School Effectiveness and School Improvement*, which attracts educational researchers, practitioners, and policy-makers from more than 50 nations to its annual international congress (Walker *et al.*, in press).

Type 2: University-sponsored partnerships

As noted earlier, universities have a long history of promoting international exchange and collaboration, which usually consists of faculty and student exchange programmes, collaborative research, professional development, and medical training (Duke University, 2009). Within the education discipline, the most common university-sponsored international opportunities are faculty-led programmes (for example, study abroad), visiting professors, and professor and student exchanges (Williamson, 2009). Often, these partnerships include faculty and/or student research and exchange programmes, such as those sponsored by the Fulbright Foundation, which are 'designed to increase mutual understanding between the peoples of the United States and the peoples of other countries' (Fulbright Foundation, 2009, p. 1). Another popular programme, the Fund for the Improvement of Postsecondary Education (FIPSE), provides grants to universities and government agencies to increase student access to higher education and improve the quality of post-secondary education. Currently, FIPSE-sponsored international cooperative programmes focus on curriculum reform and undergraduate study programmes in North America, Brazil, the European Union, and Russia (FIPSE, 2009).

A recent survey of UCEA member institutions (Barnett, 2009; Barnett *et al.*, forthcoming) indicated high levels of international involvement of educational leadership departments, particularly in delivering degrees and programmes. Doctoral and Master's degree programmes are being offered in North America as well as in Central America, the Middle East, and Asia. Departments also are conducting collaborative projects with international organizations in Kenya, Jordan, Norway, Bulgaria, Mexico, Peru, and South Korea. Not only do these partnerships support faculty, teacher, and graduate student exchanges, but they also bolster curriculum development projects, such as language and culture development, gifted education, and school improvement.

Type 3: Faculty-driven partnerships

Despite the challenges of language differences, cost, and distance, many individual university faculty form alliances with colleagues from other countries to conduct research and deliver professional development programmes (Murakami-Ramalho *et al.*, 2008). A particularly good example of cooperative international research is the set of beginning principals' studies coordinated by Parkay *et al.* (1992), which provide a unique comparative perspective on the transition of novices into the principalship in different cultural contexts. In addition, a recent survey of UCEA faculty members indicates they are conducting studies on diversity, organizational citizenship, the superintendency, principal preparation, democratic schooling and student achievement, and professional socialization and identity (Barnett, 2009). Other types of faculty-sponsored, cross-national activities include conducting study tours of practitioners to visit other countries, delivering professional development programmes, co-teaching university courses, and disseminating research (for example, Barnett *et al.* in press).

Higher education partnerships in educational leadership

Clearly, collaborative partnerships between organizations, universities, and individual faculty have been in existence for years. In an effort to illustrate how these three types of partnerships are occurring within the field of educational leadership, this section describes: (a) the International Intervisitation Programme (an organization-sponsored partnership), (b) the faculty and student exchange programme at the UC and the UW (a university-sponsored partnership), and, (c) the International Successful School Principal Project (a faculty-driven partnership). For each collaborative arrangement, we provide an overview of the history and description of the partnership, advantages, and cautions and limitations.

Organization-sponsored partnership: International Intervisitation Programme

History and description. In its early years, Culbertson (1995) envisioned UCEA making a substantive contribution to the internationalization of administrator preparation and practice, so with support from the Kellogg Foundation, he developed the first International Intervisitation Programme (IIP). The plan was that IIP was intended to bring scholars from Australia, Canada, England, and Scotland to institutions of higher education in the United States that had well-established administrator preparation programmes. At the time of the first IIP in 1966, America was the only country in the world with a system of formal, university-based, pre-service preparation. (In recent years, others countries, including England, Scotland, and South Africa, have adopted polices requiring aspiring administrators to complete accredited programmes offered by universities and other educational authorities.) Over the course of the three-week IIP66, 78 participants from the five nations visited UCEA member institutions, ending with three days of evaluation and follow-up discussions. William Walker of Australia noted that the most important outcome of the experience was 'helping to break down national insularity and provincialism, which would then lay the groundwork for a more international conception of administration' (Culbertson, 1995, p. 183).

Based on the success of the first IIP, a second conference was held in Australia in 1970, this time focusing on the themes of bureaucracy and centralization, planning and systems analysis, accountability and assessment, and teacher negotiations. Paper presentations and symposia were complemented with visits to several Australian state capitals. So powerful was the emerging idea of international organizational partnerships within educational administration circles that the Commonwealth Council for Educational Administration (later the Commonwealth Council for Educational Administration and Management) was founded at this event.

Ultimately, the IIP took place every four years for 32 years, with the last conference held in 1998 in Barbados. Over that span of time, hundreds of international scholars came together to share ideas and insights about school leadership preparation and practice. These quadrennial gatherings produced some of the most important organizational partnerships for studying and improving leadership preparation and development around the world. This 1970 conference, which revolved around the theme, 'Educational administration: New directions in practice and theory', featured three weeks of presentations and visitations in England and Scotland. IIP74 was where Thomas Greenfield presented 'Theory about Organization: A New Perspective and its Implications for Schools', a paper which challenged the basic assumptions underlying systems theory, offering an alternative 'phenomenological' perspective (Greenfield, 1975). Greenfield's subsequent exchanges with Dan Griffiths, referred to as the 'Greenfield-Griffiths debate', arguably may have had the greatest impact of any such scholarly exchange in our field and certainly helped to reshape research in educational administration to this very day. Moreover, the spirit of organizational partnership continued unabated at IIP74 with the formation of both the European Forum on Educational Administration and the British Educational Administration Society (currently the British Educational Leadership, Management and Administration Society).

Subsequent IIPs were held in Canada (1978); Nigeria (1982); Hawaii, Fiji and New Zealand (1986); Manchester (1990); Toronto and Buffalo (1994); and finally in Barbados (1998). Unfortunately, attendance at IIPs declined markedly over the years, especially among Americans after the inception of UCEA's own annual conference in 1987. With fewer than ten Americans attending IIP98 in Barbados, the CCEAM governing board voted to change IIP to a Commonwealth biennial conference for the next scheduled conference in 2002 in Sweden. Sweden's hosting of the conference was originally to have been an IIP event, but instead became a CCEAM conference, the only time CCEAM has been held in a non-Commonwealth nation. Although IIP has disappeared, subsequent CCEAM events have been held in Hong Kong and Shanghai (2004), Cyprus (2006), South Africa (2008), and Australia (2010), while UCEA continues to hold its annual meetings at major cities throughout the United States.

However, interest in revitalizing more broadly-based international events and partnerships has re-emerged. At a meeting in the summer 2007 at the University of North Carolina at Chapel Hill, several members of UCEA's leadership team drafted a transformative agenda for the Council's future. Among the key items listed in that document was the Internationalization of the Educational Leadership Preparation Conversation, which included the recommendation that UCEA once again foster greater international collaboration and cooperation by expanding its international membership; enhancing the ability of educational leaders to deal with greater cultural diversity and develop a deeper understanding of the appropriate role of preparation for citizenship; and developing comparative research projects that inform educational leadership and educational policy-making across the globe. Subsequently, the Executive Committee approved the creation of the position of Associate Director of International Affairs in 2008.

ADVANTAGES

The major advantage of nurturing international organizational partnerships between and among existing associations is that the fundamental start-up costs have already been incurred. The key is to identify common and compelling interests for such relationships. In this regard, Culbertson's initial case for engaging globally still provides the best set of objectives, because when working across contexts:

- we gain a deeper understanding of school administration in our own culture by examining other cultures;
- leaders and policy-makers have more options and insights when they access ideas from other countries;
- the limits and uses of educational ideas can be better identified in cross-nation analyses as compared to single national contexts;
- working cooperatively across nations, it is possible to achieve research and development objectives that may not be possible if pursued alone.

CAUTIONS AND LIMITATIONS

These potentially positive outcomes notwithstanding, several concerns arise; most importantly that an association such as UCEA might impose its Western viewpoints on potential partners (Brown *et al.*, 2007; Hallinger *et al.*, 2000; Walker *et al.*, 2000). Instead such partnerships must consider and respect the cultures and values of other participants, a sentiment expressed by Benno Sander in 1979, when he argued that if the InterAmerican Society for Educational Administration was to be successful, interactions had to be transactional, not interventionist, '. . . otherwise, the builders of schools and educational systems run the risk of destroying national cultural values' (Culbertson, 1995, p. 199). Another often-expressed concern is that international initiatives take resources and attention away from existing problems in a nation's schools. This is not an inconsequential issue, especially if one views such endeavours from a zero-sum perspective. However, Culbertson's (1995) four objectives for international collaboration imply that a variable-sum perspective is far more applicable since international experiences almost always inform domestic educational leadership research and practice (Lumby *et al.*, 2008; Webber *et al.*, 2004).

University-sponsored partnership: the University of Calgary and the University of Waikato, history and description.

Beginning in 1996, two educational faculty members, one from the UC in Canada (Charles Webber) and one from the UW in New Zealand (Jan Robertson) began a partnership between their two departments to allow students from their respective universities to interact with each other and learn about leadership in another culture (Webber *et al.*, 2003). During her sabbatical at the UC, Jan met Charles and they began sharing ideas of ways for their students to connect with one another. After Jan returned to New Zealand, they decided to provide opportunities for students in their respective courses to interact electronically using a shared email discussion group. They created the Change Agency listserv as a mechanism for students to share their reactions to common readings introduced by both professors. Despite only interacting for four weeks, students on both campuses appreciated the experience, and urged the faculty to arrange face-to-face interactions between students from Canada and New Zealand. Based on these positive reactions, the first student travel study tour included three UW students who attended a summer school course taught at the UC in 1998. Following the course, ten UC students travelled to New Zealand for two weeks, visiting schools, engaging in workshops and seminars, and experiencing the local culture.

During the next year, several events took place to solidify the partnership. First, Jan and Charles continued to have students in their programmes interact via the Change Agency listserv, which had expanded to over 300 subscribers from a host of countries. Second, efforts were made to create a formal partnership agreement between the two universities. The process included consultations with colleagues in other academic units, university legal experts, Faculty Graduate Studies administrators, and representatives from graduate student associations and the registrar's office. Issues needing clarification included intellectual property, copyrights, and the financial obligations of the universities. Obtaining these agreements took longer than expected; however, the final partnership documents were signed in 2001.

As these discussions and agreements were taking place, additional exchanges occurred. In 2000, Jan brought several graduate students from the UW to Calgary to learn about the Canadian educational context and culture. During this two-week travel study tour, students participated in learning activities attended by local teachers and principals as well as UC graduate students. Jan and Charles coordinated the programme with the assistance of two visiting professors from Australia and two school superintendents from Alberta, Canada. The focus for the exchange programme was educational accountability and students were exposed to research, participated in focus groups and large group discussions, and documented their learning in reflective journals. After the UW students returned home, the UC students travelled to England to interact with a mutual colleague who was involved in comparative studies of international leadership programmes. Jan and Charles were invited to present keynote addresses in one another's countries and they both were appointed as adjunct professors at the other's university.

Following the formal agreement between the UC and the UW, the partnership evolved in several ways. For example, Jan taught an online course for graduate students from both institutions. Students were able to complete projects in a variety of cultural contexts, including the Solomon Islands, Papua New Guinea, Taiwan, China, and Mexico. In addition, in July 2002, UC faculty members went to the UW to team-teach a course attended by students from North America, New Zealand, Australia, Asia, Papua New Guinea, and England. Finally, an online refereed academic journal, *International Electronic Journal for Leadership in Learning*, was established and is housed at the UC. This publication has become an outlet for reporting studies and programmes aimed at providing international experiences as well as a possible publishing source for students. Regional editors from the USA, UK, Europe, and Oceania solicit articles from their respective parts of the world, which provides an international flavour to the journal.

ADVANTAGES

Webber *et al.* (2003) report a series of benefits accruing to students, faculty, and institutions that are willing to engage in university-sponsored partnerships. Students' thinking can be expanded, especially in better understanding their own viewpoints and contexts, valuing other perspectives, and clarifying their views on how educational leaders can affect student learning (Webber *et al.*, 2004). Study tour participants from Australia who have visited other countries to investigate leadership practices and school improvement report: (a) building a sense of common purpose and commitment to making a difference in their own schools, (b) serving as resource teams for school networks engaged in school improvement, (c) distributing samples, exemplars, videos and photos, and booklets for use by the group, and (d) forming long-term relationships for personal and professional support (Barnett *et al.*, forthcoming). Faculty not only have the opportunity to expand their research productivity and professional learning experiences, but also can be exposed to new teaching strategies, including online learning, flexible teaching schedules, and co-teaching (Barnett *et al.*, forthcoming). Finally, institutions stand to benefit through these partnerships by increasing the types of learning experiences for students, expanding their teaching staff to include international faculty, and developing formal partnership agreements that can be modified for subsequent university-sponsored collaborations.

CAUTIONS AND LIMITATIONS

Like organizational partnerships, university-sponsored partnerships are fragile and can be difficult to sustain. As these partnerships are formed, faculty must consider if the collaborating organizations have the capacity to perform the required services (Swan *et al.*, 1993), are willing to share authority and responsibility (Hannay *et al.*, 1984), and understand the sustained effort that will be required (Intrilligator, 1992; Lugg, 1994). Webber *et al.* (2003), in reflecting on their university-sponsored partnership, note the following types of problems can be encountered: (a) graduate students not being able to afford the time and cost to visit other countries, (b) criticism regarding the lack of academic rigor associated with an international experience, (c) university policies and bureaucratic decision-making processes, and (d) how to sustain the partnership as faculty depart and university priorities change.

Faculty-driven partnership: International Successful School Principal Project

History and description. Having organizational and/or institutional support to help forge partnerships is clearly advantageous, but not an absolute prerequisite for international partnerships to flourish. Individuals with common interests also can create productive partnerships to advance the knowledge base in school leadership preparation and practice. A case in point is the International Successful School Principalship Project (ISSPP), which began in 2001 as an eight-nation study of the practices of principals who had successfully improved the academic performance of students in their schools. The project focuses specifically on the practices of a school's formal leader and then expands this inquiry transnationally by addressing the following questions:

1 What practices do successful principals use?
2 Do these practices vary across contexts?
3 Under what conditions are the effects of such practices heightened or diminished?
4 What variables link a principal's leadership to student achievement?

The original research teams from Australia, Canada, China, Denmark, England, Norway, Sweden, and the United States (a complete listing of the national participants can be found at: www.ils.uio.no/english/research/project/ssl/index.html) reported their initial findings in a special issue of the *Journal of Educational Administration* devoted to the ISSPP (Jacobson *et al.*, 2005). The first round of reporting produced a total of 65 case studies of successful school principals. The findings from these qualitative, primarily descriptive, cases are limited in how much transference can be made to other contexts; however, the ISSPP is one of the largest international studies ever undertaken in educational leadership, which begins to address this limitation. What is especially noteworthy about the ISSPP is that it was begun and continues to function without an overarching funding source. Although some of the national research teams have had institutional and/or governmental funding, there has never been financial support for the entire project. Instead, individual and collective commitments to the project have allowed the ISSPP to expand to over 15 member nations and to conduct longitudinal studies that will allow researchers to address the question of how school success is sustained over time. Needless to say, members of the ISSPP teams would appreciate financial support for their multinational research; however, concerns about fiscal shortfalls have clearly been outweighed by the potential gains of such cross-national analyses, as witnessed by the increasing level of interest the project has generated among new teams of researchers.

The first phase of ISSPP findings supported both the existence of a set of core leadership practices – setting directions, developing people, and redesigning the organization – necessary for improved student achievement in most contexts (Leithwood *et al.*, 2005), and an understanding that principals adapt these practices to their specific contexts in order to achieve the desired effects. For example, in the United States, direction-setting tends to be short-term, as principals address mandatory annual achievement gains (Jacobson *et al.*, 2005). In contrast, successful principals in Australia are interested in learning over a lifetime (Gurr *et al.*, 2005), while principals in Norway (Moller *et al.*, 2005), Denmark (Moos *et al.*, 2005), and Sweden (Hoog *et al.*, 2005) focus their school's direction on the development of democratic values, rather than on academic performance.

ADVANTAGES

In addition to informative comparative findings, the expansion of the ISSPP's membership has been the result of honest conversations about the benefits and pitfalls of conducting this type of transnational research among team members during their presentations at AERA, UCEA, and CCEAM. One of the greatest challenges that had to be overcome was the development of a common survey instrument for multinational research that needed to be produced in five languages. The teams were never entirely sure whether the translations that emerged were understood the same way from country to country, or even within English-speaking countries like Australia, England, and the USA. Also, common conceptions of what defines a 'challenging' school were elusive and varied across contexts. In the United States, a 'challenging' school was synonymous with socio-economic status: explicitly high-need, high-poverty schools. Similar schools could be found in Australia and England; however, in Denmark, Norway, and Sweden, the definition of a challenging school had more to do with the number of different languages spoken in a school than disparities in community wealth. Despite these contextual differences, the study has drawn the international research teams into examinations of broader policy issues that subsume governance and polices issues in education. In fact, these broader analyses reveal one final and quite significant benefit of comparative research: the study addresses concerns about social justice beyond the borders of any one nation in order to improve the life chances of all children, irrespective of where they live. The ISSPP has proven to be so successful that the National College for School Leadership at Nottingham University, England will be hosting an international conference in May 2010 devoted entirely to the work of the ISSPP.

CAUTIONS AND LIMITATIONS

ISSPP teams are receiving little internal or external support, placing a financial strain on their participation (Murakami-Ramalho *et al.*, 2008). Given the distance between team members and the costs associated with coordinating long-distance communication and meetings, faculty have had to use personal funds or seek support on an ongoing basis. In addition, the concerns expressed earlier about potential drawbacks to organization-sponsored partnerships also are applicable to faculty-driven partnerships (that is, danger of cultural arrogance and hegemony and/or lack of attention to local problems). Yet, if the experiences of the ISSPP teams are any indication, these concerns can be addressed directly. For example, two teams' research on culturally responsive leadership (Johnson, 2007; Vedoy *et al.*, 2007) have pushed the collective conversation toward cultural insensitivity. Furthermore, the ongoing examination of domestic and international practices of successful principals means that one neither ignores local issues nor fails to put those problems into a comparative perspective. In almost every way, these faculty-driven partnerships have proven to be 'win-win' relationships.

Summary and conclusion

Given the increasing emphasis on global communication and interaction (Friedman, 2005), we anticipate an increase in transnational collaboration across all three types of partnerships. For instance, professional interdependency is on the rise, as evidenced by the increasing number of international journals and conferences. As a result, colleagues from around the world are finding ways to combine their talents to conduct research, publish findings, and develop professional development programmes. In addition, many universities are formulating strategic plans explicitly focusing on globalization and have created administrative structures to oversee international projects (Duke University, 2009). Finally, computerized communication systems, such as Skype, allow individuals to hold virtual face-to-face conversations in real time at minimal or no cost, reducing some of the logistical barriers to cooperative endeavours.

Despite projected growth in organization-sponsored, university-sponsored, and faculty-driven partnerships, various regulatory, cultural, and personal obstacles can compromise their development (Barnett *et al.*, 1999; Huxham *et al.*, 2000). First, institutional regulations and policies can circumvent collaboration, particularly for organization- and university-sponsored partnerships. The UCEA-sponsored IIP spawned other educational organizations; however, as these new organizations grew, they established their own identities, policies, and structures, moving away from the original conception of the IIP (Culbertson, 1995). Similarly, university faculty attempting to mount collaborative partnerships can run into a host of bureaucratic structures and hurdles. On one hand, university admission policies may not accommodate international applicants and workload policies may deter faculty from being able to formulate long-distance partnerships. On the other hand, the time and energy required to navigate the institution's bureaucratic decision-making process can be extensive, as exemplified by Webber *et al.*'s (2003) two-year effort to obtain formal university approval for their partnership between their two universities.

Second, if these types of partnerships are to thrive and expand, organizers must understand how certain cultural factors may affect their progress, particularly differences in the social norms, customs, and jargon between international participants. When partnerships include individuals with a Western perspective, they need to be aware that their conceptualizations of research and development programmes may tend to dominate projects, marginalizing the contributions of individuals with other perspectives (Brown *et al.*, 2007; Walker *et al.*, 2000). This concern is particularly relevant for Western-based professional organizations and universities involved in educational leadership research, development, and preparation. For instance, cultural sensitivity needs to occur when international students enrol in university leadership preparation programmes, such as the UC–UW partnership. Organizers not only need to consider ways in which the perspectives of the non-dominant group can be expressed in productive ways, but they also should ensure social and organizational arrangements (for example, housing, food, transportation) of the host institution enrich the experiences of non-natives.

Finally, personal barriers, including financial expenditures for travel and accommodations, distance between partners, and lack of knowledge of local programmes, can constrain involvement in these partnerships. Whether organizations, universities, or individuals are attempting to collaborate, they need assistance from 'cultural insiders' from other countries who can help to navigate local customs, policies, and norms (Barnett *et al.*, forthcoming). A common theme of the success of the IIP, UC–UW partnership, and the ISSPP is the importance of key individuals who are dedicated to leading and managing the collaboration. Without the vision and drive of Jack Culbertson and a few international colleagues, the IIP would never have emerged or been sustained for over three decades. Similarly, the UC–UW partnership has flourished because Charles Webber and Jan Robertson have been willing to devote incredible time and energy to developing curriculum, navigating their university's bureaucracies, and supporting students. And despite little or no financial and institutional support, the ISSPP relies on the good-faith efforts of individual faculty in countries around the world. Clearly, all three partnership types exemplify the importance of having key individuals who are motivated to collaborate and follow through on their commitments; however, their stories also point out the susceptibility of partnerships to being person-dependent, rather than becoming institutionalized. As these individuals leave the partnership, others need to step into their roles, making succession planning a critical aspect for sustaining collaboratives.

Therefore, we contend that the partnerships described in this chapter – organization-sponsored, university-sponsored, and faculty-driven – have the potential to thrive if these regulatory, cultural, and personal barriers are acknowledged and addressed. We conclude by considering the implications for organizations and individuals interested in implementing each type of partnership.

Organization-sponsored partnerships

Based on the histories of CCEAM and ICSEI, Walker *et al.* (forthcoming) have identified important characteristics of how these two organization-sponsored partnerships have evolved:

- The formation of an international partnership depends on a small group of 'like-minded energetic people' who are able to locate funding, create a vision, and establish political support.
- Successful international partnerships rely on linkages with existing professional networks and must adapt in order to remain relevant.
- Diversity and difference must be embraced for international partnerships to flourish.

- Partnerships need to establish high-profile events (for example, conferences, seminars) in different locations and produce relevant products (for example, publications, websites) to publicize the partnership's efforts and contribute to the discipline's knowledge base.
- To be considered an 'international organization', partnerships must demonstrate their value by promoting activities, events, and products that support colleagues from different countries who would otherwise not be able to participate.

The IIP, an example of an organization-sponsored partnership, models many of these qualities. Beginning with the vision of Jack Culbertson and other influential international colleagues, the IIP began as a modest enterprise. Over the years, the programme expanded and moved to different continents around the world (Australia and New Zealand, North America, Africa, and Europe). A major outcome of IIP is that it spawned other important professional organizations devoted to educational administration, including the British Education Leadership Management and Administration Society, the Commonwealth Council for Educational Administration and Management, and the European Forum on Educational Administration, all of which are vibrant organizations operating today.

Furthermore, as UCEA strives to re-establish a foothold as an internationally sponsored organization, members have suggested two major roles UCEA can play to support international networks: (a) disseminating information and (b) advocating for resources and visibility (Barnett, 2009; Barnett *et al.*, forthcoming). In serving as a clearing house, information can be communicated electronically (websites, email blasts, blogs) and in print media (newsletters, journals) to publicize existing international collaboratives, potential funding sources, and international research findings. Because of the networks of the organization and its members, UCEA, similar to CCEAM and ICSEI, is in a prime position to advocate for international partnerships. Examples include co-sponsoring conferences; allocating small seed grants to support comparative research studies, and travel expenses for faculty, student, and practitioner exchanges; and hosting meetings of professional organizations from different countries. As a step in this direction, formal agreements are being created between UCEA and the Australian Council for Education Leaders (ACEL), BELMAS, CCEAM, and the New Zealand Educational Administration and Leadership Society (NZEALS) to disseminate information about one another's organizations, develop visiting scholar programmes, create reciprocal symposia at their annual conferences, provide reduced rates for conference attendance and publications, and coordinate collaborative research projects.

University-sponsored partnerships

Similar to organization-sponsored partnerships, various ingredients are necessary for university-sponsored international partnerships to form, grow, and be sustained. As universities seek to expand their international presence, additional resources and administrative processes are needed to support study abroad programmes, global research projects, and international faculty exchange. International projects require personal and financial resources. Traveling to other countries is expensive and arranging study tours is extremely time-consuming. Therefore, universities can promote and support international research and development by:

- funding faculty and student travel to other countries to conduct research, attend conferences, engage in study abroad experiences, and network with colleagues;
- authorizing in-state tuition for international students;
- preparing formal memoranda of agreements between the partnering institutions;
- communicating information about external funding (for example, the Fulbright Foundation Scholars Programme, FIPSE grants);
- partnering with other universities to bring international scholars to campus;
- organizing forums for international students to share their experiences regarding educational and social developments in their home countries;
- hiring staff to coordinate international travel and logistics;
- publicizing international initiatives on the website, in newsletters, during symposia, and with local, regional, and national media.

In reflecting on their university-sponsored partnership, Webber *et al.* (2003) acknowledge several essential ingredients when creating and maintaining international collaboratives. First, each institution must have a faculty member who is a partnership 'champion', willing to invest time, talent, and energy into the collaborative. These champions must have sufficient interest in the substance of the partnership (for example, leadership preparation, educational reform), have credible reputations within their institutions, understand their university's decision-making processes, and be able to work with people in the other institutions. Second, university-wide support is necessary, and the role of campus leaders cannot be underestimated in securing resources (Huxham *et al.*, 2000). The bureaucratic nature of universities requires various levels to be navigated, including department faculty and leadership, college deans, graduate programme administrators, and executive leaders. Similarly, the university's international centre staff play a central role in obtaining information, maintaining lines of communication, and garnering resources. Finally, important academic, policy, and practical issues need to be addressed, such as providing evidence to faculty and administrators about the academic integrity and rigor of partnership activities and products; negotiating equitable costs for international students (for example, tuition, housing); adhering to university policies regarding intellectual property and copyright laws; ensuring appropriate technological support is available at each institution; and having the patience to oversee the formal partnership approval process, which can take two to three years to finalize.

Faculty-driven partnerships

The implementation of transnational research activities with minimal external funding will make what seemed almost impossible two decades ago a far more common occurrence. Rather than making large-scale plans, international partners start with small, modest goals (Barnett *et al.*, in press). The rapid growth of ISSPP team membership is a good illustration of how a small endeavour can grow and expand in a relatively short period of time. Robertson (2008) suggests several issues must be attended to when individuals are considering whether to enter a partnership: (a) collaborative capacity – the willingness and ability of individuals to engage in partnership activities and (b) collaborative capability – resources and tools that support partnership ventures. The willingness, or personal capacity, to engage in partnerships needs to be gauged early. On one hand, faculty members need to assess how their skills, background, and personality may affect their ability to engage in international collaboration. On the other hand, they need to determine how their existing social and interpersonal relationships within and outside the organization can contribute to the formation of a meaningful international partnership. To gauge their initial level of commitment to and interest in developing a collaborative relationship, individuals should consider their responses to these questions: Is this venture a good match for my talents? What might I gain or lose by participating? (Barnett *et al.*, 1999).

The capacity to form meaningful alliances also rests on partners establishing mutual trust and understanding the realities of collaboration. High-quality relationships evolve as partners come to trust one others' motives and actions (Hoffman *et al.*, 1994). 'Collaborative and collective approaches create trust in alliances; competitive and individualistic approaches create distrust. This trust is an essential glue that holds strategic alliances together, but it is very difficult to develop and maintain' (Judge *et al.*, 2001, p. 75). Trust not only can help partners navigate cultural differences and conflict, but also helps them cope with unanticipated events and situations. As trust develops, partners gain a common understanding about the rationale for collaborating, a critical component for any multi-party partnership (Bechky, 2003; Miranda *et al.*, 2003; Standifer *et al.*, 2006). The development of shared meaning is not something that occurs immediately; however, if the collaboration is successful, partners will establish common understanding about the partnership's goals, purposes, and operating procedures (Barnett *et al.*, forthcoming).

Attention also must be given to the capacity of individuals and their organizations to create the tools and administrative processes to facilitate partnership implementation. Once the decision to form a partnership occurs, these questions require answers: What should we invest? How should we organize ourselves? (Barnett *et al.*, 1999). Robertson (2008) contends that partnership capacity depends on constant communication (for example, face-to-face contacts, electronic exchanges, group meetings) and support (for example, travel funds, administrative staff) to enable partners to connect and build relationships within and outside the organization. As Davies (2001) suggests, 'The merging of interests, the sharing of privileged information, and intimate collaboration and cooperation are all dependent on the ability of the partners to communicate' (p. 187). As communication and information exchange improves, partners understand their roles and relationships and different levels of the organization become connected to the enterprise (Hutt *et al.*, 2000).

Undoubtedly, global partnerships in higher education are here to stay. We see no let-up in partnership opportunities being resourced by governmental and non-governmental agencies, private foundations, and professional associations. Similarly, as university faculty expand their professional networks beyond their nation's borders, interest in ways of globalizing teaching, learning, and research will increase. As organization-sponsored, university-sponsored, and faculty-driven partnerships become more prolific, several trends are likely to occur. First, information clearing houses that publicize partnership opportunities will be in high demand. Handling this information explosion will create entrepreneurial opportunities, and at the same time will present challenges in maintaining reliable databases. Second, the knowledge base regarding the skills, structures, and outcomes associated with successful international higher education partnerships will need to be gathered and disseminated. This is particularly true for the field of educational leadership, which has a rather recent history of international collaboration. The examples of the International Intervisitation Programme, the Calgary–Waikato exchange, and the International Successful School Principal Project capture the realities associated with global university partnerships aimed at preparing, developing, and studying educational leaders. We encourage other university-based researchers and practitioners to share their international experiences in the professional and popular literature, at conferences and seminars, and through websites and blogs. These dissemination mechanisms not only legitimize global partnerships within the leadership education and research community, but have the potential to help teachers, administrators, and policy-makers appreciate the value of non-indigenous values and practices (Lumby, 2008), the ultimate reason for international collaboration.

References

Academic Cooperation Association (2009), *About ACA*, at http://www.aca-secretariat.be/01about/general_info.htm (accessed 4 August 2009).

Akiba, M. (2008), 'Working conditions of middle school mathematics teachers: A comparison of the United States, Australia, and Japan', in University Council for Educational Administration Convention, 30 October–2 November 2008, Orlando, Florida.

Appiah, K. A. (2006), *Cosmopolitanism: Ethics in a World of Strangers*. New York: W. W. Norton and Company.

Barnett, B. (2009), 'UCEA's involvement in international research and development: Current trends and future implications', *UCEA Review*, 50, (1), 31–2.

Barnett, B. G., Hall, G. E., Berg, J. H., and Camarena, M. M. (1999), 'A typology of partnerships for promoting innovation', *Journal of School Leadership*, 9, 484–510.

Barnett. B. G. and O'Mahony, G. R., (forthcoming) 'Unlocking the door to international collaboration: The power of interpersonal relationships and learning communities', in C. Boske and A. Tooms (eds), *Building Bridges:*

Connecting Educational Leadership and Social Justice to Improve Schools. Charlotte, NC: Information Age Publishing.

Bechky, B. A. (2003), 'Shared meaning across occupational communities: The transformation of understanding on the production floor', *Organization Science*, 14, 312–30.

Bickel, W. E. and Hattrup, R. A. (1995), 'Teachers and researchers in collaboration: Reflections on the process', *American Educational Research Journal*, 32, (1), 35–62.

Brown, L. and Conrad, D. A. (2007), 'School leadership in Trinidad and Tobago: The challenge of context', *Comparative Education Review*, 51, (2), 181–201.

Bodinger-deUriarte, C., Tushnet, N. C., and Manuel, D. 1995. *Educational Partnerships: Case Studies.* Los Alamitos, CA: Southwest Regional Laboratory.

Chapman, J. (1989), 'Australian network grows from international beginning', *Network News*, 1, (1), 1.

Culbertson, J. (1995), *Building Bridges: UCEA's First Two Decades.* University Park, PA: University Council for Educational Administration.

Davies, W. (2001), *Partner Risk: Managing the Downside of Strategic Alliances.* West Lafayette, IN: Purdue University Press.

DeBevoise, W. (1986), 'Collaboration: Some principles of bridgework', *Educational Leadership*, 43, (5), 9–12.

Dolby, N. and Rahman, A. (2008), 'Research in international education', *Review of Educational Research*, 78, (3), 676–726.

Dunn, R. E. (2002), 'Growing good citizens with a world-centered curriculum', *Educational Leadership*, 60, (2), 10–13.

Duke University (2009), *Global Duke Data*, at http://www.international.duke.edu/globaldata/partnerships/php (accessed 3 August 2009).

European Commission (2009), *Erasmus Programme*, at http://ec.europa.eu/education/lifelong-learning-programme/doc80_en.htm, accessed 5 August 2009.

Fund for the Improvement of Postsecondary Education (2009), *Office of Postsecondary Education*, at http://www.ed./about/offices/list/ope/fispes/index.html (accessed 3 August 2009).

Friedman, T. L. (2005), *The World is Flat: A Brief History of the Twenty-First Century.* New York: Farrar, Straus and Giroux.

Fulbright Foundation (2009), *Find the Right Fulbright for You*, at http://www.fubrightonline.org/ (accessed 5 August 2009).

Galligani, D. J. 1987. *Effective Relationships for School/College Partnerships: A Qualitative Evaluation of the Curriculum Enhancement Projects Participating in the California Academic Partnership Program 1984–1987.* Los Angeles, CA: California Academic Partnership Program.

Greenfield, T. (1975), 'Theory about organization: A new perspective and its implications for schools', in M. Hughes (ed.), *Administering Education: International Challenge.* London: Athlone Press of the University of London, 71–99.

Grobe, T. 1990. *Synthesis of Existing Knowledge and Practice in the Field of Educational Partnerships.* Washington, DC: Office of Educational Research and Improvement.

Gurr, D., Drysdale, L., and Mulford, B. (2005), 'Successful principal leadership: Australian case studies', *Journal of Educational Administration*, 43, (6), 539–51.

Hallinger, P. and Kantamara, P. (2000), 'Educational change in Thailand: Opening a window onto leadership as a cultural process', *School Leadership and Management*, 20, (2), 189–205

Hannay, L. M. and Stevens, K. W. (1984), 'The principal's world: A case study of collaborative research', in American Educational Research Association Conference, March, New Orleans, Louisiana.

Hoffman, J. D., Sabo, D., Bliss, J., and Hoy, W. (1994), 'Building a culture of trust', *Journal of School Leadership*, 4, (5), 484–502.

Hoog, J., Johansson, O., and Olofsson, A. (2005), 'Successful principalship: The Swedish case', *Journal of Educational Administration*, 43, (6), 595–606.

Hutt, M., Stafford, E., Walker, B., and Reingen, P. (2000), 'Case study defining the social network of a strategic alliance', *Sloan Management Review*, Winter, 51–62.

Huxham, C. and Vangen, S. (2000), 'Leadership in the shaping and implementation of collaboration agendas: How things happen in a (not quite) joined-up world', *Academy of Management Journal*, 43, (6), 1159–75.

Intrilligator, B. A. (1992). 'Establishing interorganizational structures that facilitate successful school partnerships', at the American Educational Research Association Conference, March, San Francisco, California.

Jacobson, S., Day, C., and Leithwood, K. (2005), 'The international successful school principalship project' (guest eds), *Journal of Educational Administration*, 43, (6).

Jacobson, S. L., Johnson, L., Yimaki, R., and Giles, C. (2005), 'Successful leadership in challenging us schools: Enabling principles, enabling schools', *Journal of Educational Administration*, 43, (6), 607–18.

Johnson, L. (2007), 'Rethinking successful school leadership in challenging US schools: Culturally responsive practices in school-community relationships', *International Studies in Educational Administration*, 35, (3), 49–57.

Judge, W. and Ryman, J. (2001), 'The shared leadership challenge in strategic alliances: Lessons from the US healthcare industry', *The Academy of Management Executive*, 15, (2), 71–9.

Kelo, M. (2006), *Support for International Students in Higher Education*, Bonn, Germany: Lemmens Verlags- and Mediengesellschaft.

Leithwood, K. and Riehl, C. (2005), 'What do we already know about educational leadership?', in W. Firestone and C. Riehl (eds), *A New Agenda for Research in Educational Leadership*. New York: Teachers College Press, 12–27.

Lugg, C. A. (1994), 'Schools and achieving integrated services: Facilitating utilization of the knowledge base', in University Council for Educational Administration Convention, November, Philadelphia, Pennsylvania.

Lumby, J. (2008), 'International perspectives on developing educational leaders', in Commonwealth Council for Educational Administration and Management Conference, 8–12 September, Durban, South Africa.

Lumby, J., Crow, G., and Pashiardis, P. (eds) (2008), *International Handbook on the Preparation and Development of School Leaders*. New York: Routledge.

Miranda, S. M. and Saunders, C. S. (2003), 'The social construction of meaning: An international perspective on information sharing', *Information Systems Research*, 14, (1), 87–106.

Moller, J., Eggen, A., Fuglestad, O., Langfeldt, G., Presthus, A., Skrovset, S., Stjernstrom, E., and Vedoy, G. (2005), 'Successful school leadership: The Norwegian case', *Journal of Educational Administration*, 43, (6), 584–94.

Moos, L., Kresjsler, J., Koford, K., and Jensen, B. (2005), 'Successful school principalship in Danish schools', *Journal of Educational Administration*, 43, (6), 563–72.

Morrison, M., Gorard, S., Lumby, J., Briggs, A., Hall, I., Maringe, F., See, B. H., Shaheen, R., and Wright, S. (2009), 'Citizens now and for the future? Leaders, learners, and 14–19 reform in England: Messages from research', in American Educational Research Association Conference, 13–17 April, San Diego, California.

Murakami-Ramalho, E. and Barnett, B. (2008), 'Globalizing conversations in educational leadership', *UCEA Review*, XLIX, (2), 1–4.

Parkay, F. W. and Hall, G. E. (eds) (1992), *Becoming a Principal.* Boston, MA: Allyn and Bacon.

Pashiardis, P. (2008), 'The dark side of the moon: Being locally responsive to global issues, in Commonwealth Council for Educational Administration and Management Conference, September 8–12, Durban, South Africa.

Regional Laboratory for Educational Improvement of the Northeast and Islands (1986), *Business Education Partnerships: Strategies for Improvement.* Andover, MA: Author.

Robertson, J. (2008), *Three Tiers of Collaboration,* at: http://www.steptwo.com.au/columntwo/three-tiers-of-collaboration (accessed 12 November 2008).

Robertson, J. M. and Webber, C. F. (2002), 'Boundary-breaking leadership: A must for tomorrow's learning communities', in K. Leithwood and P. Hallinger (eds), *Second International Handbook of Educational Leadership and Administration.* Dordrecht, The Netherlands: Kluwer Academic Publishers, 519–56.

Saffu, K. (2000), 'Contradictions in international tertiary strategic alliances: The case from down under', *International Studies in Educational Administration,* 28, (2), 36–47.

Standifer R. and Bluedorn, A. (2006), 'Alliance management teams and entrainment: Sharing temporal mental models', *Human Relations,* 59, (7), 903–27.

Swan, W. W. and Morgan, J. L. (1993), *Collaborating for comprehensive services for young children and their families: The local interagency coordinating council.* Baltimore, MD: Paul H. Brooks Publishing Company.

Thomas, A. R. (1971), 'The Commonwealth Council for Educational Administration: A new centre for educational leadership', *Journal of Educational Administration,* 9, (2), 128–34.

Turbowitz, S. (1986), 'Stages in the development of school-college collaboration', *Educational Leadership,* 43, (5), 18–21.

United Nations Educational Scientific and Cultural Organization, (2009), *Higher Education,* at http://www.unesco.org/en/higher-education (accessed 4 August 2009).

Vedoy, G. and Moller, J. (2007), 'Successful school leadership for diversity? Examining two contrasting examples of working for democracy in Norway', *International Studies in Educational Administration,* 35, (3), 58–66.

Walker, A. and Dimmock, C. (2000), 'Mapping the way ahead: Leading educational leadership into a globalised world', *School Leadership and Management,* 20, (2), 227–33.

—— (2002), 'Moving school leadership beyond sterile boundaries: Developing a cross-cultural approach', in K. Leithwood and P. Hallinger (eds), *Second International Handbook of Educational Leadership and Administration.* Dordrecht, The Netherlands: Kluwer Academic Publishers, 167–202.

Walker, A. and Townsend, T. (forthcoming), 'International networks on specific areas in school management: International Congress for School Effectiveness and Improvement, Commonwealth Council for Educational Administration and Management', in B. McGaw, E. Baker,, and P. Peterson (eds), *International Encyclopedia of Education,* 3rd edn. Oxford, England: Elsevier.

Webber, C. F. and Robertson, J. M. (2003), 'Developing an international partnership for tomorrow's educational leaders', *International Studies in Educational Administration,* 31, (1), 15–32.

—— (2004), 'Internationalization and educators' understanding of issues in educational leadership', *The Educational Forum,* 68, 264–75.

Williamson, W. (2009), *The Joys and Opportunities of Faculty Travel-Study Abroad,* at http://cgi.stanford.edu/~dept-ctl/cgi-bin/tomprof/postings/php (accessed 1 May 2009).

Wiseman, A. W. (2008), 'What are we training educational leaders for? A cross-national analysis of school principals' activities by school type and context' in University Council for Educational Administration Convention, 30 October–2 November, Orlando, Florida.

de Wit, H. (2002), *Internationalization of Higher Education in the United States of America and Europe: A Historical, Comparative, and Conceptual Analysis*. Westport, CT: Greenwood.

The World Bank (2009), *About Us*, at http://web.worldbank.org/WBSITE/ EXTERNAL/EXTABOUTUS (accessed 4 September 2009).

Chapter 18

International Organizations and the Tertiary Education Sector: Understanding UNESCO, the OECD, and the World Bank Linking-pin Organizations

Roberta Malee Bassett

Introduction

In light of the current atmosphere of economic crises, political instability and unrest, and the expansion of global education, international organizations are becoming increasingly important in shaping the relationships that drive progress, promote research, expand dialogues, and establish policies. Most international leaders have recognized the necessity of rethinking the many forms of international cooperation and acting more towards finding common solutions to face the numerous challenges posed by the perceived instability across societies and economies. In different ways this chapter aims to contribute to the larger dialogue on redefining ideas of international cooperation, particularly the roles and purposes of international organizations. The understanding of international organizations as monolithic, static organizations is obsolete; international organizations are complex, dynamic, and intrinsically polemic.

The ideas for this chapter emerged from my recent book (co-edited with Alma Maldonado-Maldonado), *International Organizations and Higher Education Policy: Thinking Globally, Acting Locally?* Fundamentally, the goal of that work and this chapter is to provide greater insights into the impact of international organizations – in particular what are deemed the big three: UNESCO, the World Bank, and the OECD – on higher education. Unlike the book, which explored the myriad perspectives on the impact global organizations can have on higher education in the form of an insider–outsider 'conversation', this chapter will present a more theory-based examination of the capacities these organizations have to serve as agents for influence, cooperation, and programme facilitation in a comprehensive higher education policy environment, utilizing the theory of linking-pin organizations (as explored by Doreian *et al.*, 2004, among others). And, while acknowledging the complexity of these organizations and the variety of opinions about their legitimacy and utility as drivers of education policy, this chapter seeks to reinterpret the roles international organizations play and their capacity to bridge and merge the interests of myriad stakeholders in higher education policies and reforms.

After UNESCO's Education for All conference in 1990, most of the literature on international organizations and their education work was dedicated to analyzing the situation at the basic education level. This chapter, on the other hand, seeks to examine the different ways international organizations impact higher education. The main area of inquiry follows the questions of what and how are the main activities developed by organizations like the World Bank, UNESCO, and the OECD, and to what extent do the efforts of these organizations create dynamic interchanges between each other and other stakeholders, including other organizations, governments, institutions, and individuals? It will initially introduce the history of these three organizations and the background of their efforts regarding higher education. It will then explore the ways in which international organizations have contributed to the development of the field of higher education and the expansion of the global higher education dialogue. And, finally, it will present the mechanisms these organizations use to link policy-makers with scholarship and data-supported research to promote effective innovations and developments in higher education globally.

Background: the organizations

A key foundational aspect of examining international organizations as autonomous actors within the sphere of international higher education is establishing the basis for their authority to act and influence. Rather than being funnels for their funding states, international organizations such as the 'big three' (UNESCO, the World Bank, and the OECD) examined in this chapter have assumed independent roles as drivers within the international development and policy arenas. Organizational theories developed by Max Weber in the early twentieth century support the idea of international organizations as powerful independent entities, as opposed to mouthpieces for their member states (Ness *et al.*, 1988; Barnett *et al.*, 1999). This independence stems from 'power flowing from at least two sources: (1) the legitimacy of the rational-legal authority they embody, and (2) control over technical expertise and information' (Barnett *et al.*, 1999, p. 707).

With regard to the big three, these two key components of power seem particularly relevant. Higher education, though a relatively small area of concern within the overall operations of each of these large organizations, has proven particularly open and responsive to the big three's efforts. The capacity for each of these organizations to drive the global discourse has been enormous, resulting in both support and criticism for their power within the field. One can surmise that their international stature, coupled with the talent among their staff has provided these three organizations with particularly powerful positioning in the global discourse on tertiary education.

Though these organizations serve many of the same constituencies and address many overlapping issues, their organizational purposes are often very different. In some cases, these organizations have quasi-governing roles; in others, they serve as advisors and consultants; and in some, they act as lobbyists between and outside of their membership countries. In each case, the organizations represent global power and, in some eyes, potentially neo-colonial and patriarchal power dynamics from developed economies to developed and emerging economies.

Such critical perspectives on the motives and impact of these organizations on higher education policy development are important and vital to any true interpretation of the roles these organizations can and do perform within the global tertiary education context. It is outside the realm of this chapter to delve into the multitudes of critical concerns of the impacts of these organizations. Instead, this chapter will seek to explore the work these organizations do with regard to tertiary education and interpret their influence on the global sphere of tertiary education through the theory of linking-pin organizations, in which these 'big three' organization serve as hubs around which spheres of tertiary education activities occur and are connected.

The Big Three: UNESCO, the OECD, and the World Bank

UNESCO, the OECD, and the World Bank have contributed to the academic field of higher education by financing studies, promoting methodologies, generating data, publishing materials, and conducting research on higher education and, especially, comparative higher education. Given their international scope, it is not surprising that these agencies play significant and evolving roles in the development of higher education in the countries and regions in need of their expertise.

The United Nations and its branches, including the Educational, Scientific, and Cultural Organization (UNESCO), serve in a supra-governmental role, in which representatives of member states come together to form governing bodies whose authority is, by and large, willingly recognized and respected by independent nations. While independent self-interest is, of course, primary among the member nations of the UN, the actions and decisions of the UN often supersede national self-interest for the benefit of the international community at large. At its core, the most basic purpose of the UN is to promote world peace.

An organization like the Organization for Economic Development and Co-operation (OECD), on the other hand, also seeks international input into multilateral accords, but its outputs are not so much a matter of governmental authority as they are working in the best interests of their member states. The OECD, being economically oriented, does not purport to encompass the same broad commitment to international peace as the UN or development and poverty reduction, like the World Bank, so much as it seeks to promote mutually beneficial international relations through effective economic, market, and trade relations. As the UN continues to focus on diplomacy and security, the OECD's purposes are more directly related to economic exchange and the promotion of free markets and exchange between nations. Bridging the divergent missions of the UN and the OECD is the World Bank.

The World Bank (the Bank) exists primarily as an agent for poverty reduction (Psacharopoulos, 2006) and has the highly complicated role of distributing loan funds from industrialized nations to emerging and developing nations. The Bank also serves as a 'knowledge bank',contracting out the expertise of its staff for individualized programmes with member nations. In its lending and consulting capacities, the Bank bridges the operations of the market and the public sector. In this era of globalized higher education, this tension between free market initiatives and managed development among nations has a genuine impact on higher education throughout the world.

Though there certainly are other important international and regional organizations addressing higher education policy issues – the European Union (EU), the Asian Development Bank (ADB), the Organization of African States (OAS), and the Association of Southeast Asian Nations (ASEAN) for example – their policies tend to focus on issues within their regions. This chapter, however, seeks to illustrate higher education policy influence on the more global scale, using organizations that link the higher education interests of communities across developed and developing countries. UNESCO, the OECD, and the World Bank are among the most visible and proficient international organizations incorporating education in their operations and, therefore, are the key actors analysed below.

The United Nations Educational, Scientific, and Cultural Organization (UNESCO)

Following its establishment in 1945, the United Nations (UN) began a long evolution of developing initiatives and establishing internal organizations that meet the needs and realities of cross-national interactions and relationships. One such internal arm developed by the UN, the United Nations Educational, Scientific, and Cultural Organization (UNESCO), focuses on broad social and cultural issues. Formed after the end of World War II and chartered in November of 1945 to promote peace and security, UNESCO evolved out of a 1942 meeting of the Conference of Allied Ministers of Education (CAME) of the European wartime allies against Nazi Germany. This meeting was called during World War II to prepare for the reconstruction of education sectors across Europe. Out of these discussions emerged the idea that an organization, ultimately UNESCO, would be able to address directly issues of transnational education. It was the first major international body to introduce education as a broadly defined area of international concern (Daniel, 2002).

Representatives of 37 countries signed the UNESCO constitution in November 1945, and it was ratified in November 1946, by 20 of the original signatory nations: Australia, Brazil, Canada, China, Czechoslovakia, Denmark, the Dominican Republic, Egypt, France, Greece, India, Lebanon, Mexico, New Zealand, Norway, Saudi Arabia, South Africa, Turkey, the United Kingdom, and the United States – developed and developing countries, from the North and the South. With a constitution that specifically addresses education and advocates education as an important part of the promotion of positive international relations, UNESCO became the first, and continues as the most, prominent multinational organization to include education in its organizational charter (Daniel, 2002). Initially, however, the initiatives of UNESCO focused on primary and basic education.

Noteworthy predecessors of UNESCO include: the International Committee of Intellectual Co-operation (CICI), Geneva 1922–46; its executing agency, the International Institute of Intellectual Co-operation (IICI), Paris, 1925–46; and the International Bureau of Education (IBE), Geneva, 1925–68, which has, since 1969, been part of the UNESCO Secretariat under its own statutes (UNESCO, 2004). These earlier organizations had acknowledged that there were issues specifically around international education, including the sharing of knowledge and emerging scholarship among nations, that deserved international attention and oversight. UNESCO's efforts include focusing on non-political areas of international exchange, such as the protection of significant cultural landmarks, the promotion of copyright protection and intellectual property rights, and the preservation of library treasures and collections, as well as promoting basic education for all. Advanced scholarship and higher education also remain important programmatic and policy areas for UNESCO.

Since the 1960s, the major issue regarding transnational higher education for UNESCO has concerned the recognition of earned degrees across international borders, and the organization continued to examine this particular issue area through the 1970s and 1980s. At the same time, UNESCO sought to broaden its scope of attention to a myriad of other higher education issues (Uvalić-Trumbić, 2002), including academic mobility, international exchanges of excellence, research on education systems and knowledge production, curriculum innovation, leadership roles for women educators, teacher development, and the defence of quality in higher education qualifications (UNESCO, 2004).

UNESCO continues to serve as a forum for examining issues within international higher education, presenting itself as an important leader in recognizing the importance of higher education in the development of individual nations, in the emerging realm of globalized higher education, and in promoting transnational education as a mechanism for economic development and improved international relations. 'UNESCO is the only UN body with a *mandate* [emphasis added] to support national capacity-building in higher education' (UNESCO, 2004).

The Organization plays a leading role in the worldwide reflection on higher education reform. It also provides a platform for dialogue on how best to adapt education systems to the emergence of knowledge societies and the new social, cultural and economic challenges of an increasingly globalized world.

That the UN has established investment in higher education as a core activity – a mandate – worthy of specific attention and investment of resources points to the potential of higher education to promote, or even compel, change. As both a national investment in its own development and an international industry with cross-national significance, higher education has been deemed worthy of major policy direction.

With a directorate for higher education in Paris and a separate research centre working on higher education in Romania (UNESCO-CEPES), UNESCO has made significant investments in the development of its higher education initiatives. UNESCO also incorporates issues such as democracy, women's rights, economic development, and scholarship into their higher education endeavors, expanding the sphere of influence of higher education from merely that of the relatively small numbers of students who actually enter into higher education worldwide. Current international concerns regarding higher education, such as massification, the burgeoning for-profit sector, and trade liberalization initiatives, will likely impact national capacities to expand higher education and increase access to larger segments of their populations; issues that are of interest and concern to UNESCO as well as many other international and higher education organizations.

In particular, UNESCO has established globalization as a specific and significant focus in its work in higher education:

> Globalization: Once viewed as mainly economic in nature, this phenomenon has profound social and cultural aspects. Borders between countries have become more open to intellectual exchange, and the search for uniformity and for common solutions continues to increase in many domains. In the field of higher education, the international aspects reach into numerous university activities. Many universities are part of international agreements, and mobility is facilitated by the rapid increase in international exchanges. In the field of research, there is an increased interest in the concerns of global governance e.g. democracy and human rights, collective social responsibility, the rising impact and interconnectedness of phenomena such as conflict-resolution, multiculturalism, environmental matters and the advent of technology. (UNESCO, 2004)

UNESCO has established the Conventions on the Recognition of Qualifications, which, according to UNESCO, 'represent the only existing regulatory frameworks for trans-border mutual recognition of qualifications. These Conventions have been ratified by over a hundred Member States in Africa, Asia and the Pacific, the Arab States, Europe and Latin America' (UNESCO, 2004). The UNESCO Conventions seek to promote cross-border recognition of degrees and qualifications between the countries that have ratified them. Ideally, such international cooperation in higher education would reduce actual and perceived obstacles to the mobility of teachers and students, with such mobility being increasingly popular and significant as higher education becomes more thoroughly globalized.

The Organization for Economic Co-operation and Development (OECD)

As with UNESCO, the foundations of the Organization for Economic Co-operation and Development (OECD) also emerged from World War II, in this case from initiatives developed out of the European Aid Program – the Marshall Plan. The Marshall Plan, named after US Secretary of State George C. Marshall, was initiated in June of 1947 and outlined the United States' commitment, through multilateral cooperation, to help rebuild Europe following the devastation of the two World Wars. The Organization for European Economic Co-operation (OEEC) emerged out of the Marshall Plan as the multinational format for administering aid most effectively in rebuilding the economies of Europe. The OEEC became the OECD in 1961, with the ratification of the OECD charter in September of that year.

Unlike UNESCO, the OECD is not a 'culturally' oriented organization but, instead, is an economic- and market-oriented one; a significant distinction for understanding how these organizations target their projects and conduct their research. The Convention that established the OECD stipulates three main aims the organization is to consider as it promotes policies:

- to achieve the highest sustainable economic growth and employment and a rising standard of living in member countries, while maintaining financial stability, and thus contribute to the development of the world economy;
- to contribute to sound economic expansion in member as well as non-member countries in the process of economic development;
- to contribute to the expansion of world trade on a multilateral, non-discriminatory basis in accordance with international obligations. (OECD, 2004, p. 4)

By including education, higher education in particular, the OECD has established its stance on education as being a significant driver in economic development. In so doing, the OECD has positioned itself as a leader in pursuing international educational initiatives.

Education has been a core issue for the OECD from its inception (OECD, 2004). During 1960s – the early years of the Cold War, and the 'race to space' – the OECD focused its efforts in education on developing scientific personnel. Later, as the unemployment levels and economic woes of many OECD nations became severe in the 1970s, the OECD moved its educational focus away from scientific innovation towards more general employment issues. And, in September 2002, the Secretary-General of the OECD, Donald J. Johnston, announced the creation of an independent Directorate for Education to raise the profile of the OECD's work. He noted that 'education is a priority for OECD Member countries and the OECD is playing an increasingly important role in this field. Society's most important investment is in the education of its people. We suffer in the absence of good education: we prosper in its presence' (OECD, 2004, p. 5).

The OECD Directorate for Education established six 'strategic objectives' to help orient the focus of their education initiatives within member countries. The six objectives are:

- Connecting lifelong learning policy with other socio-economic policies
- Evaluating and improving outcomes of education
- Promoting quality teaching
- *Rethinking tertiary education in a global economy* [emphasis added]
- Building social cohesion through education
- Building new futures for education (OECD, 2004, p. 6)

The global economy (also known as globalization) is, again, a core issue for this international organization. The OECD understands that education worldwide is not immune to the impact of international economic influences. Indeed, the OECD has advocated strongly that higher education must evolve along with the global economy, to ensure that all elements of the global higher education industry continue to serve its expanding, indeed global, constituents well. For the OECD (and other similarly influential international organizations), globalization is a force so strong that it requires a re-examination of existing modes of tertiary (higher) education provision to ensure that the current models of higher education remain relevant.

The current director of education at the OECD, Barbara Ischinger, has acknowledged the tension between domestic initiatives and institutionalizing globalization at the institutional level. Recognizing that 'the international higher education trade has reached the level of a quasi-export industry . . . worth about $40 billion (£21.7 billion)' (THES, 2006), Ischinger charged that the scale of higher education is too significant to ignore, and she admonished those campus leaders who remain so focused on localized issues that they ignore the implications and challenges of globalized higher education at their systems' peril. No campus or system can remain inured from the forces of globalization for much longer, and seeking ways to profit from those forces is a smarter approach then waiting to see what may happen. On behalf of the OECD, Ischinger has called attention to the scale of higher education as an important economic engine and has specifically acknowledged the directorate's commitment to influencing international perspectives and initiatives on higher education through its data production and comparative research capacities (THES, 2006).

The OECD focuses efforts regarding tertiary education on market forces currently impacting higher education in its member countries. 'Governments are major players in the (tertiary education) sector, but they are not the only stakeholders: there is competition on the supply side and greater sophistication in demand' (OECD, 2004, p. 16). Using terms like supply and demand, stakeholders, and players in describing modern higher education, the OECD is purposefully evoking economic and strategic terminology. Unlike education policy-brokers who examine economics and markets, the OECD has economic and market specialists to focus on education. Without the cultural 'baggage' or domestic limitations that educators often have, the OECD can situate education in the broad context of globalization and compare its endeavours to those of other industries.

With this focus on understanding the market for higher education internationally, the OECD has established five 'activities' in which they are conducting research and focusing their work on tertiary higher education: evaluating tertiary education policy, monitoring internationalization and trade in tertiary education, improving governance and management of higher education institutions, improving indicators on tertiary education, and building future scenarios of universities (OECD, 2004, p. 16). The OECD produces research that fills a void by generating data on macro and micro level shifts in both domestic and cross-border markets for higher education as supply (institutions and governments) and demand (students, employers) pressures continue to impact the international tertiary education market. By examining national and international policies, as well as the roles and impacts of 'suppliers' and 'consumers', the OECD provides important data and analysis of the 'numbers' behind the often emotional and anecdotal responses to the evolving globalized nature of higher education today.

The World Bank

Formed originally in 1944 in Bretton Woods, New Hampshire, USA, as the International Bank for Reconstruction and Development (IBRD), the World Bank ('the Bank') arose, like many of these other significant international agencies, out of the recognized need to rebuild the world after the destructive chaos of the wars in the first half of the twentieth century. The World Bank was developed as and remains an organization that provides low-cost loans to nations working to improve their economic conditions. The original twenty-eight governments that signed the IBRD's Articles of Agreement (Belgium, Bolivia, Canada, China, Czechoslovakia, Ethiopia, France, Greece, Honduras, Iceland, India, Iraq, Luxembourg, the Netherlands, Norway, Philippines, South Africa, Egypt, the United Kingdom, the United States, and Yugoslavia) largely overlap original memberships of the organizations discussed here. The Bank currently counts 184 countries as members, including developed and developing countries. Members provide oversight and accountability to the Bank regarding distribution of funds and scope of operations.

With regard to education, the Bank takes its cues from its members as well as from partner organizations engaged in similar works. 'Along with the rest of the development community, the World Bank centres its efforts on . . . reaching the Millennium Development Goals, agreed to by UN members in 2000 and aimed at sustainable poverty reduction' (World Bank, 2004). Addressing poverty, improving outputs and quality, and making systems more efficient are all primary goals of education funding from the Bank. And, in understanding the impact education has on sustainable development, the Bank has sought avenues for making long-term improvements to and investment in education. In so doing, the Bank has become the largest external financial source supporting education around the world (World Bank, 2004).

Teritary education, as part of the full compendium of educational areas funded through World Bank loans, has fluctuated in significance over the past forty years. According to the Bank's website, tertiary education (in the form of teacher education) was an element of the Bank's very first educational loan in 1963, to Tunisia. From teacher education and the development of buildings and ground-level operations, the World Bank's funding for higher education has focused more on 'systemic reforms and capacity building' (World Bank, 2004). In its history, the World Bank has loaned over $84 billion to over 107 countries for 336 education projects with tertiary education components, and over the past decade, lending for tertiary education projects has averaged $343 million per year (World Bank, 2004).

The position of higher education among other education priorities at the Bank, however, has not always been secure. Bank policies that prioritized primary and secondary education over tertiary were the norm after a published study on the rate of return on investment showed better returns from primary education (Psacharopoulos, 2006). In the past 15 years or so, however, the Bank has shifted its position again, seeking more balance and with a stronger commitment to its education efforts on post-secondary education:

The Bank is commonly perceived as supporting only basic education;

systematically advocating the reallocation of public expenditures from tertiary to basic education; promoting cost recovery and private sector expansion;
and discouraging low-income countries from considering any investment in
advanced human capital. Given these perceptions, the rapid changes taking
place in the global environment, and the persistence of the traditional problems
of tertiary education in developing and transition countries, re-examining the
World Bank's policies and experiences in tertiary education has become a matter of urgency. (Salmi, 2002, p. 52)

Explaining its commitment to higher education, particularly in contrast to the
long-standing priority given to primary and basic education, the World Bank
(2004) states:

Higher education is a key piece to the holistic puzzle of a country's entire
education system, providing the advanced skills required by teachers, doctors,
scientists, civic leaders, technicians and entrepreneurs. Adequate education
capacity is key to a competitive workforce, and that includes higher-order skills.
Even to promote literacy, good health, and other aspects of human development
in disadvantaged segments of the population, countries require good quality
tertiary education – teacher training institutes, nursing schools, medical colleges, universities, and local avenues for lifelong learning – so that sufficient
numbers of appropriately trained professionals are generated to support these
development goals that are proven to reduce poverty. Investments are being
made at all levels of education to support the comprehensive and equitable
expansion of human capital needed to better the lives of all people. (World
Bank, 2004)

The World Bank also supports research on higher (tertiary) education and
produces publications, conferences, and other mechanisms for disseminating
their research findings. Starting in the mid-1990s, the World Bank undertook new policy reviews on its decades-old position that marginalized tertiary
education, resulting first in the publication of *Higher Education: The Lessons
of Experience* in 1994, which began the World Bank's redeployment of efforts
into the tertiary education sector. This undertaking was soon followed by the
convening of the Task Force on Higher Education and Society, which was an
international body of higher education leaders and researchers from across the
developed and developing world, assigned to focus their attention specifically
on the state of higher education in developing countries. *Higher Education in
Developing Countries: Peril and Promise* (Task Force, 2000) was the outcome of
two years of collaboration by the task force.

This report is noteworthy in the context of this research as it examines a
breadth of concerns and challenges facing higher education worldwide and
offers suggestions for re-investing in higher education, particularly in the developing world. It also touches briefly on the impact of globalization, specifically,
on higher education in noting: 'The globalization of higher education can
have damaging as well as beneficial consequences. It can lead to unregulated
and poor-quality higher education, with the worldwide marketing of fraudu-
lent degrees or other so-called higher education credentials a clear example'

(Task Force, 2000, p. 43). This perspective on globalization – here referring to the economic pressures to expand for-profit higher education in worldwide markets and the ramifications of such expansion – provides a skepticism about the benefits of unchecked growth in higher education, even where a real need for expansion of opportunities for higher education exist. With trade policies and agreements that facilitate the expansion of the higher education service industry worldwide, such skepticism is, itself, a useful check on the value of globalized higher education today.

A 2002 World Bank publication regarding international higher education is the most pointed and developed rationale for World Bank support for tertiary education initiatives to date. *Constructing Knowledge Societies: New Challenges for Tertiary Education* specifically addresses globalization and the need for a well-educated work force in order to participate in the new global economy and establishes a pointed strategy towards tertiary higher education for operations across the Bank. The report 'describes how tertiary education contributed to building up a country's capacity for participation in an increasingly knowledge-based world economy, and investigates policy options for tertiary education that have the potential to enhance economic growth and reduce poverty' (Salmi, 2002, p. 52).

The World Bank, though a lending body with high levels of accountability to the most powerful and wealthiest nations, examines issues that affect the least powerful nations, and the expansion of globalization in educational services through trade is one area that will likely continue to receive attention from the Bank in the future. The Bank has the potential to dramatically affect the course of investment in and policy directions for tertiary education through its linking-pin role between developed, middle-income, and low-income countries. This high level of influence is perceived as both positive and negative, depending upon political leanings and philosophical perspectives, but it its existence is undeniable, regardless.

The Big Three as linking-pin higher education organizations

In light of the history and contexts of these three global organizations, their positions as linking-pins in the web of tertiary education actors is unsurprising given the environment in which the discourse on tertiary education is taking place. Aldrich (1979) finds that linking-pin organizations serve as agents for information and resource exchanges between and across organizations. Doreian *et al.* (2004) find that 'linking-pin organizations are structurally critical in their role of . . . connecting inter-organization networks' (p. 46) and establish three defining elements to any linking-pin organization: their centrality to the networks they link, their position as bridging agents among the other members of the network, and the uniqueness of the organizations themselves. Utilizing this three-part definition of a linking-pin organization, it is clear that the influence and utility of the three organizations examined in this chapter in the realm of tertiary education can be explained by their positions as 'focal organizations' (Doreian *et al.*, p. 45) among the myriad other actors and organizations in their networks.

Within the first defining point (centrality) UNESCO's role as a linking organization in the tertiary education sector is perhaps the most obvious, given the two World Conferences on Higher Education (1998 and 2009) that it has hosted. Bringing together thousands of practitioners, policy-makers, government officials, academics, and others across the spectrum of stakeholders, these two conferences illustrate most clearly the impact of a linking-pin organization. Both conferences created a forum for the exchange of ideas, as well as networking, across the enormous pool of participants (over a thousand at both conferences), and these two conferences remain unique in providing such a hub for exchange in the global tertiary education sphere. Indeed, the UNESCO World Conferences on Higher Education illustrate the linking-pin idea in such a literal way that it is easy to envision a diagram of the global tertiary community as a wheel with UNESCO as a core hub from which the spokes of myriad actors are connected. Biannual conferences at the OECD (through their affiliated Programme on Institutional Management of Higher Education – IMHE) situate the OECD as a central actor in the tertiary sphere, as well, while the World Bank's centrality stems more from its role as a source for extensive global technical advice and analytical research.

UNESCO, the World Bank, and the OECD also situate themselves as central providers of global data and tertiary education statistics, and it is often this data, as well as the accompanying analytical works, that also establish these organizations as bridges to the rest of the tertiary education community. The annual publication of the *Global Education Digest* (UNESCO) and *Education at a Glance* (OECD), as well as the web-based data tool EdStats (the World Bank), all contribute to these organizations' serving as the primary locations for international tertiary education data. Researchers, policy-makers, and other stakeholders in the field of tertiary education rely on the data produced and/or synthesized by the big three organizations. All three organizations coordinate their data generation and presentation in varying degrees, to refine and address the data needs for their own purposes, as well as for the perceived needs of their client countries and funders.

Finally, the uniqueness of these three organizations is well established in the history section above. Indeed, it is challenging to imagine the circumstances that could bring about a similar building of central, global organizations as those that existed at the end of World War II. That these three groups emerged at a time of global redevelopment and continue to redefine their missions in light of both their historically prescribed roles and the current global conditions illustrates the relevance of global interrelationships.

At this time of expansion in tertiary education, particularly in developing and emerging economies, the role of these multinational powers should not be overlooked or underestimated. As tertiary education expands as a global industry, so too does the influence of these global organizations on the policies and priorities of localized tertiary systems. The World Bank, the OECD, and UNESCO will continue to promote poverty reduction, world peace, economic development, or other grand ambitions while also promoting localized equity initiatives, improved data collection for informed decision-making, and improvements in quality assurance at the institutional level. The decades ahead will include initiatives to promote expansion of access and opportunity through both public and private providers and the need for quality assurance training and investments to develop localized capacity.

The twenty-first century opened with tertiary education expanding in its global significance, and these three multinational and highly influential organizations emerged as hubs for research and policy influence. At the time of this publication, there is no indication that their roles will change in the near future. Their activities as linking-pin organizations in the global sphere of tertiary education are more pronounced than ever, and this dynamic will continue to merit further analysis and research in the years and decades ahead.

References

Aldrich, H. E. (1979), *Organizations and Environment*. Englewood Cliffs, NJ: Prentice-Hall.

Barnett, M. N. and Finnemore, M. (1999), 'The politics, power, and pathologies of international organizations', *International Organizations*, 53, (4), 699–732.

Daniel, J. S. (2002), 'Quality assurance, accreditation and the recognition of qualifications in higher education in an international perspective', in S. Uvalić-Trumbić (ed.), *Globalization and the Market in Higher Education*. Paris: UNESCO, 11–20.

Doreian, P. and Fujimoto, K. (2004), 'Identifying linking-pin organizations in inter-organizational networks', *Computational & Mathematical Organization Theory*, 10, (1), 45–68.

Ness, G. D. and Brechin, S. (1988), 'Bridging the gap: International organizations as organizations', *International Organization*, 2, 245–73.

OECD, *History of the OECD*, at http://www.oecd.org/document/63/0,2340,en_2649_201185_1876671_1_1_1_1,00.html (accessed 12 November 2004).

—— *Marshall Plan Speech*, at http://www.oecd.org/document/10/0,2340,en_2649_20 1185_1876938_1_1_1_1,00.html (accessed 12 November 2004).

—— *Convention of the Organisation for Economic Co-operation and Development*, at http:// www.oecd.org/document/7/0,2340,en_2649_201185_1915847_1_1_1_1,00.html (accessed 12 November 2004).

—— (2002), *GATS: The Case for Open Services Markets*. Paris: OECD.

—— (2004a), *Internationalisation and trade in higher education: Opportunities and Challenges*. Paris: Organization for Economic Co-operation and Development – Center for Educational Research and Innovation.

—— (2004b), *Policy Brief: Internationalisation of Higher Education*, from www.oecd.org/ publications/Pol_brief (accessed 12 November 2004).

OECD/CERI. (2002), 'Background document: Current commitments under the GATS in educational services', paper presented at the OECD/US Forum on Trade in Educational Services, Washington, DC, Appendix B(3) 1–47.

Psacharopoulos, G. (2006), 'World Bank policy on education: A personal account', *International Journal of Educational Development*, 26, (3), 329–38.

Salmi, J. (2002), 'Constructing knowledge societies: New challenges for tertiary education', in G. Breton and M. Lambert (eds), *Universities and Globalization: Private Linkages, Public Trust*. Paris: UNESCO Publishing, 51–68.

Task Force on Higher Education and Society. (2000), *Higher Education in Developing Countries: Peril and Promise*, from http://www.tfhe.net/report/readreport.htm (accessed 25 July 2008).

THES (2006), 'Think globally, urges Ischinger', 7 July, from http://www.timeshigher

education.co.uk/story.asp?sectioncode=26&storycode=204165 (accessed 10 July 2008).

UNESCO, *UNESCO Education-Objectives*, from http://portal.unesco.org/education/ en (accessed 22 November 2004).

—— *UNESCO Forum on Higher Education, Research, and Knowledge*, from http://portal. unesco.org/education.en (accessed 22 November 2004).

—— *Constitution of the United Nations Educational, Scientific and Cultural Organization.* from http://portal.unesco.org/en/ev.php-URL_ID=3328&URL_DO=DO_ TOPIC&URL_SECTION=201.html (accessed 22 November 2004).

—— *UNESCO Milestones.* http://portal.unesco.org/en/ev.phpURL_ID=1 (accessed 12 November 2008).

Uvalić-Trumbić, S. (ed.) (2002) *Globalization and the Market in Higher Education: Quality, Accreditation and Qualifications.* Paris, France: UNESCO/Economica.

Chapter 19

Intercultural Experience in English Universities: A Case Study of Chinese Students

Mei Tian and John Lowe

Introduction

The expansion of international student numbers in UK universities is probably the most immediately obvious manifestation of their internationalization. Among this general expansion of students from outside the UK, the explosion in the number of Chinese students over the last ten years or so is perhaps the most remarkable phenomenon, reflecting in a microcosm the rapid growth of China on the world stage more generally. From less than three thousand in 1998–99, the number of Chinese students studying at all levels in UK universities had increased to almost fifty thousand by 2006–07 (HESA, 2009). This chapter examines the experiences of some of these students at various universities in England, using this to raise questions about both our interpretations of 'internationalization' in higher education (HE) and its actual impact on campuses and those who study there.

As a somewhat simplified analytical starting point, we see two broad perspectives on the origins, meaning and significance of internationalization of HE. Turner and Robson's (2008) distinction between 'symbolic' and 'transformative' internationalization captures particularly well the institutional implications of these two perspectives. The first perspective regards internationalization as an epiphenomenon of globalization, a systemic and institutional response driven largely by economic forces backed up by a neo-liberal political agenda. This is explicit in some earlier definitions and accounts of HE internationalization (for example, the influential early definition offered by Knight, 1997) and has been identified as a dominant rationale in practice by several researchers (Matthews, 2002; Toyoshima, 2007; Bolsmann *et al.*, 2008; Haigh, 2008). It has assumed a particular significance in the context of the marketization of HE and a gradual erosion of state funding in many countries, forcing many institutions to turn to the global student market as a means of enhancing their financial viability (Naidoo, 2003; Jiang, 2008). Of particular concern for this chapter, with its focus on intercultural exchange, is that the current era of globalization is also associated with Western cultural hegemonic assimilation (Sidhu, 2004; Tikly, 2001), so that internationalization seen as a derivative of such global forces may also involve implicit assumptions of cultural dominance.

The second perspective on internationalization in HE may accept globalization as a context within which internationalization is taking place (Gacel-Ávila, 2005) but seeks to distinguish the two by presenting a rationale for the latter which is cultural and personal, rather than economic and institutional (Yang, 2002; Turner *et al.*, 2008, p. 33). Of particular interest to us in this respect is Sanderson's (2004) concept of 'existential internationalisation', in which he sees the need to improve our ability to deal with the increased contact with the 'Cultural Other' that is one consequence of globalization: 'It is to internationalize our personal selves in a bid to produce a very different relationship between internationalization and globalization than the biased, instrumental one offered by neo-liberal globalism' (p. 14). Sanderson draws on Appadurai's (2001) notion of 'globalization from below' to suggest an alternative view of internationalization, in which 'humanistic advancement in the face of the domination of neo-liberal, neo-conservative and implicit neo-colonial agendas' is possible. This, he argues, promotes engagement with and greater understanding of the 'Cultural Other', through which one is better enabled to deconstruct and reconstruct one's understanding of national identity and less likely to retreat into a stereotyped, chauvinistic nationalism (Tian *et al.*, 2009). One consequence of such internationalization would be to substitute enhanced intercultural engagement and communication for the cultural hegemony implicit in notions of assimilation of the 'outsider' to the dominant 'insider' culture.

Our concern in what follows is to examine empirically whether the experiences of a group of international students in England suggest that internationalization of the universities they are attending could be considered 'transformative' or merely 'symbolic', using Turner *et al.*'s (2008) terms. If it is the former, we would expect to find evidence of successful intercultural interaction and communication that has an impact at the personal level, making individuals more empathetic to the Cultural Other, leaving those who arrive as 'outsiders' with a sense of being 'insiders' and perhaps promoting a greater sense of a cosmopolitan (Gunesch, 2004), rather than uncritical national identity. If it is the latter we might expect to find little overall effect, or only incidental effect, on our international students' cross-cultural interaction and understanding, since institutional attitudes would tend to be that the presence of international students is a sufficient indicator of internationalization and it is the responsibility of those students to adapt to their new environment and not for the institution to change (Luxon *et al.*, 2009; see also Baty, 2009, for an example of how the proportion of international students enrolled is used as a measure of internationalization in the production of global university rankings).

Our studies

The data we present and discuss below are taken from two empirical investigations of the experiences of Chinese students in English universities. One is an intensive, longitudinal study of thirteen Chinese students on taught Master's programmes in a single university; the other is a study of undergraduate students at seven universities, with data obtained through interviews with four-teen students on a range of courses. Despite the very different nature of the courses, age and experience of the students, their location and the length of time they spent in the UK, we found striking similarities across the two samples that allow us to suggest a categorization of their experiences of intercultural interactions during that time. This is based on Berry's (1997) identification of four acculturation strategies, but in using these we are not in any sense sug-gesting that the goal of internationalization should be some sort of assimilation of the 'outsider' through a process of more-or-less successful acculturation. Rather, we find these four strategies to be useful summaries of the different degrees of intercultural engagement that our subjects experienced, and the influence this had on their behaviour, values and beliefs. We go further, how-ever, in proposing that these categories are better thought of as being domains on a continuum, ranging from 'cultural isolation' to 'cultural assimilation' and that individuals may – and probably will – change their position on this continuum in response to their experiences.

Findings

To illustrate these four domains, we have chosen to describe the experiences and responses of four individuals, rather than compiling composite pictures within each. One of our purposes in doing this is to emphasize our concern to retain a view of our subjects as individuals whose personal histories and char-acteristics do influence their particular responses and strategies when dealing with the experiences of being an international student in England. The labels we have chosen for the domains are intended to give some indication of the start- and end-points of individuals' aspirations and outcomes, while recogniz-ing that these 'end-points' may represent temporary positions at the time our studies were carried out and subsequent movement along the continuum in either direction remains possible.

Separation/marginalization

Separation/marginalization refers to the situations where students experi-enced very limited intercultural interaction, partly from choice or partly forced by (perceived or real) social exclusion and discrimination (Berry, 1997). Such students rarely sought friendship with those from other countries and remained in a very restricted social network of a small number of Chinese students.

   These students declared themselves to be independent learners with confi-dence in their own academic learning ability. They were less likely to socialize for the purpose of English learning. Some had a stable relationship with a girlfriend or boyfriend in China; others lived with their partners or parents in the UK, either of which could diminish both the desire and opportunity for cross-cultural engagement. These students were either unaware of social events on campus for promoting intercultural communications, or showed little interest in such events. They described themselves as somewhat introverted and were all sensitive to prejudiced treatment in their everyday lives.

Lin

At the age of 17, Lin arrived in the UK for a language course. An agency had arranged for him to live in a homestay with a UK family and he was initially excited at the prospect of opportunities to interact with the host family. His experiences, however, did not match his expectations.

> We [the landlord and I] had few interactions in everyday life . . . The rent covered breakfast . . . I was a 17-year-old boy but I [usually] got only two pieces of toast for breakfast, which was not enough. One morning, there were six pieces of bread [on the table]. I finished two but wanted some more. The landlady said: 'stop eating, those are for other people.' In the house there lived two boys and a girl, that is why [there were] six pieces in total. Why did she provide so little food? I always felt hungry. I paid £110 per week. I paid so much so I deserved to be treated better.

'Homestay myth' is used to describe a belief that by living with host families, foreign students will instantly become immersed in an authentic environment of cross-cultural interactions, which will facilitate acquisition of the target language and understanding of the host culture (Wilkinson, 1997). Pellegrino has questioned the 'myth' by pointing out the potentially negative influences from the host on foreign students. In our interviews, Lin repeatedly talked about life with the host family. His unhappy memories 'damaged the image of the British in my mind'. Although he admitted he might 'just have met with a very mean person', the behaviour of the landlady had clearly hurt him and reduced his desire for further interaction. Six months later, he moved out to share a house with other Chinese students; then, he declared, he 'started feeling better'.

From his second year in the UK, Lin's parents visited Britain once a year and each time stayed with him for six months. Living with his parents minimized difficulties in his everyday life, in terms of cooking and cleaning and other house chores: 'I need to worry about nothing but study.' Lin was frustrated, however: 'My parents control everything . . . [I] prefer an independent life . . ..
I don't feel very happy when living with them.' Thus, on the one hand, his family provided comfort and emotional support, and Lin adapted easily to life in the university; on the other hand, with his parents dealing with everyday life for him, Lin lost the chance to participate in the host society.

With the subject he was studying being delivered mainly through lectures, Lin had few opportunities within his course to interact with other students. Like other students in this group, Lin reported few problems with studying and, knowing 'the tricks of examinations', he was confident that he would pass the degree course. From his words, it was evident that there was no particular incentive for Lin to communicate with the host students for the purpose of improving learning outcomes.

Off-campus, Lin worked part-time in a fast-food restaurant, where he reported unfair racially biased treatment: 'They [local employees] rarely do dirty or exhausting work. Such jobs are always done by the Chinese.' To protect himself, he transferred to another store where 'there are twenty to thirty Chinese employees . . . if something happens, we help each other'.

Even among his immediate Chinese network, Lin rarely socialized, preferring to spend his time in online forums, created and managed by Chinese students overseas for sharing information and opinions. Here Lin found many other people similar to him and he clearly felt comfortable and had a sense of belonging in such a situation. He shared with online friends his dilemmas and frustrations in interactions with local people:

> As we discussed in online forums, we find it difficult to get into a British circle of friendship. Nor can they easily get into our circle of friends . . .. [We agree] that [Chinese] can only interact naturally with British if they are boy- or girlfriends, or if they are colleagues. Otherwise, it is not easy to interact with them. I don't know whether some British will behave better or whether this is a national way of behaving.

Furthermore, Lin described himself as a 'pure Chinese', who 'cares about the changes in China . . . [I] only watch Chinese news through Chinese media . . . and will finally return to China'. To some extent, Lin resembles the 'strangers', described by Simmel (1950, cited in Coates, 2004), who live a foreign country but feel no attachment to it.

Among most of the participants in both of our studies, we noted a shared 'national mentality' emerging during their stay in the UK, characterized by an increasing stress on an essence of 'the Chinese' and their essentialist distinguishing of themselves from 'the British others'. This 'self-essentializing' stereotyping of self and others was primarily a response to their perceptions of experiences of behaviour and attitudes among 'locals' with whom they interacted rather than being a reflection of any fixed cultural or ethnic characteristics shared by Chinese learners.

Integration/separation

Integration/separation refers to situations where students had actively sought cross-cultural interactions, but for various reasons increasingly socialized with Chinese students only, although they retained an interest in intercultural friendship. Most of our participants fall into this group. They generally stated that they came to the UK with expectations of enriching intercultural experiences through meeting people from diverse backgrounds. They tended, initially at least, to respond actively to social events organized by the university and often tried to initiate friendships with host or other international students. For these students, however, interaction with the host people was largely campus-bound and tended not to lead to sustained intercultural friendships. Over time, they gradually withdrew into a Chinese social network, though generally remaining open to the possibility of friendships outside this network.

Xin

Coming from one of China's largest cities and one of its top universities, Xin held great expectations when arriving at the UK for her postgraduate study; important among these was meeting and making friends with people from other countries. Once again, however, the dominant teaching approach on her course gave her few opportunities to interact with her classmates. Furthermore, she had been given university accommodation with mostly Chinese neighbours and she did not take on a part-time job, so her chances to meet locals remained sparse.

Hoping to increase her contacts with British or other international students, Xin attended various social events organized by the department, the student union, the international office, the graduate school and local churches. Although she was motivated to make contacts, on most occasions Xin had little success at such events.

> . . . we had a party today. Many tutors and students attended it, eating and drinking together. It was interesting to talk with others but we still have troubles in communication. My classmates, particularly those from Greece and Italy, have a strong accent, which makes their expressions difficult to understand. And on the other hand, they may feel that we have a strong accent and are hard to be understood as well. So in the end it was still Chinese students sitting together with other Chinese, or at least Asian students. I feel we have more common topics with other Asian students, perhaps because our background is a bit similar. It is different regarding European students, to whom we just asked several key questions and then we don't know what to say.

Xin tried to initiate communications, particularly with native English speakers. Despite the willingness to talk with others, a different accent, the lack of topics of common interest or background similarities pushed her back to the co-nationals or 'at least Asian students'.

Before she left China, Xin had applied for a 'mentor programme', organized by the university's international office to help new international students settle down and enjoy their lives in the UK. Joanna, an undergraduate female student who had been introduced to Xin as her mentor, was in fact the only British person with whom Xin had regular contacts throughout the year. Her response to their first meeting was very promising:

> . . . I met with Joanna today . . . .. She looked like a boy, but very warm. We had tea together and chatted for an hour. She said my English was good, which was really encouraging. She told me that in her spare time she did a paid job and worked part-time as a volunteer. She also told me how she changed her major recently and why. We decided to meet each other every week in the future.

Meeting and talking with her mentor did help Xin's initial adjustment. Subsequent meetings were described as interesting and Xin learned valuable information and insights from Joanna. Joanna also showed her pictures of her family and shared with Xin the happiness of getting engaged. Although speaking in English was 'a bit strange' for Xin because she felt unable to 'chat as freely as in Chinese', her anxiety was reduced on finding Joanna understood her linguistic troubles, was encouraging and made great efforts to facilitate their communication.

Despite this, the contacts did not develop into a lasting friendship, as the programme organizers hoped, but ended with the completion of the programme.

> . . . If you are active enough, you could become good friends with your mentor, and probably integrate into their lives. But I gradually reduced our interaction – we are just too busy. It is a good chance – at least you know a local. But gradually we all gave up.

With the increasing academic pressure over time, especially in pre-examination periods, Xin had to prioritize academic work, which was her main reason for coming to the UK. Conscious of the expense of this overseas study and the loss of face if she failed, she deferred interaction with the host nationals.

Integration/identity retention

Integration/identity retention refers to the situations where the students aimed to participate closely in the host society and were able to do so to a greater extent than those in the previous category. At the same time, however, they maintained close friendships with other Chinese and remained comfortable with but not uncritical of their own sense of being Chinese.

Michael

Michael was a self-assured young man who enjoyed photography, travelling and meeting people from different backgrounds. As with most of our participants, his spoken English was not very good and although he was able to express himself, he had difficulties in freely sharing his thoughts when speaking English. In his childhood, he had been greatly influenced by his parents' 'Westernized' value system and he knew 'what kind of life I want', which was 'to enjoy more freedom'.

Michael's account of his family and his relationship with his parents contradicts the hierarchical picture often portrayed in the literature (for instance, Chao, 1994, 2000; Xu *et al.*, 2005). He saw his parents as reliable sources of advice and emotional support: '. . . I like talking with them when I have problems and they always give me better solutions'. But it was not one-way dependency in this respect: 'whoever was in trouble would speak it out and then we discussed together to find solutions . . .. I have been seeing my parents as friends since I was young. I feel we are a quite democratic family. We talk with each other about almost everything.' The lure of essentialized accounts of Chinese students prevents us from appreciating the diversity that exists in their backgrounds and will in turn negatively influence our exploration of possible interpretations of Chinese students' actions and perceptions.

Michael pointed out that, since coming to the UK, he had learned to appreciate friendship and viewed it as a crucial step in his personal growth. He now regarded friends as sources of information, partners in study and helpers in life, but he also stressed the importance of non-instrumental emotional attachment to friends. In particular, Michael talked about making friends with other international students:

> . . . I get along well with my housemate. She is a Korean student. She learned sculpture in Korea and now is studying Psychology. She loves cooking and we usually had dinner and chatting together.

Simple proximity, such as sharing a kitchen and having dinner together, may help to increase students' interactions with other international students (Gareis, 2000). This point was reinforced by other participants, who reported that cross-cultural contacts usually took place in the shared kitchen in residence and always occurred when Chinese students and their housemates made food together or when they cooked Chinese dishes and invited others to join in.

Michael was interviewed together with a female friend and his response to her account of an experience of racial prejudice is illuminative of a characteristic that we wish to capture of this third category of students. Commenting on her experience, he said:

> I would get cross if such things happened to me. But I don't think we should then link it to national pride . . . In every country, there are 'rubbish' people; but also kindly people. Once I took bus. There were some teenagers of around 16/17 year old on the bus. They swore and said Chinese bla bla bla. Several British people were sitting near me. They talked with me and they said they could not understand how these teenagers behaved like that. They also told me: 'Don't mind' . . .. You see they are all British but they hold different attitudes. Among British people, some are better educated. Those who have been to universities, like us, will behave better. These [their attitudes] relate to their education and the contexts they grow up in . . .. I have been in Britain for several years and I just encountered such things once or twice. Most British are kind to us. They don't look down on you just because you are Chinese.

Adler (1975) suggests people living outside their 'home' country tend to experience cultural marginality but one can make a difference by choosing either to remain isolated or to develop a more open sense of self and build relationships with diverse groups of people in the host country. Michael, compared with his classmate, was more tolerant of (perceived) social biases and ready to change himself to meet new challenges brought about by his trans-border journey.

The point is further illustrated by his opinions on 'Chineseness':

> . . . currently the world is becoming smaller and smaller. If you insist that you are Chinese and want to emphasize your Chinese culture, you will find that you pay much [more] than what you get.

Living abroad is certainly difficult, especially when it is compounded with demanding study. Aware of this, Michael was positive about diversity and was enthusiastic to explore such diversity by, for example, travelling and making friends with different groups of people. He tended to view cultures as somewhat interchangeable and societies as interdependent, and was willing to adopt a more international lifestyle and improve his ability to settle down in different places other than his home country.

Integration/assimilation

Integration/assimilation refers to the situation where Chinese students successfully built and maintained a friendly or intimate relationship with the host people. Students in this group had strong expectations of establishing local friendships and were likely to initiate interaction with host people in different social events. Their close Chinese friends also showed a strong tendency to meet and socialize with host people. They introduced new friends to each other, and therefore, had greater chances to extend their social network with British people, commonly diminishing their association with other Chinese. These students were found either to have limited communication with parents and consequently a strong need for emotional support; or were brought up in a family where intercultural experiences were encouraged.

LingLing

LingLing was an outgoing young female student with excellent English language skills. Socially very active, she spent her leisure time in diverse extracurricular activities. LingLing was also very determined to make friends with the locals. Her motivation, at least initially, was highly oriented to learning English. Aiming to become a professional interpreter, she reminded herself of the importance of 'keeping speaking in English'. Informal conversations with the natives, in particular, were believed to be 'a necessity' because 'fluency and accuracy cannot be simply acquired in class'. To improve her English she found a language partner with the help of the English Language Centre. This British girl, who had a great interest in China and desired to know more about the country, became LingLing's first local acquaintance.

LingLing was also well aware of the harm caused by spending too much of her time with other Chinese. In fact, 'sticking to the Chinese', as some of her Chinese classmates did, was seen by LingLing as 'purely a shame'. This, for her, inhibited language improvement and cultural assimilation, which she saw as complementary goals. Hence she consciously avoided interacting with co-nationals and gave preference to communication with the locals.

LingLing's great passion for dancing led her to join the university salsa dancing society, which in turn gave her more opportunities than other participants to get involved with the locals. In LingLing's words, it enabled her to 'develop a cosmopolitan view of the world'. More importantly, it was in this society that LingLing met with Simon and Mat. As LingLing gradually developed her dancing skills, her relationship with Simon and Mat deepened, from student and teacher to dancing partners and to intimate friends.

Among all participants in both studies, LingLing was the only one who embraced the 'pubbing and clubbing' culture of the locals, although her initial reaction to the local student social culture was far from positive:

> Yesterday evening at around 10 o'clock, [I] received a call from Amy saying a party was being held in the Physics Department. I went there but, my goodness, found the place was like a hell. So many people crowded into a small room. So noisy. The floor is dirty and damp. And boys and girls kiss each other after just saying a few sentences. A boy held two girls in his arms. I cannot believe it. How will they feel when meeting each other on the next day? Wouldn't they feel embarrassed? And I saw a boy wanted to kiss a girl. He was refused. But immediately he turned around and kissed another girl. What a hell! It was really a disordered primitive society! I will never go there again!

This experience is interesting in terms of Lingling's getting to 'know' local customs. In spite of the desire for closer integration into the host culture, which was a key aim in coming to the UK, her initial experiences of attending students' parties shocked and repelled her. The activities she observed seemed to LingLing a waste of time, meaningless and perhaps immoral. She gradually changed her mind, however, partly due to her love of dancing and partly due to her determination to participate fully in the host culture. Having agreed with her local friends that pubbing and clubbing were parts of the British lifestyle, she believed it necessary to get herself involved. Otherwise 'you don't need to come to the UK; you should have taken a long distance course and studied in China'. LingLing's acceptance of the new lifestyle, which she further commented on as a 'very relaxed way of life', made it easier to have host friends and going to pubs and clubs became LingLing's main form of entertainment. Her contacts with salsa friends expanded dramatically, and her relationships with some reached various levels of intimacy.

The four people with whom LingLing had most frequent contacts were male and the relationships were all somewhere between good friend and lover. Her case illustrates how sexual attraction can facilitate and accelerate intercultural interaction and, among our participants, we did find that those who did participate most in and were most familiar with local culture had a local partner. These students were all female, in line with Gao's (1998) findings that female Chinese students in Australia are more likely to be sought after by the local students and hence make friends more easily than male Chinese students. This brings in a very interesting gender dimension which is potentially very complex, based on expectations of gender roles and appropriate gendered behaviour.

Summary and conclusion

The Chinese students in our studies were exposed to a diverse range of challenges during their time in the UK. Academically, they encountered difficulties caused by inadequate English proficiency, gaps in their subject knowledge and a lack of familiarity with UK higher education teaching and learning conventions. Socially, they were faced with problems of living in a society based on unfamiliar norms, customs and expectations. Many, if not all, had expected to encounter such novelty and had even looked forward to it, but the reality often came as something of a shock and most had difficulty in engaging with and participating in their new social environment. Pressure from their studies became entangled with pressure from other aspects of life such as financial troubles, as for many students whether home or international, but presenting them with particular psychological and emotional challenges. Difficulties in dealing with these challenges tended to be worsened by the fact of living far away from family and lacking a sense of belonging in the host society.

The majority, but not all, of our participants came to the UK with aspirations and expectations of meeting and mixing with members of the host population, particularly other students. They actively sought an intercultural experience and hoped to develop cross-cultural communication, understanding and friendships. For most, however, the stresses posed by life in this new context led to their abandoning such aspirations. Help in dealing with these stresses was more easily and effectively found among the Chinese student community and the energy required to make closer cross-cultural contacts was soon dissipated by the effort needed to manage daily life. A variety of factors, both personal and institutional, led to eventual disappointment and disillusionment and, in some cases, to a sense of isolation, 'otherization' and an enhanced sense of national cultural distinction. We have suggested a model of a continuum of intercultural experience, with most students initially arriving somewhere vaguely in the middle of this continuum but tending over their time in the UK to drift or be forced towards the 'isolationist' end.

From our own perspective of a genuinely internationalized university, we would not, however, advocate occupation of the opposite end of this continuum – characterized by cultural assimilation – as the 'ideal' outcome of this process. Such an outcome implies a loss of cultural diversity and a compromise only on the part of the overseas students, with a further implication of a loss of opportunity for home students to expand their own intercultural experience and competence. Turner *et al.*'s (2008) concept of transformative internationalization, or Sanderson's (2004) notion of existential internationalization demands that space remains for the 'cultural other' to retain a cultural identity that is valued rather than rejected, so that the opportunity for intercultural communication and understanding permeates the lives of all students – and staff, we might add. Undoubtedly, a contributing factor to the majority of our Chinese students' abandonment of serious attempts at meaningful relationships with the host community was a perception that there was little will among the hosts to meet them halfway, and to accept the need for the hosts to enter and engage with the Chinese 'cultural space'. In this respect we note Donati's (2009) suggestion of an interesting and potentially valuable alternative to assimilationist (culturally homogenous) and multiculturalist (culturally isolationist) models of cross-cultural interaction in which this space between culturally diverse individuals (and, we would argue, communities and institutions too) becomes a fertile ground for interaction that allows the retention of distinct cultural identities while simultaneously informing the development of those identities.

The accounts of our participants suggest considerable common experience in being a Chinese student in England. Although responses to this common experience did vary across the sample, there was a broad tendency among our Chinese students eventually to admit defeat in their hopes and attempts to achieve greater cultural contact with their English peers and local inhabitants in the wider community. We simply do not have enough data from such a relatively small sample to make definitive comments on what brings about this tendency to settle towards the 'separatist end' of our continuum, although we can make tentative suggestions. Individual personalities and characteristics of individuals' backgrounds and their circumstances when in the UK seem to play a significant role, as Gu *et al.* (2006) similarly found in their study. Those students who, for example, came with or rapidly found a Chinese partner – spouse or lover – were less likely to need or to seek local contacts with whom to socialize or to seek emotional support. We initially expected to find that undergraduate students would have succeeded better in establishing cross-cultural friendships and in feeling more accepted by and more comfortable with the host culture, on the grounds that they had spent a longer time living in the UK than the postgraduate students in our study. We found, however, that experiences and responses to those experiences were remarkably similar in both groups.

It was also clear from our data that programmes offered by the universities themselves to promote cross-cultural contact and communication, including social events as well as 'buddy' or 'mentor' schemes, tended to have limited and usually temporary impact at best, although we are anecdotally aware of more successful programmes and are reluctant to label and condemn them more widely. Indeed, experience of social events such as 'welcome parties' could have a negative impact on the Chinese students' perceptions of the host culture and the possibility of engaging with home students (see Tian *et al.*, 2009 for further accounts of such experiences). Similarly, activities in class, such as mixed-culture group-working, rarely did much to promote intercultural empathy and understanding (Tian *et al.*, 2009). Finally, it is also important to note that experiences off-campus, including several reports among our participants of blatantly racist abuse, often had an impact that exacerbated a sense of rejection and inhibited contacts within the university. Attempts by the university to develop a 'transformatively international' community will be hampered unless such experiences of the students in the wider community are also addressed through liaison with local communities and authorities.

We are very well aware that our own studies suffer from being one-sided research into the experiences of international – and more narrowly, Chinese – students only, and that there is an urgent need to complement this with the views of home students. Anecdotal evidence from our own experience suggests that an 'international experience' is not one of the attractions of university life for the majority of UK students and that many of these students themselves see Chinese students as tending to prefer to work and socialize with their compatriots, rather than engaging with host students or others. We would argue that in the contemporary world of increasing globalization of work and cultural contacts and the increased imperative to engage with the cultural other who is no longer 'over there', this lack of intercultural experience is particularly detrimental to the home students and their future lives. For those students coming to the UK from other countries, their experience is, at least in some sense, automatically 'international', but we need to ensure that their presence also offers the opportunity for an international, intercultural experience for all. From both institutional and personal perspectives this demands that the presence of large numbers of international students on our campuses be no longer seen as a 'problem', but as an opportunity and a valuable resource for developing intercultural understanding.

References

Adler, P. (1975), 'The transitional experience: An alternative view of culture shock', *Journal of Humanistic Psychology*, 15, 13–23.

Appadurai, Arjun (ed.), (2001), *Globalization*. Durham: Duke University Press.

Baty, P. (2009), 'Rankings 09: Talking points', *Times Higher Education*, 8 October, available at http://www.timeshighereducation.co.uk/story.asp?storycode=408562.

Berry, J. (1997), 'Immigration, acculturation, and adaptation', *Applied Psychology: An International Review*, 46, (1), 5–68.

Bolsmann, C. and Miller, H. (2008), 'International student recruitment to universities in England: Discourse, rationales and globalisation', *Globalisation, Societies and Education*, 6, (1), 75–88.

Chao, R. K. (1994), 'Beyond parental control and authoritarian parenting style: Understanding Chinese parenting through the cultural notion of training', *Child Development*, 65, 1111–20.

—— (2000), 'The parenting of immigrant Chinese and European American mothers: Relations between parenting styles, socialization goals, and parental practices', *Journal of Applied Developmental Psychology*, 21, 233–48.

Coates, N. (2004), *The 'Stranger', the 'Sojourner' and the International Student*. Proceedings of Education in a Changing Environment Conference, University of Salford, 13–14 September.

Gacel-Ávila, J. (2005), 'The internationalisation of higher education: A paradigm for global citizenry', *Journal of Studies in International Education*, 9, (2), 121–36.

Gao, M. (1998), 'Influence of native culture and language on intercultural communication: The case of PRC student immigrants in Australia', paper presented at the Symposium of Intercultural Communication, Gothenburg University, 28–29 September, available at http://www.immi.se/intercultural/nr4/gao.htm.

Gareis, E. (2000), 'Intercultural friendship: Five case studies of German students in the USA', *Journal of Intercultural Studies*, 21, (1), 67–91.

Gu, Q. and Schweisfurth, M. (2006), 'Who adapts? Beyond cultural models of "the" Chinese learner', *Language, Culture and Curriculum*, 19, (1), 74–89.

Gunesch, K. (2004), 'Education for cosmopolitanism', *Journal of Research in International Education*, 3, 251–75.

Haigh, M. (2008), 'Internationalisation, planetary citizenship and higher education, Inc.', *Compare*, 38, (4), 427–40.

HESA (Higher Education Statistics Agency) (2009), *Institutional level statistics, 1997 to 1998 and 2006 to 2007*, available at http://www.hesa.ac.uk/index.php?option=com_datatables&Itemid=121&task=show_category&catdex=34606&URL_DO=DO_TOPIC&URL_ SECTION=201.html.

Jiang, X. (2008), 'Towards the internationalisation of higher education from a critical perspective', *Journal of Further and Higher Education*, 32, (4), 347–58.

Knight, J. (1997), 'Internationalisation of higher education: A conceptual framework', in J. Knight and H. de Wit (eds) *Internationalisation of Higher Education in Asia Pacific Countries*. Amsterdam: European Association for International Education.

Luxon, T. and Peelo, M. (2009), 'Internationalisation: Its implications for curriculum design and course development in UK higher education', *Innovations in Education and Teaching International*, 46, 51–60.

Matthews, J. (2002), 'International education and internationalisation are not the same as globalisation: Emerging issues for secondary schools', *Journal of Studies in International Education*, 6, (4), 369–90.

Naidoo, R. (2003), Repositioning higher education as a global commodity: Opportunities and challenges for future sociology of education work, *British Journal of Sociology of Education*, 24, (2), 249–59.

Pellegrino, A. V. (2005), *Study Abroad and Second Language Use: Constructing the Self.* Cambridge: University of Cambridge Press.

Sanderson, G. (2004), 'Existentialism, globalisation and the cultural other', *International Education Journal*, 4, (4), 1–20.

Sidhu, R. (2004), 'Governing international education in Australia', *Globalisation, Societies and Education*, 2, (1), 47–66.

Simmel, G. (1950), 'The stranger', in K. Wolff, *The Sociology of Georg Simmel.* London and New York: Free Press/Collier MacMillan.

Tian, M. and Lowe, J. (2009), 'Existentialist internationalisation and the Chinese student experience in English universities', *Compare*, 39, (5), 659–76.

Tikly, L. (2001), 'Post-colonialism and comparative education research', in K. Watson (ed.), *Doing Comparative Education Research: Issues and Problems.* Oxford: Symposium Books.

Toyoshima, H. (2007), 'International strategies of universities in England', *London Review of Education*, 5, (3), 265–80.

Turner, Y. and Robson, S. (2008), *Internationalizing the University.* London: Continuum.

Wilkinson, S. (1997), 'Separating fact from myth: A qualitative perspective on language learning during summer study abroad'. MLA Convention, Toronto. 29 December.

Xu, Y., Farver, J., Zhang, Z., Zeng, Q., Yu, L. and Cai, B. (2005), 'Mainland Chinese parenting styles and parent–child interaction', *The International Society for the Study of Behavioural Development*, 29, (6), 524–31.

Yang, R. (2002), 'University internationalisation: Its meanings, rationales and implications', *International Education*, 13, (1), 81–95.

Uvalić-Trumbić, S. (2002), 'Globalization and quality in higher education: An introduction', in S. Uvalić-Trumbić (ed.), *Globalization and the Market in Higher Education.* Paris: UNESCO, 1–10.

The World Bank (1999), *Higher Education: The Lessons of Experience.* Washington, DC: The World Bank.

—— *What is the World Bank?* from http://web.worldbank.org/WBSITE/EXTERNAL/EXTABOUTUS/0,contentMDK:20040558~menuPK:34559~pagePK:51123644~piPK:329829~theSitePK:29708,00.html (accessed 13 October 2008).

—— *World Bank History*, from http://web.worldbank.org/WBSITE/EXTERNAL/EXTABOUTUS/EXTARCHIVES/0,contentMDK:20053333~menuPK:63762~pagePK:36726~piPK:36092~theSitePK:29506,00.html (accessed 13 October 2008).

Chapter 20

The Internationalization of Higher Education: A Prospective View

Nick Foskett and Felix Maringe

Introduction

The internationalization of higher education (HE) has been a key feature of the first decade of the twenty-first century (Weber *et al.*, 2008). This chapter seeks to draw together the themes explored by authors within this book to examine the future evolution of the sector in the context of internationalization, and to explore briefly how the international HE scene may evolve in response to changing global political and economic circumstances.

Facing the future

The future of HE has become a significant focus for debate. From individual universities, to national governments, to international policy organizations, recognition of the importance of universities to the social and economic well-being of states and communities has stimulated a fundamental questioning of how the benefit and impact of HE can be channelled and optimized. In 2008 the UK government, for example, commissioned a range of reports on future scenarios and responses to change for the HE sector (DIUS, 2008), which provided a backdrop to a new framework for the sector published in 2009 (*Higher Aspirations*, DBIS, 2009). At the same time, the Australian government undertook a fundamental review of its HE system (Commonwealth of Australia, 2009), raising key questions about regulation and deregulation, the state's ability to fund growing demand for HE, and the contribution of the sector to the Australian economy.

Similar initiatives are emerging from international organizations engaged with higher education. In late 2008 the Organization for Economic Co-operation and Development (OECD) began a series of international debates on the theme of 'Higher Education to 2030', drawing together academics, national policy-makers and transnational organizations to consider a range of key policy issues. At the heart of these debates lie four themes which the OECD believes will be of central importance to policy development at national and institutional level – issues of access, attainment and achievement; the role of higher education in addressing issues of social inequality; the challenges of funding HE; and the impact of globalization on the role and governance of the HE sector. Underpinning these issues, the OECD's first report in the series (OECD, 2008) recognizes that responses to these policy issues will be shaped by a number of meta trends:

a   The expansion of student participation in HE
b   The increasing diversity in the profile of students as participation begins to provide access to groups currently under represented
c   The increasing international mobility of students
d   The increasing international mobility of graduates as the graduate labour market is less constrained by national boundaries
e   The increasing international mobility of academic staff

The OECD's identification of the key trends reiterates perspectives from earlier in the decade about the broad direction of travel, suggesting that some of the patterns of change are sufficiently well established to use them as a basis for prediction of future scenarios. Tilak, for example, writing in 2003 (Tilak, 2003) identified a number of international trends in HE which have emerged strongly in the themes within this book:

Rapid increase in demand for HE, with both absolute numbers and participation rates increasing in almost every country.

Fundamental changes to the financial models underpinning HE, as governments seek to enhance the rate of return from their investment in education and drive down unit costs as a way of funding more students. At the same time, governments are seeking to increase their cost recovery on such expenditure, with the increasing expectation that students will fund part or all of their own tertiary education.

The rise of privatization, as recognition that meeting the increasing demand for HE while reducing public sector expenditure can best be achieved through models of increasing privatization.

The internationalization of the sector, in terms of student mobility, in terms of the economic engagement of universities, and in terms of their intellectual and ideological positioning.

While some of these changes are intrinsic and are the product of an emerging self-awareness by universities of what their role can be for society, most are the result of extrinsic market forces and government intervention. At the root of this lies the global economic imperative, for the economic importance of universities is now strongly recognized. In the UK, for example, over one per cent of all full-time jobs are within universities, and the sector contributes directly and indirectly over 5 per cent of GDP. As Berglund (2009, pp. 7–8) indicates, 'Governments, and arguably electorates, now perceive and measure university activities within a framework of cost-benefit analysis and direct accountability to funders'.

Boulton *et al.* (2008, p. 6), in their review of the nature and purpose of universities, refer to this change as 'the new discourse of the primacy of direct economic benefit', and identify that 'increasingly, discussions about the organisation of research and indeed of university systems across Europe have become dominated by analyses of the ways in which they can best fulfil an immediate economic function'. This economic focus is well illustrated in two perspectives.

In a recent analysis of future labour market requirements in the USA, Karoly *et al.* (2004, p. 1) have emphasized the importance of tertiary-level education as underpinning economic performance, as 'shifts in the nature of business organisations and the growing importance of knowledge-based work . . . favour strong, non-routine cognitive skills such as abstract reasoning, problem-solving, communication and collaboration'. Similarly, a report commissioned for the British prime minister on the role of universities in the world's leading economies concludes that:

> Universities and colleges have a profound responsibility to ensure that they supply young citizens from around the world with the deep understanding and the intellectual tools which they will need to become wise leaders of commerce, industry and politics in a world that is at once conceptually borderless and yet in some ways more fraught than ever by national conflicts. (UK/US Study Group, 2009, p. 2)

Recognition of the economic importance of HE to national governments has encouraged the adoption of policies to encourage the growth of HE participation. These have been enthusiastically adopted by individuals who have bought into the idea of the individual economic and lifestyle benefits of a university education. The global trends in HE growth, both recent and projected, are indicators of a strong and significant role for universities within the economic, social and cultural aspirations of individuals, communities and states. Growth in the developed countries of the world has been substantial – in the UK, for example, the number of students in British universities grew from 500,000 to 2.4 million between 1980 and 2008. However, in emerging economies the growth rates have been even stronger, with governments investing larger proportions of GDP into expanding their university sectors. UNESCO (2008) has estimated that domestic demand for university places in India and Malaysia doubled between 2003 and 2008. In China, the number of PhD students graduating from Chinese universities grew from 5000 in 1996 to 30,000 in 2008, while between 1985 and 2007 the number of students in Chinese universities grew from 5 million to 25 million (Berglund, 2009). At the global scale, Bhandari *et al.* (2008) estimate that the number of HE students grew from 13 million in 1960 to 68 million in 1991 to 150 million by 2008. UNESCO (2009) estimates that participation grew from 28 million in 1970 to 152 million in 2007, with an annual growth rate over that period of 4.6 per cent, and a rapid increase of some 33 per cent since 2000, so that the number of students at universities has grown by over 51 million since the turn of the century. Projections for the future are less secure, of course, but conservative estimates of growth in the context of demographic predictions and perceptions of economic rates of return to the individual would suggest that a global HE student population of 250 million by 2030 is realistic.

The analysis above provides the overall context of change for universities. Within all the trends identified here, the theme of increasing internationalization is strong. Universities are faced, therefore, with the task of developing strategies and operations with a clear awareness of how the 'international' is shaping the 'local' and 'national', and will need to identify how they can respond to international opportunities to secure a strong economic, intellectual and academic future. In the sections that follow we shall return to our propositions from Chapter 1 about how HE is being shaped by the 'international' and how each might change in the next two decades – and we shall then propose a picture for what the global HE system of the third decade of the twenty-first century might look like, and how internationalization will have shaped that pattern.

Propositions revisited

In shaping the organization of this book we began by drawing some general conclusions about the current shape of HE in the context of emerging internationalization. These have provided a framework for the contributors to provide perspectives and empirical evidence about how universities are behaving in a globalized HE system and how leaders and managers in individual institutions are responding to change. Here we revisit those propositions to comment on their future evolution.

Proposition 1. The global system is not uniform and homogeneous

That universities are diverse is a truism. Within the national landscapes of HE there is considerable variation, from small regional institutions to national premier institutions, from monotechnics to comprehensive universities, from teaching-focused to research-led, from small to large – and also, of course, from those which deliver education and research of a consistent, recognizable global quality to those which do not. The growth of HE over the coming decades and the challenge of responding to competitive markets will, we believe, lead to increasing differentiation – and this differentiation will be in the context of global markets, rather than simply local markets. Many universities will grow to encompass the global, internationalized HE arena, but others will adapt or emerge to respond to those sectors of the market which are local and regional by definition.

Proposition 2. HE is increasingly subject to international trades and services law and international law

The transformation of HE towards operating as market-focused service enterprises will continue, as state funding decreases, either in relative terms or in absolute terms. In pursuing economic security, universities will need to acquire more of their income from international students and from enterprise activities ranging from consultancy to establishing spin-out companies – and both directions of travel will require an increasingly international perspective, shaped by the legal rights and obligations of international trade law.

Proposition 3. Student and staff mobility is predominantly from poor, less developed countries to richer developed countries

In terms of international student mobility, the American Council on Education (2006) has predicted a growth in students seeking to undertake undergraduate or graduate studies in another country from 1.8 million in 2001 to 7 million in 2020. This market has traditionally been based on students moving to universities in North America, Europe or Australasia from Asia, Africa and Latin America. While we must expect that the direction of travel will continue to be from less developed to more developed nations, the emergence of China, Singapore and Malaysia as destinations for students from elsewhere in Asia, from the Islamic realm and from Africa, has been an emerging theme of the last five years. Hence the pattern of international student mobility will become more diverse, and the previous hegemony in the marketplace will be increasingly challenged.

Concern for the consequences of graduates not returning to their own country has also stimulated some governments to consider strategies for providing education from international providers in their home country, through the development of branch campuses or multi-institutional campuses. We would expect this trend to continue.

Proposition 4. HE is increasingly under the influence of international organizations

The role of international organizations such as UNESCO and The World Bank has become significant in the development of HE globally, as Roberta Bassett has shown in her chapter in this volume. Their role will continue to be important as a basis for sharing good practice and promoting good leadership. However, the traditional expectation that their role has been to export good practice from West to East will be increasingly challenged as the political validity of such a perspective is questioned, and as the value of sharing good practice from wherever it is found to wherever it is needed becomes the basis of their influence.

Proposition 5. Demand for HE will increase in years to come

For those countries which have reached high levels of HE participation among their high school leavers, the challenge for universities has been how to grow and increase demand for their education provision. A key market, of course, is international students, for much of the rapid growth in participation will be among young people from countries whose domestic HE provision cannot satisfy demand. In addition, however, the UNESCO report on demographic projections and HE (UNESCO, 2008) notes the importance of new growth sectors as a result of under-represented segments of the population beginning to participate in tertiary education. This will include mature students, those from lower socio-economic groups, and those seeking further training or Continuing Professional Development (CPD) as part of their career development. The drive towards internationalization of each of these trends will be significant for, not only will international student number growth require engagement with international markets, there will be a clear expectation from other 'growth' groups that the education provided will equip them to engage in the global economy.

Proposition 6. Global HE is characterized by increasing competition for students, resources, staff and funding

Although the overall global market for HE is set to expand, it will do so in the context of a highly marketized and competitive environment. The reduction in public sector funding and the resulting obligation for universities to pursue alternative income streams means that global HE will be a market in which the key leadership challenges will be the same for universities as for other global businesses, with a premium on responsiveness, careful market positioning and attentive market scanning.

Proposition 7. Universities are increasingly focusing on notions of global citizenship and related graduate attributes

The emphasis in most of the propositions above has been on the economic survival of the university as a corporation. However, international engagement is strongly rooted in a commitment to equipping students with the skills and knowledge to help them make a positive contribution to the global economy and as global citizens. Citizenship has long been an aspiration universities have had for their students, but within the context of their own national civic society. With the globalization of almost all sectors of economic and social life, having the skills of a global graduate will be important to students and a positive dimension of what they demand from their university. While some will acquire this from studying abroad, most will expect it from the education and experience they have at a university in their own region or country, an expectation that governments will also have of the education they buy from their own 'home' universities. The obligation to internationalize the curriculum and the institutional ethos will be strong drivers for change for universities over the next two decades.

Higher education 2025

In the context of the key trends that we have identified, therefore, it is appropriate to consider what the global HE scene will look like by 2025 and how the current internationalization developments will have shaped universities. The two most significant factors in change will be the continuing growth in student numbers and the constraints on public funding for either maintaining current resourcing levels or for supporting that growth in participation. The consequence of both will be an increasing marketization of the global HE system, with competition for growth a key characteristic. For those universities in national systems where participation rates have already reached high levels, the only response in the market is to compete for students internationally or to adopt a niche strategy of specialization. Such specialization may be sectoral or geographic, and the response of some smaller institutions will be to focus on their local regions as an alternative to being absorbed by a much larger national-scale institution. Increased internationalization is therefore the inevitable future path for universities to enable them to operate in the global markets to which they will be exposed.

This pressure will show itself not just in the educational domain, of course. Financial constraint will mean that public funding for research is reduced, at least in relative if not absolute terms, and the funding that is available will be increasingly channelled to those with very large research capacity, strong track records in research quality measures and robust and extensive international networks, providing access to the 'best' facilities and academic talent around the world. Furthermore, increasingly the emphasis in research funding will be on generating economic and social impact, and so the research themes to be funded will be those of large international significance around issues such as health, environmental change, and global economic and political relations. Substituting private research funds for public funds to sustain research capacity will, of course, simply intensify such a trend. As with the changes in education, the consequence is a strong pressure towards international profile and networks, and the priority for internationalization will be further underlined.

In terms of the wider enterprise engagement of universities, similar trends will be clear. Generating income from consultancy, the establishment of trading companies and the provision of continuing professional development will be seen by most universities as important 'third stream' sources of funding, but all require a strong engagement with the international arena. Enterprise, whether economic or social enterprise, means engaging with communities at local, national and international scales – and in a globalized society the requirements of those communities are for students and services with an international perspective.

Within the cultural and economic context we describe, what will the global system look like? The picture we present below reflects the strong marketization of the system and is considered in terms of the supply side of the market (the universities) and the demand side, including the range of 'customers' seeking the services of HE.

In terms of the supply side of the global HE market, the pressures towards growth or specialization will firmly establish a number of distinctive tiers of universities. While the boundaries of these tiers may be 'fuzzy', and those institutions close to the upper boundaries will certainly aspire to be part of a higher tier, in reality the tiers will act as largely closed systems, with competition principally between the universities within specific tiers rather than between institutions in different tiers. Such a pattern of market shape is well established in educational markets as they mature, and has been noted elsewhere in the context of schools and colleges (for example, Foskett *et al.*, 2001).

At the top of the hierarchy will be a relatively small number of global universities whose reputation and markets are global and which operate with limited constraint from domestic national policies and markets. These are the transnational corporations (TNCs) of the HE world, and will themselves be distinguishable in two groups. One group will be the stronglyand long-established universities with a global reputation, typified perhaps by Harvard University. The second will be the private corporations, established as profit-based educational institutions, perhaps best typified by the University of Phoenix. The shared characteristic of these two groups will be the global stage on which they play, but the differentiation will be in the markets they seek to access. To such universities internationalization will be innate, with programmes designed to reach across cultural boundaries, whether delivered on residential campuses in their home country, on overseas campuses, or by distance learning. For those with a research profile, academic staff will be global leaders in their field, recruited blind to national background and engaged with the leading academic and political networks around the world. The number of universities in this tier will be small, perhaps less than five traditional foundations and one or two business corporations.

The second tier of internationalized universities will also operate in the global arena, but from a base which is strongly rooted in their own national HE system. Such institutions may still retain dominance in numerical terms of students and staff from their own country, and will receive significant funding from national government. However, their programmes will be focused in terms of quality and market on the international arena, and their research will be engaged in the same networks as those of the top-tier institutions. In these top two tiers will sit the global elite universities, including those currently occupying the top positions in the range of international university league tables (Dehon *et al.*, 2009). Their spread across the top two tiers will reflect a diversity of strategy for, while all will be distinctive by their global quality, some will have chosen to remain strongly connected within their national and local setting as a key distinctor of their strategic position. This group, too, will be relatively small in number, perhaps no more than one to two hundred institutions. However, their global strategic power within the HE arena will be very strong indeed, and they will dominate the high-reputation end of the education, research and enterprise markets, with brands emphasizing quality and international perspective. Internationalization will be at the core of such institutions, with international student recruitment being the consequence of the internationalization process rather than the key component within it.

The third tier of universities will be those that operate principally at national level, drawing students and resources largely from their own national context, but providing some opportunities for international engagement. The group will be diverse, for there will be many that retain a traditional comprehensive academic profile and continue to promote a research-led philosophy, while there will be others which move towards a more specialized niche, or focus predominantly on the educational function. In terms of internationalization there will also be diversity, with some largely eschewing the challenges of internationalization while others engage in a clearly strategic way (see Foskett, 2010, in this volume). A key feature of these universities will be a financial constraint reflecting national government funding priorities – and all will be in competition with an emerging number of private, for-profit institutions.

The fourth tier will be those universities which operate almost entirely within sub-national or regional contexts, engaging comparatively little with global markets, but demonstrating internationalization in terms of curriculum design and content or links with regional employers operating in international markets. These will typically have more limited academic range, akin to the concept of community colleges, and with a strong focus on education and little engagement with research. Teaching will be research-informed rather than research-led.

An interesting feature of the system will be among the second, third and fourth tier of global universities, where an emerging group of 'super universities' will appear. These universities will be the product of regional mergers and partnerships, created to operate with large economies of scale but distinguished by strong internal segmentation to enable them to reach out to the full diversity of aspiring students within their region and beyond. Such universities will dominate large regions, but will be characterized by separate campuses or even sub-brands, with distinctive educational or research missions. The local community college, for example, may simply be a subsidiary of the large international university in the region. The growth of the region rather than the nation state as the focus of economic power has been identified by the OECD as an emerging trend, so that by 2030 regional economies may be more important than national economies. Some of these will be transnational regions by current definitions (for example, southern Malaysia and Singapore), but many will be within existing nation states. At the heart of strong regional economies lie strong internationally focused universities, which provide both intellectual and knowledge-based power to those economies but also, as Florida (2005) has so strongly stressed, the connection to the creative, cultural and community 'capital' that underpins the social and lifestyle energy of the region. Regional super-universities will be both the product of and the driving force behind such regional development.

The demand side of the HE marketplace will also change substantially over the next two decades, both in terms of the nature of university students and in relation to the diversity of customers that HE must serve. The rise of the employability agenda and the centrality of national governments in driving the growth of university funding mean that the status of government, business and employers as university customers will grow. Students and independent knowledge creation will no longer be the only masters to be served in developing institutional strategy, and managing a complex set of external relationships will become a business-critical process for university leaders. Diversity of the marketplace requires increasingly sophisticated understanding of the wants and needs of each of the groups of stakeholders. As students are no longer predominantly 17–21 year olds from the local community, but more diversified by age, educational background, cultural and socio-economic characteristics, so the design of curriculum and the management of student services must become more responsive. Similarly, as national government becomes less important as the provider of funding, so the skills of engaging with business (locally, regionally and internationally), and managing the institution as a business, become more important.

In terms of students, we might identify a segmentation model which reflects the tiering of global universities, although it is important to recognize that there will also be many other segmentation models that apply. Each tier will be focused on a distinctive group of students, who will probably be self-selecting in terms of the tier in which they choose to seek HE. The value added by an education in a Tier 1 or Tier 2 university will enable strong selection by such universities, with the key characteristics of their students being their extremely high prior educational achievement and their financial resources to pay high fees and other costs. To compensate, however, we would expect the private rates of return to those attending such institutions to be substantially higher than those attending Tier 3 or Tier 4 institutions, making such investment a sound economic decision. The market for high-status services and for investments with a high rate of return is a global market, and the reach of institutions in these tiers will be essentially international.

Engagement with government and business will also reflect the tiering of universities. The priorities of most national administrations include making the national economy strong in global markets. In relation to universities, this will include promoting the development of economic skills within HE curricula and supporting the 'employability' agenda for students and the 'impact' agenda for research funded by the state. For those countries with universities already within the top two tiers of global HE, there will be a strong incentive for government to promote strategies which further enhance their position, hence disproportionate investment in one or two leading universities to sustain their position. This strategy is already strongly present in many countries, for example in China and South Korea. For those countries that feel unable to acquire such profile through their own institutions, the strategy will be to draw in global leading universities to operate within their own country. Such strategies are an important feature, for example, of states in the Middle East including Dubai, Qatar and Kuwait, where wealthier states can support the buying-in of reputable universities to develop a strong HE profile in the country.

Finally, the relationship between universities and business will see a strong engagement between global corporations and global universities. Global corporations provide a strong outlet for the innovations of universities, while strong universities provide the knowledge and research resource to enable large corporations to optimize their own business development. Managing relationships with leading corporations will be an increasingly important challenge for leading universities, therefore, and will oblige such universities to scan the globe for the most valuable and significant relationships within their own areas of expertise.

Modelling globalization and internationalization in HE

We provide a brief summary of the ideas explored above in what we propose as a model for conceptualizing and analyzing the impact of globalization in HE. Four broad elements are identified in the model (Figure 20.1). The first is a set of analytic elements which identify the context and drivers of change. These are based on the four broad dimensions of globalization including the

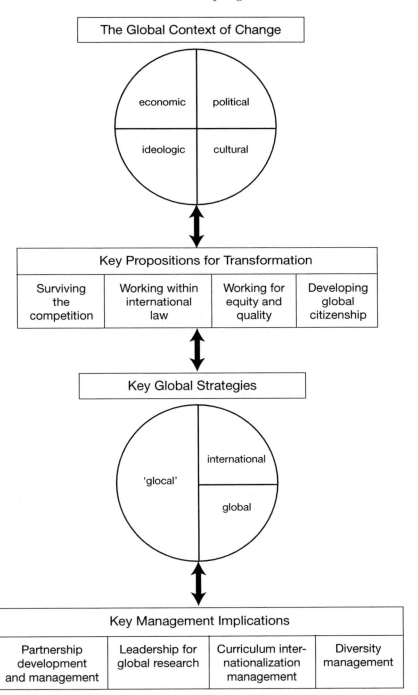

Figure 20.1 Modelling globalization impact in universities

economic, political ideological and cultural elements. We believe that these elements provide a useful framework for universities to examine the nature of the forces for change in this globalization era.

The second set of elements includes the propositions for institutional transformation under globalization. Although the discussion identifies seven such propositions, these have been grouped into four key areas as shown in Figure 20.1. It has been argued that these key propositions provide what we see as key areas of growth and transformation in universities. An examination of each of these provides a useful framework for individual institutions to assess the direction and success of their endeavours under globalization.

Our analysis shows that in the global era, universities will have three key strategic options. The first option is to strive to become 'glocal' universities, with a strong local focus but with a global reach in which key local decisions are informed by global developments. This option relates to a position in either Tier 3 or Tier 4 of the hierarchy of institutions identified earlier, with the distinction lying in whether the university chooses to be locally focused or nationally focused. The second strategic choice is to become an international institution, and this relates to Tier 3 in our hierarchical model. In such universities, there will be clear progress towards strong partnership working with a range of international institutions and organizations. Such universities tend to be strongly involved in cross-border educational activity and also driven in their mission by a strong desire to be leaders in interrogating global challenges such as global climate change, global terrorism, global financial relations, global political relations and global labour markets, trade, commercial and financial activity. The final option, which we believe will be adopted by only a few of the elite universities, will be to become global universities. Such universities (Tier 1 in our hierarchical model, apart from having a very sharp focus both in research terms and in teaching on issues of global relevance, will also develop strong links with powerful global commercial/political institutions which fund their programmes.

The last set of elements in this model identifies key management implications for universities transforming under globalization. New management competences for strong partnership working, for leadership in research of global issues and for working with increasing diversity will become central to the management of the new global university of the future.

Summary and conclusion

This chapter has drawn together a picture of the future evolution of HE on a global scale. It presents a confident picture of a service business which is increasingly seen as a key driver to both future global economic development and the ability of human society to tackle some of the major global social, cultural and environmental challenges of the century. However, the scenario we have built is not simply a description of what might be seen around the world as we move towards 2025. More importantly, it has demonstrated that the essential feature of the changes we shall see is the process of internationalization itself. Internationalization is both cause and consequence of the emerging system, a positive feedback loop which obliges universities to engage increasingly in the international arena. This will not only weave together the network that is the global HE system, but will engender processes which shape the exact form and organization of that system. The HE system of 2025 will be global in organization and international in culture.

References

American Council on Education (2006), *Students on the Move: The Future of International Students in the USA*. Washington, DC: ACE.

Berglund, E. (2009), *Growing by Degrees: Universities in the Future of Urban Development*. London: Royal Institution of British Architects.

Bhandari, R. and Blumenthal, P. (2008), *The Europa World of Learning*. London: Routledge.

Boulton, G. and Lucas, C. (2008), *What are Universities for?* Leuven: League of European Research Universities.

Commonwealth of Australia (2009), *Transforming Australia's Higher Education System*. Canberra: Commonwealth of Australia.

Department of Business, Innovation and Skills (DBIS) (2009), *Higher Aspirations*. London: DBIS.

Dehon, C, Jacobs, D. and Vermandele, C. (eds) (2009), *Ranking Universities*. Brussels: Universite Libre de Bruxelles.

Department for Innovation, Universities and Skills (DIUS) (2008), *The Debate on the Future of Higher Education*. London: DIUS.

Florida, R. (2005), *Cities and the Creative Class*. New York: Routledge.

Foskett, N. H. and Hemsley-Brown, J. (2001) *Choosing Futures*. London: FalmerRoutledge.

Karoly, L. A. and Panis, C. W. A. (2004), *The 21st Century at Work: Forces Shaping the Future Workforce and Workplace in the United States*. Los Angeles: Rand Corporation.

Organization for Economic Cooperation and Development (OECD) (2008), *Higher Education to 2030: Volume 1 – Demography*. Paris: OECD.

Tilak, J. (2003), Higher education and development. *Paper presented to an international seminar at Paris XXI University*, at www.mec.gov.br/univxx1/pdf/Jandhyala.pdf

UK/US Study Group (2009), *Higher Education and Collaboration in Global Context: Building a Global Civic Society*. A Private Report to Prime Minister Gordon Brown.

UNESCO (2008), *Global Education Digest*. Montreal: UNESCO Institute of Statistics.

Weber, L. E. and Duderstadt, J. (eds) (2008), *The Globalisation of Higher Education*. London: Economica.

Index